CompTIA.
Security+™
Certification Practice Exams, Fourth Edition (Exam SY0-601)

Daniel Lachance
Glen E. Clarke

McGraw Hill is an independent entity from CompTIA® and is not affiliated with
CompTIA in any manner. This publication and accompanying media may be used
in assisting students to prepare for the CompTIA Security+ exam. Neither CompTIA
nor McGraw Hill warrants that use of this publication and accompanying media will
ensure passing any exam. CompTIA and CompTIA Security+™ are trademarks or
registered trademarks of CompTIA in the United States and/or other countries. All
other trademarks are trademarks of their respective owners. The CompTIA Marks are
the proprietary trademarks and/or service marks of CompTIA and its affiliates used
under license from CompTIA.

McGraw Hill

New York   Chicago   San Francisco
Athens   London   Madrid   Mexico City
Milan   New Delhi   Singapore   Sydney   Toronto

T0200730

McGraw Hill books are available at special quantity discounts to use as premiums and sales promotions, or for use in corporate training programs. To contact a representative, please visit the Contact Us pages at www .mhprofessional.com.

CompTIA Security+™ Certification Practice Exams, Fourth Edition (Exam SY0-601)

Copyright © 2021 by McGraw Hill. All rights reserved. Printed in the United States of America. Except as permitted under the Copyright Act of 1976, no part of this publication may be reproduced or distributed in any form or by any means, or stored in a database or retrieval system, without the prior written permission of publisher, with the exception that the program listings may be entered, stored, and executed in a computer system, but they may not be reproduced for publication.

All trademarks or copyrights mentioned herein are the possession of their respective owners and McGraw Hill makes no claim of ownership by the mention of products that contain these marks.

1 2 3 4 5 6 7 8 9   LCR   24 23 22 21 20

ISBN   978-1-260-46797-0
MHID   1-260-46797-X

Sponsoring Editors
Tim Green

Editorial Supervisor
Patty Mon

Project Manager
Parag Mittal,
KnowledgeWorks Global Ltd.

Acquisitions Coordinator
Emily Walters

Technical Editor
Nick Mitropoulos

Copy Editor
Lisa Theobald

Proofreader
Tricia Lawrence

Production Supervisor
Thomas Somers

Composition
KnowledgeWorks Global Ltd.

Illustration
KnowledgeWorks Global Ltd.

Art Director, Cover
Jeff Weeks

Information has been obtained by McGraw Hill from sources believed to be reliable. However, because of the possibility of human or mechanical error by our sources, McGraw Hill, or others, McGraw Hill does not guarantee the accuracy, adequacy, or completeness of any information and is not responsible for any errors or omissions or the results obtained from the use of such information.

For Roman and Trinity, who make a father proud and enrich life beyond measure.

—Dad

ABOUT THE AUTHORS

Daniel Lachance, CompTIA Cloud Essentials, CompTIA Server+, CompTIA A+, CompTIA Network+, CompTIA Security+, MCT, MCSA, MCITP, MCTS, is the owner of Lachance IT Consulting, Inc., based in Halifax, Nova Scotia. Dan has delivered technical IT training for a wide variety of products for more than 20 years. He has recorded IT support videos related to security and various cloud-computing platforms. Dan has developed custom applications and planned, implemented, troubleshot, and documented various network configurations and conducted network security audits. He has worked as a technical editor on a number of certification titles and has authored titles including *CompTIA Server+ Certification All-in-One Exam Guide (Exam SK0-004)* and *CompTIA Security+ Certification Practice Exams, Second Edition (Exam SY0-401)*.

Glen E. Clarke, MCSE, MCSD, MCT, CCNA, CEH, CHFI, PenTest+, Security+, Network+, A+, is a technical trainer and owner of DC Advanced Technology Training (DCATT), an IT training company based out of Atlantic Canada that delivers live instructor training online and at the customer's site. Glen spends most of his time delivering courses on Cisco CCNA, CompTIA A+, Network+, Security+, and PenTest+. He also delivers certified training on Windows Server, SQL Server, SharePoint, Office 365, Exchange Server, Visual Basic .NET, and ASP.NET. Glen teaches a number of security-related courses covering topics such as ethical hacking and countermeasures, penetration testing, vulnerability testing, firewall design, and packet analysis. Glen is author of the *CompTIA Security+ Certification Study Guide, CompTIA Network+ Certification Study Guide*. He also designed and coauthored the *CCT/CCNA Routing and Switching All-In-One Exam Guide*.

About the Technical Editor

Nick Mitropoulos is the CEO of Scarlet Dragonfly and has more than a decade of experience in security training, cybersecurity, incident handling, vulnerability management, security operations, threat intelligence, and data loss prevention. He has worked for a variety of companies (including the Greek Ministry of Education, AT&T, F5 Networks, JP Morgan Chase, KPMG, and Deloitte) and has provided critical advice to many clients regarding various aspects of their security. He's SC/NATO security cleared, a certified (ISC)^2 and EC-Council instructor, Cisco champion, senior IEEE member as well as a GIAC advisory board member, and has an MSc (with distinction) in Advanced Security and Digital Forensics from Edinburgh Napier University. He holds more than 25 security certifications including GCIH, GPEN, GWAPT, GISF, Security+, SSCP, CBE, CMO, CCNA Cyber Ops, CCNA Security, CCNA Routing & Switching, CCDA, CEH, CEI, Palo Alto (ACE), Qualys (Certified Specialist in AssetView and ThreatPROTECT, Cloud Agent, PCI Compliance, Policy Compliance, Vulnerability Management, Web Application Scanning), and Splunk Certified User. If you have any questions or want to provide any feedback, please feel free to reach out via feedback@scarlet-dragonfly.com, LinkedIn (https://www.linkedin.com/in/nickmitropoulos) or Twitter (@MitropoulosNick).

CONTENTS

Welcome to *CompTIA Security+ Certification Practice Exams, Fourth Edition*! This book serves as a preparation tool for the CompTIA Security+ certification exam (SY0-601) as well as for your work in the IT security field. After you've gone through the *CompTIA Security+ Certification Study Guide, Fourth Edition* thoroughly, you can test your knowledge using this practice exams book.

The CompTIA Security+ Exam (Exam SY0-601)

The CompTIA Security+ certification exam is a vendor-neutral exam that validates your skills in risk identification and management, the application of physical and digital security controls for devices and networks, disaster recovery, the adherence to rules set forth by legal and regulatory bodies, as well as cloud computing. This certification is aimed at individuals who have a minimum of two years of experience in IT administration, focusing on security.

The CompTIA Security+ exam consists of five domains (categories). CompTIA represents the relative importance of each domain within the body of knowledge required for an entry-level IT professional taking this exam.

1.0 Attacks, Threats, and Vulnerabilities	24 percent
2.0 Architecture and Design	21 percent
3.0 Implementation	25 percent
4.0 Operations and Incident Response	16 percent
5.0 Governance, Risk, and Compliance	14 percent

Your CompTIA Security+ certification is valid for three years from the date you are certified, after which time you must take the most current version of the exam to keep your certification. Detailed information regarding the CompTIA Security+ certification and exam is available at www.comptia.org.

In This Book

The objective of this book is to prepare you for the CompTIA Security+ exam by familiarizing you with the technology and body of knowledge tested on the exam. Because the primary focus of this book is to help you pass the test, we don't always cover every aspect of the related technology. Some aspects of the technology are covered only to the extent necessary to help you understand what you need to know to pass the exam, but we hope this book will serve you as a valuable professional resource after your exam as well.

CompTIA Security+ Certification Practice Exams, Fourth Edition (Exam SY0-601), provides a battery of practice test questions organized by the official exam objectives. The 21 chapters contain more than 600 questions that cover all the objectives for the SY0-601 exam. Additionally, the accompanying media contains 300 questions in a customizable test engine that enables you to take three full practice exams in a simulated testing environment or customized exams by chapter or exam domain.

This book was developed and written in conjunction with the *CompTIA Security+ Certification Study Guide, Fourth Edition (Exam SY0-601)*, by Glen E. Clarke. The order in which the objectives are presented is identical, as are the chapter titles. These books were designed to work together as a comprehensive program for self-study.

Pre-assessment Exam

This book features a pre-assessment exam in Appendix A. The pre-assessment exam will gauge your areas of strength and weakness so you can tailor your studies based on your needs. We recommend that you take the pre-assessment test before starting the questions in Chapter 1.

In Every Chapter

This book is organized in such a way as to serve as an in-depth review for the CompTIA Security+ exam for both experienced IT security professionals and newcomers to security technologies. Each chapter covers a major aspect of the exam, with practice questions to test your knowledge of specific exam objectives. The SY0-601 exam will present you with some performance-based questions that will test your ability to carry out a task to solve a problem. This could be in the form of typing in a command, placing network devices in the correct positions on a network map, or matching terms with definitions.

Each chapter contains components that call your attention to important items and reinforce salient points. Take a look at what you'll find in every chapter:

- Every chapter begins with **certification objectives**, a list of the official CompTIA exam objectives covered in that chapter.

■ Practice **questions**, similar to those found on the actual exam, are included in every chapter. By answering these questions, you'll test your knowledge while becoming familiar with the structure of the exam questions.

■ The **Quick Answer Key** section follows the questions and enables you easily to check your answers.

■ **In-Depth Answers** at the end of every chapter include explanations for the correct and incorrect answer choices and provide an opportunity for reviewing the exam topics.

Practice Exams

In addition to the more than 600 questions included in this book, 300 questions are included in the customizable test engine on the accompanying media. You can create practice exams by objective or by chapter, or you can take full-length practice exams. Like the questions in the chapters, these practice exams also include detailed explanations for the correct and incorrect answer choices. For more information about the accompanying media, please see Appendix B.

Strategies for Use

You can use this book a variety of ways, whether simultaneously with the *CompTIA Security+ Certification Study Guide, Fourth Edition*, or as a stand-alone test prep tool.

■ **With the Study Guide**   Taking a chapter-by-chapter approach, you can opt to read a *Study Guide* chapter and then practice what you have learned with the questions in the corresponding *Practice Exams* chapter, alternating between books throughout your course of study.

■ **The Practice Exams book alone**   Using the *Practice Exams* book after you have read the Study Guide, or as a stand-alone test prep tool, you can work through the book cover to cover and take the three practice exams as the final step in your preparation.

Alternatively, by means of the "Exam Readiness Checklist" in the next section, you can gauge your level of expertise and determine which objectives to focus on and then work through the book by objectives. The checklist notes which questions pertain to which objectives, enabling you to tailor your review.

Exam Readiness Checklist

This "Exam Readiness Checklist" has been constructed to enable you to reference the official CompTIA Security+ objectives and refer to the order in which these objectives are covered in this book. You can check your progress and ensure that you spend the time you need on more difficult or unfamiliar sections. The objectives are listed as CompTIA has presented them with the corresponding book chapter number.

Exam Readiness Checklist

Official Objective	Chapter Number
1.0 Threats, Attacks, and Vulnerabilities	
1.1 Compare and contrast different types of social engineering techniques.	4
1.2 Given a scenario, analyze potential indicators to determine the type of attack.	4, 5
1.3 Given a scenario, analyze potential indicators associated with application attacks.	15
1.4 Given a scenario, analyze potential indicators associated with network attacks.	4, 9
1.5 Explain different threat actors, vectors, and intelligence sources.	2, 5
1.6 Explain the security concerns associated with various types of vulnerabilities.	5
1.7 Summarize the techniques used in security assessments.	19, 20
1.8 Explain the techniques used in penetration testing.	20
2.0 Architecture and Design	
2.1 Explain the importance of security concepts in an enterprise environment.	8, 16
2.2 Summarize virtualization and cloud computing concepts.	16
2.3 Summarize secure application development, deployment, and automation concepts.	15
2.4 Summarize authentication and authorization design concepts.	10
2.5 Given a scenario, implement cybersecurity resilience.	5, 18
2.6 Explain the security implications of embedded and specialized systems.	5
2.7 Explain the importance of physical security controls	14
2.8 Summarize the basics of cryptographic concepts	12

Exam Readiness Checklist

Official Objective	Chapter Number
3.0 Implementation	
3.1 Given a scenario, implement secure protocols.	12
3.2 Given a scenario, implement host or application security solutions.	6, 7, 15
3.3 Given a scenario, implement secure network designs.	1, 8
3.4 Given a scenario, install and configure wireless security settings.	9
3.5 Given a scenario, implement secure mobile solutions.	7
3.6 Given a scenario, apply cybersecurity solutions to the cloud.	16
3.7 Given a scenario, implement identity and account management controls.	11
3.8 Given a scenario, implement authentication and authorization solutions.	10, 11
3.9 Given a scenario, implement public key infrastructure.	13
4.0 Operations and Incident Response	
4.1 Given a scenario, use the appropriate tool to assess organizational security.	20, 21
4.2 Summarize the importance of policies, processes, and procedure for incident response.	21
4.3 Given an incident, utilize appropriate data sources to support an investigation.	21
4.4 Given an incident, apply mitigation techniques or controls to secure an environment.	21
4.5 Explain the key aspects of digital forensics.	21
5.0 Governance, Risk, and Compliance	
5.1 Compare and contrast various types of controls.	11
5.2 Explain the importance of applicable regulations, standards, or frameworks that impact organizational security posture.	3
5.3 Explain the importance of policies to organizational security.	3
5.4 Summarize risk management processes and concepts.	17, 18
5.5 Explain privacy and sensitive data concepts in relation to security.	2, 3

Chapter Overview

The following list provides a general overview of what you can expect from each of the 21 chapters in this book.

- **Chapter 1: Networking Basics and Terminology**   You'll explore how to configure IPv4 and IPv6 environments properly, how load balancing provides application high availability and improved performance, and how to configure load balancing, including active/active and active/passive.

- **Chapter 2: Introduction to Security Terminology**   You'll explore various threat actor types and their motivations, sources of cybersecurity threat intelligence, and data roles and responsibilities.

- **Chapter 3: Security Policies and Standards**   You'll explore how data privacy industry standards and regulations influence how data is classified and protected in accordance with organizational security policies.

- **Chapter 4: Types of Attacks**   You'll explore how social engineering can compromise systems and entire networks; how various attacks such as password, cryptographic, and physical attacks can be executed; and how malicious code can be triggered.

- **Chapter 5: Vulnerabilities and Threats**   You'll explore various types of malware such as spyware and ransomware, system configuration vulnerabilities, and threats related to IoT devices, industrial control systems, and embedded devices.

- **Chapter 6: Mitigating Security Threats**   You'll explore how to harden network devices and hosts to reduce the attack surface using methods such as disk encryption and patch management.

- **Chapter 7: Implementing Host-based Security**   You'll explore how to secure endpoint devices by hardening databases, enabling TPM, preventing data loss, and using MDM tools to secure mobile devices with remote wipe and storage segmentation configurations.

- **Chapter 8: Securing the Network Infrastructure**   You'll explore how network security can be achieved using HSMs, TLS, honeypots, and honeynets; how data sovereignty influences data privacy practices; and how to use network security solutions such as NAC, VPNs, and VLANs to control and secure network access.

- **Chapter 9: Wireless Networking and Security**   You'll explore how to install and configure secure wireless networks using solutions such as EAP, WPA3, and IEEE 802.1x to mitigate wireless network threats such as bluesnarfing and radio-frequency jamming.

■ **Chapter 10: Authentication**   You'll explore authentication protocols such as CHAP and 802.1x, authentication methods including one-time passwords and token keys, and how multifactor authentication enhances user sign-in security.

■ **Chapter 11: Authorization and Access Control**   You'll explore various types of security controls such as detective and compensating controls, the role that identity providers play in authorizing resource access, and how to grant resource permissions and harden user accounts.

■ **Chapter 12: Introduction to Cryptography**   You'll explore cryptographic concepts related to keys, encryption and hashing, and steganography, and how network security protocols such as DNSSEC and HTTPS are implemented.

■ **Chapter 13: Managing a Public Key Infrastructure**   You'll explore PKI concepts including certificate authorities and certificate signing requests, the certificate lifecycle, and various types of certificates and how they are issued and used.

■ **Chapter 14: Physical Security**   You'll explore various types of physical controls such as security guards, cable locks, and USB data blockers, as well as secure data destruction techniques including shredding and degaussing.

■ **Chapter 15: Application Attacks and Security**   You'll explore common application attacks such as SQL injection and integer overflows, automated code testing for efficient quality assurance, and common application threat mitigation techniques such as block lists and secure coding techniques.

■ **Chapter 16: Virtualization and Cloud Security**   You'll explore the relationship between virtualization and cloud computing, how to secure the use of cloud computing services using options such as security groups and replication, and how to secure the use of virtual machines.

■ **Chapter 17: Risk Analysis**   You'll explore risk management strategies such as risk acceptance and risk transfer, how to establish a risk register, and how to calculate the cost of realized threats and compare them against the cost of security controls.

■ **Chapter 18: Disaster Recovery and Business Continuity**   You'll explore how to ensure business continuity through redundancy options such as RAID and data replication; using data backups on-premises and in the cloud; as well as determining how negative incidents may affect the organization through a business impact analysis.

■ **Chapter 19: Understanding Monitoring and Auditing**   You'll explore how to configure logging for various types of devices and hosts, how to centrally monitor for security incidents using SIEM, and how to automate incident response using SOAR.

■ **Chapter 20: Security Assessments and Audits**   You'll explore the importance of periodic host and network security audits; the different between reconnaissance, vulnerability scanning, and penetration testing; and some of the techniques used when conducting security assessments.

■ **Chapter 21: Incident Response and Computer Forensics**   You'll explore digital forensics, including how to gather, store, and analyze evidence in accordance with evidence standards such as chain of custody; and you'll examine the importance of incident response planning and execution.

Chapter 1

Networking Basics and Terminology

QUESTIONS

Disruption of connectivity to applications presents a risk for both on-premises and cloud-based apps. App performance can influence the effectiveness of IT solutions used to address business needs.

Load balancing addresses both application reachability and performance needs. A load balancer accepts client app requests and routes them to a pool of backend servers, where the least busy server services the request. Because there are multiple servers serving up the app, a backend server failure does not disrupt user connections to apps; instead, the load balancer does not route client requests to the unresponsive host.

Internet Protocol version 4 (IPv4) and the newer IPv6 are the protocol foundations on which network services are available. IPv6 uses a 128-bit hexadecimal addressing scheme as well as device discovery and communication techniques that differ from IPv4.

1. Which of the following benefits are realized from implementing a load balancer? (Choose two.)
   A. Improved app performance
   B. Increased app security
   C. Increased app regulatory compliance
   D. Increased app availability

2. A busy web site has not been responding well because of the large volume of HTTP requests sent to the web server. Which solution would be the most optimal to improve current and future web server performance?
   A. Add more RAM to the web server.
   B. Use two web servers hosting the same content. Configure a load balancer to distribute incoming HTTP connections between the two web servers.
   C. Place a router between the web server and the Internet to throttle incoming HTTP connections.
   D. Enable SSL on the web server.

3. You would like to prevent client requests from being serviced by busy backend servers hosting user sessions. Which load balancer scheduling algorithm should you configure?
   A. Round robin
   B. Weighted round robin
   C. Random
   D. Least connections

4. During an IT meeting, your colleague Trinity suggests that there is a single point of failure in the single load balancer in place for the company web site ordering system. She suggests having two load balancers configured, with only one in service at a given time. What type of load balancing configuration has Trinity described?

   A.   Round robin

   B.   Active-active

   C.   Active-passive

   D.   Least connections

5. An active-passive load balancer solution is configured on your network. When the standby load balancer determines that the primary load balancer is down, what attribute does it take control of?

   A.   Load balancer MAC address

   B.   Load balancer IP address

   C.   First backend server MAC address

   D.   First backend server IP address

6. Your public cloud–based load balancer uses Linux backend servers to host a web application. Each backend Linux host is configured with only a single private IPv4 address. You need to be able to manage each Linux backend host remotely from your on-premises network without exposing each backend server directly to the Internet. Which options should you consider? (Choose two.)

   A.   Assign a public IP address to each backend Linux instance.

   B.   Assign an IPv6 address to each backend Linux instance.

   C.   Configure inbound NAT rules on the load balancer.

   D.   Configure a jump box solution.

7. To improve application performance for a public-facing web application, you want to reduce the amount of processing for each backend Windows server configured in a load balancer backend server pool. HTTPS is currently configured on each server. HTTPS is required to protect traffic web application traffic. What should you do?

   A.   Enable SSL/TLS pass-through on the load balancer.

   B.   Configure IPSec on the load balancer.

   C.   Configure SSL/TLS termination at the load balancer.

   D.   Generate a new certificate for the load balancer DNS name.

8. How does an OSI layer 7 load balancer differ from a layer 4 load balancer?

   A.   Layer 7 load balancers can inspect IP addresses to make load balancing decisions.

   B.   Layer 7 load balancers can inspect URLs to make load balancing decisions.

   C.   Layer 7 load balancers can examine MAC addresses to make load balancing decisions.

   D.   Layer 7 load balancers can examine port numbers to make load balancing decisions.

9. Refer to Figure 1-1. Which type of load balancing is being depicted?
    A. Fixed weighted
    B. Source IP hash
    C. Least connection
    D. Round robin

FIGURE 1-1

Load balancer
connections

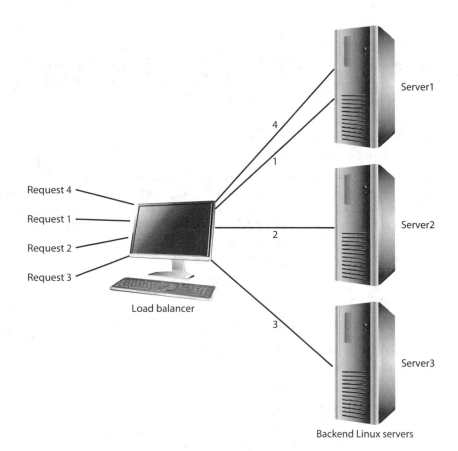

Request 4

Request 1

Request 2

Request 3

Load balancer

Server1

Server2

Server3

Backend Linux servers

10. What is the primary purpose of a load balancer health probe configuration?
    A. To check Internet connectivity
    B. To check load balancer responsiveness
    C. To check backend server responsiveness
    D. To compare performance baselines to current metrics

11. While testing a custom load balanced application, you determine that the app depends on client devices being connected to the same backend server throughout a session. Which load balancer option should you enable to support this kind of behavior?

   A. Source IP affinity
   B. Health probe
   C. Round robin
   D. Fixed weight

12. IPv6 addresses consist of how many bits?

   A. 8
   B. 16
   C. 32
   D. 128

13. You need to test to determine whether a local IPv6 stack is functioning on a Windows 10 host. Which command should you issue?

   A. **ping 127.0.0.1**
   B. **ipconfig –test 127.0.0.1**
   C. **ping 0:0:0:0:0:0:0:1**
   D. **ipconfig –test 0:0:0:0:0:0:0:1**

14. An IT technician issues the Windows **ipconfig** command and is concerned after noticing an address with an FE80 prefix. What should you tell the technician?

   A. IPv6 hosts always have a link-local unicast address beginning with FE80.
   B. IPv6 hosts with an FE80 address are unable to communicate on the Internet.
   C. FE80 is similar to an IPv4 169.254 prefix; it means the host could not reach a DHCP server.
   D. The IPv4 FE80 prefix is the local loopback address.

15. Which IPv6 protocol is primarily responsible for error and status information?

   A. TCP
   B. ICMP
   C. UDP
   D. IP

16. Refer to Figure 1-2. What is wrong with the listed configuration? (Choose two.)

   A. The load balancer is using a link-local IPv6 address instead of a public IPv6 address.
   B. IPv6 addresses can use double colon notation only once within an IPv6 address.
   C. Load balancer backend servers cannot be configured with IPv6 addresses.
   D. Load balancer public IP addresses must be IPv4, not IPv6.

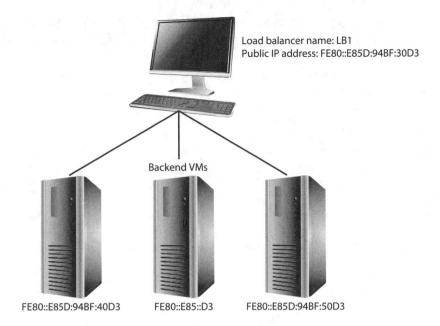

FIGURE 1-2

Load balancer addressing

Load balancer name: LB1
Public IP address: FE80::E85D:94BF:30D3

Backend VMs

FE80::E85D:94BF:40D3   FE80::E85::D3   FE80::E85D:94BF:50D3

17. One backend server named HOST 2 is used by a load balancer in a backend pool. HOST 2 has more RAM and CPU processing power than others in the same backend pool. You need to ensure that more client requests are serviced by this powerful server. What should you do?

   A. Assign a lower priority weight value to HOST 2.
   B. Assign a low priority weight value to the load balancer.
   C. Assign a high priority weight value to the load balancer.
   D. Assign a higher priority weight value to HOST 2.

18. Which load balancing scheduling algorithm treats all backend servers equally when it comes to client request processing capabilities?

   A. Round robin
   B. Weighted round robin
   C. Random
   D. Least connections

19. Which of the following terms is the most closely related to a load balancer?

   A. Reverse proxy
   B. Forward proxy
   C. Jump box
   D. Content delivery network

20. Which of the following load balancing solutions is best suited for routing incoming video-streaming requests to specific backend servers optimized for streaming?

   A. Layer 4 load balancer

   B. Round robin

   C. Fixed weight

   D. Layer 7 load balancer

21. You are configuring a load balancer to support a backend pool of FTP servers using standard port numbers. Which TCP ports should the load balancer accept FTP requests on?

   A. 20, 21

   B. 21, 23

   C. 21, 80

   D. 80, 443

22. Users complain that when they access a load balanced shopping web site, periodically the contents of their shopping cart is lost. What should you configure in the load balancer to alleviate the issue?

   A. Active-passive

   B. Virtual IP

   C. Persistence

   D. Active-active

23. You are configuring load balancer support for an HTTPS custom web application. Which of the following statements regarding this scenario are correct? (Choose two.)

   A. Backend servers can listen on any port number.

   B. Traffic between the load balancer and backend servers does not have to be encrypted.

   C. The backend server port number must be the same as the load balancer VIP port number.

   D. HTTPS requires an active-active load balancer configuration.

24. You are designing a load balancing strategy for a multi-tiered web app named APP1 that uses frontend publicly accessible web servers, application servers, and database servers. APP1 experiences a large number of requests each day. You need to ensure that the performance of each web app tier is optimized. What should you do?

   A. Configure an internal load balancer in front of the web servers, an internal load balancer between web servers and app servers, and a public load balancer between app servers and database servers.

   B. Configure a public load balancer in front of the web servers, an internal load balancer between web servers and app servers, and another internal load balancer between app servers and database servers.

   C. Create a load balancer active-active configuration.

   D. Create a load balancer active-passive configuration.

25. Refer to Figure 1-3. To ensure proper load balanced web app functionality, what should be configured where a question mark appears in the diagram?

  A. Database backup

  B. Active-active load balancer configuration

  C. Active-standby load balancer configuration

  D. Database replication

FIGURE 1-3

Load balanced multi-tiered web application

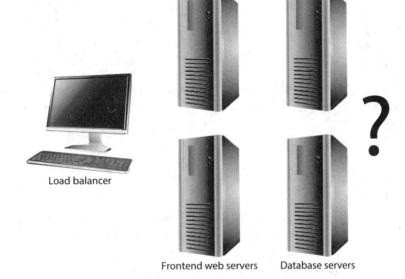

Load balancer

Frontend web servers   Database servers

26. Which IPv6 protocol is used to discover neighboring hosts on a local area network?

  A. ARP

  B. TCP

  C. UDP

  D. NDP

27. Refer to Figure 1-4. Which statements about this configuration are correct? (Choose two).

  A. An IPv4 DHCP server was not reachable.

  B. The FE80 IPv6 address will still appear if a static IPv6 address is configured.

  C. The FE80 IPv6 address will not appear if a static IPv6 address is configured.

  D. Network traffic can be routed to remote IP networks (no default gateway is set).

FIGURE 1-4

IP configuration

```
Connection-specific DNS Suffix  . :
Link-local IPv6 Address . . . . . : fe80::e85d:94bf:30d3:dba5%5
Autoconfiguration IPv4 Address. . : 169.254.219.165
Subnet Mask . . . . . . . . . . . : 255.255.0.0
Default Gateway . . . . . . . . . :
```

28. Refer to Figure 1-5. The nature of the load balanced application is such that users must connect to the same backend server for the duration of their connection. Which option should be configured?

    A. The protocol should be set to UDP.

    B. The port should be 443.

    C. The backend port should be 443.

    D. Session persistence should be enabled.

FIGURE 1-5

Load balancer configuration

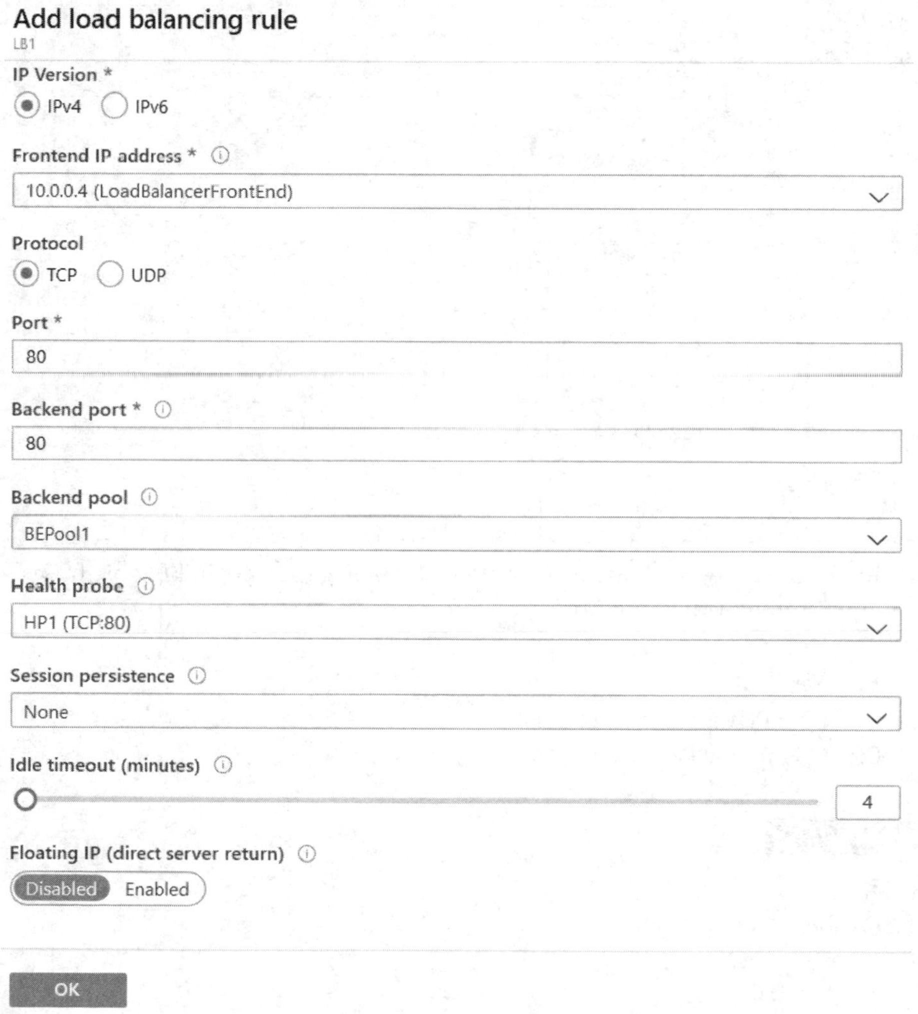

Add load balancing rule
LB1

IP Version *

(●) IPv4   ( ) IPv6

Frontend IP address * ⓘ

| 10.0.0.4 (LoadBalancerFrontEnd) | ⌄ |

Protocol

(●) TCP   ( ) UDP

Port *

| 80 |

Backend port * ⓘ

| 80 |

Backend pool ⓘ

| BEPool1 | ⌄ |

Health probe ⓘ

| HP1 (TCP:80) | ⌄ |

Session persistence ⓘ

| None | ⌄ |

Idle timeout (minutes) ⓘ

O――――――――――――――――――――――― | 4 |

Floating IP (direct server return) ⓘ

(Disabled Enabled)

[OK]

29. Refer to Figure 1-6. Which aspect of a load balancer configuration does this apply to?
   A.   Session persistence
   B.   Frontend IP address
   C.   Health probe
   D.   Backend server pool

FIGURE 1-6

Load balancer
configuration

Name *

Config1

Protocol ⓘ

HTTP

Port * ⓘ

80

Path * ⓘ

/

Interval * ⓘ

5

seconds

Unhealthy threshold * ⓘ

2

consecutive failures

30. Refer to Figure 1-7. You need the ability to manage servers in BEPool1 from a remote network. What should you configure?
   A.   Session persistence
   B.   NAT rule
   C.   IPv6 Private IP address
   D.   SSH public key

FIGURE 1-7

Load balancer
configuration
settings

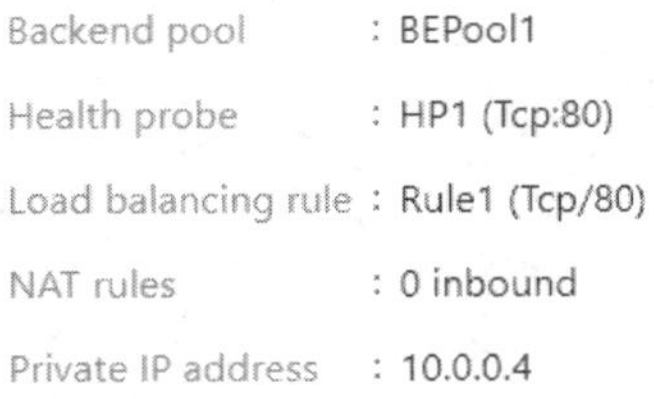

Backend pool   : BEPool1

Health probe   : HP1 (Tcp:80)

Load balancing rule : Rule1 (Tcp/80)

NAT rules   : 0 inbound

Private IP address : 10.0.0.4

31. You have an active-active load balancer configuration for a web app using a backend Microsoft SQL Server database. How many SQL database instances are active concurrently?

A. None

B. One

C. Two

D. It depends on the backend pool configuration

32. You have configured two load balancers to work together. The first load balancer routes all client traffic to backend servers, while the second load balancer is idle. What type of configuration is this?

A. Active-active

B. Active-passive

C. Active-scheduled

D. Active-persistent

QUICK ANSWER KEY

1.	A, D	**9.**	D	**17.**	D	**25.**	D
2.	B	**10.**	C	**18.**	A	**26.**	D
3.	D	**11.**	A	**19.**	A	**27.**	A, B
4.	C	**12.**	D	**20.**	D	**28.**	D
5.	B	**13.**	C	**21.**	A	**29.**	C
6.	C, D	**14.**	A	**22.**	C	**30.**	B
7.	C	**15.**	B	**23.**	A, B	**31.**	D
8.	B	**16.**	A, B	**24.**	B	**32.**	B

IN-DEPTH ANSWERS

1. ☑ **A** and **D.** Load balancers improve app performance because a pool of backend servers is available to handle client requests instead of a single server, which means that these servers can handle the additional request load that may occur. App availability is increased because a pool of backend servers is available to service client requests. A backend server failure means client requests will be serviced by backend servers that remain up and running.

   ☒ **B** and **C** are incorrect. Load balancing is not directly related to increasing the security of an app, even with Secure Sockets Layer/Transport Layer Security (SSL/TLS) termination. Compliance with regulations is not necessarily achieved with the deployment of a load balancer.

2. ☑ **B.** Configuring multiple servers behind a load balancer allows for the distribution of incoming network traffic among those servers. This improves the performance of busy web applications and increases availability because more than one server is hosting the same application.

   ☒ **A, C,** and **D** are incorrect. Adding more RAM can sometimes improve the performance of a computing device, but the problem here is network performance based. Routers determine the best path to be used when transmitting data between networks. They are not used to increase network performance to a web server. SSL secures network transmissions and is not related to improving network performance to a web server.

3. ☑ **D.** The least connections algorithm ensures that traffic is sent to the backend server with the smallest amount of active connections.

   ☒ **A, B,** and **C** are incorrect. The round robin algorithm sends traffic to the first backend node, then the second, the third, back to the first, and so on. Weighted round robin is similar to round robin but differs in that it also takes the overall computing power into consideration, so the beefiest servers get sent traffic first. Random algorithms, as the name suggests, route client traffic to backend servers randomly.

4. ☑ **C.** Active-passive configurations consist of two load balancers, one of which is active. When the active load balancer is unresponsive, the second load balancer takes over.

   ☒ **A, B,** and **D** are incorrect. Round robin and least connections are load balancer scheduling algorithms and are not related to fault tolerance with multiple load balancers. Active-active means that both load balancers function at the same time and work together to distribute incoming traffic to backend nodes.

5. ☑ **B.** A virtual IP address (load balancer IP address) is assigned to the active load balancer. This is the externally exposed address that the DNS names must resolve to.
   ☒ **A, C,** and **D** are incorrect. MAC addresses are not exchanged in an active-passive load balancer configuration; neither is the first backend server IP address.

6. ☑ **C** and **D.** Load balancer inbound NAT rules allow incoming traffic to the load balancer on a given port, such as SSH for Linux management, to be mapped to internal hosts configured with only private IP addresses. A jump box is a physical or virtual server with at least two network interfaces with routing between the interfaces disabled. One jump box interface has a connection to a public network and the second interface has a connection to an internal network. Once authenticated to the jump box, administrators can use it as a launch pad to connect to internal hosts.
   ☒ **A** and **B** are incorrect. For security reasons, each backend Linux instance should not be directly exposed to the Internet with a public IPv4 or IPv6 address.

7. ☑ **C.** Configuring SSL/TLS termination at the load balancer offloads this computationally expensive operation from each backend server. This means network connections to and from the load balancer are protected using HTTPS. Traffic between the load balancer and backend servers is not protected with HTTPS.
   ☒ **A, B,** and **D** are incorrect. SSL/TLS pass-through uses HTTPS configurations on each backend server; this needs to be disabled in this scenario to reduce the workload on each backend server. IPSec is not as well suited for protecting public-facing web applications as HTTPS, so IPSec should not be configured on the load balancer for this purpose. Load balancers can be configured with custom DNS names to match existing DNS names in PKI certificates. DNS records would need to be changed to resolve the DNS name to the IP address of the load balancer.

8. ☑ **B.** Layer 7 of the OSI model, the application layer, enables access to all packet contents including the payload; therefore, URLs can be examined by the load balancer to determine which backend servers should receive the request.
   ☒ **A, C,** and **D** are incorrect. OSI layer 7 does not apply to IP addresses (layer 3), MAC addresses (layer 2), or port numbers (layer 4).

9. ☑ **D.** With round robin load balancing, each client request to the load balancer is routed to the next backend server in sequence, one after the other.
   ☒ **A, B,** and **C** are incorrect. Fixed weighted load balancing uses an assigned "weight" value, and servers with higher priority weight values receive the most requests. Source IP hashing generates a hash value from the source and destination IP addresses of a request to determine which backend server will service a request; it is not sequential, as shown in the figure. Least connection load balancing ensures that traffic is sent to the backend server with the smallest amount of active connections.

10. ☑   **C.** A load balancer can be configured to test connectivity to backend servers periodically on a given port number using health probes. Unresponsive backend servers are marked as unhealthy and do not receive client app requests.

    ☒   **A, B,** and **D** are incorrect. None of the listed items defines the purpose of configuring load balancer health probes. Health probes are used to ensure that load balanced backend servers are responsive, not to check Internet or load balancer connectivity or compare performance metrics.

11. ☑   **A.** Load balancer source IP affinity, also called client IP affinity, ensures that clients remain connected to the same backend host during an app session.

    ☒   **B, C,** and **D** are incorrect. A load balancer can be configured to test connectivity to backend servers periodically on a given port number using health probes. Unresponsive backend servers are marked as unhealthy and do not receive client app requests. With round robin load balancing, each client request to the load balancer is routed to the next backend server in sequence, one after the other. Fixed weighted load balancing uses an assigned "weight" value, and servers with higher priority weight values receive the most requests.

12. ☑   **D.** IPv6 addresses are 128 bits long, represented as eight 16-bit groups of hexadecimal characters, where each group is separated with a colon.

    ☒   **A, B,** and **C** are incorrect. None of the listed values correctly represents the number of bits in an IPv6 address.

13. ☑   **C.** The Windows **ping** command can be used to test IPv6 functionality for the IPv6 local loopback address of 0:0:0:0:0:0:0:1, also referred to as ::1. The double colons represent a series of consecutive zeroes.

    ☒   **A, B,** and **D** are incorrect. The **ipconfig** command is not used to test IPv6 connectivity; 127.0.0.1 is the IPv4 local loopback address; and 0:0:0:0:0:0:0:1 is the IPv6 local loopback address.

14. ☑   **A.** The IPv6 FE80 prefix is used for link-local unicast addresses. IPv6 hosts always have this type of IP address, whether or not they are configured with a static IP address or are configured to use DHCP.

    ☒   **B, C,** and **D** are incorrect. All IPv6 hosts have an FE80 link-local unicast address for local network purposes; this does not prevent Internet connectivity. FE80 addresses are not the same as IPv4 168.254 addresses, which result when a DHCP server is not reachable. The IPv6 local loopback address is 0:0:0:0:0:0:0:1 and does not begin with FE80. The IPv4 local loopback address is 127.0.0.1.

15. ☑   **B.** The Internet Control Message Protocol (ICMP) is responsible for error and status information in IPv4 and IPv6.

    ☒   **A, C,** and **D** are incorrect. Transmission Control Protocol (TCP) is responsible for the establishing and maintaining of TCP sessions as well as the acknowledging of the receipt of transmissions. User Datagram Protocol (UDP) is a best-effort transmission method that does not establish sessions or acknowledge receipt of sent packets. Internet Protocol (IP) is responsible for routing traffic to destinations.

16.   ☑   **A** and **B.** IPv6 addresses using the FE80 prefix are automatically assigned to network interfaces and are used for local area network connectivity, not public Internet connectivity. The double colon notation in IPv6 represents a series of zeroes and can be used only once within an IPv6 address.
☒   **C** and **D** are incorrect. Load balancers and backend servers can use either IPv4 or IPv6 addresses.

17.   ☑   **D.** Assigning a higher priority weight value to HOST 2 as compared to other backend hosts in the same pool means HOST 2 will service more requests than other servers in the pool.
☒   **A, B,** and **C** are incorrect. Lower priority weight values would result in less requests being sent to HOST 2. Weight values apply to backend pool hosts, not the load balancer itself.

18.   ☑   **A.** Round robin sends traffic to the first backend node, then the second, the third, back to the first, and so on. All servers are treated equally when it comes to client processing capability.
☒   **B, C,** and **D** are incorrect. Weighted round robin is similar to round robin but differs in that it also takes the overall computing power into consideration, so that the beefiest servers get sent traffic first. Random, as the name suggests, routes client traffic to backend servers randomly. Least connections ensures that traffic is sent to the backend server with the smallest amount of active connections.

19.   ☑   **A.** A reverse proxy accepts clients requests and forwards them to an internal host or hosts for processing, thus hiding the true identity of the internal host(s).
☒   **B, C,** and **D** are incorrect. Forward proxies accept client requests and forward them to external services such as Internet web sites, thus hiding the true identity of requesting client devices. Although a load balancer could behave as a jump box to enable external connectivity to internal hosts for management purposes, this is rare compared to much more common load balancing configuration of acting as a reverse proxy. A content delivery network (CDN) replicates content geographically to place it close to the users requesting it, thus reducing network latency.

20.   ☑   **D.** OSI layer 7 (the application layer) load balancers can inspect URL requests, such as those that may include references to media, and send those requests to specific backend hosts configured to stream media.
☒   **A, B,** and **C** are incorrect. OSI layer 4 (the transport layer) cannot inspect URLs and so would not be able to determine which requests are media-related. Round robin sends traffic to the first backend node, then the second, the third, back to the first, and so on. Fixed weighted load balancing uses an assigned "weight" value, so that servers with higher priority weight values receive the most requests.

21.   ☑   **A.** FTP normally uses TCP ports 20 and 21.
☒   **B, C,** and **D** are incorrect. Port 23 is used by Telnet daemons. Port 80 is HTTP and port 443 is HTTPS, both of which are used for web servers.

22. ☑ **C.** Configuring the load balancer persistence setting ensures that client session traffic continues to the same backend server. This can be especially important when server-side storage is used for user sessions.

☒ **A, B,** and **D** are incorrect. Active-passive load balancer configurations, also called active-standby, provide redundancy in the event that the active load balancer fails, in which case the standby becomes active. A load balancer virtual IP (VIP) is the IP address that receives client requests. A single VIP can be used to load balance an application with many backend servers. In an active-active load balancer configuration, both load balancers can accept traffic on either the same VIP or different VIPs, depending on the configuration and solution being used.

23. ☑ **A** and **B.** Backend web servers may be configured to listen on TCP port 400, while the load balancer VIP configuration listens on the standard HTTPS port, TCP 443. Load balancers can be configured as SSL/TLS termination points to offload the extra encryption/decryption processing from the backend servers.

☒ **C** and **D** are incorrect. Backend server port numbers do not have to match the load balancer VIP port number. HTTPS does not require multiple load balancers.

24. ☑ **B.** To ensure that each web app tier performs optimally, each tier should have a load balancer; a public load balancer between the Internet and the frontend web servers, an internal load balancer between web servers and apps servers, and another internal load balancer between app servers and database servers.

☒ **A, C,** and **D** are incorrect. Public load balancers are placed between clients and the frontend web servers. Internal load balancers in this scenario are used for the application and database tiers. Redundant load balancer configurations such as active-active or active-passive will not ensure that each web app tier performs optimally.

25. ☑ **D.** The backend databases should have replication enabled so that if one frontend web server fails, the second frontend web server will point to a database that has up-to-date data.

☒ **A, B,** and **C** are incorrect. Although database backups are important, they are not required for a proper load balanced web application. Active-active and active-standby load balancer configurations do not apply to backend database servers.

26. ☑ **D.** Neighbor Discovery Protocol (NDP) is used by IPv6 to discover nodes on a local are network.

☒ **A, B,** and **C** are incorrect. Address Resolution Protocol (ARP) is used by IPv4 to translate IP addresses to MAC addresses. Transmission Control Protocol (TCP) is responsible for the establishing and maintaining of TCP sessions as well as the acknowledging of the receipt of transmissions. User Datagram Protocol (UDP) is a best-effort transmission method that does not establish sessions or acknowledge receipt of sent packets.

27.   ☑   **A and B.** An IPv4 address with a 169.254 prefix results from being unable to reach a DHCP server. IPv6 uses the FE80 prefix for local network discovery and communication. An IPv6 address with the FE80 prefix exists even if a static IPv6 configuration is applied.
      ☒   **C and D** are incorrect. IPv6 FE80 prefix address are always attached to a network interface and do not disappear if static IPv6 addresses are configured. Because a default gateway is not configured, traffic cannot be routed to remote IP networks.

28.   ☑   **D.** Session persistence is enabled when clients need to connect to the same backend server throughout a session.
      ☒   **A, B,** and **C** are incorrect. None of the listed items links a client to the same backend server for the duration of a session.

29.   ☑   **C.** Health probes are used periodically to test the reachability of backend servers to determine when they are unhealthy. The load balancer does not route client requests to unhealthy backend servers.
      ☒   **A, B,** and **D** are incorrect. None of the listed items is indicated in Figure 1-6. The Unhealthy Threshold field indicates this is a health probe configuration.

30.   ☑   **B.** Inbound Network Address Translation (NAT) rules allow traffic external to the load balancer to come in through the load balancer and be mapped to backend servers for management purposes.
      ☒   **A, C,** and **D** are incorrect. None of the listed options would allow management access to backend servers through a load balancer.

31.   ☑   **D.** Each backend server may have a replicated SQL database, or each backend server may refer to shared storage or a dedicated server hosting the SQL database.
      ☒   **A, B,** and **C** are incorrect. There is no definitive number of active SQL database instances implied just because there is an active-active load balancer configuration. There are, however, two load balancers active concurrently (active-active).

32.   ☑   **B.** An active-passive load balancer configuration links two load balancers together for high availability, but only one load balancer is active at any time.
      ☒   **A, C,** and **D** are incorrect. An active-active load balancer configuration means both load balancers are active at the same time and can route client traffic to backend servers. Active-scheduled and active-persistent are invalid load balancer configuration terms.

Chapter 2

Introduction to Security Terminology

QUESTIONS

Threat actors are the entities that enact malicious activities. Identifying threat actor types and their motivations is the first step in planning threat countermeasures.

Information is power. Sharing cybersecurity intelligence helps organizations craft meaningful security policies, and it enhances the efficacy of security monitoring and reporting tools. This includes identifying threat vectors such as e-mail systems, removable media, or cloud services. The protection of data assets is undertaken by a variety of roles, such as data custodians, data controllers, data processors, and data owners.

1. Your manager, Wayne, is concerned about malicious users who might compromise servers and remain undetected for a period of time. What type of threat is Wayne concerned about?
   A. Insider threat
   B. Hacktivist
   C. Advanced persistent threat
   D. State actor

2. Which type of malicious users or groups attempt to promote a political or ideological view?
   A. Hacktivist
   B. Advanced persistent threat
   C. State actor
   D. Insider threat

3. Your organization has begun quarterly lunch-and-learn sessions to educate employees about current scams and computer security threats to increase their awareness and help prevent security issues such as data leaks. To which of the following items does this initiative best apply?
   A. Hacktivist
   B. Advanced persistent threat
   C. State actor
   D. Insider threat

4. Which type of malicious entity is most likely to launder the proceeds of illegal activities through online gambling sites?
   A. State actor
   B. Criminal syndicate

    C.   Hacktivists

    D.   Script kiddie

5. You are part of a team that has been hired to conduct penetration tests. Which term best describes your team?

    A.   Unauthorized hackers

    B.   Semi-authorized hackers

    C.   Script kiddies

    D.   Authorized hackers

6. You are an IT technician responsible for defining and implementing IT solutions throughout the organization. You have discovered that users in a remote branch office have configured a Wi-Fi network for use only in their location without approval from headquarters. Which term best describes this scenario?

    A.   Authorized hacking

    B.   Hacktivists

    C.   Hardening

    D.   Shadow IT

7. Which type of malicious actor is the most likely to have the most resources and funding?

    A.   Hacktivist

    B.   Criminal syndicate

    C.   State actor

    D.   Script kiddie

8. You have enabled firewall rules to allow only HTTPS connections to a web server that resides in your company's server room. The company's web site stores sensitive customer data in a backend database stored on the same host. Which types of potential security problems do company IT technicians present in this scenario? (Choose two.)

    A.   On-path attacks

    B.   Direct physical access

    C.   Phishing

    D.   Insider threat

9. Your organization has deployed mission-critical applications to a public cloud service provider (CSP) platform. The CSP recently disclosed a security flaw in the underlying network switches that was exploited by malicious users. The network switches were missing a firmware update that addressed security vulnerabilities. From your organization's perspective, what is the source of this security issue?

    A.   Update management

    B.   Network switch vendor

    C.   CSP organizational security policies

    D.   Supply chain

10. You manage an air-gapped secure network named NET1 for a utility provider. NET1 does not connect in any way to any other network. You have scheduled the automatic scanning of the network for unauthorized network devices. Recently, new malware that is active on the Internet was discovered on NET1. What is the most likely explanation for how the malware made its way to NET1?

    A. A rogue Wi-Fi router introduced the malware.
    B. Users on NET1 downloaded infected files from the Internet.
    C. Users on NET1 clicked a malicious link on a social media site.
    D. Removable media was infected.

11. After running a vulnerability scan of your entire network because of newly reported vulnerabilities on the Internet, you notice that Linux-based honeypots on your network that are intentionally configured to appear vulnerable were not reported as vulnerable. What is the most likely cause of this behavior?

    A. A credentialed scan was not run.
    B. The honeypots have an OS-level firewall enabled.
    C. Vulnerability scanners cannot identify vulnerabilities on Linux hosts.
    D. The vulnerability database is not up-to-date.

12. You are reviewing network analysis reports for signs that could suggest malicious activity. What are you looking for?

    A. Threat map
    B. Automated indicator sharing (AIS)
    C. Indicators of compromise
    D. Predictive analysis

13. You are researching potential vulnerabilities with the way that Session Initiation Protocol (SIP) Voice over IP (VoIP) calls are established over the network. Which documentation source explains the standardized inner workings of SIP VoIP calls?

    A. Open source intelligence
    B. RFCs
    C. Vendor documentation
    D. Automated indicator sharing

14. What is the primary purpose of the Tor web browser?

    A. Accessing media content in foreign countries
    B. Downloading music
    C. Web application vulnerability scanning
    D. Accessing the Web anonymously

15. Which role is responsible for managing data in alignment with policies set forth by data owners?

    A. Data owner

    B. Data custodian

    C. Data analyst

    D. Data privacy officer

16. Which role is ultimately responsible for a data asset?

    A. Data owner

    B. Data custodian

    C. Data analyst

    D. Data privacy officer

17. Your organization collects, processes, and stores EU customer data. As a result, a Data Privacy Officer (DPO) role has been established to ensure regulatory compliance. To which European digital privacy legislation does this role apply?

    A. PCI DSS

    B. HIPAA

    C. PIPEDA

    D. GDPR

18. An online retailer legally collects and stores sensitive customer data that it then sells to marketing firms. Which data role is the online retailer partaking in?

    A. Data processor

    B. Data privacy officer

    C. Data custodian

    D. Data controller

19. A marketing firm legally purchases sensitive customer data from a data collection agency. Which data role is the marketing firm partaking in?

    A. Data processor

    B. Data privacy officer

    C. Data custodian

    D. Data controller

20. Which phrase best encompasses the mapping out of specific malicious user activity from beginning to end?

    A. Automated indicator sharing

    B. Adversary tactics, techniques, and procedures

    C. Indicator of compromise

    D. Predictive analysis

21. You are researching the potential of an employee e-mail account breach. You suspect these accounts may have been used to sign up to a variety of social media sites. After searching and viewing multiple web pages related to this issue, you become overwhelmed with information. What type of public-sourced security intelligence tool should you use to facilitate further testing of your suspicions?

A. Open source intelligence

B. Academic journals

C. File and code repositories

D. Conferences

22. Which of the following are standards related to the sharing of threat intelligence information? (Choose two.)

A. TAXII

B. OSINT

C. STIX

D. RFC

23. Which statements regarding the usage of the Tor web browser are correct? (Choose two.)

A. The Tor network is an Internet overlay network.

B. The Tor network requires the use of IPv6 addresses.

C. The Tor browser host IP address is hidden.

D. Usage of the Tor network requires signing up with an account.

24. Which of the following are normally considered potential insider threats? (Choose two.)

A. Port scanning of firewall interfaces

B. Contractors

C. Infected e-mail file attachments

D. Brute-force username and password web site attacks

25. Which type of hacker may discover and exploit vulnerabilities, yet lacks malicious intent?

A. Authorized

B. Red hat

C. Semi-authorized

D. Unauthorized

26. Which type of hacker has malicious intent and attempts to discover and exploit vulnerabilities?

A. Authorized

B. Red hat

C. Semi-authorized

D. Unauthorized

27. Which type of active security testing attempts to exploit discovered vulnerabilities?

A. Penetration testing

B. Vulnerability scanning

   C.   Port scanning

   D.   Network scanning

28. Which of the following wireless cryptographic protocols are the most vulnerable? (Choose two.)

   A.   WEP

   B.   WPA

   C.   WPA2

   D.   Default Wi-Fi router credentials

29. Refer to Figure 2-1. You are reviewing the configuration of a wireless router used in an executive boardroom. Which items should be changed to harden the wireless network? (Choose two.)

   A.   Do not use WEP.

   B.   Change the wireless network name.

   C.   Change the wireless channel to a different value.

   D.   Enable extended range mode.

FIGURE 2-1   Wireless router configuration

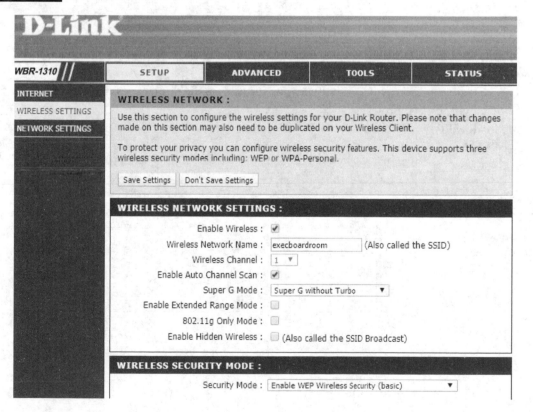

30. Refer to Figure 2-2. You are configuring notifications on a company mobile device app. To which of the following terms does this configuration best apply?

    A. Device hardening

    B. Shadow IT

    C. TAXII

    D. STIX

FIGURE 2-2

Mobile device
network change
notifications

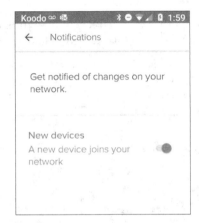

31. Refer to Figure 2-3. To which of the following terms does the display message apply?

    A. Anonymous web browsing

    B. Shadow IT

    C. TAXII

    D. STIX

FIGURE 2-3

Tor web browser
connection reset

32. Refer to Figure 2-4. To which of the following terms does the display message apply?
- A. Data processor
- B. Data custodian
- C. Data controller
- D. Data analyst

FIGURE 2-4

Windows NTFS
file system
security
permissions

QUICK ANSWER KEY

1. C	**9.** D	**17.** D	**25.** C
2. A	**10.** D	**18.** D	**26.** D
3. D	**11.** D	**19.** A	**27.** A
4. B	**12.** C	**20.** B	**28.** A, D
5. D	**13.** B	**21.** A	**29.** A, B
6. D	**14.** D	**22.** A, C	**30.** B
7. C	**15.** B	**23.** A, C	**31.** A
8. B, D	**16.** A	**24.** B, C	**32.** B

IN-DEPTH ANSWERS

1. ☑ **C.** An advanced persistent threat (APT) implies a compromised network or device, whereby malicious actors, such as competitors or hacking groups, retain control of the compromised system for a period time before being detected.
    ☒ **A, B,** and **D** are incorrect. Insider threats result from an actor within the organization who has knowledge of internal procedures, configurations, or details that would be unknown to external users. Hacktivists exploit vulnerable systems with the intention of promoting awareness of social, political, or ideological views. State actors are hacking groups supported by nations for the purposes of intelligence gathering or computer system disruption of other nations. State actors have considerable resources and sophisticated capabilities for hacking.

2. ☑ **A.** Hacktivists exploit vulnerable systems with the intention of promoting awareness of social, political, or ideological views.
    ☒ **B, C,** and **D** are incorrect. An APT implies a compromised network or device, whereby malicious actors, such as competitors or hacking groups, retain control of the compromised system for a period of time before being detected. State actors are hacking groups supported by nations for the purposes of intelligence gathering or computer system disruption of other nations. Insider threats result from an actor within the organization who has knowledge of internal procedures, configurations, or details that would be unknown to external users.

3. ☑ **D.** Insider threats result from an actor within the organization who has knowledge of internal procedures, configurations, or details that would be unknown to external users. Internal user training and awareness help protect digital assets from unintentional security breaches.
    ☒ **A, B,** and **C** are incorrect. Hacktivists exploit vulnerable systems with the intention of promoting awareness of social, political, or ideological views. An APT implies a compromised network or device, whereby malicious actors, such as competitors or hacking groups, retain control of the compromised system for a period time before being detected. State actors are hacking groups supported by nations for the purposes of intelligence gathering or computer system disruption of other nations.

4. ☑ **B.** A criminal syndicate is related to organized crime, which is likely to profit through illegal means and therefore must "clean" the proceeds through laundering.
    ☒ **A, C,** and **D** are incorrect. State actors are hacking groups supported by nations for the purposes of intelligence gathering or computer system disruption of other nations. Hacktivists exploit vulnerable systems with the intention of promoting awareness of social, political, or ideological views. Script kiddies have limited technical sophistication, and as opposed to creating their own exploit tools, they use exploit tools created by others.

5. ☑ **D.** Authorized hackers are the "good guys"; they are hired to perform penetration tests to identify exploitable security weaknesses.

    ☒ **A, B,** and **C** are incorrect. Unauthorized hackers steal sensitive data or break into systems and are usually motivated by profit, revenge, or other nefarious motives. Semi-authorized hackers sit between Authorized and Unauthorized; they do not have malicious intent but may cross legal or ethical boundaries, such as breaking into computer systems at an airport and then notifying officials that their systems are vulnerable. Script kiddies have limited technical sophistication, and as opposed to creating their own exploit tools, they use exploit tools created by others.

6. ☑ **D.** The term "shadow IT" refers to non-IT staff who install or configure networked devices without central approval from the IT department; this would include adding a Wi-Fi router to a network without approval.

    ☒ **A, B,** and **C** are incorrect. Authorized hackers are the "good guys"; they are hired to perform penetration tests to identify exploitable security weaknesses. Hacktivists exploit vulnerable systems with the intention of promoting awareness of social, political, or ideological views. Hardening is the process of securing a network or device by applying updates, removing unnecessary features, changing default settings, and so on.

7. ☑ **C.** State actors are likely to have ample funding for their activities. These hacking groups are supported by nations for the purposes of intelligence gathering or computer system disruption of other nations.

    ☒ **A, B,** and **D** are incorrect. Hacktivists exploit vulnerable systems with the intention of promoting awareness of social, political, or ideological views. A criminal syndicate is related to organized crime, which often generates profits through illegal means, and would have plenty of resources and funding available for malicious activities. Script kiddies have limited technical sophistication and are often individuals who are hacking a system for fun; they are not likely to be funded.

8. ☑ **B** and **D.** Technicians who can gain access to the server room have direct access to the physical server and storage arrays, and physical access bypasses firewall rules. This is considered a potential insider threat.

    ☒ **A** and **C** are incorrect. On-path attacks involve a malicious user inserting themselves in network conversation between two unsuspecting victims. Phishing involves the attempt to acquire sensitive data from unsuspecting victims, usually through deception, such as by sending an SMS text message or e-mail message that looks legitimate but is not.

9. ☑ **D.** In this case, the cloud service provider (CSP) is a part of the supply chain, or service delivery platform (SDP), in the sense that the CSP supplies the IT services infrastructure used by the cloud customer.

    ☒ **A, B,** and **C** are incorrect. Applying updates and reading security documentation from vendor web sites for network switches are activities specific to the CSP, not you as the cloud customer. Cloud customers have no detailed knowledge of CSP organizational security policies and whether those policies mention applying updates nor would customers know if this is a case in which policies were not adhered to.

10.   ☑   **D.** Since NET1 has no connections to other networks, the most likely explanation is that the malware was transmitted through infected files on removable media.
  ☒   **A, B,** and **C** are incorrect. Since automatic network scanning is in place, a rogue Wi-Fi router would get detected. Users on NET1 do not have access to the Internet or social media sites.

11.   ☑   **D.** Vulnerability scanning tools use a database of known vulnerabilities as a comparison mechanism when scanning hosts and apps. Scanning tools can be configured to subscribe to vulnerability and threat feeds for automatic updating. If this database is not kept up-to-date, newer vulnerabilities may not be detected during scanning.
  ☒   **A, B,** and **C** are incorrect. A credentialed scan will provide a more in-depth scan of hosts that use those credentials, and OS-level firewalls can block some scanning traffic, but since the scan was initiated because of a newly reported vulnerability, these are not as likely as an out-of-date vulnerability database. Vulnerability scanners normally support many different OS platforms, including Linux.

12.   ☑   **C.** Indicators of compromise (IoCs) suggest that malicious activity may be taking place or has taken place.
  ☒   **A, B,** and **D** are incorrect. Threat maps allow for the visualization of active threats geographically. Automated indicator sharing (AIS) allows for the exchange of cybersecurity intelligence information between entities. Predictive analysis is used to analyze vast amounts of network and host activity logs to determine if a security incident is imminent.

13.   ☑   **B.** Requests for comment (RFCs) are publicly available technical standardization documents stemming from various international technical bodies that detail how specific types of technologies such as HTTP, DNS, or the ASCII character set work. Vendors building software and hardware products generally adhere to RFCs.
  ☒   **A, C,** and **D** are incorrect. Open source intelligence (OSINT) tools ingest cybersecurity intelligence data from various public sources to facilitate cybersecurity hardening activities. Vendor documentation is proprietary and will not provide as much standardized information about network protocols as RFCs will; vendor documentation will focus on how that vendor implemented RFC standards. Paying customers will often acquire access to closed source intelligence, such as after purchasing IT security solutions. Automated indicator sharing (AIS) uses information that can stem from open source as well as closed source, or proprietary origins, as well as local industry groups that focus on identifying suspicious activity. AIS focuses on the exchange of cybersecurity intelligence information between entities.

14.   ☑   **D.** The Tor web browser enables anonymous connectivity to the Web.
  ☒   **A, B,** and **C** are incorrect. While the Tor browser can be used to access media and download music, this is not its primary purpose. Tor is not a web app vulnerability scanning tool.

15. ☑ **B.** The data custodian, or data steward, role involves managing data assets in accordance with policies set forth by data owners. An example of a data custodian is a file server administrator that can set file system permissions.

 ☒ **A, C,** and **D** are incorrect. Data owners set policies on how data will be managed; they are ultimately responsible for the data. Data analysts collect data from multiple sources in order to gain meaningful insights that may not otherwise be derived. A data privacy officer (DPO), also referred to as a data protection officer, is a role put in place to ensure compliance, such as with the European Union (EU) General Data Protection Regulation (GDPR) to protect sensitive EU citizen data.

16. ☑ **A.** Data owners set policies on how data will be managed; they are ultimately responsible for the data.

 ☒ **B, C,** and **D** are incorrect. The data custodian, or data steward, role involves managing data assets in accordance with policies set forth by data owners. Data analysts collect data from multiple sources to gain meaningful insights that might otherwise not be derived. A data privacy officer (DPO) ensures compliance with the EU General Data Protection Regulation (GDPR) to protect sensitive EU citizen data.

17. ☑ **D.** The EU GDPR is an act of legislation designed to protect sensitive EU citizen data. A data privacy officer ensures compliance with regulations such as the GDPR.

 ☒ **A, B,** and **C** are incorrect. The Payment Card Industry Data Security Standard (PCI DSS) provides guidance on securing environments where credit card information is processed. The Health Insurance Portability and Accountability Act (HIPAA) is an American act of legislation designed to protect sensitive medical patient information. The Personal Information Protection and Electronic Documents Act (PIPEDA) is a Canadian data privacy act of legislation.

18. ☑ **D.** The data controller determines how data can be used, such as providing it to other parties.

 ☒ **A, B,** and **C** are incorrect. The data processor role, in this example, is assumed by the marketing firm that purchases data for processing purposes, such as to enhance targeted marketing campaigns. A data privacy officer (DPO) ensures compliance with security standards and regulations such as the EU GDPR to protect sensitive EU citizen data. The data custodian manages data assets in accordance with policies set forth by data owners.

19. ☑ **A.** The data processor role, in this example, is assumed by the marketing firm that purchases data for processing purposes, such as to enhance targeted marketing campaigns.

 ☒ **B, C,** and **D** are incorrect. A data privacy officer ensures compliance with security and regulatory standards such as the EU GDPR to protect sensitive EU citizen data. The data custodian manages data assets in accordance with policies set forth by data owners. The data controller role determines how data can be used, such as providing it to other parties.

20. ☑ **B.** Adversary tactics, techniques, and procedures (TTP) is used to define how malicious attacks are carried out.

☒ **A, C,** and **D** are incorrect. Automated indicator sharing (AIS) uses information that can stem from open source, closed source, or proprietary origins, as well as local industry groups that focus on identifying suspicious activity. AIS focuses on the exchange of cybersecurity intelligence information between entities. Indicators of compromise (IoCs) suggest that malicious activity may be taking place, or has taken place. Predictive analysis is used to analyze vast amounts of network and host activity logs to determine if a security incident is imminent.

21. ☑ **A.** Open source intelligence (OSINT) tools ingest cybersecurity intelligence data from various public sources to facilitate cybersecurity activities.

☒ **B, C,** and **D** are incorrect. Academic journals and conferences can provide valuable security information, but they are not security intelligence tools that can be used for testing. File and code repositories such as GitHub and Bitbucket serve as centralized programming code repositories and can provide security tools, but OSINT is more specific to gathering security information from many sources and using it for security purposes.

22. ☑ **A and C.** The Trusted Automated Exchange of Indicator Information (TAXII) standard defines how cybersecurity intelligence information is shared among entities. The Structured Threat Information eXpression (STIX) standard defines the data exchange format for cybersecurity information.

☒ **B and D** are incorrect. Open source intelligence (OSINT) tools ingest cybersecurity intelligence data from various public sources to facilitate cybersecurity hardening activities. Requests for comment (RFCs) are publicly available technical standardization documents stemming from various international technical bodies that detail how specific types of technologies such as HTTP, DNS, or the ASCII character set work.

23. ☑ **A and C.** The Tor network is considered an overlay network in that it sits on the existing public Internet infrastructure; it is designed to use encryption and multiple global relay points to protect user activity from traffic analysis. As a result, using the Tor web browser for Tor network connectivity hides the IP address of the machine running the Tor web browser.

☒ **B and D** are incorrect. IPv6 is not required on the Tor network, and there is no requirement for setting up a user account.

24. ☑ **B and C.** Contractors working for an organization may have knowledge of or access to company processes and systems. Users opening infected file attachments from e-mail messages means the infection would then be on the inside. Both of these present potential insider threats.

☒ **A and D** are incorrect. Port scanning of firewall interfaces is commonplace and is not specifically conducted from internal networks, but is normally conducted from outside the network by external users. Using brute-force techniques in an attempt to compromise user accounts can be conducted internally but it can also involve an external perspective, such as against a public-facing web site by malicious users.

25. ☑ **C.** Semi-authorized hackers discover vulnerabilities and can compromise systems, which could cross legal or ethical boundaries, but their intent is not malicious. Often Semi-authorized hackers will compromise systems and let the system owners know about the vulnerabilities.

    ☒ **A, B,** and **D** are incorrect. Authorized hackers attempt to identify and sometimes exploit vulnerabilities as part of security testing, such as when teams are hired to conduct penetration tests. "Red-hat hackers" is not a valid security term. Unauthorized hackers are users with malicious intent who attempt to exploit systems.

26. ☑ **D.** Unauthorized hackers are individuals with malicious intent that attempt to exploit systems.

    ☒ **A, B,** and **C** are incorrect. Authorized hackers attempt to identify and sometimes exploit vulnerabilities as part of security testing, such as when teams are hired to conduct penetration tests. "Red-hat hackers" is not a valid security term. Semi-authorized hackers discover vulnerabilities and can compromise systems, which could cross legal or ethical boundaries, but their intent is not malicious.

27. ☑ **A.** Penetration tests (pen tests) identify and attempt to exploit vulnerabilities.

    ☒ **B, C,** and **D** are incorrect. Vulnerability scans only identify vulnerabilities; no attempt is made to exploit discovered weaknesses. Port scanning is a reconnaissance technique used to learn which network services are running on hosts. Network scanning is used to identify which devices are up and running on a network, and also to identify any services they may be running.

28. ☑ **A and D.** Wired Equivalent Privacy (WEP) is an older, deprecated wireless encryption protocol and should not be used, because many freely available tools can compromise WEP. Using default credentials always presents a security risk because these are widely known.

    ☒ **B and C** are incorrect. Wi-Fi Protected Access (WPA) and its successor, WPA2, are wireless encryption protocols that succeed WEP. Although they can be compromised, this is not done as quickly or as easily as it is with WEP or with the use of default Wi-Fi router credentials.

29. ☑ **A and B.** Wired Equivalent Privacy (WEP) should not be used because of its many known security flaws; instead, use WPA2 or, if supported by the device, WPA3. Wireless network names, or service set identifiers (SSIDs), should never truly reflect the location in which they are used, because this provides malicious users with more details they can use for nefarious purposes.

    ☒ **C and D** are incorrect. Changing a wireless channel can reduce interference but does not increase security. Extending wireless range could decrease security, such as in the case of allowing wireless signals to propagate beyond an office space.

30. ☑ **B.** Shadow IT relates to the non-IT staff implementation of network devices and configurations without centralized IT department approval, such as adding unauthorized devices to the network. Many available tools can notify IT staff when new devices are added to a network.
☒ **A, C,** and **D** are incorrect. Device hardening involves reducing the device's attack service with activities such as applying updates, removing unnecessary components, and changing default settings. The Trusted Automated Exchange of Indication Information (TAXII) standard defines how cybersecurity intelligence information is shared among entities. The Structured Threat Information EXpression (STIX) standard defines the data exchange format for cybersecurity information.

31. ☑ **A.** The Tor web browser is used to connect to the Dark Web and the Internet anonymously by routing browsing traffic through a variety of servers in different geographical regions.
☒ **B, C,** and **D** are incorrect. Shadow IT relates to the non-IT staff implementation of network devices and configurations without centralized IT department approval, such as adding unauthorized devices to the network. The TAXII standard defines how cybersecurity intelligence information is shared among entities. The STIX standard defines the data exchange format for cybersecurity information.

32. ☑ **B.** The data custodian, or data steward, role involves managing data assets in accordance with policies set forth by data owners. In this case, setting file system permissions is a responsibility of the data custodian. The listed file system permissions are applied locally on the machine as well as over the network via the server message block (SMB) protocol when the folder is shared.
☒ **A, C,** and **D** are incorrect. The data processor role applies actions to data within the confines of parameters specified by the data controller, such as data transformations between file formats, the secure use and storage of data, data versioning and archiving. The data controller role determines how data can be used, such as providing it to other parties. Data analysts collect data from multiple sources to gain meaningful insights that may not otherwise be derived.

Chapter 3

Security Policies and Standards

QUESTIONS

Security policies provide the framework from which all types of users can learn the proper procedures in using computing devices and accessing data. Policies are often influenced by laws, regulations, and security standards. Management support is crucial to ensure that the security policies are understood and enforced to mitigate risk. User awareness and training provide users with this knowledge, and metrics, such as thorough testing, must be gathered to determine training effectiveness.

1. Your online retail business accepts PayPal and credit card payments. You need to ensure that your company is compliant with the relevant security standards. Which payment security standard should you focus on?

    A. GDPR

    B. PCI DSS

    C. HIPAA

    D. PIPEDA

2. Your legal consulting services company is headquartered in Berlin with a branch office in Paris. You are determining how to comply with applicable data privacy regulations. Which of the following security standards must your company comply with?

    A. GDPR

    B. PCI DSS

    C. HIPAA

    D. PIPEDA

3. You have been hired to review security controls for a medical practice in rural Tennessee. Which of the following data privacy frameworks must the medical practice be compliant with?

    A. GDPR

    B. PCI DSS

    C. HIPAA

    D. PIPEDA

4. Which action will have the largest impact on mitigating against SQL injection attacks?

    A. Enable HTTPS

    B. Change default web server settings

    C.   Enable input validation

    D.   Apply web server host OS updates

5.   You are planning the secure management of servers and network infrastructure devices on your corporate LAN. Which design will best protect these devices from RDP and SSH attacks?

    A.   Enabling HTTPS

    B.   Periodic vulnerability scanning

    C.   SSH public key authentication

    D.   Dedicated network management interface

6.   You need to manage cloud-based Windows virtual machines (VMs) from your on-premises network. Which option presents the most secure remote management solution?

    A.   Enable HTTPS for RDP

    B.   Configure each VM with a public IPv6 address

    C.   Use PowerShell remoting for remote management

    D.   Manage the VMs through a jump box

7.   During customer support calls, customer service representatives periodically pull up customer details on their screens, including credit card numbers. What should be enabled to prevent the disclosure of credit card numbers?

    A.   Tokenization

    B.   Anonymization

    C.   Data minimization

    D.   Data masking

8.   You have been tasked with creating a corporate security policy regarding smart phone usage for business purposes. What should you do first?

    A.   Issue smart phones to all employees.

    B.   Obtain support from management.

    C.   Get a legal opinion.

    D.   Create the first draft of the policy.

9.   Match the security policy terms with the appropriate definitions:

Security Policy Terms	Definitions
Scope _____	A. Describes how the security policy improves security
Overview _____	B. Consequences of policy nonadherence
Policy _____	C. Explanation of terms used throughout the security policy
Definitions _____	D. Collection of dos and don'ts
Enforcement _____	E. Defines which set of users a security policy applies to

10. Christine is the server administrator for your organization. Her manager provided step-by-step security policies outlining how servers should be configured to maximize security. Which type of security policy will Christine be implementing?

    A. Mail server acceptable use policy

    B. VPN server acceptable use policy

    C. Procedural policy

    D. File server acceptable use policy

11. Which of the following are examples of PII? (Choose two.)

    A. Public IP address of a NAT router

    B. Mobile phone number

    C. Digital certificate

    D. Gender

12. After a lengthy background check and interviewing process, your company hired a new payroll clerk named Tammy. Tammy will be using a web browser on a company computer at the office to access the payroll application on a public cloud provider web site over the Internet. Which type of document should Tammy read and sign?

    A. Internet acceptable use policy

    B. Password policy

    C. Service level agreement

    D. Remote access acceptable use policy

13. You are configuring a password policy for users in the Berlin office. Passwords must be changed every 60 days. You must ensure that user passwords cannot be changed more than once within the 60-day interval. What should you configure?

    A. Minimum password age

    B. Maximum password age

    C. Password complexity

    D. Password history

14. Your company has decided to adopt a public cloud device management solution whereby all devices are centrally managed from a web site hosted on servers in a data center. Management has instructed you to ensure that the solution is reliable and always available. Which type of document should you focus on?

    A. Password policy

    B. Service level agreement

    C. Remote access acceptable use policy

    D. Mobile device acceptable use policy

15. Which of the following options best describe the proper use of PII? (Choose two.)
    A. Law enforcement tracking an Internet offender using a public IP address
    B. Distributing an e-mail contact list to marketing firms
    C. Logging into a secured laptop using a fingerprint scanner
    D. Practicing due diligence

16. Your company restricts firewall administrators from modifying firewall rules unless they make the modifications with a member of the IT security team. What is this an example of?
    A. Due care
    B. Separation of duties
    C. Principle of least privilege
    D. Acceptable use

17. You are the network administrator for a legal firm. Users in Vancouver must be able to view trade secrets for patent submission. You have shared a network folder called Trade Secrets and allowed the following NTFS permissions:

    ▪ Vancouver_Staff: Read, List Folder Contents
    ▪ Executives: Write
    ▪ IT_Admins: Full Control

    Regarding Vancouver staff, which principle is being adhered to?
    A. Job rotation
    B. Least privilege
    C. Mandatory vacations
    D. Separation of duties

18. The Accounts Payable department notices large out-of-country purchases made using a corporate credit card. After discussing the matter with Juan, the employee whose name is on the credit card, they realize that somebody has illegally obtained the credit card details. You also learn that Juan recently received an e-mail from what appeared to be the credit card company asking him to sign in to their web site to validate his account, which he did. How could this have been avoided?
    A. Provide credit card holders with smartcards.
    B. Tell users to increase the strength of online passwords.
    C. Install a workstation-based firewall.
    D. Provide security awareness training to employees.

19. Which of the following statements are true? (Choose two.)
    A. Security labels are used for data classifications, such as restricted and top secret.
    B. PII is applicable only to biometric authentication devices.
    C. Forcing user password changes is considered change management.
    D. A person's signature on a check is considered PII.

20. What is the primary purpose of enforcing a mandatory vacation policy?
    A. To adhere to government regulation
    B. To ensure employees are refreshed
    C. To enable other employees to experience other job roles
    D. To prevent improper activity

21. Which of the following is an example of PHI?
    A. Education records
    B. Employment records
    C. Fingerprints
    D. Credit history

22. As the IT security officer, you establish a security policy requiring that users protect all paper documents so that sensitive client, vendor, or company data is not stolen. What type of policy is this?
    A. Privacy
    B. Acceptable use
    C. Clean desk
    D. Password

23. Which of the following best illustrates potential security problems related to social media sites?
    A. Other users can easily see your IP address.
    B. Talkative employees can expose a company's intellectual property.
    C. Malicious users can use your pictures for steganography.
    D. Your credit card number is easily stolen.

24. Margaret, the head of HR, conducts an exit interview with a departing IT server technician named Irving. The interview encompasses Irving's view of the organization, such as the benefits of the job he held and suggestions of improvements that could be made. Which of the following issues should also be addressed in the exit interview? (Choose two.)
    A. Background check
    B. Job rotation
    C. Nondisclosure agreement
    D. Property return form

25. You are a file server administrator for a health organization. Management has asked you to configure your servers appropriately to classify files containing unique manufacturing processes. What is an appropriate data classification for these types of files?

    A. Proprietary

    B. PII

    C. PHI

    D. Public

26. Your organization must observe the appropriate cloud security ISO compliance standards. Which ISO standard must be observed?

    A. ISO 27001

    B. ISO 27017

    C. ISO 27002

    D. ISO 27701

27. Which of the following security standards focuses on assessing and managing risk?

    A. CIS

    B. SOC 2

    C. NIST CSF

    D. NIST RMF

28. Your organization hosts a public-facing web application using the architecture depicted in Figure 3-1. Which solutions would enable the secure remote management of DB1 from the Internet? (Choose two.)

    A. Jump box

    B. Expose DB1 directly to the Internet

    C. VPN

    D. Encryption of data at rest on DB1

FIGURE 3-1

Multi-tiered web application

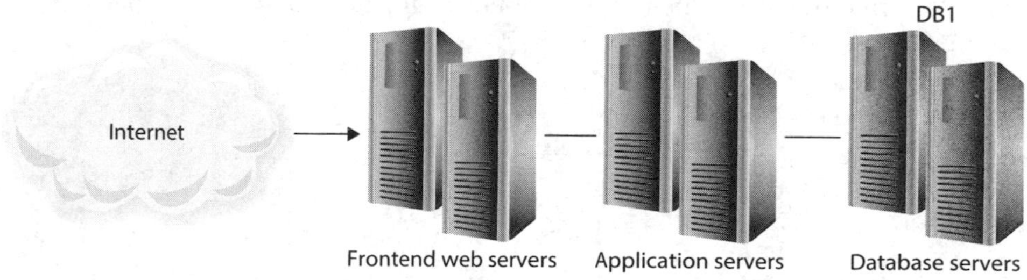

Internet

Frontend web servers   Application servers   Database servers

DB1

29. Refer to Figure 3-2. You have been tasked with hardening Internet access to Windows web server hosts. The web servers must be managed remotely using Remote Desktop Protocol. Standard TCP port number are in use. Which changes will enhance security? (Choose two.)
   A. On the Windows web servers, disable SSL v3 and enable TLS v1.2 or higher.
   B. On the firewall device, block all traffic destined for port 443.
   C. Deploy a jump box.
   D. On the Windows web servers, disable RDP.

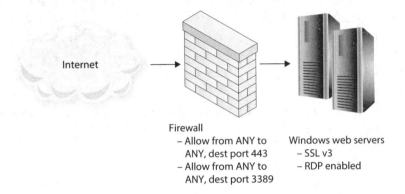

FIGURE 3-2

Public web server and firewall configuration

Internet

Firewall
– Allow from ANY to ANY, dest port 443
– Allow from ANY to ANY, dest port 3389

Windows web servers
– SSL v3
– RDP enabled

30. To enhance your organization's security posture, management has decided that new and existing security technician employee IT security awareness will be implemented through gamification. What is the best way to achieve this?
   A. User onboarding procedures
   B. Computer-based training
   C. Role-based training
   D. Capture the flag

31. Which type of document is a nonbinding agreement between two parties?
   A. BPA
   B. MSA
   C. MOU
   D. EOSL

32. In Figure 3-3, match the terms on the left with the descriptions on the right. Note that some descriptions on the right do not have matching terms on the left.

FIGURE 3-3

Security terms and descriptions

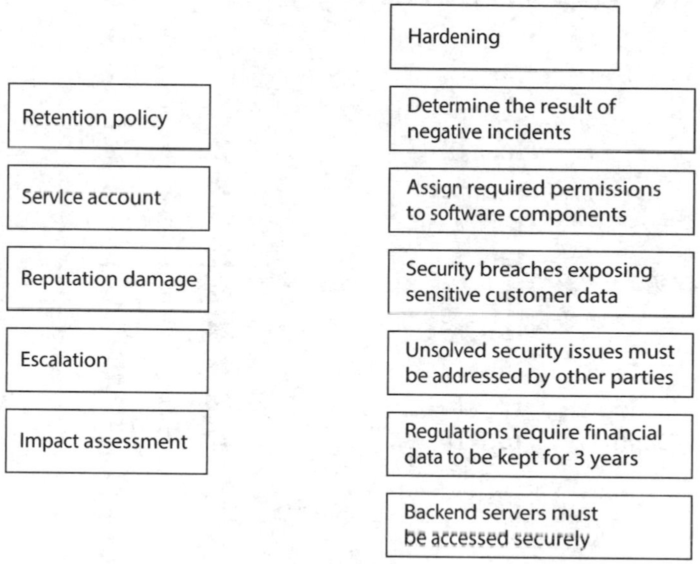

| Retention policy |
| Service account |
| Reputation damage |
| Escalation |
| Impact assessment |

| Hardening |
| Determine the result of negative incidents |
| Assign required permissions to software components |
| Security breaches exposing sensitive customer data |
| Unsolved security issues must be addressed by other parties |
| Regulations require financial data to be kept for 3 years |
| Backend servers must be accessed securely |

33. You have instructed your web app developers to include a message for web site visitors detailing how their data will be processed and used. What should web app develops add to the site?

A. Information life cycle document

B. Terms of agreement

C. Public disclosure

D. Privacy notice

QUICK ANSWER KEY

1. B
2. A
3. C
4. C
5. D
6. D
7. D
8. B
9. See "In-Depth Answers."

10. C
11. B, C
12. A
13. A
14. B
15. A, C
16. B
17. B
18. D

19. A, D
20. D
21. C
22. C
23. B
24. C, D
25. A
26. B
27. D

28. A, C
29. A, C
30. D
31. C
32. See "In-Depth Answers."
33. D

IN-DEPTH ANSWERS

1. ☑ **B.** The Payment Card Industry Data Security Standard (PCI DSS) provides guidance on securing environments where credit card information is processed.
☒ **A, C,** and **D** are incorrect. The European Union (EU) General Data Protection Regulation (GDPR) is designed to protect sensitive EU citizen data. In the United States, the Health Insurance Portability and Accountability Act (HIPAA) is designed to protect sensitive medical patient information. The Personal Information Protection and Electronic Documents Act (PIPEDA) is Canadian legislation designed to protect data privacy.

2. ☑ **A.** The GDPR is designed to protect sensitive EU citizen data.
☒ **B, C,** and **D** are incorrect. The PCI DSS provides guidance on securing environments where credit card information is processed. In the United States, HIPAA is designed to protect sensitive medical patient information. PIPEDA is Canadian legislation that applies to how organizations manage personally identifiable information (PII) as opposed to sensitive government data.

3. ☑ **C.** HIPAA is American legislation designed to protect sensitive medical patient information.
☒ **A, B,** and **D** are incorrect. The GDPR is designed to protect sensitive EU citizen data. PCI DSS provides guidance on securing environments where credit card information is processed. PIPEDA is Canadian legislation designed to protect data privacy.

4. ☑ **C.** Input validation is used to prevent unexpected characters or data from being sent to a server in a SQL injection attack. This can prevent sensitive data disclosure.
☒ **A, B,** and **D** are incorrect. Enabling HTTPS increases the security of network transmissions. Changing default settings hardens the web server, as does applying OS updates. None of these is a SQL injection attack countermeasure.

5. ☑ **D.** A dedicated network management interface connects to a dedicated secure network used only for management purposes. Because no user traffic is present, this will protect devices from Remote Desktop Protocol (RDP) and Secure Shell (SSH) attacks.
☒ **A, B,** and **C** are incorrect. Although enabling HTTPS increases the security of network transmissions, it does not specifically protect against RDP and SSH attacks. Periodic vulnerability scanning is important for identifying weaknesses, but it is not focused on remote management, so it will not protect against these attacks. SSH public key authentication improves upon Linux username and password authentication, and in conjunction with dedicated management network interfaces it provides a secure remote management solution.

6. ☑ **D.** A jump box is a host with a connection to a public and a private network. After successfully authenticating to the jump box, administrators can remotely connect to hosts on the private network. This prevents the direct exposure of hosts to the public network.

   ☒ **A, B,** and **C** are incorrect. None of the listed solutions presents as secure a remote management solution as a jump box, which prevents direct access to private hosts from the Internet. Allowing direct, externally-initiated access to internal Windows VMs via HTTPS, IPv6, or PowerShell remoting presents more security risks than allowing indirect access through a jump box. One reason for this is that the jump box may only be accessible using nonstandard port numbers or through a VPN.

7. ☑ **D.** Data masking replaces sensitive characters (such as credit card number digits) with other characters, such as asterisks (*). Normally, only the last four digits of a credit number are shown. Data masking is an option available in many database solutions.

   ☒ **A, B,** and **C** are incorrect. Data tokenization substitutes sensitive data for something that cannot be traced back to that sensitive data (the "token"). The token can then be presented to apps instead of the original sensitive data (such as credit card information). Anonymization modifies data so that it cannot be traced back to its original form; data masking and tokenization are forms of data anonymization. Data minimization is a strategy of collecting and processing only required data.

8. ☑ **B.** Management support is crucial in the successful implementation of corporate security policies.

   ☒ **A, C,** and **D** are incorrect. Smart phones should be issued only after having obtained management approval and having created the appropriate policies. Legal counsel can be an important part of the policy creation process, but management approval must be obtained first, even before the first draft of the policy.

9. ☑ Scope: **E,** Overview: **A,** Policy: **D,** Definitions: **C,** Enforcement: **B**

10. ☑ **C.** Procedural policies provide step-by-step instructions for configuring servers.

    ☒ **A, B,** and **D** are incorrect. Acceptable use policies are usually user-centric documents outlining rules and regulations for appropriate computing use, and they do not provide step-by-step instructions.

11. ☑ **B** and **C.** Personally identifiable information (PII) is data that uniquely identifies a person, such as a mobile phone number or digital certificate. The appropriate security controls must be put in place to prevent identify theft, which can include pseudo-anonymization to prevent tracing data back to an individual.

    ☒ **A** and **D** are incorrect. NAT device public IP addresses identify a network, but not a specific host that initiated a connection from that private network. The same private IP address could be used on separate private networks. Gender is a generic categorization that alone does not uniquely identify a person.

12. ☑ **A.** Because Tammy will be using company equipment to access the Internet, she should read and sign an Internet acceptable use policy.

☒ **B, C,** and **D** are incorrect. Password policies are rules stating how often passwords must change and so on. Service level agreements are contractual documents guaranteeing a specific quality, availability, and responsibility agreed upon between a service provider and the service user. Remote access acceptable use policies define how remote access to a network, such as through a VPN, is to be done securely.

13. ☑ **A.** The minimum password age is a period of time that must elapse before a password can be changed. This prevents users from changing passwords multiple times in a short period to reuse old passwords.

☒ **B, C,** and **D** are incorrect. The maximum password age defines the interval by which the password must be changed—in this case, 60 days. Password complexity prevents users from using simple passwords, such as a variation of the username. Password history prevents the reuse of passwords.

14. ☑ **B.** A service level agreement is a contract stipulating what level of service and availability can be expected from a third party.

☒ **A, C,** and **D** are incorrect. Password policies specify how user password behavior will be implemented. Remote access acceptable use policies dictate how users will securely access corporate networks remotely—for example, access from home or from hotels when traveling. Mobile device acceptable use policies dictate how mobile devices are to be used to conduct business.

15. ☑ **A** and **C.** Proper use of PII means not divulging a person's or entity's personal information to other parties. Law enforcement tracking criminals using IP addresses and logging in with a fingerprint scanner are proper uses of PII.

☒ **B** and **D** are incorrect. Distributing e-mail contact lists is an improper use of PII. Due diligence does not imply PII.

16. ☑ **B.** Separation of duties requires more than one person to complete a process such as controlling a firewall and its rules.

☒ **A, C,** and **D** are incorrect. Due care means implementing policies to correct security problems. The principle of least privilege requires users to have only the rights they need to do their jobs; although this answer could apply in this case, separation of duties is a much stronger answer. Acceptable use refers to proper conduct when using company assets.

17. ☑ **B.** The principle of least privilege states that people should be granted access based on the minimum access required to do their job. In this case, Vancouver staff members have only read access to the Trade Secrets because they should not be allowed to make changes.

☒ **A, C,** and **D** are incorrect. Job rotation refers to the practice of periodically moving people from one job role to a different role for a variety of reasons, such as employee skill enhancement or exposure to a wider range of business processes. Like job rotation, mandatory vacations are used as a tool to help detect potential fraud or privilege abuse while a user fulfilling a role is not actively working. Separation of duties is not related to file system security; it prevents a single person from having end-to-end control of a single business process.

18. ☑ **D.** If Juan had been made aware of phishing scams by attending phishing training campaigns or by being shown phishing simulations, he would have ignored the e-mail message. Perpetrators of this type of crime can be charged with fraud, which can result in fines or imprisonment, depending on applicable laws.

    ☒ **A, B,** and **C** are incorrect. Smartcards enable users to authenticate to a resource but would not have prevented this problem. Even the strongest password means nothing if the user willingly reveals it. Although very important, a workstation-based firewall will not prevent phishing scams.

19. ☑ **A** and **D.** Restricted and top secret are examples of security data labeling. A signature on a check is considered PII, since it is a personal characteristic.

    ☒ **B** and **C** are incorrect. PII also applies to other personal traits such as speech, handwriting, tattoos, and so on. Change management ensures standardized procedures are applied to the entire life cycle of IT configuration changes.

20. ☑ **D.** Knowledge that vacation time is mandatory means employees are less likely to engage in improper business practices, because when a different employee fills a job role while the vacationing employee is out of the office, he or she is likely to notice any irregularities.

    ☒ **A, B,** and **C** are incorrect. Adhering to regulations is not the primary purpose of mandatory vacations as they pertain to security policies. Refreshed employees tend to be more productive, but this is not the primary reason for mandatory vacations. A job rotation policy enables other employees to gain experience in additional job roles; although this would occur for a vacationing employee, this is not the best answer.

21. ☑ **C.** Fingerprints are considered protected health information (PHI) under the American HIPAA rules.

    ☒ **A, B,** and **D** are incorrect. Although education and employment records and credit history are considered PII, they are not considered to be PHI.

22. ☑ **C.** A clean desk policy requires paper documents to be safely stored (and not left on desks) to prevent malicious users from acquiring them.

    ☒ **A, B,** and **D** are incorrect. Although the clean desk policy is one of several privacy policies that protect sensitive information, the question refers specifically to the clean desk policy, so this is not the best answer. Acceptable use policies govern the proper use of corporate assets. Password policies control all aspects of passwords for authentication, not securing paper documents.

23. ☑ **B.** People tend to speak more freely on social networking sites than anywhere else. Exposing sensitive company information could pose a problem.

    ☒ **A, C,** and **D** are incorrect. Knowing a computer's IP address has nothing to do with social networking risks. Secretly embedding messages in pictures is not a threat tied specifically to social networks. Credit card numbers are not normally stolen through social networks.

24. ☑ **C** and **D.** Nondisclosure agreements (NDAs) are used to ensure that sensitive data an employees or contractor may have been exposed to is not revealed outside of the organization. An NDA is signed during employee onboarding, when other contracts are signed; reminding employees leaving the organization of their responsibility of not violating NDAs is important. Any equipment, access codes, passes, and keys must be surrendered to the company when an employee leaves the organization (employee offboarding). This is formalized and recorded on a property return form.

☒ **A** and **B** are incorrect. Background checks are a part of the hiring process and can reveal past problems related to a potential employee's credit or criminal record. In job rotation, employees periodically switch job roles with other employees to ensure broad expertise in various job roles or to identify suspicious activity from previous job role occupants.

25. ☑ **A.** Company trade secrets such as unique manufacturing processes should be labeled as proprietary.

☒ **B, C,** and **D** are incorrect. PII refers to private user information that can be traced back to an individual. PHI refers to private healthcare information. Public is not an appropriate label.

26. ☑ **B.** International Organization for Standardization (ISO) 27017 provides guidelines related to the secure use of cloud computing.

☒ **A, C,** and **D** are incorrect. While ISO 27001, 27002, and 27701 are all related to information security, they do not focus on cloud computing security.

27. ☑ **D.** The National Institute of Standards and Technology (NIST) Risk Management Framework (RMF) provides guidance regarding how to assess, frame, monitor, and respond to risks, including how to apply security controls to mitigate risk. The Cloud Security Alliance (CSA) Reference Architecture can also be used to assess risk, and the Cloud Controls Matrix can be used to organize risk mitigations.

☒ **A, B,** and **C** are incorrect. The Center for Internet Security (CIS) is a nonprofit entity providing guidance for securing IT systems and data. SOC 2 is a standard for measuring data availability and confidentiality protection provided by service providers such as public cloud providers. The NIST Cyber Security Framework (CSF) consists of security best practices and recommendations for hardening the use of IT systems and related data.

28. ☑ **A** and **C.** A jump box solution is a host (physical or virtual) that has two network interfaces: one allows connections from the Internet, and the other allows connectivity to an internal private network. To manage internal hosts remotely from the Internet, connections first go to the jump box, and from there remote management to internal hosts is possible. Another option is using a virtual private network (VPN) to establish a secure tunnel between two endpoints such as an IT technician station and the networking hosting the public-facing web application. VPN clients are assigned IP addresses from a known pool that can enable them to access the private IP address of internal hosts such as DB1.

☒ **B** and **D** are incorrect. Exposing a web site database directly to the Internet presents unacceptable security risks. While encrypting data at rest on DB1 is a good idea, it is not related to the secure remote management of that host.

29. ☑ **A and C.** Secure Sockets Layer (SSL) is a network security protocol that uses security certificates. SSL has been deprecated since 2015 because of many known vulnerabilities and should not be used on clients or servers. Transport Layer Security (TLS) version 1.2 or higher supersede SSL and provide network security that has not been deprecated. Like SSL, TLS must be enabled on clients and servers, just as SSL should be disabled on clients and servers. Deploy a jump box to enable indirect Windows remote management through the jump box instead of directly to each Windows host from the Internet.

    ☒ **B and D** are incorrect. Blocking port 443 traffic would not enable HTTPS secured traffic to access the web servers. Disabling RDP would not enable remote management of the Windows web servers using this protocol, which is a stated requirement.

30. ☑ **D.** Gamification involves using game-style drills to prepare for cybersecurity incident response, or using a reward system that provides some kind of incentive for demonstrating cybersecurity acumen. Capture the flag security competitions work by awarding a flag when a team overcomes a security problem. The flag owner submits the flag to a central authority to earn points. Individuals or teams with the highest number of points win the competition.

    ☒ **A, B,** and **C** are incorrect. User onboarding refers to processes related to the hiring and training of new employees. Computer-based training (CBT) can help in achieving security goals, but this is not gamification. Role-based training focuses on the skills necessary to complete specific job tasks.

31. ☑ **C.** A memorandum of understanding (MOU) is a document outlining an agreement between entities such as business partners; unlike a contract, it is not legally binding. An example of how a MOU is used between organizations that connect IT environments together is an interconnection security agreement (ISA) which can be put in place to ensure the secure transmission of sensitive data between organizations.

    ☒ **A, B,** and **D** are incorrect. A business partnership agreement (BPA) is a contract between two or more business partners to create a joint business venture; a BPS is legally binding. Measurement systems analysis (MSA) is used to determine the accuracy of a system used to collect data metrics, such as capturing web site metrics through usage activity and user surveys. It is not an agreement document. End of service life (EOSL) refers to the point at which a hardware or software product will no longer be supported by its creator or manufacturer; it has nothing to do with a document.

32. ☑ Figure 3-4 shows the terms matched to correct answers. A retention policy may be a regulation requiring financial data to be kept for three years. Regulatory compliance will often influence IT activities such as the retention of specific types of data for periods of time. Service accounts assign required permissions to software components. They are similar to user accounts but are instead used by software components that require special permissions to resources. Reputation damage can be caused by security breaches that expose sensitive customer data. Such exposure can negatively affect the reputation and shareholder confidence in the organization. In incident escalation, unsolved security issues must be addressed by other parties. Incident response plans must include details on how to escalate an incident when the first responders cannot contain the breach. Impact assessments are tools that determine the result of negative incidents. They are used to measure the negative impact of realized threats. This in turn can be used to prioritize threats and ultimately resources and time to mitigate the threats.

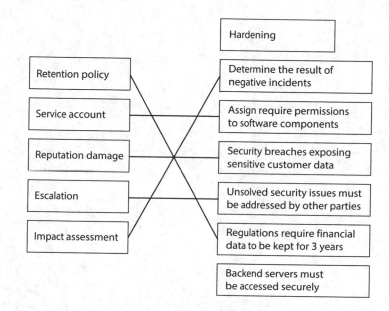

FIGURE 3-4

Security terms and descriptions— the answers

Retention policy

Service account

Reputation damage

Escalation

Impact assessment

Hardening

Determine the result of negative incidents

Assign require permissions to software components

Security breaches exposing sensitive customer data

Unsolved security issues must be addressed by other parties

Regulations require financial data to be kept for 3 years

Backend servers must be accessed securely

33. ☑ **D.** A privacy notice provides details regarding how sensitive data will be collected, stored, used, and shared and may be required for legal or regulatory compliance.

☒ **A, B,** and **C** are incorrect. The information life cycle relates to the creation, processing, usage, reporting, archiving, and deletion of information during its useful life. A variety of hardware and software solutions can apply to information at different stages, such as data retention policies for financial records. Terms of agreement is a generic term that normally applies to contractual terms, such as how a subcontractor will provide materials and services. In the realm of IT security, public disclosure deals with the reporting of discovered product vulnerabilities or the reporting of a cybersecurity incident that may involve a data breach.

Chapter 4

Types of Attacks

QUESTIONS

Understanding different types of attacks is important for any security professional in the workforce, but it is also important for the CompTIA Security+ certification exam, because you are sure to see questions related to different types of attacks on the exam.

Social engineering attacks involve the attacker contacting a person through e-mail, via a phone call, or in person, and trying to trick the person into compromising security. You also need to be familiar with the different types of application attacks, such as buffer overflow attacks, which are popular today, and SQL injection attacks, which are typically performed against web sites that have been developed without considering programming best practices. You also should be familiar with the different password attacks for the exam, such as dictionary attacks, hybrid attacks, and brute-force attacks. This chapter is designed to help you review these critical points.

1. You are inspecting a user's system after she has complained about slow Internet speeds. After analyzing the system, you notice that the default gateway in the ARP cache is referencing an unknown MAC address. What type of attack has occurred?
   A. Brute force
   B. DNS poisoning
   C. Buffer overflow
   D. ARP poisoning

2. You want to implement a security control that limits tailgating in a high-security environment. Which of the following protective controls would you use?
   A. Swipe cards
   B. Mantrap
   C. Locked door
   D. CMOS settings

3. Which of the following descriptions best describes a buffer overflow attack?
   A. Injecting database code into a web page
   B. Using a dictionary file to crack passwords
   C. Sending too much data to an application that then enables the attacker to run arbitrary code
   D. Altering the source address of a packet

4. You are analyzing web traffic in transit to your web server and you notice someone logging on with a username of Bob with a password of "pass' or 1=1--". Which of the following describes what is happening?

   A. XML injection
   B. A SQL injection attack
   C. LDAP injection
   D. Denial of service

5. A user on your network receives an e-mail from the bank stating that there has been a security incident at the bank. The e-mail asks the user to log on to her bank account by following the link provided and verify that her account has not been tampered with. What type of attack is this?

   A. Phishing
   B. Spam
   C. Dictionary attack
   D. Spim

6. What type of attack involves the attacker modifying the source IP address of the packet?

   A. Xmas attack
   B. Spear phishing
   C. Spoofing
   D. Pharming

7. Which of the following files might an attacker modify after gaining access to your system in order to achieve DNS redirection?

   A. /etc/passwd
   B. Hosts
   C. SAM
   D. Services

8. What type of attack involves the attacker sending too much data to a service or application that typically results in the attacker gaining administrative access to the system?

   A. Birthday attack
   B. Typosquatting/URL hijacking
   C. Eavesdrop
   D. Buffer overflow

9. Which of the following methods could be used to prevent ARP poisoning on the network? (Choose two.)

   A. Static ARP entries
   B. Patching
   C. Antivirus software
   D. Physical security
   E. Firewall

10. As a network administrator, what should you do to help prevent buffer overflow attacks from occurring on your systems?
    A. Static ARP entries
    B. Antivirus software
    C. Physical security
    D. Patching

11. Which of the following is the term for a domain name that is registered and deleted repeatedly so that the registrant can avoid paying for the domain name?
    A. DNS redirection
    B. Domain poisoning
    C. Domain kiting
    D. Transitive access

12. You receive many calls from customers stating that your web site seems to be slow in responding. You analyze the traffic and notice that you are receiving a number of malformed requests on that web server at a high rate. What type of attack is occurring?
    A. Eavesdrop
    B. Denial of service
    C. Man-in-the-middle
    D. Social engineer

13. What type of attack is a smurf attack?
    A. Distributed denial of service (DDoS)
    B. Denial of service (DoS)
    C. Privilege escalation
    D. Malicious insider threat

14. Your manager has ensured that a policy is implemented that requires all employees to shred sensitive documents. What type of attack is your manager hoping to prevent?
    A. Tailgating
    B. Denial of service
    C. Social engineering
    D. Dumpster diving

15. What type of attack involves the attacker inserting a client-side script into the web page?
    A. XSS
    B. Watering hole attack
    C. ARP poisoning
    D. SQL injection

16. Your manager has read about SQL injection attacks and is wondering what can be done to protect against them for applications that were developed in-house. What would you recommend?
    A. Patching
    B. Antivirus
    C. Input validation
    D. Packet filtering firewall

17. An attacker sitting in an Internet café ARP poisons everyone connected to the wireless network so that all traffic passes through the attacker's laptop before she routes the traffic to the Internet. What type of attack is this?
    A. Rainbow tables
    B. Man-in-the-middle
    C. DNS poison
    D. Spoofing

18. Which of the following best describes a zero-day attack?
    A. An attack that modifies the source address of the packet
    B. An attack that changes the computer's system date to 00/00/00
    C. An attack that never happens
    D. An attack that uses an exploit that the product vendor is not aware of yet

19. What type of file on your hard drive stores preferences from web sites?
    A. Cookie
    B. Hosts
    C. LMHOSTS
    D. Attachment

20. What type of attack involves the attacker disconnecting one of the parties from a communication and continues the communication while impersonating that system?
    A. Man in the browser
    B. Denial of service (DoS)
    C. SQL injection
    D. Session hijacking

21. What type of password attack involves the use of a dictionary file and modifications of the words in the dictionary file?
    A. Dictionary attack
    B. Brute-force attack
    C. Hybrid attack
    D. Modification attack

22. Which of the following countermeasures is designed to protect against a brute-force password attack?

    A. Patching
    B. Account lockout
    C. Password complexity
    D. Strong passwords

23. Three employees within the company have received phone calls from an individual asking about personal finance information. What type of attack is occurring?

    A. Phishing
    B. Whaling
    C. Tailgating
    D. Vishing

24. Tom was told to download a free tax program to complete his taxes this year. After downloading and installing the software, Tom notices that his system is running slowly and he receives a notification from his antivirus software. What type of malware has he installed?

    A. Keylogger
    B. Trojan
    C. Worm
    D. Logic bomb

25. Jeff recently reports that he is receiving a large number of unsolicited text messages to his phone. What type of attack is occurring?

    A. Bluesnarfing
    B. Whaling
    C. Bluejacking
    D. Packet sniffing

26. An employee is suspected of sharing company secrets with a competitor. After seizing the employee's laptop, the forensic analyst notices that a number of personal photos on the laptop have been e-mailed to a third party over the Internet. When the analyst compares the hashes of the personal images on the hard drive to what is found in the employee's mailbox, the hashes do not match. How was the employee sharing company secrets?

    A. Digital signatures
    B. Steganography
    C. MP3Stego
    D. Whaling

27. You arrive at work today to find someone outside the building digging through her purse. As you approach the door, the person says, "I forgot my pass at home. Can I go in with you?" What type of attack could be occurring?
    A. Tailgating
    B. Dumpster diving
    C. Brute force
    D. Whaling

28. Your manager has requested that the combo padlocks used to secure different areas of the company facility be replaced with electronic swipe cards. What type of social-engineering attack is your manager hoping to avoid with this change?
    A. Hoaxes
    B. Tailgating
    C. Dumpster diving
    D. Shoulder surfing

29. Your manager has been hearing a lot about social-engineering attacks and wonders why such attacks are so effective. Which of the following identifies reasons why the attacks are so successful? (Choose three.)
    A. Authority
    B. DNS poisoning
    C. Urgency
    D. Brute force
    E. Trust

30. Jane is the lead security officer for your company and is monitoring network traffic. Jane notices suspicious activity and asks for your help in identifying the attack. Looking at Figure 4-1, what type of attack was performed?
    A. Integer overflow
    B. Directory traversal
    C. Malicious add-on
    D. Header manipulation

FIGURE 4-1   Identify the attack type.

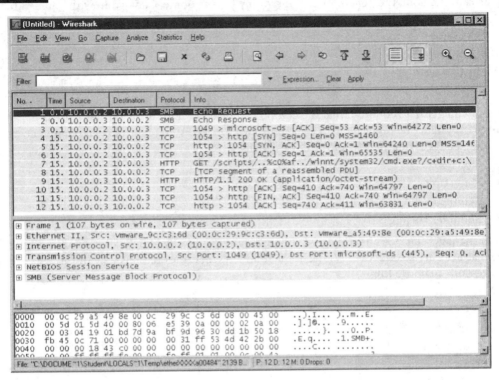

31. A user calls and asks you to send sensitive documents immediately because a salesperson needs them to close a multimillion-dollar deal and the salesperson's files are corrupted. She demands you do this immediately, or she'll have you fired. What form of social engineering is this?

   A. Familiarity

   B. Intimidation

   C. Consensus

   D. Scarcity

32. An attacker tricks a user into clicking a malicious link that causes an unwanted action on a web site the user is currently authenticated to. What type of exploit is this?

   A. Cross-site request forgery

   B. Cross-site scripting

   C. Replay

   D. Pass the hash

33. Your server is being flooded with DNS lookup requests, which is causing the server to be unavailable for legitimate clients. What sort of general attack is this?

   A. Buffer overflow
   B. Domain hijacking
   C. Man in the browser
   D. Amplification

34. A user calls you stating that his browser performed an unintended action after he clicked a button on a web page. What sort of attack has taken place?

   A. Replay
   B. Shimming
   C. Click-jacking
   D. Integer overflow

35. A downloaded hardware driver does not match the checksum from the manufacturer, yet it installs and seems to behave as it should. Months later, you learn that sensitive information from your device has been leaked online. Which term best describes this type of attack?

   A. Refactoring
   B. Collision
   C. ARP poisoning
   D. Typosquatting

36. A user is attempting to log into a web application but notices that the version of TLS being used is lower than expected. What sort of attack is this?

   A. Weak implementations
   B. Known plain text/cipher text
   C. Downgrade
   D. Replay

37. You have received a SMS text message from the bank stating that access to your bank account has been blocked. The message asks you to click a link to reactivate the account right away. What type of attack is this?

   A. Spraying
   B. Skimming
   C. Card cloning
   D. Smishing

38. An attacker obtains a connection to your LAN and then uses SETH to perform a MiTM attack between your system and the company RDP server, which enables the attacker to collect the logon information for the RDP server. What type of attack has occurred?

A. Reconnaissance

B. Credential harvesting

C. Impersonation

D. Hybrid warfare

39. Which of the following mechanisms can be used by an attacker as a method in an influence campaign to trick the victim into compromising security?

A. Intimidation

B. Malicious flash drive

C. Social media

D. Identity fraud

40. Which of the following represent reasons why social-engineering attacks are so effective? (Choose two.)

A. URL redirection

B. Consensus

C. Domain reputation

D. Scarcity

E. Malicious code execution

41. You receive a call from the network administrator who was supposed to be on vacation. She informs you that there was an update to the financial system, and she needs you to temporarily change your password to "N3wSyst3m" so that the software can receive initial updates. What type of social-engineering technique is being used here?

A. Impersonation

B. Eliciting information

C. Prepending

D. Invoice scams

42. Which of the following is a layer 2 attack that involves the attacker sending a large number of frames to the switch in order to trick the switch into sending all new frames to every port on the switch?

A. ARP poisoning

B. MAC cloning

C. MAC spoofing

D. MAC flooding

43. What type of physical attack involves the attacker creating a component that contains a wireless controller embedded inside it that enables the attacker to send commands to the device from a nearby phone or PC?

- A. Card cloning
- B. Spraying
- C. Malicious USB cable
- D. Whaling

44. Which of the following attack types involves an attacker manipulating data input in order to exploit vulnerabilities in the algorithm used by the system?

- A. Adversarial AI attack
- B. Supply-chain attack
- C. Cloud-based attack
- D. On-premises attack

45. What type of DDoS attack involves consuming bandwidth with traffic coming from many different sources so that the company cannot access the Internet?

- A. Application
- B. Network
- C. Operational technology
- D. Physical

46. To execute a script you created, you first run the **set-executionpolicy unrestricted** command. What type of script file are you about to execute?

- A. Bash
- B. Python
- C. PowerShell
- D. Macros
- E. VBA

QUICK ANSWER KEY

1.	D	**13.**	A	**25.**	C	**37.**	D
2.	B	**14.**	D	**26.**	B	**38.**	B
3.	C	**15.**	A	**27.**	A	**39.**	C
4.	B	**16.**	C	**28.**	D	**40.**	B, D
5.	A	**17.**	B	**29.**	A, C, E	**41.**	A
6.	C	**18.**	D	**30.**	B	**42.**	D
7.	B	**19.**	A	**31.**	B	**43.**	C
8.	D	**20.**	D	**32.**	A	**44.**	A
9.	A, D	**21.**	C	**33.**	D	**45.**	B
10.	D	**22.**	B	**34.**	C	**46.**	C
11.	C	**23.**	D	**35.**	A		
12.	B	**24.**	B	**36.**	C		

IN-DEPTH ANSWERS

1. ☑ **D.** ARP poisoning occurs when the attacker alters the ARP cache to redirect communication to a particular IP address to the wrong MAC address, which maps to the attacker's machine. This is a popular attack on wireless networks.

    ☒ **A, B,** and **C** are incorrect. A brute-force attack is a type of password attack that involves the attacker calculating all potential passwords until a match is found. DNS poisoning occurs when the attacker poisons the DNS cache so that the DNS server gives out the wrong IP address. Buffer overflow happens when the amount of data sent to a target system exceeds the size of data allocated by the target buffer, thus causing neighboring memory areas to be overwritten. As a result of the buffer overflow, the attacker gains access to the system with the privilege level of the account associated with the software being exploited, which is sometimes admin-level access.

2. ☑ **B.** Tailgating occurs when an unauthorized person tries to slip through a secured door after an authorized person opens it. A mantrap helps prevent tailgating; it is the area between two locked doors, in which the second door does not open until the first door closes. This enables you to watch who enters the building with you, or it can prevent two people from entering the door at the same time.

    ☒ **A, C,** and **D** are incorrect. Swipe cards are mechanisms used to unlock doors, but they do not prevent someone from tailgating. A locked door does not prevent someone from tailgating through the door after you open it. CMOS settings are a way to implement a level of security to prevent someone from booting from removable media and bypassing the security of the local system.

3. ☑ **C.** A buffer overflow attack occurs when an attacker sends more data to an application or service than it is expecting. The extra data that is sent flows out of the area of memory (the buffer) assigned to the application. It has been found that if the attacker can write information beyond the buffer, he can run whatever code he wants. Attackers typically write code that gives them remote shell access to the system with administrative capabilities.

    ☒ **A, B,** and **D** are incorrect. Injecting database code into a web page is an example of an SQL injection attack. Using a dictionary file to crack passwords is known as a dictionary attack—a form of password attack. Altering the source address of a packet is known as spoofing, specifically IP spoofing in this example.

4.   ☑   **B.** A SQL injection attack occurs when the attacker inserts database (SQL) statements into an application, such as a web site, which then passes the SQL commands to a backend database to be processed. The end result could lead to the attacker bypassing the authentication or manipulating data in the backend database. In this example, the attacker is trying to bypass the logon by typing **"pass' or 1=1--"** into the password box.

☒   **A, C,** and **D** are incorrect. An XML injection attack aims at attacking the application's logic by inserting XML content into XML messages. An LDAP injection aims at inserting an LDAP call, through the web application, to the underlying LDAP service so the LDAP call is executed. Denial of service occurs when the attacker tries to overload your system or network so that it cannot service valid request from clients.

5.   ☑   **A.** Phishing occurs when a attacker e-mails a victim and hopes she clicks the link that leads her to a fake site (typically a bank). At this point, the attacker hopes the user types information into the fake site (such as bank account information) that he can use to gain access to her real account.

☒   **B, C,** and **D** are incorrect. Spam is unsolicited e-mails you receive that try to encourage you to buy a product or a service. A dictionary attack is a type of password attack that reads a dictionary file and uses all words in the text file as password attempts. Spim is spam-type messages sent via instant messaging instead of e-mail.

6.   ☑   **C.** A spoofing attack occurs when the attacker modifies the source address of the packet. In IP spoofing, the source IP address is modified; in MAC spoofing, the source MAC address is modified; and in e-mail spoofing, the attacker alters the source e-mail address of the message.

☒   **A, B,** and **D** are incorrect. An Xmas attack is a type of port scan that has the FIN, URG, and PSH flags set in the TCP header. Spear phishing is a phishing e-mail that is targeting a specific individual or group within the company. Pharming occurs when the attacker modifies the hosts file or poisons DNS to lead a victim to a bogus web site that attempts to collect personal information from the user such as logon credentials or account numbers.

7.   ☑   **B.** The hosts file on the local hard drive of the computer is used to resolve fully qualified domain names (FQDNs) to IP addresses and could be used to redirect an unsuspecting person to the wrong site.

☒   **A, C,** and **D** are incorrect. The /etc/passwd file is where passwords are stored in Linux. The SAM file is where the user passwords in Windows are stored. The services file is a file that maps ports to actual friendly names of services.

8.   ☑   **D.** Buffer overflow happens when the amount of data sent to a target system exceeds the size of data allocated by the target buffer, thus causing neighboring memory areas to be overwritten. If the buffer overflow is successful, the attacker is able to execute code in the security context of the software being exploited, potentially gaining admin-level access.

☒   **A, B,** and **C** are incorrect. A birthday attack is an example of a cryptographic attack type on hashing functions to generate the same hash value from different data input. Typosquatting/URL hijacking occurs when the attacker foresees common typos of common URLs and runs a bogus site at those URLs in hopes that a victim will think he is at the real site, when he is actually on the attacker's site. An eavesdrop attack occurs when the attacker listens in on a conversation or captures traffic on the network with a packet analyzer such as Wireshark.

9. ☑ **A** and **D.** ARP poisoning can be countered by adding static ARP entries to your ARP cache and by implementing physical security so that unauthorized persons cannot gain access to the network and poison everyone's ARP cache.

   ☒ **B, C,** and **E** are incorrect. Patching a system will not prevent ARP poisoning, because system patching removes vulnerabilities in software. Antivirus software will not prevent ARP poisoning, because there is no virus involved. A firewall is not the solution either, because you will need to ensure that ARP messages can reach all the stations, which will allow ARP poisoning messages.

10. ☑ **D.** The best countermeasure to buffer overflow attacks is to ensure that you keep up to date with system and application patches. As the vendor finds the vulnerabilities, that vendor will fix the issues through a patch.

    ☒ **A, B,** and **C** are incorrect. Static ARP entries will help protect against ARP poisoning, antivirus software will protect against viruses and other malicious software as long as you keep the virus definitions up to date, and physical security will help control who gets physical access to an asset such as a server, but buffer overflow attacks are typically network-based attacks where physical access to the asset is not required by the attacker.

11. ☑ **C.** Domain kiting is a vulnerability in the domain name system in which the attacker registers a DNS name and then cancels it within the five-day grace period to avoid paying for the domain. After a few days, he deletes the name and re-creates it to get the five-day grace period again.

    ☒ **A, B,** and **D** are incorrect. With DNS redirection, the attacker ensures that your system is given an incorrect IP address for a DNS name. Domain poisoning is a method of ensuring that your system is given the wrong IP address for a specific domain name. Transitive access is a type of attack that is based on trust models: if machine A trusts machine B and machine B trusts machine C, then in some environments machine C would trust machine B by default, granting potential access to unwanted sources.

12. ☑ **B.** The fact that you are receiving a high number of malformed requests at a high rate is a great indication that someone is trying to perform a denial of service (DoS) attack on your system. The results of a DoS could be to keep your system so busy servicing bogus requests that it cannot service valid requests from customers, or the attacker may try to crash your system.

    ☒ **A, C,** and **D** are incorrect. Eavesdropping is a passive-type attack, which involves the attacker capturing traffic, not sending traffic to your system. A man-in-the-middle attack involves the attacker inserting herself into a conversation so that all traffic passes through the attacker. A social engineering attack occurs when someone tries to trick you into compromising security through social contact (e-mail or phone call).

13. ☑ **A.** A smurf attack is a distributed denial of service (DDoS) attack, which is a DoS attack involving multiple systems. The smurf attack involves the attacker pinging a number of systems but spoofing the address of the ICMP packet so that all those systems reply to an intended victim. The victim would be so overburdened with the ICMP replies that it would cause a denial of service.

    ☒ **B, C,** and **D** are incorrect. A denial of service (DoS) attack involves only one system performing the attack, but the smurf attack has many systems performing the attack. Privilege escalation occurs when someone with user-level access is able to exploit a vulnerability within the system and gain elevated privileges. A malicious insider threat occurs when someone inside the company purposely destroys or intentionally discloses sensitive company data.

14. ☑ **D.** Dumpster diving occurs when the attacker goes through a company's garbage trying to locate information that can help him perform an attack or gain access to the company assets.
☒ **A, B,** and **C** are incorrect. Tailgating occurs when an unauthorized person tries to follow behind an authorized person to sneak through a locked door. Denial of service occurs when a attacker overloads a system causing it to become unresponsive or crash, and social engineering occurs when the attacker tries to trick someone into compromising security through social contact, such as phone call or e-mail.

15. ☑ **A.** Cross-site scripting (XSS) is an attack that involves the attacker inserting script code into a web page so that it is then processed and executed by a client system.
☒ **B, C,** and **D** are incorrect. A watering hole attack occurs when an attacker plants malicious code on a site you may visit often so that when you navigate to the site, the code attacks your system from a site you trust. ARP poisoning occurs when the attacker manipulates the ARP cache to add his or her own MAC address, thus leading systems to the attacker's system. In SQL injection SQL code is inserted into an application in order to manipulate the underlying database or system.

16. ☑ **C.** A SQL injection attack involves the attacker inserting database code into an application (such as a web site) where it is not expected. The best countermeasure to this is to have your programmers validate any information (check its accuracy) passed into an application.
☒ **A, B,** and **D** are incorrect. Although patching system solves a lot of problems, it will not protect against a SQL injection attack for applications that you build. Antivirus software is not going to help you in this instance either, because this is not a virus problem—it is a problem based on your own coding habits. Packet filtering firewalls are not going to help you, because you need to allow people access to the application and the problem is not about the type of traffic reaching the system—the problem is about the data that is being inserted into the application.

17. ☑ **B.** When a attacker poisons everyone's ARP cache in order to have them send any data destined for the Internet through the attacker's system, this is a man in the middle attack, because the attacker is receiving all traffic before it is sent to the Internet. The attacker will do this to see what you are doing on the Internet and ideally capture sensitive information.
☒ **A, C,** and **D** are incorrect. A rainbow table is a file that contains hashed representations of mathematically calculated passwords so that a brute-force attack can be performed quickly. DNS poisoning involves the attacker modifying the DNS cache to lead victims to the wrong web sites. Spoofing in general is the altering of a source address; IP spoofing is altering the source IP address to make a packet look as if it is coming from somewhere different.

18. ☑ **D.** A zero-day attack is considered a new exploit that the vendor is not aware of yet, but the hacking community is.
☒ **A, B,** and **C** are incorrect. An attack that involves the source address being modified is known as a spoofing attack. There is no such attack as one that modifies the system date to 00/00/00, and an attack that never happens is not really an attack.

19. ☑ **A.** A cookie is a text file on the hard drive of your system that stores preferences for specific web sites.
☒ **B, C,** and **D** are incorrect. The hosts file stores the FQDNs and matching IP addresses, the LMHOSTS file in Windows stores the computer names and matching IP addresses, and attachments are files included in e-mail messages. Note that attachments could contain malicious code and are a potential avenue of attack.

20. ☑ **D.** Session hijacking involves the attacker taking over a conversation by impersonating one of the parties involved in the conversation after the attacker kicks that party off. The attacker typically launches a DoS attack to kick out one of the parties of the communication.
☒ **A, B,** and **C** are incorrect. A man in the browser (MiTB) attack occurs when Trojan code is run on the system by leveraging vulnerabilities in the browser. This Trojan code acts as a proxy, placing the attacker in the middle of the browser and the web site being visited. A denial of service occurs when an attacker overloads a system, causing it to become unresponsive or to crash. SQL injection involves inserting SQL code into an application in order to manipulate the underlining database or system.

21. ☑ **C.** In a hybrid password attack, the attacker uses a dictionary file and a brute-force attack to try to guess a user's password; the software uses modifications of the dictionary words by placing numbers at the end of each word, and a brute-force attack then attempts to apply each password as it is created.
☒ **A, B,** and **D** are incorrect. Although a dictionary attack does use a dictionary file, it uses only the entries found in the file and does not try modifications of the words in the file. A brute-force attack is a trial-and-error technique of password cracking and is one component of a hybrid attack. There is no such thing as a modification attack.

22. ☑ **B.** Because brute-force attacks mathematically aim to calculate all possible passwords, if you give the attacker enough time, the attacker will crack passwords, including complex passwords. The key point here is you need to take the time away from the attacker, and you do that by enabling account lockout—after a certain number of bad logon attempts, the account is locked. Note that passwords should be stored in an encrypted format so if someone gets access to the database storing the passwords, they are not seeing the passwords in plaintext.
☒ **A, C,** and **D** are incorrect. Patching will not protect against any type of password attack, while strong passwords and password complexity (which are the same thing) constitute a countermeasure to dictionary attacks, not brute-force attacks.

23. ☑ **D.** Vishing is a form of social-engineering attack in which the attacker calls a user trying to trick the person into divulging secure information over the phone or a Voice over IP (VOIP) call. "Vishing" as a term comes from the fact that it is similar to phishing, but instead of the attack coming through e-mail, it is using the phone (voice).
☒ **A, B,** and **C** are incorrect. Phishing occurs when the victim receives an e-mail that typically asks the user to click a link to visit a site. Whaling is a form of phishing attack, but it is designed to target executives within the company (the big fish!). Tailgating occurs when an unauthorized person tries to follow behind an authorized person to sneak through a locked door.

24. ☑ **B.** Tom has installed a Trojan virus, a program disguised to do one thing that actually does something else or something additional.
☒ **A, C,** and **D** are incorrect. A keylogger is a program that records keystrokes and sends them to the attacker. A worm is self-replicating malware, and a logic bomb is malicious code that is triggered by an event such as a specific date.

25. ☑ **C.** Bluejacking occurs when the attacker sends unsolicited text messages to a Bluetooth device such as a phone.
☒ **A, B,** and **D** are incorrect. Bluesnarfing is the exploiting of a Bluetooth device such as a phone with the intention of stealing data such as call logs or contact lists. Whaling is a form of phishing attack aimed at company executives. Packet sniffing involves the attacker capturing traffic from the network and trying to find sensitive information.

26. ☑ **B.** Steganography involves hiding information inside a file—for example, hiding text data in an image file—and is a common technique used by attackers to share information.
☒ **A, C,** and **D** are incorrect. Digital signatures are used to verify the sender of a message. MP3Stego is a program used to hide text information in MP3 files (not image files), and whaling is a type of phishing attack that targets company executives.

27. ☑ **A.** Tailgating occurs when an unauthorized person tries to follow behind an authorized person to sneak through a locked door.
☒ **B, C,** and **D** are incorrect. Dumpster diving occurs when the attacker goes through the garbage looking for sensitive information. Brute force is a type of password attack that mathematically calculates all possible passwords to guess the correct one. Whaling is a form of phishing attack that targets the executives of a company.

28. ☑ **D.** Shoulder surfing is a form of social-engineering attack that involves someone looking over your shoulder to spy your passcode or other sensitive information.
☒ **A, B,** and **C** are incorrect. Hoaxes are e-mail messages that describe a false story and are sent to users to ask them to take some form of action, such as forwarding the message on to others. Tailgating occurs when an unauthorized person tries to follow behind an authorized person to sneak through a locked door. Dumpster diving occurs when the attacker goes through the garbage looking for sensitive information.

29. ☑ **A, C,** and **E.** There are a number of reasons why social-engineering attacks are successful, including these three reasons: The victim believes he is receiving communications from a person of authority. Also, the attacker speaks with a sense of urgency, which makes the victim want to help out as quickly as possible. Trust is correct because social engineering works based on the fact that we trust people, especially people in need or people of authority. Social engineering is effective for a number of other reasons, such as intimidation, consensus or social proof, scarcity of the event, and familiarity or liking of a person. Most social-engineering experts have mastered being likeable, which transforms into trust.
☒ **B** and **D** are incorrect. DNS poisoning occurs when the attacker alters the DNS data to redirect victims to a malicious web site. Brute force is a type of password attack that mathematically calculates all potential passwords to guess the right one. Online brute-force attacks involve performing the attack against a live system, and offline brute-force attacks involve obtaining a copy of the password database and performing the password cracking later on the attacker's system.

30. ☑ **B.** Directory traversal occurs when the attacker navigates the folder structure of the web server in the URL to call upon commands found in the operating system of the web server.

☒ **A, C,** and **D** are incorrect. Integer overflow is a form of attack that presents security risks because of the unexpected response of a program when a mathematical function is performed, and the integer used to store the result is larger than the space in memory allocated by the programmer. In a malicious add-on attack, your system downloads a piece of software used by the browser and slows down the system or exploits a vulnerability in the system. Header manipulation occurs when the attacker modifies the header data in the packet in order to manipulate how the application processes the information.

31. ☑ **B.** Intimidation occurs when an attacker threatens the victim using bullying tactics or threats to get the victim to take an action.

☒ **A, C,** and **D** are incorrect. Familiarity involves an attacker creating some sort of connection with the victim ahead of time or impersonating a person that the victim deals with on a regular basis. Consensus is a tactic that involves an attacker fabricating fake testimonials to convince the victim that other people have used the software or web page that the attacker is offering, making it seem safe. Scarcity is an attack that involves making what the attacker is offering seem very rare or likely not found elsewhere. For example, an attacker could get a victim to click a link by saying that the software offered at the link cannot be found anywhere else.

32. ☑ **A.** Cross-site request forgeries occur when an attacker tricks a user into executing unwanted actions on a web site she is currently authenticated to.

☒ **B, C,** and **D** are incorrect. Cross-site scripting enables an attacker to insert client-side scripts into a web page that other users will see. A replay attack occurs when legitimate network traffic is delayed or repeated maliciously. Pass the hash is an attack that involves intercepting a hash from a legitimate user and using it to authenticate as that user to other resources.

33. ☑ **D.** An amplification attack involves sending a small amount of data to an unsuspecting third party, which sends a larger amount of data to the target.

☒ **A, B,** and **C** are incorrect. A buffer overflow attack is used in an attempt to execute arbitrary code on a target machine by overflowing the target's buffer with data. Domain hijacking is a Domain Name System (DNS) attack that occurs when registration information of a domain name is changed without the permission of the registrant. A man in the browser attack occurs when the browser the user is running is infected and manipulates user requests without either the user's or the receiving server's knowledge.

34. ☑ **C.** A click-jacking attack involves tricking the user into clicking an object that causes some evil action as a result. Users think they are clicking a link for a legitimate purpose, but they are unwittingly downloading malware or performing some other malicious activity with the click.

☒ **A, B,** and **D** are incorrect. A replay attack involves legitimate network traffic being delayed or repeated maliciously. Shimming, in terms of driver manipulation, is an attack whereby a piece of software acts as a driver and intercepts and changes commands coming to and from the hardware. An integer overflow occurs when the integer storing the expected result of a mathematical formula consumes more memory space that was allocated to it.

35. ☑ **A.** A refactoring attack involves changing the internal code of the driver while maintaining the external behavior so it appears to be behaving normally.

☒ **B, C,** and **D** are incorrect. A collision attack is an example of a cryptographic attack in which the attacker attempts to find additional input that results in the same output hash value as different origin data. ARP poisoning alters the ARP cache and redirects communication associated with an IP address to an attacker's MAC address. Typosquatting is an attack that involves registering domain names that are misspellings of legitimate web sites to lure victims to those sites, who think they are browsing legitimate web sites. It also can involve sending phishing e-mails using those domains to trick a victim into thinking that the e-mail originated from the legitimate domain.

36. ☑ **C.** A downgrade attack involves forcing a connection to abandon a high-quality encryption protocol for a lower quality, more insecure protocol.

☒ **A, B,** and **D** are incorrect. A weak implementation is an encryption method that has been implemented in a way that is easily broken, such as Wired Equivalent Privacy (WEP) on Wi-Fi networks. A known plain text/cipher text attack occurs when the attacker has access to the plain text and encrypted versions, or access to the cipher text in the cases of a known cipher text attack. A replay attack, in terms of cryptography, occurs when legitimate network traffic is fraudulently or maliciously delayed or re-sent.

37. ☑ **D.** A smishing attack occurs when the attacker uses SMS text messaging to send a phishing style message to a user's mobile phone, trying to trick the user into compromising security.

☒ **A, B,** and **C** are incorrect. Spraying is a type of password attack that involves trying to hack into a large number of user accounts with a single, commonly used password, in order to prevent locking the accounts by performing multiple access attempts on each account. Skimming, also known as card skimming, occurs when the attacker uses a device to extract information from the magnetic strip on a credit card, typically a bank card. That information is then put on a new blank card so that the attacker can attempt to use the card to access your account. Card cloning is another term for skimming, which involves copying the card information off the magnetic strip and putting it on a blank card so that the attacker can use that card to make purchases.

38. ☑ **B.** Credential harvesting occurs when the attacker collects logon information and then uses that information to gain access to system at a later time.

☒ **A, C,** and **D** are incorrect. Reconnaissance is part of the hacking process that involves the attacker discovering information about the victim that aids in the attack. Impersonation is one of the techniques used during social-engineering attacks that involves the attacker pretending to be someone else in order to trick you into compromising security. Hybrid warfare occurs when traditional military tactics and nontraditional methods such as organized crime, terrorism, and the use of civilian actors to perform different types of actions, including propaganda, during times of conflict.

39. ☑ **C.** Social media is a tool that can be used as an influence campaign during a social-engineering attack.

☒ **A, B,** and **D** are incorrect. Intimidation is a tactic used during social-engineering attacks, but not within an influence campaign. A malicious flash drive is used in a physical attack whereby the attacker tricks the user into inserting a flash drive into the system that runs malware. Identity fraud occurs when a person's identity information such as a Social Security number or credit card information is stolen and used by the attacker.

40. ☑ **B** and **D.** There are a number of reasons why social engineering is effective, such as intimidation, consensus or social proof, scarcity of the event, and familiarity or liking of a person. ☒ **A, C,** and **E** are incorrect. URL redirection is a DNS attack that involves the attacker sending request to your domain to a different location such as an attacker's web site. Domain reputation represents your e-mail domain's reputation on message hygiene. If your domain sends a lot of spam messages, the domain reputation is rated poorly, versus a domain that does not send spam messages. Malicious code execution is the execution of malware such as a Trojan virus or keylogger that is used to compromise the security of the system.

41. ☑ **A.** Impersonation is when the attacker pretends to be a different individual in order to trick someone into compromising security. It is common for the attacker to impersonate the network administrator in order to get users to make changes, but it is also common for the attacker to impersonate a frustrated user so that the administrator helps give the user access to the network. ☒ **B, C,** and **D** are incorrect. Eliciting information occurs when the attacker uses social-engineering techniques to obtain information from a user that could be used in an attack. Prepending occurs when the attacker adds information to the beginning of some malicious data in order to trick the user to trust the data. For example, www.trustedsite.com@192.168.1.1 was a common method in the past to get you to click a link that you thought would go to the trusted site, but older browsers would ignore everything to the left of the @ sign and navigate to whatever address was shown on the right side of the @ sign, which could be a malicious site set up by the attacker. In invoice scams, e-mails are sent out by the attacker requesting payment for an overdue invoice, but in reality, those invoice files are infected with some type of malware; or the victim is invited to click a malicious URL to view the invoice.

42. ☑ **D.** MAC flooding occurs when the attacker sends a large number of frames to the switch, causing it to fill its MAC address table so old entries are removed from the table to make space for the new entries. This causes known MAC addresses to be removed from the MAC address table, which results in the switch flooding all frames (sends the frames to all ports on the switch). ☒ **A, B,** and **C** are incorrect. ARP poisoning occurs when the attacker alters the ARP cache of a system in order to redirect communication to a particular IP address to the attacker's MAC address (used for MiTM attack). MAC cloning occurs when the attacker copies an existing MAC address on the network and uses that MAC address to send network communication. MAC spoofing occurs when the attacker alters his source MAC address, which is common to help bypass access control lists such as MAC filtering on a wireless router.

43.   ☑   **C.** A malicious USB cable is used as a physical attack on systems because the USB cable must be physically connected to the system that an attacker wishes to exploit. Once the cable is connected, it can receive commands wirelessly to execute payloads on the target system.
☒   **A, B,** and **D** are incorrect. Card cloning is another term for skimming, which involves copying the card information off the magnetic strip and putting it on a blank card so that the attacker can use that card to make purchases. Spraying is a type of password attack that involves trying to hack into a large number of user accounts with a single, commonly used password. Whaling is a form of social-engineering attack that targets the executives of a company (the big fish).

44.   ☑   **A.** Artificial intelligence (AI), also known as machine learning, may be vulnerable to adversarial machine-learning attacks, in which the attacker sends malicious input into the learning system in order to compromise the system. The attack is based on the fact that machine-learning systems use models of data for their training, which may be tainted training data for machine learning (ML). The learning system may respond differently in production scenarios to different data input during an attack. This attack type is designed to test the security of the machine-learning algorithm.
☒   **B, C,** and **D** are incorrect. A supply-chain attack occurs when the attacker attacks the supply chain of a business. A supply chain of a business involves any vendors and any activities that are needed to get goods into the hands of the customer. It is now common for cybersecurity attacks to go after the supply chain of an organization, which can have devastating affects on the business. Cloud-based attacks affect cloud resources such as data or services running in the cloud. For example, an attacker may create malware that deletes data of a cloud data storage account the user is using. An on-premises attack occurs when the attack affects a system or data at the company's site.

45.   ☑   **B.** A network-based distributed denial of service attack involves using up network resources such as bandwidth or processing power of network devices such as routers and switches so that network access is slow or crashes.
☒   **A, C,** and **D** are incorrect. Application-based DDoS are attacks on a specific piece of software cause the application or service to no longer work. Operational technology–based DDoS are attacks target hardware and software that is required to run industrial equipment. And physical attacks are not DDoS-based attacks, but attacks against physical security, such as attacking (or disabling) a physical lock to break into a facility.

46.   ☑   **C.** To execute PowerShell scripts on a Windows system, you must first set the execution policy on the system to allow scripts to execute. You can configure the execution policy on many systems at once with Group Policies, or you can use the **set-executionpolicy** cmdlet in PowerShell.
☒   **A, B, D,** and **E** are incorrect because they do not require the **set-executionpolicy** command to be run. Bash shell scripts are created in Linux or Unix environments to automate task within those operating systems. Python scripts are common scripts that run on different platforms such as Linux or Windows and have a .py extension. Macros scripts are created in software with a small programming language, known as a macros language. VBA stands for Visual Basic for Applications and is a type of macro script available in Microsoft Office applications.

Chapter 5

Vulnerabilities and Threats

QUESTIONS

IT security threats can apply to software or hardware. Software threats include the exploitation of vulnerabilities and the wide array of malware such as worms and spyware. Hardware threats apply when a malicious entity gains physical access, for example, to a handheld device or a server hard disk.

IoT and specialized embedded devices are widely used and can transmit sensitive data over the Internet, where industrial control systems are normally not connected to external networks. Identifying these threats is an important step in properly applying security policies.

1. A previous cloud administrator has deployed a cloud-hosted web application that uses HTTPS communications over TCP port 443 through the SSL network protocol. The web application is accessed over the Internet by customers. The underlying cloud Linux virtual machine supporting the web application defaults to employing username and password authentication. You have been tasked with hardening the web application. What should you recommend? (Choose two.)

   A. Use TLS instead of SSL.

   B. Change the default HTTPS port 443 to a different value.

   C. Host the web application on an underlying Windows virtual machine instead of Linux.

   D. Configure Linux public key authentication instead of username and password authentication.

2. Which of the following statements are true? (Choose two.)

   A. Worms log all typed characters to a text file.

   B. Worms propagate themselves to other systems.

   C. Worms can contain additional malware.

   D. Worms infect the hard disk MBR.

3. While conducting an assessment of network devices, you discover legacy and modern IoT devices that do not allow administrative credentials to be reset, they do not support TLS, and they do not allow firmware updates. What should you do to secure the continued use of these devices?

   A. Enable HTTPS on the devices.

   B. Patch the IoT operating system.

   C. Place the discovered devices on a firewalled and isolated network.

   D. Enable alerts for suspicious device activity.

4. Which description *best* defines a fileless virus?

   A. A computer program that replicates itself

   B. A file with a .vbs file extension

   C. A computer program that gathers user information

   D. A malicious computer program that loads directly into computer memory

5. You are developing a custom software component for a web application that will retrieve real-time stock quote feeds over the Internet using HTTPS. Your solution will consist of custom programming code as well as code from an existing code library using the C# programming language. The data feed will originate from a cloud storage repository. Which of the following presents the biggest potential security risk for this scenario?

   A. Cloud storage

   B. Data transmission over the Internet

   C. Vulnerabilities in C#

   D. Component integration

6. James is a software developer for a high-tech company. He creates a program that connects to a chat room and waits to receive commands that will gather personal user information. James embeds this program into an AVI file for a current popular movie and shares this file on a P2P file-sharing network. Once James's program is activated as people download and watch the movie, what will he created?

   A. Botnet

   B. DDoS

   C. Logic bomb

   D. Worm

7. A user reports USB keyboard problems. You check the back of the computer to ensure that the keyboard is properly connected and notice a small connector between the keyboard and the computer USB port. After investigating, you learn that this piece of hardware captures everything a user types in. What type of hardware is this?

   A. Smartcard

   B. Trojan

   C. Keylogger

   D. PS/2 converter

8. What is the difference between a rootkit and privilege escalation?

   A. Rootkits propagate themselves, while privilege escalation gives attackers additional resource permissions

   B. Privilege escalation can result from the installation of a rootkit.

   C. Rootkits are the result of privilege escalation.

   D. Each uses a different TCP port.

9. Which of the following are true regarding backdoors? (Choose two.)

   A. They are malicious code.

   B. They enable remote users access to TCP port 25.

   C. They are often used by rootkits.

   D. They provide access to the Windows root account.

10. Which of the following is NOT an example of a smart (or IoT) device?

   A. A wearable device

   B. A light sensor

   C. A UAV/drone

   D. System on a chip

11. You have discovered that a driver's license was mistakenly left on a scanner that was remotely compromised by a malicious user who scanned the document and used it to secure a bank loan. Further investigation reveals that the attacker identified vulnerabilities in the unpatched web application component built into the multifunction printer, which was revealed through web app error messages. Which terms best describe the nature of this attack? (Choose two.)

   A. Brute force

   B. Data exfiltration

   C. Identity theft

   D. Reputation loss

12. You have been tasked with hardening Wi-Fi networks in your office building. You plan on seeking potential Wi-Fi vulnerabilities. What should you look for? (Choose two.)

   A. Open Wi-Fi networks

   B. MAC address filtering

   C. WPA2 encryption

   D. Default settings

13. In Figure 5-1, match the terms on the left with the descriptions on the right. Note that two of the descriptions on the right do not have a matching term on the left.

FIGURE 5-1		
Security terms and descriptions	Outsourcing	Harden Raspberry Pi
	Reset root password	Task-specific firmware that supports updates
	Field programmable gate array	VoIP
	Packetizing phone calls	Windows OS hardening
		SIM card
		Supply chain

14. _____ is best suited for IoT sensors with small data transmission requirements.
   A. IPSec
   B. Narrowband IoT
   C. A VPN
   D. TLS

15. Which term describes a digital signal before it is encoded for transmission over radio frequencies?
   A. Broadband
   B. 5G
   C. Baseband
   D. Zigbee

16. Botnets can be used to set what type of coordinated attack in motion?
   A. DDoS
   B. Cross-site scripting
   C. Privilege escalation
   D. Rootkit

17. Refer to the Wireshark packet capture in Figure 5-2. What type of network traffic resulted in this audio wave?

    A. Baseband

    B. 5G

    C. TLS

    D. VoIP

FIGURE 5-2   Wireshark packet capture

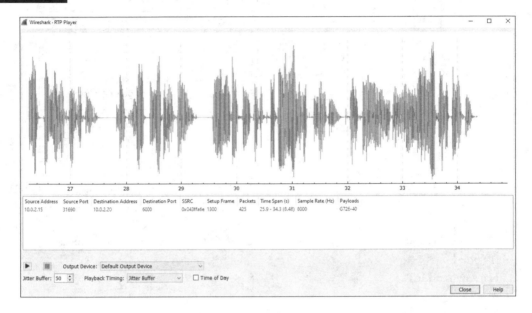

18. The Michelangelo virus was said to be triggered to overwrite the first 100 hard disk sectors with null data each year on March 6, the date of the Italian artist's birthday. What type of virus is Michelangelo?

    A. Zero-day

    B. Worm

    C. Trojan

    D. Logic bomb

19. The Stuxnet attack's primary function is to hide its presence while reprogramming industrial computer systems such as programmable logic controllers (PLCs) within a SCADA IDS environment. The malware was spread through USB flash drives, where it transmits copies of itself to other hosts. To which of the following does Stuxnet relate? (Choose two.)

    A. Rootkit
    B. Spam
    C. Worm
    D. Adware

20. Refer to Figure 5-3. You are connecting to an internal network printer for management purposes. What should be done to avoid this security message while minimizing cost?

    A. Use TLS instead of SSL.
    B. Acquire a certificate from a public certification authority.
    C. Block TCP port 443 on the printer.
    D. Install the root CA certificate on the connecting host.

FIGURE 5-3

Web browser
warning message

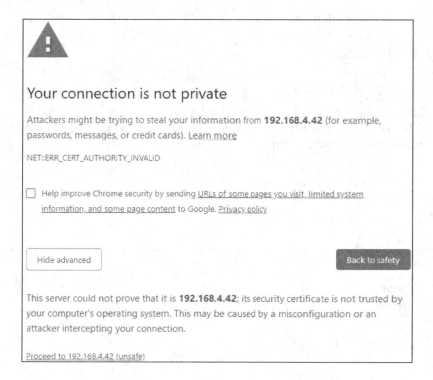

21. You need to harden the firewall rules for a network printer, as shown in Figure 5-4. The printer and management stations exist on the 192.168.4.0/24 network, and the printer will be managed using HTTPS standard port numbers. What should you do?

    A. Do nothing; the current firewall rules follow security best practices.
    B. Allow TCP port 80 management traffic to the printer
    C. Block 192.168.4.0/24.
    D. Allow TCP port 443 management traffic to the printer.

FIGURE 5-4

Network printer firewall rules

Firewall Rules
Step 4: Rules

Status	Address Template	Services Template	Action
Enable	All IPv4 Addresses	All Services	Allow
Enable	All IPv6 Addresses	All Services	Allow

22. Which of the following items are most affected by worm malware?

    A. Memory
    B. IP address
    C. Computer name
    D. Network bandwidth

23. Refer to Figure 5-5. Your network printer resides on the 192.168.4.0/24 network. The printer will receive its IP configuration automatically from the network. You are hardening the network printer configuration. What should you change?

    A. Uncheck all items except DHCPv4/BOOTP.
    B. Uncheck all items except DHCPv6.
    C. Uncheck all items except ICMPv4.
    D. Uncheck all items except NTP.

FIGURE 5-5

Network printer firewall bypass options

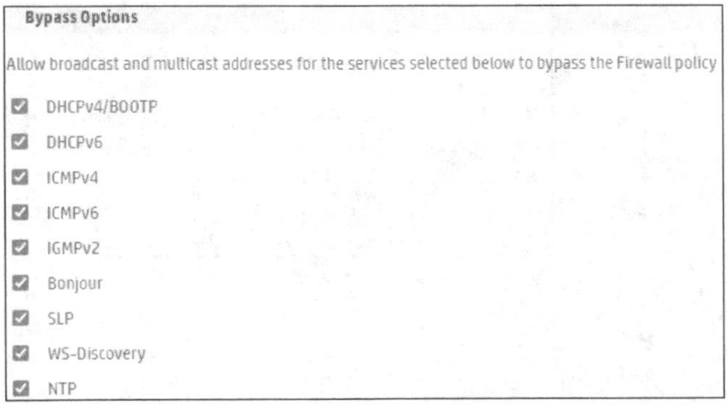

Bypass Options

Allow broadcast and multicast addresses for the services selected below to bypass the Firewall policy

- ☑ DHCPv4/BOOTP
- ☑ DHCPv6
- ☑ ICMPv4
- ☑ ICMPv6
- ☑ IGMPv2
- ☑ Bonjour
- ☑ SLP
- ☑ WS-Discovery
- ☑ NTP

24. Which of the following is true regarding Trojan malware?

A. It secretly gathers user information.

B. It encrypts user data files.

C. It can be propagated through peer-to-peer file-sharing networks.

D. It automatically spreads through Windows file- and print-sharing networks.

25. While attempting to access documents in a folder on your computer, you notice all of your files have been replaced with what appear to be random filenames. In addition, you notice a single text document containing payment instructions that will result in the decryption of your files. What type of malicious software is described in this scenario?

A. Trojan

B. Fileless virus

C. Worm

D. Ransomware

26. What should be done to help mitigate the threat of ransomware? (Choose two.)

A. Modify packet-filtering firewall rules.

B. Perform online backups.

C. Conduct user awareness training.

D. Use offline backups.

27. After reviewing perimeter firewall logs, you notice a recent change in activity, where internal stations are now connecting to the same unknown external IP address periodically. You are suspicious of this network traffic. Which explanation is the most likely to be correct?

A. Internal stations are infected with worm malware.

B. Weak encryption is being used by the internal stations.

C. Operating system updates are being installed.

D. Bots are contacting a command and control server.

28. Which network standard is designed for connecting and controlling smart home devices?

A. 5G

B. Zigbee

C. Narrowband IoT

D. Baseband

29. A user complains that his system has suddenly become unresponsive and ads for various products and services are popping up on the screen and cannot be closed. Which user actions could have led to this undesirable behavior? (Choose all that apply.)

A. Clicking a web search result

B. Viewing a web page

C. Watching a move in AVI file format

D. Inserting a USB flash drive

30. A server at your place of work has had all of its files encrypted after an attacker compromised a device on the network. Which attack has taken place?

A. Virus

B. Worm

C. Crypto-malware

D. Keylogger

31. After installing a new piece of software from an online web site and then reviewing system logs, you notice that programs have been running without your consent. You also realize that files have been added and removed to the system at times when you were not using the computer. Which of the following items was most likely used to result in these logged messages?

A. Remote access Trojan

B. Adware

C. Logic bomb

D. Backdoor

A

QUICK ANSWER KEY

1.	A, D	**12.**	A, D	**22.**	D
2.	B, C	**13.**	See "In-Depth Answers."	**23.**	A
3.	C			**24.**	C
4.	D	**14.**	B	**25.**	D
5.	D	**15.**	C	**26.**	C, D
6.	A	**16.**	A	**27.**	D
7.	C	**17.**	D	**28.**	B
8.	B	**18.**	D	**29.**	A, B, C, D
9.	A, C	**19.**	A, C	**30.**	C
10.	D	**20.**	D	**31.**	A
11.	B, C	**21.**	D		

IN-DEPTH ANSWERS

1. ☑   **A and D.** The same security issues apply to web applications hosted on-premises as well as in the public cloud. Transport Layer Security (TLS) supersedes the unsecure deprecated Secure Sockets Layer (SSL) network security protocol and should be used instead of SSL. Public key authentication enhances Linux user sign-in security by requiring the user to have knowledge of a username, as well as possessing a private key that is related to the public key stored with the Linux host. Public key authentication should always be enabled for the Linux root account.
    ☒   **B and C** are incorrect. Since the web application is public-facing, the default HTTPS port 443 should not be changed; otherwise, users would be required to enter the port number in the URL when connecting to the site. Changing default settings is not always appropriate. Hosting a web application on Windows instead of Linux does not in itself improve security.

2. ☑   **B and C.** Worms are malicious programs that do not require human interaction to multiply and self-propagate over the network, and they sometimes carry additional malware (the worm is the delivery mechanism).
    ☒   **A and D** are incorrect. Keyloggers capture data as it is typed. Boot sector viruses infect the MBR, not worms.

3. ☑   **C.** Legacy devices and IoT devices that have limited security configuration options should be placed on an isolated network that has strict firewall rules in place to limit traffic to other networks. This way, a compromised device would not be on the same network with other, more sensitive, systems. IoT devices include smart devices, such as those used for commercial and residential lighting automation, heating, ventilation and air conditioning (HVAC), motion detection and video surveillance, and wearable devices such as fitness watches.
    ☒   **A, B,** and **D** are incorrect. Because HTTPS using SSL is not the best solution (TLS should be used) compared to network isolation, this option is not correct. The IoT operating system is normally embedded in the firmware along with other functions, often called system on a chip (SoC), which in this scenario cannot be updated. Many embedded systems are specialized and have limited compute, cryptographic, and network authentication options. Embedded systems are often low cost and used for specialized tasks. Enabling alerts for suspicious activity is important in terms of notifications, but it is not as effective as network isolation in the secure, continued use of such devices.

4. ☑ **D.** A fileless virus is a type of malware that resides exclusively in a target system's memory and is not stored in the infected computer's file system. A traditional virus attaches itself to a file, such as a portable executable (PE), which is an executable (EXE) or dynamic linked library (DLL) file used in Windows operating systems.

☒ **A, B,** and **C** are incorrect. Worms replicate themselves. A .vbs file extension does not always mean the file is malicious; it is a valid Visual Basic script file extension. Spyware is a computer program that gathers user information.

5. ☑ **D.** Integrating systems and components into an existing environment can present security risks if the integrated items are not from a trusted source or are not themselves hardened.

☒ **A, B,** and **C** are incorrect. Cloud storage can protect data at rest using strong encryption ciphers. Data transmitted over the Internet using HTTPS is considered secure if newer versions of the TLS protocol are used as opposed to SSL. The use of the C# language itself does not present a security risk; software developers that do not adhere to secure coding practices, however, do present a risk, regardless of the language being used.

6. ☑ **A.** Botnets are applications that infect computers with malware that is under a malicious user's control. The malicious user uses command and control (C2) servers to issue commands to infected bots.

☒ **B, C,** and **D** are incorrect. DDoS attacks can be facilitated with botnets, but they do not gather personal user information; they render network services unusable by legitimate users. Logic bombs are malware triggered by specific conditions. Worms are malicious aps that replicate and proliferate.

7. ☑ **C.** Hardware keyloggers capture the user's every keystroke and store them in a chip.

☒ **A, B,** and **D** are incorrect. Smartcards are the size of a credit card, contain a microchip, and are used to authenticate a user. A Trojan is malware posing as legitimate software; the question is referring to hardware. The question refers to a USB keyboard and port, not a PS/2 keyboard.

8. ☑ **B.** Rootkits conceal themselves from operating systems and enable remote access with escalated privileges.

☒ **A, C,** and **D** are incorrect. Worms propagate themselves, not rootkits. Privilege escalation is the result of a rootkit. Privilege escalation does not refer to network software that uses a TCP port.

9. ☑ **A** and **C.** Malicious code produces undesired results, such as a rootkit providing access to a backdoor.

☒ **B** and **D** are incorrect. Backdoors do not have to allow malicious connections to any specific TCP port. Windows has an administrator account, while Unix and Linux have a root account.

10. ☑ **D.** A system on a chip (SoC) can be a component of a smart/Internet of Things (IoT) device, but SoC is not a smart/IoT device, much like firmware can be used in a firewall device, but firmware is not a firewall.

☒ **A, B,** and **C** are incorrect. A watch (wearable device), a lightbulb (light sensor), and an unmanned aerial vehicle (UAV) or drone could all potentially be smart devices (aka IoT devices) that connect to the Internet, providing telemetry data and remote management.

11. ☑ **B** and **C.** Because the driver's license was used to secure additional services, identity theft occurred as well as the potential for personal financial loss for the victim. The unauthorized scanning of the driver's license is considered data exfiltration, also referred to as data loss or a data breach.

    ☒ **A** and **D** are incorrect. Brute force refers to the continuous attempt to compromise something of value, such as trying password combinations to break into a user account. Reputation loss is applicable when a security breach at an organization is made public.

12. ☑ **A** and **D.** An open Wi-Fi network does not require authentication for connecting devices. This means anybody could access the Wi-Fi network and then scan for vulnerable hosts/devices, flood the network with useless traffic thus affecting network and service availability, and so on. The network should at the very least be protected with an encryption passphrase. The use of default settings is a security risk because anybody could easily research the hardware or software solution to determine what the default settings are and use them to access the network.

    ☒ **B** and **C** are incorrect. Despite the fact that MAC addresses are easily spoofed, MAC address filtering is a good security measure because it can either allow or block devices based on the network interface MAC address. WPA2 secures Wi-Fi networks by providing secure data encryption for network transfers.

13. ☑ See Figure 5-6 for the correct answers.

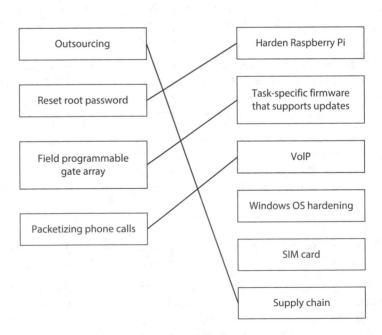

FIGURE 5-6

Security terms and descriptions— the answers

14. ☑ **B.** Narrowband Internet of things (IoT) falls under the fifth-generation (5G) mobile network standard. It is designed to support a large number of IoT devices with small data transmission requirements while preserving device battery life for extended periods of time. The wireless transmission of video and other data-intensive applications uses wideband communication channels.

☒ **A, C,** and **D** are incorrect. IP security (IPSec) is a network security protocol used to secure communications in a variety of ways, such as by ensuring that transmissions are authentic (via authentication headers, or AHs) and encrypting packet data through encapsulating security payload (ESP). IPSec differs from other network security mechanisms such as HTTPS in that it does not require a PKI certificate (but can use one) and it is not specific to an application such as an HTTP web server; IPSec can be configured to secure all IP traffic on a network. Virtual private networks (VPNs) create an encrypted communication channel between two end-points over an untrusted network such as the Internet but are not specifically related to IoT data transmissions. Transport layer security (TLS) is a network security protocol that supersedes the deprecated Secure Sockets Layer (SSL) network security protocol and is commonly used to secure web application traffic.

15. ☑ **C.** Baseband transmissions are used in radio-frequency (RF) systems including cellular communications. The signal originates as a digital signal but is then converted to an analog signal to be transmitted wirelessly using radio waves.

☒ **A, B,** and **D** are incorrect. Broadband refers to using multiple channels or frequencies to transmit simultaneously a larger amount of data than was possible with baseband. Fifth generation (5G) is a mobile network standard superseding 4G. 5G is designed to accommodate higher device density with faster data transmissions rates than were possible with 4G and its predecessors. Zigbee is a wireless personal area network (WPAN) standard used for smart home automation devices that communicate over small distances up to approximately 100 meters (about 328 feet) as opposed to wireless cellular signals, which theoretically can be used over distances of up to approximately 70 kilometers (about 43 miles). The specific equipment used determines the actual maximum transmission distance.

16. ☑ **A.** Botnets (groups of computers under singular control) can be used to dispatch distributed denial of service (DDoS) attacks against hosts or other networks.

☒ **B, C,** and **D** are incorrect. Cross-site scripting attacks trick users into running malicious scripts, often in the form of a malicious URL that is placed on a server susceptible to XSS attacks, which the victim accesses, resulting in malicious code being executed on the victim's browser. Privilege escalation refers to an attacker having more rights than she normally would have, usually by means of malware or leveraging an exploit. Rootkits are malware that replace existing system files to enable malicious use persistent access while remaining undetected by the OS.

17. ☑ **D.** Voice over IP (VoIP) uses packetizing, in which analog data (voice sound waves) is converted to transmittable network packets, such as encoding voice into an IP packet for transmission.

☒ **A, B,** and **C** are incorrect. Baseband transmissions are used in radio-frequency (RF) systems including cellular communications. The signal originates as a digital signal but is then converted to an analog signal to be transmitted wirelessly using radio waves. Fifth generation (5G) is a mobile network standard superseding 4G. 5G is designed to accommodate higher device density with faster data transmissions rates than were possible with 4G and its predecessors. Transport layer security (TLS) is a network security protocol that supersedes the deprecated Secure Sockets Layer (SSL) network security protocol and is commonly used to secure HTTPS web application traffic.

18. ☑ **D.** Logic bombs trigger malicious code when specific conditions are satisfied, such as a particular date.

☒ **A, B,** and **C** are incorrect. Zero-day exploits are not triggered by certain conditions; they are exploits that are unknown to the software vendor and the wider security community and, as such, no patch or countermeasure exists. Worms are self-replicating types of malware. Trojans are malicious code posing as legitimate code that may be performing a benign operation in the foreground and something malicious in the background.

19. ☑ **A** and **C.** Stuxnet replicates itself, as worm malware does, and masks itself while running, like rootkits do. This malware was designed to attack a specific type of industrial control system (ICS) in a system control and data acquisition (SCADA) environment, specifically, Siemens PLCs used to control centrifuges for uranium enrichment in nuclear power plant facilities in Iran. PLCs run a real-time operation system (RTOS), which is designed to perform specific tasks in a timely and reliable manner. ICSs and SCADA environments are also used to control machinery in manufacturing environments. Industrial networks should not be connected to external networks as a security measure, even though it can complicate the logistics of data transfer, software update, and so on.

☒ **B** and **D** are incorrect. Spam refers to the bulk sending of unsolicited email. Stuxnet is not triggered by any specific conditions.

20. ☑ **D.** The message is appearing because the web browser does not trust the certificate issuer for the certificate being used by the network printer. Installing the correct root CA certificate that issued the printer certificate will avoid this warning message in the future.

☒ **A, B,** and **C** are incorrect. Using TLS instead of the deprecated SSL network security protocol is a good security practice, but this will not remove future occurrences of the warning message. Acquiring a public certification authority (CA) certificate would prevent the warning message since the web browser would trust the public CA, but this incurs a cost. Blocking TCP port 443 is not recommended, since this is the default port number used for HTTPS connectivity, which secures network communications.

21. ☑ **D.** If remote printer management will occur over HTTPS, TCP port 443 traffic must be allowed to the printer instead of allowing all services. Firewalls rules should allow only what is required.

☒ **A, B,** and **C** are incorrect. The current firewall rules do not follow security best practices, because all network service traffic is allowed to the printer; only the required traffic should be allowed. The default HTTPS TCP port number is 443, not 80. Blocking the 192.168.4.0/24 network blocks all IP addresses on the subnet, which would prevent management of the printer.

22. ☑ **D.** Worms are malware that self-propagate over a network. As such, they consume bandwidth more so than the other listed resources.

☒ **A, B,** and **C** are incorrect. Neither the IP address nor the computer name gets changed by worms. While worms are programs that consume memory, this is not as pronounced as network bandwidth utilization is.

23. ☑ **A.** The printer will use the Dynamic Host Configuration Protocol (DHCP) for IPv4 to acquire its IP configuration from the network, so this traffic must be allowed (it must remain checked on in the configuration settings).

☒ **B, C,** and **D** are incorrect. The network is using an IPv4 network range, so DHCPv6 will not be used. Internet Control Message Protocol (ICMP) is used for network testing and error reporting by tools such as the **ping** and **tracert** commands. Network Time Protocol (NTP) is used to keep network device time synchronized to a central and reliable time source.

24. ☑ **C.** Trojans are malicious code that appears to be useful software. For example, a user may use a peer-to-peer file-sharing network on the Internet to illegally download pirated software. The software may install and function correctly, but a Trojan may also get installed. This Trojan could use a backdoor for attackers to gain access to the system.

☒ **A, B,** and **D** are incorrect. Trojans don't secretly gather user information; spyware does that. Ransomware, and not a Trojan, is malware that can encrypt user data files. Trojans are not self-replicating on Windows file and print sharing or any other network as worms are; they are spread manually.

25. ☑ **D.** Ransomware makes data or an entire system inaccessible until a ransom is paid.

☒ **A, B,** and **C** are incorrect. Trojans are malicious code that appears to be useful software. For example, a user may use a peer-to-peer file-sharing network on the Internet to illegally download pirated software. The software may install and function correctly, but a Trojan may also get installed. A fileless virus loads malicious code directly into memory, thus never writing to the host file system. This can occur in many ways, such as malicious users taking advantage of hardware or software vulnerabilities, so that instructions are piggy-backed onto existing system files to download and run malicious code in memory only. Worms are malicious programs that do not require human interaction to multiply and self-propagate over the network.

26. ☑ **C and D.** User awareness and training can help prevent users from falling prey to scams that involve users clicking file attachments that could be used to launch a ransomware attack. Frequent backups should be taken but stored offline so that a ransomware-infected device cannot also infect data backups.

☒ **A and B** are incorrect. Packet-filtering firewalls can examine only packet headers for network protocol types and a variety of source and destination addresses (IP and port addresses); they cannot detect and block ransomware. Online backups present a risk in the sense that a ransomware-infected device could potentially infect the data backup.

27. ☑ **D.** Because the change is recent and many internal stations are connecting to the same external IP address, this could indicate bots contacting a command and control server.

☒ **A, B,** and **C** are incorrect. The traffic is not initiated from the Internet, but is instead from the internal network, so internal stations are not allowing backdoor traffic initiated from the Internet. A change in network traffic patterns is not normally associated with the use of weak cryptographic solutions. Operating system updates would have been applied in the past; the scenario states the network activity is a recent change.

28. ☑ **B.** Zigbee is a wireless personal area network (WPAN) standard used for smart home automation devices that communicate over small distances up to approximately 100 meters (approximately 328 feet).

☒ **A, C,** and **D** are incorrect. Fifth generation (5G) is a mobile network standard superseding 4G. 5G is designed to accommodate higher device density with faster data transmissions rates than is possible with 4G and its predecessors. Narrowband Internet of things (IoT) falls under the fifth-generation (5G) mobile network standard. It is designed to support a large number of IoT devices with small data transmission requirements while preserving device battery life for extended periods of time. Baseband transmissions are used in radio-frequency (RF) systems including cellular communications. The signal originates as a digital signal but is then converted to an analog signal to be transmitted wirelessly using radio waves.

29. ☑ **A, B, C,** and **D.** All listed items have the potential of infecting a computer. Certain controls may be in place, such as limits on which web sites can be viewed or which files can execute, but this type of preventative measure must have been in place before an infection occurred.

30. ☑ **C.** Crypto-malware gains access to a computer system and encrypts all files.

☒ **A, B,** and **D** are incorrect. A virus is an application that performs malicious actions without the user's consent. A worm is a piece of malicious software that can replicate itself. A keylogger intercepts and stores every keystroke from the machine on which it is installed.

31. ☑ **A.** A remote access Trojan (RAT) presents itself as legitimate software that can infect a host and enable an attacker to gain privileged access to that host over a network.

☒ **B, C,** and **D** are incorrect. Adware is a type of malware that bombards the victim with advertisements. A logic bomb is a type of malware that functions normally until a predetermined condition is met, which will cause its malicious functionality to start. Backdoors enable undetected persistent malicious user access to the compromised host.

Chapter 6

Mitigating Security Threats

QUESTIONS

Threat mitigation techniques help harden the computing environment by reducing the attack surface. Threats include unauthorized access to sensitive data and standard network service ports exposed to the Internet.

Disk encryption protects sensitive data at rest by providing confidentiality; only the possessors of the correct decryption passphrase or key can decrypt encrypted data. Disabling unused network services and changing default listening port numbers make it more difficult for attackers to determine which network services are in use.

The Windows registry contains thousands of settings, some of which are related to security. Knowing the methods by which registry settings can be managed helps security professionals harden an environment. Enterprises also need a centralized mechanism for automatic update deployment, whether in a Windows or a Linux environment.

1. You have enabled encryption for cloud-based virtual machine hard disks. To which term does this configuration apply?
   A. Availability
   B. Integrity
   C. Authentication
   D. Confidentiality

2. Your manager suggests using laptop hardware to store cryptographic keys that are used to protect disks in a Windows 10 laptop. Which type of hardware is required to implement this plan?
   A. HSM
   B. Load balancer
   C. TPM
   D. Key vault

3. You have decided to use a centralized hardware solution for storing cryptographic keys. The keys will be used to protect data at rest. Which type of hardware is required to implement this plan?
   A. HSM
   B. Load balancer
   C. TPM
   D. Key vault

4. Your Windows laptop has a single disk containing operating system files and data. The machine does not support TPM, and a local cryptographic key must be used to encrypt and decrypt the drive. What should you configure?

   A. HSM

   B. Group policy

   C. A removable USB drive containing the key

   D. IPSec

5. To which OSI model layer do port numbers apply?

   A. Network

   B. Session

   C. Data link

   D. Transport

6. You are attempting to use SSH to remotely manage a running Linux server hosted in the cloud, but the connection is never made. Standard TCP port numbers are being used. What is the most likely cause of the problem?

   A. Port 23 traffic is blocked.

   B. Port 389 traffic is blocked.

   C. Port 443 traffic is blocked.

   D. Port 22 traffic is blocked.

7. You are part of a penetration testing team hired to test an organization's network security. The first phase of the test involves reconnaissance to discover which network services might be exposed to the Internet. Which tool should be used to complete this phase as quickly as possible?

   A. Vulnerability scanner

   B. HSM

   C. Port scanner

   D. Packet analyzer

8. Your load balancer is configured with a TLS certificate and contacts backend web application servers listening on TCP port 8081. Users must be able to access the web application using standard TCP port numbers in their web browsers. Which listening port should you configure on the load balancer?

   A. 25

   B. 80

   C. 443

   D. 3389

9. Your IoT video surveillance device allows remote management connections over HTTPS. To increase security, you want to use a nonstandard port number exposed to the Internet for managing the IoT device. What should you configure?

   A. Port forwarding
   B. TLS
   C. Load balancer
   D. VPN

10. You are configuring port forwarding to an internally-hosted Internet mail server as per Figure 6-1. The mail server is listening on standard port numbers. You must complete the configuration by specifying the start and end port number(s) as well as the traffic type. What should you specify?

    A. 80, 80, TCP
    B. 25, 25, TCP
    C. 0, 25, TCP
    D. 25, 0, TCP

FIGURE 6-1

Port forwarding
configuration

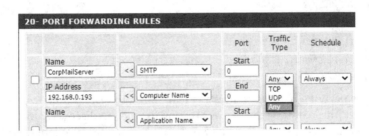

11. Refer to Figure 6-2. You are enabling HTTP remote access to a wireless router from an Internet host at 74.56.245.21. You do not want to use standard port numbers. Which port number should you *not* use?

    A. 80
    B. 88
    C. 1080
    D. 8080

FIGURE 6-2

Remote
management
configuration

12. What should you recommend to harden a Linux computer that is currently configured and being used in the following way?

- The computer administrator signs in using the default root account.
- Remote SSH management is done using the default port number.
- For confidentiality purposes, file hashes of customer financial transaction data have been generated on a local disk volume where the source data is also stored.

A. Use the **sudo** command, change port 22 to a nonstandard port, and encrypt customer data.

B. Change port 22 to a nonstandard port and regenerate updated customer data file hashes.

C. Change port 80 to a nonstandard port and regenerate updated customer data file hashes.

D. Use the **sudo** command and change port 80 to a nonstandard port number.

13. You need to apply security settings to the registry on a Windows server. Which command should you use?

A. **cipher**

B. **certutil**

C. **regedit**

D. **regex**

14. An application named APP1 runs on a domain-joined Windows server named SERVER1. When APP1 runs, it reads and writes to a specific registry key. You need to harden APP1's access to the registry. What should you do?

A. Create a service account for APP1 and assign the service account the appropriate registry permissions using regedit.exe.

B. Create a service account for SERVER1 and assign the service account the appropriate registry permissions using regedit.exe.

C. Create a service account for APP1 and add it as a member to the Domain Admins group.

D. Create a service account for SERVER1 and add it as a member to the Domain Admins group.

15. You need to use a command line tool to disable the Windows AutoRun feature in the Windows registry on Microsoft Windows Server Core computers. You have exported the appropriate registry settings to a file named DISABLEAUTORUN.REG. Which command should you issue on Server Core computers?

A. **ssh disableautorun.reg**

B. **cipher disableautorun.reg**

C. **msconfig disableautorun.reg**

D. **regedit disableautorun.reg**

16. Which regedit.exe command line parameter is used to export a registry subkey?

A. **regedit /S**

B. **regedit /Export**

C. **regedit /E**

D. **regedit /Save**

17. Your organization uses Windows desktop computers. You need to implement an efficient solution for deploying updates to the Windows computers. What should you deploy?

    A. HSM

    B. WSUS

    C. TLS

    D. EFS

18. Your organization uses Windows client machines connected to an on-premises Active Directory domain. You need to configure all client machines to point to the newly deployed WSUS update server. What should you do?

    A. Create a Bash script.

    B. Configure the registry on client machines.

    C. Configure a group policy.

    D. Create a PowerShell script.

19. You have been tasked with configuring a WSUS update server, but when you sign in to the Windows server, WSUS is unavailable in the Start menu. Why is this happening?

    A. Your user account lacks sufficient permissions.

    B. WSUS must be managed from the command line.

    C. The WSUS role has not been installed.

    D. The WSUS feature has not been installed.

20. You need to configure a network perimeter firewall to enable a newly deployed branch office WSUS server to synchronize updates over HTTP from an existing WSUS server located in the headquarters office. Standard port numbers are being used. Which TCP port number should be opened up in the firewall?

    A. 80

    B. 3389

    C. 22

    D. 8530

21. Which Red Hat Enterprise Linux command is used to apply server updates?

    A. **wsus update**

    B. **wua update**

    C. **yum update**

    D. **yum apply**

22. You have issued the **apt-get update** command on your Ubuntu Linux server, but the system returns the errors shown in Figure 6-3. What should you do?

    A. Open TCP port traffic on the Linux host.

    B. Modify Linux file system permissions.

    C. Issue the **sudo apt-get update** command.

    D. Create new file links.

FIGURE 6-3   Linux command error

```
cblackwell@Ubuntu-Srv1:~$ apt-get update
Reading package lists... Done
E: Could not open lock file /var/lib/apt/lists/lock - open (13: Permission denied)
E: Unable to lock directory /var/lib/apt/lists/
W: Problem unlinking the file /var/cache/apt/pkgcache.bin - RemoveCaches (13: Permission denied)
W: Problem unlinking the file /var/cache/apt/srcpkgcache.bin - RemoveCaches (13: Permission denied)
```

23. Your Windows stations use non-Microsoft applications. You need to ensure that patches and updates for these applications are applied on a regular basis. What should you do?

    A. Deploy WSUS.

    B. Configure yum updates.

    C. Configure apt-get updates.

    D. Deploy a third-party update tool.

24. You are about to install a new line-of-business application on sales managers' Windows computers. The new app requires a specific Windows security update to have been applied. The Windows computers download updates directly from Microsoft on the Internet. What should you do?

    A. Review WSUS server operational logs.

    B. Review network-perimeter firewall logs.

    C. View the Windows firewall log settings.

    D. View the update history on sales managers' computers.

25. Upon starting your Ubuntu Linux server, you are presented with a message asking for a disk unlock key. Nobody in the IT department has knowledge of a disk unlock key. What does this mean?

    A. The Linux disk is encrypted; the key must be retrieved from a recovery agent.

    B. The Linux disk is hashed; the key must be retrieved from a recovery agent.

    C. The Linux disk is hashed and is no longer accessible.

    D. The Linux disk is encrypted and is no longer accessible.

26. You need to allow standard HTTP traffic into an Ubuntu Linux server running the Apache web server. You are logged into the host with your user account. Which Linux command should you use?

    A. **sudo ufw allow 80/tcp**
    B. **ufw allow 80/tcp**
    C. **sudo ufw allow 443/tcp**
    D. **ufw allow 443/tcp**

27. You need to scan hosts on a network to determine which ports are open. Which TCP/IP protocols use port numbers? (Choose two.)

    A. IP
    B. ICMP
    C. TCP
    D. UDP

28. Why is UDP port scanning through firewalls considered unreliable?

    A. Most firewalls block IP packets.
    B. Most firewalls block ICMP packets.
    C. Most firewalls block HTTP traffic.
    D. Most firewalls block SSH traffic.

29. You have used the Nmap tool to scan hosts for open ports. Based on the output in Figure 6-4, what type of device is most likely in use? (Choose two.)

    A. Windows client computer
    B. Network switch
    C. Linux computer
    D. Windows server computer

FIGURE 6-4

Nmap scan
results

```
Starting Nmap 7.60 ( https://nmap.org ) at 2020-06-14 15:09 UTC
Nmap scan report for ubuntu-srv1.internal.cloudapp.net (10.1.0.4)
Host is up (0.000011s latency).
Not shown: 999 closed ports
PORT    STATE SERVICE
22/tcp open  ssh
```

30. In Figure 6-5, match the terms on the left with the descriptions on the right. Note that some descriptions on the right do not have a matching term on the left.

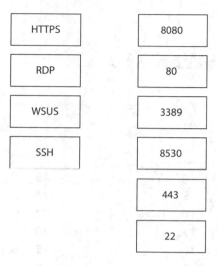

FIGURE 6-5

Network protocols and port numbers

HTTPS		8080
RDP		80
WSUS		3389
SSH		8530
		443
		22

31. You are reviewing a Linux server to ensure secure configurations. The SSH settings on the host are shown in Figure 6-6. Which conclusions can be drawn from the SSH configuration? (Choose two.)

   A. The default port number has been changed.
   B. The default port number is still being used.
   C. The host is listening on all IPv4 addresses used by the host.
   D. The host is listening on all IPv6 addresses used by the host.

FIGURE 6-6

Linux SSH configuration file

```
# $OpenBSD: sshd_config,v 1.101 2017/03/14 07:19:07 djm Exp $
# This is the sshd server system-wide configuration file.  See
# sshd_config(5) for more information.

Port 2002
#AddressFamily any
ListenAddress 199.126.129.45
#ListenAddress ::
```

32. You have placed IoT HVAC devices on an isolated subnet named SUBNET1. The IoT devices can be managed only through an HTTP connection using standard port numbers. When you're configuring the network firewall for SUBNET1, which inbound traffic should be allowed?

   A. None
   B. UDP port 80
   C. All
   D. TCP port 80

QUICK ANSWER KEY

1.	D	**12.**	A	**23.**	D	
2.	C	**13.**	C	**24.**	D	
3.	A	**14.**	A	**25.**	D	
4.	C	**15.**	D	**26.**	A	
5.	D	**16.**	C	**27.**	C, D	
6.	D	**17.**	B	**28.**	B	
7.	C	**18.**	C	**29.**	B, C	
8.	C	**19.**	C	**30.**	See "In-Depth Answers."	
9.	A	**20.**	D			
10.	B	**21.**	C	**31.**	A, D	
11.	A	**22.**	C	**32.**	D	

IN-DEPTH ANSWERS

1. ☑ **D.** Encryption of data at rest or network transmissions provides confidentiality in that only possessors of a decryption key can return the cipher text to its original plain text form.

   ☒ **A, B,** and **C** are incorrect. In IT security, availability ensures that IT systems and data remain available as much as is possible. High availability can be achieved with mechanisms such as load balancing, server clustering, and data backups. Integrity is used to ensure that data has not been tampered with, and it is accomplished commonly by generating file hashes; if the current file hash does not match an earlier file hash, the file has been modified. Authentication is used to prove the identity of an entity, such as a user logging in and providing the correct username and password.

2. ☑ **C.** Trusted platform module (TPM) security firmware is embedded in some computer systems and supports boot process integrity and the storage of cryptographic keys used by that machine.

   ☒ **A, B,** and **D** are incorrect. A hardware security module (HSM) is an appliance that is used to securely store cryptographic secrets that can be accessed by multiple hosts. Load balancers accept client app requests and route those requests to backend servers running the app. Key vaults can be defined in cloud computing environments as a centralized, secured secret store.

3. ☑ **A.** A hardware security module (HSM) is an appliance that is used to securely store cryptographic secrets that can be accessed by multiple hosts. In the cloud, managed HSM solutions are referred to as HSM as a service (HSMaaS).

   ☒ **B, C,** and **D** are incorrect. Load balancers accept client app requests and route those requests to backend servers running the app. Trusted platform module (TPM) security firmware is embedded in some computer systems and supports boot process integrity and the storage of cryptographic keys used by that machine. Key vaults can be defined in cloud computing environments as a centralized, secured secret store.

4. ☑ **C.** Many disk encryption solutions allow the decryption key to be provided through a removable USB drive, which is often used in place of trusted platform module (TPM) firmware key storage.

   ☒ **A, B,** and **D** are incorrect. A hardware security module (HSM) is an appliance that is used to securely store cryptographic secrets that can be accessed by multiple hosts; this does not apply in this scenario since a local key must be used. Group policy can be used to deploy settings to Windows computers, including those related to BitLocker disk encryption, but the answer does not specify BitLocker settings. IP Security (IPSec) is a network security protocol, not a disk encryption solution.

5.   ☑   **D.** Layer 4 of the Open Systems Interconnect (OSI) model is the transport layer, which can use User Datagram Protocol (UDP) or Transmission Control Protocol (TCP) port numbers to identify a network service running on a host. Port numbers are layer 4 addresses.
☒   **A, B,** and **C** are incorrect. Layer 3 (the network layer) of the OSI model focuses on the routing of network packets; this would apply to protocols such as Internet Protocol (IP). IP addresses are also called layer 3 addresses. Layer 5 (the session layer) of the OSI model relates to the creation, maintenance, and eventual teardown of network sessions. Layer 2 (the data link layer) of the OSI model focuses on how devices gain access to the transmission medium to transmit data. The 48-bit Media Access Control (MAC) address of a network interface is a layer 2 address.

6.   ☑   **D.** Secure Shell (SSH) is commonly used to remotely manage network equipment as well as Unix and Linux hosts. The standard SSH port number is TCP port 22.
☒   **A, B,** and **C** are incorrect. The Telnet protocol, used to connect to a Telnet daemon (this uses clear text transmissions and should be avoided) uses TCP port 23. Lightweight Directory Access Protocol (LDAP) uses TCP port 389. LDAP is used to query a network configuration database that can be distributed among multiple servers to allow user login, for example. Hypertext Transfer Protocol Secure (HTTPS) is an encrypted HTTP connection to a web server that normally uses TCP port 443.

7.   ☑   **C.** Port scanners can scan a single host or multiple hosts for open ports.
☒   **A, B,** and **D** are incorrect. While vulnerability scanners can also identify open ports, they are not as fast as port scanners because they attempt to identity many types of vulnerabilities that may be present on each host. A hardware security module (HSM) is an appliance that is used to securely store cryptographic secrets that can be accessed by multiple hosts. Packet analyzers such as Wireshark can capture network traffic, which can then be analyzed; this type of tool is not designed to identify open ports.

8.   ☑   **C.** TCP port 443 is the standard HTTPS port. Users do not have to enter in the port number in their web browser address bar when standard port numbers for HTTP and HTTPS are in use.
☒   **A, B,** and **D** are incorrect. The Simple Mail Transfer Protocol (SMTP) uses TCP port 25 to transfer e-mail messages to other SMTP hosts. Hypertext Transfer Protocol (HTTP) uses TCP port 80 to allow connectivity to a web server, where HTTPS is a secured connection, meaning the web server has been configured with a PKI certificate. TCP and UDP port 3389 is used for Remote Desktop Protocol (RDP), which allows remote GUI management of Windows hosts.

9.   ☑   **A.** Port forwarding enables a device to listen on a configured port number for an external interface, which is then sent internally to devices using either the same or a different port number. In this case, a port number other than 443 (HTTPS) should be used to increase security. If you're using a web browser to connect to IoT devices, the port number will have to follow the IP address or hostname after a full colon (:), such as https://mydevice.local:2000.
☒   **B, C,** and **D** are incorrect. Transport Layer Security (TLS) is a network security protocol that supersedes Secure Sockets Layer (SSL) and is commonly used to secure HTTPS connections. Load balancers accept client app requests and route those requests to backend servers running the app. Virtual private networks (VPNs) provide an encrypted tunnel between two end-points through which traffic can be securely transmitted over an untrusted network such as the Internet.

10. ☑ **B.** Simple Mail Transfer Protocol (SMTP) mail servers communicate by default using TCP port 25.

☒ **A, C,** and **D** are incorrect. SMTP servers do not listen on TCP port 80. Both the start and end files must contain port 25, even though it is a single port number and not a range.

11. ☑ **A.** Hypertext Transfer Protocol (HTTP) normally uses TCP port 80, so this port should not be used in this case.

☒ **B, C,** and **D** are incorrect. UDP port 88 is normally used by the Kerberos network authentication protocol; Microsoft Active Directory Domain Services uses Kerberos for authentication. The Socket Secure (SOCKS) protocol proxies user connections, often to bypass firewall filtering. This means that all communications between two end-points are funneled through the SOCKS proxy and the IP address of the originating devices is changed to that of the SOCKS proxy to enable connections to other devices on remote networks. SOCKS normally uses TCP port 1080. Explicit HTTP proxy servers normally use TCP port 8080 and are used for HTTP connections from client devices to HTTP web servers; SOCKS servers are not limited to HTTP connectivity. On the other hand, HTTP proxies can cache requested content to speed up subsequent requests. Transparent HTTP proxies normally listen on TCP port 80 or 443 and do not require the client to be configured with the proxy server name or IP address and port number.

12. ☑ **A.** The **sudo** command is used to run other commands with escalated privileges when you're not logged in using the root account (logging in as root is not recommended for security reasons). Changing default port numbers, such as TCP 22 for SSH, is one way to harden network services. Hashing customer data files can be used to determine whether the data has been tampered with, but encryption ensures that only authorized parties can even read customer data.

☒ **B, C,** and **D** are incorrect. The **sudo** command should be used to run commands requiring elevated privileges instead of staying logged in as the root user. File hashing provides data integrity but not data confidentiality, as encryption does. The default SSH port number (22) is being used, so changing port 80 to another does not apply.

13. ☑ **C.** The Windows **regedit** command enables Windows administrators to view and modify registry entries, import and export registry settings, and set permissions to different parts of the registry.

☒ **A, B,** and **D** are incorrect. On a Windows computer, the **cipher** command is used to manage encrypting file system (EFS) and the **certutil** command is used to manage PKI certificates. Regex is a general term that stands for "regular expressions" and is used in some command line environments for data pattern matching.

14. ☑ **A.** Software requiring specific permissions can be configured to use a service account, which can then be granted specific permissions to parts of the Windows registry using the regedit.exe tool.

☒ **B, C,** and **D** are incorrect. A service account is needed for APP1, not the entire server, SERVER1. When minimal permissions are required, membership in the Domain Admins group is not recommended, since it allows far too many rights and permissions.

15. ☑   **D.** The **regedit** command can be used to manipulate the Windows registry, including importing .reg files.

☒   **A, B,** and **C** are incorrect. The **ssh** command is built into Unix and Linux and can also be installed and run on Windows hosts. Newer Windows versions such as Windows 10 variations automatically include the **ssh** command. SSH is used to manage hosts remotely over an encrypted connection. The Windows **cipher** command is used to manage encrypting file system (EFS), while **msconfig** is a GUI tool used to control the boot environment.

16. ☑   **C.** The /**E** switch for the **regedit** command means "export." A filename must also be specified.

☒   **A, B,** and **D** are incorrect. None of the listed **regedit** command line switches are used to export registry information to a .reg file. The **regedit.exe /S** switch means "silent mode," which suppresses **regedit** output messages. /**Export** and /**Save** are invalid **regedit** command line switches.

17. ☑   **B.** Windows Server Update Services (WSUS) is a Windows Server role designed to provide updates to internal Windows hosts instead of all internal Windows hosts pulling down updates.

☒   **A, C,** and **D** are incorrect. A hardware security module (HSM) is an appliance that is used to securely store cryptographic secrets that can be accessed by multiple hosts. Transport Layer Security (TLS) is a network security protocol that supersedes Secure Sockets Layer (SSL) and is commonly used to secure HTTPS connections. Encrypting File System (EFS) is a Windows feature that enables the encryption of files on an NTFS disk volume.

18. ☑   **C.** In order for Windows clients to pull updates from a WSUS server, they must be configured to do so. This can be done centrally for Microsoft Active Directory domain-joined computers using group policy.

☒   **A, B,** and **D** are incorrect. While the other listed options could be used to configure clients to point to a WSUS host, using group policy for domain-joined machine configurations is recommended since the WSUS settings already exist in group policy.

19. ☑   **C.** The Windows Server Update Services (WSUS) role is not installed by default and can be installed using the Server Manager GUI or the Install-WindowsFeature PowerShell cmdlet.

☒   **A, B,** and **D** are incorrect. A lack of permissions would not prevent WSUS from showing up in the Start menu. WSUS is a Windows server role, not a feature, and it can be managed using the GUI or the command line.

20. ☑   **D.** Windows Server Update Services (WSUS) uses TCP port 8530 for HTTP transmissions and TCP port 8531 for HTTPS transmissions.

☒   **A, B,** and **C** are incorrect. TCP port 80 is used for Hypertext Transfer Protocol (HTTP), Remote Desktop Protocol (RDP) uses UDP and TCP port 3389, and Secure Shell (SSH) uses TCP port 22.

21.   ☑   **C.** Red Hat Enterprise Linux (RHEL) uses the **yum** command syntax to manage software, including updates.
☒   **A, B,** and **D** are incorrect. Wsus uses command line tools such as wsutil, not wsus or wua. Updates are not applied to a RHEL host using the **yum apply** command.

22.   ☑   **C.** Ubuntu Linux updates can be applied with the **apt-get update** command. The command should be prefixed with **sudo** to run it with elevated permissions instead of staying logged in with the Linux root account.
☒   **A, B,** and **D** are incorrect. The listed error is occurring because elevated privileged are required, not because of the listed potential reasons.

23.   ☑   **D.** WSUS is designed for Microsoft software updates, not third-party software updates, so a third-party update tool must be used in this case.
☒   **A, B,** and **C** are incorrect. WSUS is designed only for Microsoft software updates. Yum and apt-get are Linux-based software update tools.

24.   ☑   **D.** Windows computers retain Windows update details, including specific update names and versions. This information is accessible through the Windows update history.
☒   **A, B,** and **C** are incorrect. None of the listed options will provide details regarding applied Windows updates. WSUS server operational logs contain entries related to the WSUS server, not updates applied to client stations. Network-perimeter and Windows firewall logs contain entries related to allowed or blocked network traffic, not entries related to applied Windows updates.

25.   ☑   **D.** Disks that are encrypted with a passphrase or key are inaccessible if the passphrase or key cannot be provided. The disk could be repartitioned and formatted and used again, however.
☒   **A, B,** and **C** are incorrect. Standard Linux disk locking does not use recovery agents. Disk unlock keys are for encrypted disks and are not related to file system hashing.

26.   ☑   **A.** Linux commands that make system changes require elevated privileges, which is achieved using the **sudo** command prefix. The Linux universal firewall (**uwf**) command can allow HTTP traffic over TCP port 80.
☒   **B, C,** and **D** are incorrect. Without being logged in as root or using the **sudo** command prefix, managing the firewall will fail. HTTP uses TCP port 80, not 443, which is used by HTTPS.

27.   ☑   **C and D.** The Transmissions Control Protocol (TCP) establishes "sessions" between hosts before transmissions can occur. After session establishment, transmitted data receipt must be acknowledged by the recipient; otherwise, the data is re-sent by the sender. Many network services use TCP, and each network service on a host is uniquely identified by a port number. The User Datagram Protocol (UDP) does not use sessions; instead, it simply transmits data to a target with no receipt acknowledgments. Network services that use the UDP transport also use port numbers.
☒   **A and B** are incorrect. The Internet Protocol (IP) uses IP addresses for routing, and the Internet Control Message Protocol (ICMP) is used to test and report on network connectivity issues; neither protocol uses port numbers.

28. ☑ **B.** Common forms of UDP port scanning use ICMP, which reports if a network host is unreachable for some reason. This can indicate that the port is closed. Because ICMP is commonly blocked by most firewalls, this type of scanning is not considered reliable.
☒ **A, C,** and **D** are incorrect. UDP port scanning normally uses ICMP, not specifically IP, HTTP, or SSH.

29. ☑ **B** and **C.** Because TCP port 22 SSH is listed, the device is most likely a network device such as a network switch or a Unix/Linux host, since these types of devices often have SSH enabled by default.
☒ **A** and **D** are incorrect. The host is more likely to be a network device or a Linux host rather than Windows because of the use of TCP port 22 for SSH.

30. ☑ When default port numbers are used, it is easy to identify the running service. HTTPS uses TCP 443, RDP uses UDP and TCP 3389, WSUS uses TCP 8530 for HTTP transmissions, and SSH uses TCP 22. Figure 6-7 shows the correct answers.

FIGURE 6-7

Network protocols and port numbers— the answers

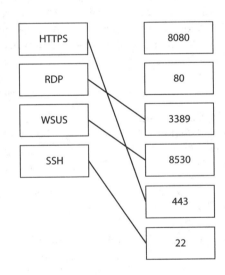

31. ☑ **A** and **D.** The default secure shell (SSH) port is TCP 22, not 2002. The default ListenAddress :: listing means that all IPv6 addresses configured on the host are listening on TCP port 2002 in this case.
☒ **B** and **C** are incorrect. 2002 is not the default SSH port number. The dual colons (::) are IPv6 shorthand for a collection of 0's and are not related to IPv4.

32. ☑ **D.** HTTP connections use the standard TCP 80 port number. Internal segmentation firewalls (ISFWs) are used to allow or block network traffic between internal network segments.
☒ **A, B,** and **C** are incorrect. HTTP normally uses TCP, not UDP.

Chapter 7

Implementing Host-based Security

QUESTIONS

While firewalls can examine network transmissions to allow or deny that traffic, intrusion detection and prevention systems can be configured to detect and report on abnormal activity occurring on a network or a specific host. Intrusion prevention systems (IPSs) have the ability to stop attacks in progress.

End-point devices are used directly by users and include desktops, laptops, tablets, smartphones, and so on. Hardening end-point device configurations and usage can be achieved with configurations such as app geofencing, disabling unneeded functionality such as Bluetooth, and context-aware authentication.

Full device encryption as well as using self-encrypting drives (SEDs) can protect sensitive data from unauthorized viewing, while hashing can be used to determine whether changes have been made, such as to individual files. Data loss prevention (DLP) software can be deployed to ensure that sensitive data is not leaked to unauthorized users inside and outside the organization.

1. You have been tasked with deploying a security solution that will monitor activity related to a specific application server. The solution must be able to detect suspicious activity and take steps to prevent the activity from continuing. What should you deploy?
   - A. NIDS
   - B. NIPS
   - C. HIDS
   - D. HIPS

2. You need to implement a tool that can be configured to detect abnormal activity for a cloud-based virtual network. The solution must be configured to send alert notifications to administrators. What should you deploy?
   - A. NIDS
   - B. HSM
   - C. HIDS
   - D. TPM

3. Your software development team is creating a custom app that will accept customer payments. The app calls upon existing third-party APIs, where those APIs result in a unique value generated from user payment methods and that unique value is sent over the network to complete payment transactions. Which technique is taking place when payments occur using this custom app?
   A. Tokenization
   B. Salting
   C. Encryption
   D. Hashing

4. Which close-range wireless system that supports "tap" payments is commonly used for debit and credit card payments with point-of-sale systems?
   A. Wi-Fi
   B. Bluetooth
   C. NFC
   D. Infrared

5. You plan on working remotely while vacationing in a rural location, where traditional wired phone service and electricity are unavailable. Your mobile phone has a data connection in this location, but the signal is very weak and unacceptably slow for work purposes over the Internet. You plan on using batteries and a power generator to run electrical devices. Which network connectivity options should you consider? (Choose two.)
   A. DSL
   B. Cable modem
   C. Cellular signal booster
   D. Satellite connectivity

6. Your company-issued smartphone is configured to accept your fingerprint as a form of authentication. What type of authentication is this?
   A. Context-aware
   B. Multifactor
   C. Biometric
   D. Gesture-based

7. Some of your technically proficient users have modified their company-issued Android smartphone to provide full device access in order to install apps requiring this permission. Which term best describes this scenario?
   A. Jailbreaking
   B. sudo
   C. Rooting
   D. Hijacking

8. You are configuring a mobile device management (MDM) solution to harden employee smartphones. The devices must be configured such that:

   ■ Device location around the world cannot be tracked.

   ■ Sensitive data cannot be viewed by unauthorized parties.

   ■ Device configuration and data can be removed when devices are lost or stolen.

   ■ Corporate apps and data are isolated from personal apps and data.

   What do you need to do?

   A. Disable GPS, enable full device hashing, enable remote wipe, and run apps in Docker containers.

   B. Disable GPS enable full device encryption, enable remote wipe, and configure containerization.

   C. Disable Bluetooth, enable full device encryption, enable remote access, and configure containerization.

   D. Disable Bluetooth, enable full device hashing, enable remote wipe, and configure containerization.

9. After sensitive data is leaked from within your organization, you decide to implement security solutions on all desktop computers that will ensure that sensitive documents are shared only with authorized parties. Desktop computers must also be protected from malicious code and must block network traffic not initiated by the desktop itself. Which of the following solutions will best address these concerns?

   A. Opal-compliant self-encrypting drive full-disk encryption, DLP, firewall

   B. DLP, full disk backup, firewall

   C. Anti-malware, disk encryption using TPM, firewall

   D. DLP, anti-malware, firewall

10. Users in your company use a web browser on their tablets to access their cloud-hosted Windows desktop and applications remotely. Which term best encompasses this scenario?

    A. TPM

    B. VDI

    C. HSM

    D. IPS

11. Users complain that as they are travelling on a commuter train to and from work, they are unable to access e-mail and cloud-based files on their laptops. However, they are able to read e-mail messages on their company-issued smartphones. Cloud-based files can be edited only using specialized software installed on laptops. The train does not offer Wi-Fi Internet connectivity. Users must have access to e-mail and cloud-based files during their commute while minimizing costs and inconvenience. What should you do?

A. Teach users how to sideload applications.
B. Teach users how to manage USB On-The-Go.
C. Teach users how to enable GPS tagging.
D. Teach users how to enable smartphone tethering.

12. You are traveling on a bus with a colleague, and you both have your laptops. You need to share files with each other during the trip with a minimum of inconvenience and minimal cost. The bus does not offer Wi-Fi connectivity. What should you do?

A. Copy the files to external USB storage media.
B. Copy the files to a MicroSD HSM.
C. Enable Wi-Fi Direct.
D. Enable satellite Internet connectivity.

13. Which technique should be employed when testing unfamiliar software to ensure it is benign?

A. Sandboxing
B. Push notifications
C. Firmware Over-The-Air updates
D. Carrier unlocking

14. Which wireless technology is commonly used for inventory control?

A. Wi-Fi
B. RFID
C. NFC
D. Cellular

15. Your manager has asked you to evaluate and recommend a single IT tool that can be used to manage desktops, laptops, as well as Android tablets and smartphones. What type of tool should you be looking at?

A. Trusted platform module
B. Unified end-point management
C. SEAndroid
D. Hardware security module

16. You have been tasked with disabling the SMS text messaging multimedia message service (MMS) on user smartphones. Which type of SMS texting risk is directly mitigated with this configuration?

A. Injection attack
B. Identity theft
C. Ransomware triggered from an e-mail message file attachment
D. Malicious code embedded in video files

17. Refer to Figure 7-1. You would like to use a payment app on your Android smartphone that allows for "tap" close range payments. What should you configure?

    A. NFC

    B. Tethering & mobile hotspot

    C. VPN

    D. Mobile networks

FIGURE 7-1

Android
smartphone
settings

18. Refer to Figure 7-2. You are working with two Windows laptops side-by-side on a desk in a new office. Wi-Fi connectivity is not yet available in the office. You need to transfer files between the laptops wirelessly. Which option should you select?

    A. Bluetooth & other devices

    B. Touchpad

    C. AutoPlay

    D. USB

FIGURE 7-2

Windows settings

Devices

🖳 Bluetooth & other devices

🖶 Printers & scanners

🖱 Mouse

⬚ Touchpad

⌨ Typing

✒ Pen & Windows Ink

▶ AutoPlay

🔋 USB

19. In Figure 7-3, match the terms on the left with the descriptions on the right. Note that one term on the left does not have a matching description on the right.

FIGURE 7-3

Mobile device
terms and
definitions

Containerization		Satellites are used to provide detailed location information
SEAndroid		Users may use their personal mobile device for work tasks
iOS		Uses policies to control mobile device resource access
GPS tagging		Remote wiping of lost or stolen devices removes only corporate apps, settings, and data
BYOD		

20. You are configuring a security appliance with the following rule:

```
alert tcp any any -> $CORP_NET 23 (msg:"Telnet connection attempt";
sid:1000002; rev:1;)
```

Which type of device are you configuring?
A. Packet filtering firewall
B. Proxy server
C. IDS
D. HSM

21. You are evaluating IoT HVAC sensors for a commercial building. One concern is how device updates can be applied wirelessly when they are available. What should you search for in the IoT sensor documentation?
A. Sideloading
B. Firmware OTA updates
C. WSUS
D. TPM

22. Upon entering your favorite hardware and tool store, the store app that you had previously installed welcomes you and lists that day's sales items for that store location. You search the app for a wrench, and the app directs you within the store to the correct location of the item. What is being used in this scenario?
A. Firmware OTA updates
B. Geotagging
C. Geofencing
D. Wi-Fi Direct

23. Your organization manages valuable pharmaceutical research data. Company security policies require Android mobile device users to use cryptographic keys to protect sensitive data. The keys cannot be stored on the device itself. What type of accompanying hardware should be used for securely storing cryptographic keys?
A. Next-generation firewall
B. USB On-The-Go
C. Secondary SIM card
D. MicroSD HSM

24. Which security issue is being addressed in Figure 7-4?
A. Data confidentiality
B. Data integrity
C. Data availability
D. Data classification

FIGURE 7-4

Microsoft
PowerShell
cmdlet output

```
PS D:\SampleFiles> Get-FileHash .\CardData.db

Algorithm       Hash
---------       ----
SHA256          9FC99C38247E777AB85234E152D45668883DEA6F223A7E5BF8423FD98627C372
```

25. To which operating system does the term "jailbreaking" apply?
    A. Android
    B. iOS
    C. Linux
    D. Windows

26. In which device provisioning strategy does an organization pay for and provide a mobile device to employees while allowing employees personal use of the device?
    A. BYOD
    B. CYOD
    C. VDI
    D. COPE

27. You no longer require data stored on a self-encrypting drive (SED). What is the quickest way to wipe the drive so that it can be reused, while ensuring data artifacts are not recoverable?
    A. Overwrite all disk sectors with random data.
    B. Overwrite all disk sectors with 0's.
    C. Remove and destroy SED cryptographic keys.
    D. Attach the SED in a different computer.

28. Which abilities are unique to end-point detection and response solutions in comparison to host-based packet filtering firewalls? (Choose two.)
    A. Block incoming traffic initiated from outside the machine
    B. Allow incoming response traffic initiated from the machine
    C. Stop attacks in progress
    D. Detect threats

29. You have decided to use a different mobile network provider. Which process must be completed to use a new provider?
    A. Containerization
    B. Carrier unlock
    C. Jailbreaking
    D. Rooting

30. Online payment services can use your credit card while never sending the actual credit card details to merchants during payment transactions. Which technique enables this to occur?
    A. Encryption
    B. Hashing
    C. Salting
    D. Tokenization

31. Which technique provides cryptographic one-way functions with randomized data in addition to the data that is to be protected?
    A. Encryption
    B. Hashing
    C. Salting
    D. Tokenization

32. You work in the IT department at a military base. The IT department has secured issued smartphones to require that users must provide not only user credentials to sign in, but they must also be present at the base. Which term best describes this scenario?
    A. Single sign-on
    B. Multifactor authentication
    C. Identity federation
    D. Context-aware authentication

QUICK ANSWER KEY

1. D
2. A
3. A
4. C
5. C, D
6. C
7. C
8. B
9. D
10. B
11. D

12. C
13. A
14. B
15. B
16. D
17. A
18. A
19. See "In-Depth Answers."
20. C
21. B

22. C
23. D
24. B
25. B
26. D
27. C
28. C, D
29. B
30. D
31. C
32. D

IN-DEPTH ANSWERS

1. ☑ **D.** A host-based intrusion prevention system (HIPS) runs on a specific host such as an application server. A HIPS can be configured to detect anomalous behavior related to that specific host and is not limited only to reporting/alerting/logging the activity; it can also be configured to take action to stop the activity, such as blocking specific types of network traffic from specific hosts.
   ☒ **A, B,** and **C** are incorrect. A network-based intrusion detection system (NIDS) is not specific to a host but instead analyzes network traffic from many sources to detect potentially malicious activity. A network-based instruction prevention system (NIPS) has the additional capability of stopping a potential attack, such as by blocking or limiting the type and amount of network traffic from hosts. A host-based intrusion detection system (HIDS) can detect and report/alert/log any host-specific suspicious activity but does not take steps to stop or prevent those malicious activities.

2. ☑ **A.** A NIDS is not specific to a host but instead analyzes network traffic from many sources to detect potentially malicious activity.
   ☒ **B, C,** and **D** are incorrect. A hardware security module (HSM) is a dedicated tamper-resistant device designed to securely store and manage cryptographic keys. A HIDS can detect and report/alert/log any host-specific suspicious activity but does not take steps to stop or prevent those malicious activities. The Trusted Platform Module (TPM) is a firmware chip within a computing device that ensures device boot integrity and stores cryptographic keys used to encrypt storage devices. TPM is part of an overall computing security strategy and is often referred to as being part of the "hardware root of trust."

3. ☑ **A.** Tokenization is a security technique that uses a trusted centralized service to create a digital representation of sensitive data, such as credit card information. This "token" can then be used to authorize resource access or payments without ever sending the actual origin sensitive data.
   ☒ **B, C,** and **D** are incorrect. Salting is a technique used to add random data to plain text data prior to all of the data being fed into a one-way cryptographic algorithm. Linux user passwords stored in the /etc/shadow file are represented as a hash value generated from the salted user password string. Encryption uses one or more keys to render plain text to cipher text (encrypted data), thus providing data confidentiality for data at rest or in transit in that only the possessor of the correct decryption key can convert the cipher text back into plain text. Hashing feeds data into a one-way hashing algorithm, which results in a unique value that can't be easily reversed. An example of hashing would be generating file hashes periodically to see if files have been corrupted or tampered with in some way. If the current hash differs from the previous hashes, you know that a change in the data has occurred.

4. ☑ **C.** Near Field Communication (NFC) is a wireless technology used to transfer small amounts of data between devices that are no more than approximately 10 centimeters (3.9 inches) apart. NFC is commonly used for "tap" contactless payment systems from smartphones or payment cards.

☒ **A, B,** and **D** are incorrect. The wireless fidelity (Wi-Fi) wireless network system uses radio waves that can be transmitted from one point and received by many Wi-Fi devices such as desktops, laptops, tablets, smartphones, gaming consoles, and so on. Wi-Fi devices can communicate directly with each other (ad-hoc mode) or they can connect to a central wireless connectivity device (wireless access point or wireless router). Wireless routers are designed to route local Wi-Fi traffic to other networks such as the Internet. Infrared is an older line-of-sight, or point-to-point, wireless technology that is used for items such as television remote controls. Modern computing devices no longer use infrared for local device connectivity or printing; instead, Bluetooth is used for these purposes. Bluetooth is a wireless technology similar to Wi-Fi but has a smaller range than Wi-Fi; most common Bluetooth implementations have a range of up to 10 meters (33 feet). Common uses of Bluetooth include hands-free mobile phone usage while driving, connecting devices such as televisions and smartphones to wireless speaker systems, and so on.

5. ☑ **C** and **D.** Cellular signal boosters can amplify a weak cellular signal many times to enable voice calls, texting, and mobile device data usage that otherwise may be unacceptably slow or not be possible in a rural area. Always check with the nearest cell tower provider to register your cellular signal booster. Satellite connectivity requires a satellite dish installation to transmit and receive data through a wireless satellite system and can also be used to provide Internet connectivity to rural areas or ships at sea.

☒ **A** and **B** are incorrect. A digital subscriber line (DSL) uses specialized transmission and reception equipment to get data over traditional copper phone wires at different frequencies than are used by standard voice conversations. Because there are no phone lines in the area, DSL is not an option. Cable modems use an existing coax cable television network to provide Internet connectivity. Because there are no phone lines and no electricity, a cable network would not exist, so this will not provide a solution.

6. ☑ **C.** Biometric authentication uses a person's physical characteristics for unique identification, such as through fingerprints, retinal scans, voice and speech recognition, and so on.

☒ **A, B,** and **D** are incorrect. Context-aware authentication uses not only standard identification mechanisms such as usernames and passwords, but also factors such as device location, device type of configuration, time of day, and so on. Multifactor authentication (MFA) uses multiple authentication categories together, such as something you know (username and password), along with something you are (fingerprint) and something you have (smartcard, key fob, unique authentication PIN derived from alternative device). Gesture-based authentication comes in the form of motions, or movement, and touchscreen gestures using one or more fingers; both of these can be used to verify a user's identity.

7. ☑ **C.** Rooting an Android device means allowing full privileged access to a device and its operating system, which is required by some apps and provides the user full device configuration ability. One common way of rooting a phone is to download a developer toolkit or specialized firmware flashing app; you may also require a separate USB-connected computer to complete the process. The term "rooting" came about because the Android operating system is based on the Linux operating system kernel, which uses the root account as the fully privileged account. Users should be aware that rooting an Android device can introduce security risks (malware getting full control of the device) and may void a mobile carrier's warranty.

    ☒ **A, B,** and **D** are incorrect. Jailbreaking applies to Apple iOS devices such as the iPhone, iPad, and iPod. Like rooting an Android device, jailbreaking can be achieved with an installed app on the device, or it can be done using a USB-connected external computer to remove device restrictions, which allows the user full configuration flexibility, such as the ability to install apps not available in the Apple App Store. **sudo** is a Linux command that allows some users to run privileged commands; the normal Linux command is simply prefixed with **sudo**. In IT security, session hijacking can refer to taking over an existing established session between two hosts.

8. ☑ **B.** Disabling a global positioning system (GPS) on a mobile device, which is often used for device tracking, geolocation media tagging, and limiting location-based app usage with geolocation, prevents the device location from being tracked through GPS, although device tracking is still possible with cell-tower triangulation within a locality. Protecting sensitive data from unauthorized parties can be achieved with full device encryption. Remote wipe enables mobile device administrators to erase the device remotely over the network if the device is lost or stolen. Mobile device containerization separates work and personal apps, settings, and data for security purposes, including remote wiping of only the corporate container (partition). Mobile device administrators can also harden devices by enabling settings such as timeout screen locking, or disabling unneeded functionality provided by cameras, microphones, Bluetooth connectivity, and so on.

    ☒ **A, C,** and **D** are incorrect. Device hashing can be used to verify whether files have been modified, but it does protect them from unauthorized access. Bluetooth is a local wireless solution; it is not global, so disabling it will not prevent device tracking globally. Enabling device remote access does not imply remote wipe capabilities.

9. ☑ **D.** Data loss prevention (DLP) software solutions can reduce the potential of intentional and unintentional sensitive data leaks, such as preventing the forwarding of confidential data to e-mail addresses outside the organization. Anti-malware, if kept up-to-date, can help protect devices from malicious code. A desktop computer with a host-based firewall configured can allow or block network traffic to or from that computer. Next-generation firewalls take this a step further by inspecting all details in the transmissions.

    ☒ **A, B,** and **C** are incorrect. The listed items, such as a self-encrypting drive (SED) that uses the Opal security specification, do not address the malicious code or sensitive data leak concerns. Answers not addressing the prevention of data leakage, malware mitigation, or network traffic control through a firewall are incorrect.

10. ☑ **B.** Virtual Desktop Infrastructure (VDI) provides remote desktop and apps access from any type of device, even if only a web browser is used.

☒ **A, C,** and **D** are incorrect. Trusted Platform Module (TPM) is a firmware chip within a computing device that ensures device boot integrity on UEFI firmware computers, which allows for measured, or integrity-checked boot-up to protect from security threats such as rootkits. TPM can also store cryptographic keys used to encrypt storage devices. A hardware security module (HSM) is a dedicated tamper-resistant device designed to securely store and manage cryptographic keys. An intrusion prevention system (IPS) can be configured to detect anomalous behavior related to a specific host and is not limited to reporting/alerting/logging the activity; it can also be configured to take action to stop the activity.

11. ☑ **D.** Smartphone tethering enables you to connect other devices, such as laptops lacking cellular connectivity, to a smartphone Internet connection through the smartphone's data services. Tethering can be done wirelessly between the smartphone and the laptop, or through a USB cable.

☒ **A, B,** and **C** are incorrect. Sideloading an application normally refers to installing an app manually on the mobile device as opposed to installing it from an app store. USB On-The-Go (USB OTG) enables a USB device to assume the role of both a USB host and a USB end-point peripheral device, as required. For example, USB OTG is often used to plug standard USB storage devices (end-point devices) into a smartphone (host) charging port through a USB OTG adapter device to enable the smartphone to access the USB storage device. Global positioning system (GPS) tagging is used to add location information to files or social media posts. It would not be used in this scenario.

12. ☑ **C.** Desktop, laptop, and mobile devices can be quickly linked together wirelessly for transferring files using Wi-Fi Direct, even when no Internet connection is available.

☒ **A, B,** and **D** are incorrect. Wi-Fi Direct is more convenient than plugging cables and devices into each computer to share files, including the use of satellite Internet connectivity. MicroSD hardware security modules (HSMs) plug directly into mobile devices to provide cryptographic authentication and management functions and are irrelevant to this discussion.

13. ☑ **A.** Sandboxing uses an isolated network, host, or app environment for testing configurations, including unfamiliar software, without the risk of unintentionally harming other systems or components.

☒ **B, C,** and **D** are incorrect. Push notifications are commonly used with mobile devices to send user notification, regardless of whether the user is currently using an app or visiting a web site. Firmware Over-The-Air (FOTA) updates enable device firmware updates to be added to a device remotely over a wireless network. Carrier unlocking refers to removing a smartphone from a specific mobile carrier network. The process to achieve this varies slightly from device to device and region to region around the world. In Canada, for example, CRTC regulations require new smartphones to be sold already unlocked.

14. ☑ **B.** Radio-frequency identification (RFID) uses wireless radio frequencies to track items or animals with RFID tags attached to them, such as for inventory control and animal location tracing.

☒ **A, C,** and **D** are incorrect. The listed wireless solutions are not normally used for inventory control. Wi-Fi is normally used to connect devices wirelessly to a network, where normally the ultimate goal is wireless Internet connectivity. Near Field Communication (NFC) is a wireless technology used to transfer small amounts of data between devices that are no more than approximately 10 centimeters (3.9 inches) apart. NFC is commonly used for "tap" contactless payment systems from smartphones or payment cards. Cellular wireless technology uses transmission towers to enable wireless connectivity from cellular network subscribers. Each radial coverage area around a cell tower is referred to as a "cell." In populated areas, cells normally overlap to provide continual coverage as cell subscribers travel.

15. ☑ **B.** A unified end-point management (UEM) solution allows for the centralized management of many types of devices and includes the functionality of mobile device management (MDM) and mobile application management (MAM) capabilities. UEM tools can deploy device configurations and apps, manage apps and security settings, and apply updates, which removes the need to work with multiple device management tools.

☒ **A, C,** and **D** are incorrect. Trusted platform module (TPM) is a firmware chip within a computing device that ensures device boot integrity on UEFI firmware computers, which allows for measured, or integrity-checked boot-up to protect from security threats such as rootkits. TPM can also store cryptographic keys used to encrypt storage devices. Security enhanced Android (SEAndroid) is a variant of the Linux-based Android operating system that focuses on using policies and mandatory access control (MAC) to secure Android devices. MAC uses security levels that users are assigned to, which allows resource access. A hardware security module (HSM) is a dedicated tamper-resistant device designed to securely store and manage cryptographic keys.

16. ☑ **D.** When MMS is enabled, malicious code embedded in media files could be distributed through MMS. Disabling MMS reduces this likelihood. MMS is also sometimes referred to as rich communication services (RCS).

☒ **A, B,** and **C** are incorrect. Injection attacks normally result from improper user input validation such that untrusted user input can be sent to a server, resulting in elevated privileges or the disclosure or sensitive data. In identity theft, an attacker assumes the identity of a victim, often for financial gain or the acquisition of legal IDs such as a driver's license. Ransomware normally encrypts data files and attackers demand a bitcoin payment to potentially receive a decryption key. None of these risks is directly mitigated by disabled SMS MMS.

17. ☑   **A.** Near-field communication (NFC) is a wireless technology used to transfer small amounts of data between devices that are no more than approximately 10 centimeters (3.9 inches) apart. NFC is commonly used for "tap" contactless payment systems from smartphones or payment cards.
☒   **B, C,** and **D** are incorrect. Smartphone tethering enables other devices, such as laptops lacking cellular connectivity, to use the smartphone Internet connection through the smartphone's data services. Tethering can be done wirelessly between the smartphone and laptop or through a USB cable. A virtual private network (VPN) provides an encrypted tunnel between two end-points over an untrusted network such as the Internet. VPNs allow for the secure connection between networks or from a single device to a network. The mobile networks option allows for the configuration of items such as roaming and network types.

18. ☑   **A.** Bluetooth allows for wireless connectivity, such as for transferring files between devices at close range, which is normally up to approximately 10 meters (33 feet).
☒   **B, C,** and **D** are incorrect. The touchpad option is used to configure the touchpad normally placed in the center of a laptop keyboard, which is used for mouse-style control of the laptop. AutoPlay is used to enable executable files on removable devices to run automatically. Universal serial bus (USB) is a device connectivity standard that uses cables and does not provide wireless connectivity.

19. ☑   See Figure 7-5 for the correct answers.

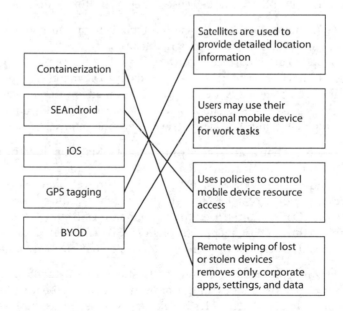

FIGURE 7-5

Mobile device terms and definitions—the answers

Containerization		Satellites are used to provide detailed location information
SEAndroid		Users may use their personal mobile device for work tasks
iOS		Uses policies to control mobile device resource access
GPS tagging		Remote wiping of lost or stolen devices removes only corporate apps, settings, and data
BYOD		

20. ☑ **C.** An intrusion detection (IDS) analyzes network or host-specific traffic for potentially malicious activity. An IDS can write alerts to logs or send notifications to administrators about the activity. In this example, when TCP port 23 (used by default from Telnet) traffic is detected from anywhere destined to the corporate network, an alert message is generated.

    ☒ **A, B,** and **D** are incorrect. A packet filtering firewall can allow or block traffic based on details such as source and destination IP addresses, protocol types, or port addresses. A proxy server (also called a forward proxy) sits between an internal network and the Internet. The proxy server accepts user requests for Internet content, fetches the content, and serves it back to the requesting internal client. Proxy servers can also be configured to cache content for quicker subsequent requests for the same content. A hardware security module (HSM) is a dedicated tamper-resistant device designed to securely store and manage cryptographic keys.

21. ☑ **B.** Firmware Over-The-Air can be used to deliver firmware updates wirelessly to devices without requiring updates to be manually downloaded or transferred using cables.

    ☒ **A, C,** and **D** are incorrect. Sideloading refers to installing an app manually on a mobile device as opposed to installing it from an app store. Windows Server Update Services (WSUS) is a Microsoft Windows Server role that is used as an update synchronization server on an internal network, which is then configured to deliver updates to internal Windows hosts. Trusted Platform Module (TPM) is a firmware chip within a computing device that ensures device boot integrity as well as storing cryptographic keys used to encrypt storage devices.

22. ☑ **C.** Geofencing uses device location tracking to present mobile device users with message when they are within a specific geographic boundary.

    ☒ **A, B,** and **D** are incorrect. Firmware Over-The-Air can be used to deliver firmware updates wirelessly to devices without requiring updates to be manually downloaded or transferred using cables. Geotagging is used to provide detailed location information metadata to files such as photos. Desktop, laptop, and mobile devices can be quickly linked together wirelessly for transferring files using Wi-Fi Direct, even when no Internet connection is available.

23. ☑ **D.** MicroSD hardware security modules (HSMs) plug directly into mobile devices to provide cryptographic authentication and management functions.

    ☒ **A, B,** and **C** are incorrect. Next-generation firewalls can inspect not only packet headers but also packet payloads to determine whether network traffic should be allowed or blocked. USB On-The-Go (OTG) is often used to plug standard USB storage devices (end-point devices) into a smartphone (host) charging port through a USB OTG adapter device to enable the smartphone to access the USB storage device. Mobile devices do not normally support more than one SIM card.

24. ☑ **B.** Hashing provides data integrity. Hashing feeds data into a one-way cryptographic algorithm, which results in a unique hash value. This can be used for purposes such as password storage or to detect whether files have changes since the last hash was generated.

    ☒ **A, C,** and **D** are incorrect. Encryption provides data confidentiality, which prevents unauthorized access to read encrypted data without possessing the correct decryption key. Data availability can be achieved with data backups and server clustering as well as load balancing. Data classification is used to assign sensitivity labels to data, which is in turn commonly used by data loss prevention (DLP) systems to prevent sensitive data leakage outside of an organization.

25. ☑ **B.** Jailbreaking applies to Apple iOS devices such as the iPhone, iPad, and iPod. Like rooting an Android device, jailbreaking can be achieved with an installed app on the device, or it can be done using a USB-connected external computer to remove device restrictions, which provides the user full configuration flexibility, such as installing apps not available in the Apple App Store. Jailbreaking can void device and carrier warranties and increases the risk of device compromise due to malicious code with full device access.

☒ **A, C,** and **D** are incorrect. Jailbreaking does not apply to these operating systems.

26. ☑ **D.** In the corporate owned personally enabled (COPE) mobile device provisioning strategy, the organization provides mobile devices to employees for both personal and business use. The organization will often pay partial or full monthly costs related to the mobile device, and in some jurisdictions this is considered an income tax benefit to the employee.

☒ **A, B,** and **C** are incorrect. Bring your own device (BYOD) is a corporate mobile device strategy that enables employees to use their own personal mobile devices for business use. BYOD organizations will often pay a portion of the monthly cost of the device usage. With choose your own device (CYOD), employees are provided a selection of mobile devices that they can choose from for business use. Virtual Desktop Infrastructure (VDI) provides remote desktop and apps access from any type of device, even using only a web browser.

27. ☑ **C.** For encrypted drives, one quick method of wiping the drive is to destroy the drive decryption key, which renders all encrypted data on the drive unreadable, since the decryption key no longer exists. The drive can then be repartitioned and formatted for continued use while ensuring that the old data is not recoverable. This technique is often referred to as crypto erase.

☒ **A, B,** and **D** are incorrect. Overwriting disk sectors takes much longer than simply destroying decryption keys. Placing the SED in a different computer does not destroy decryption keys and does not overwrite data on the drive.

28. ☑ **C** and **D.** The "response" part of end-point detection and response solution refers to the ability to stop attacks from continuing after threats have been detected.

☒ **A** and **B** are incorrect. While the listed items are important security hardening techniques, they apply to end-point detection and response solutions as well as packet filtering firewalls.

29. ☑ **B.** Carrier unlocking enables a smartphone to be switched to a different mobile network provider. This process is often executed for free by the new carrier you are switching to.

☒ **A, C,** and **D** are incorrect. Mobile device containerization separates work and personal apps, settings, and data for security purposes, including remote wiping of only the corporate container (partition). Jailbreaking applies to Apple iOS devices such as the iPhone, iPad, and iPod. Like rooting an Android device, jailbreaking can be achieved with an installed app on the device, or it can be done using a USB-connected external computer to remove device restrictions. This offers the user full configuration flexibility, such as installing apps not available in the Apple App Store. Rooting refers to the process of providing full privileged access to an Android device for purposes similar to jailbreaking an iOS device.

30. ☑ **D.** Tokenization is a security technique that uses a trusted centralized service to create a digital representation of sensitive data, such as credit card information. This "token" can then be used to authorize resource access or payments without ever sending the actual origin sensitive data.

☒ **A, B,** and **C** are incorrect. Encryption uses one or more keys to convert plain text to cipher text (encrypted data), thus providing data confidentiality for data at rest or in transit. Only the possessor of the correct decryption key can convert the cipher text back into plain text. Hashing feeds data into a one-way hashing cryptographic algorithm, which results in a unique value being output. An example of hashing would be generating file hashes periodically to see if a file has been corrupted or tampered with in some way. If the current hash differs from the previous hash, a change in the data has occurred. Salting is a technique used to add random data to unique data prior to all of the data being fed into a one-way cryptographic algorithm. Linux user passwords stored in the /etc/shadow file are represented as a hash value generated from the salted user password string.

31. ☑ **C.** Salting is a technique used to add random data to unique data prior to all of the data being fed into a one-way hashing algorithm. Linux user passwords stored in the /etc/shadow file are represented as a hash value generated from the salted user password string.

☒ **A, B,** and **D** are incorrect. Encryption uses one or more keys to convert plain text to cipher text (encrypted data), thus providing data confidentiality for data at rest or in transit. Only the possessor of the correct decryption key can render the cipher text back into plain text. Hashing feeds data into a one-way hashing algorithm, which results in a unique value being output. An example of hashing would be generating file hashes periodically to see if a file has been corrupted or tampered with in some way. If the current hash differs from the previous hash, a change in the data has occurred. Tokenization is a security technique that uses a trusted centralized service to create a digital representation of sensitive data, such as credit card information. This "token" can then be used to authorize resource access or payments without ever sending the actual origin sensitive data.

32. ☑ **D.** Context-aware authentication uses not only standard identification mechanisms such as usernames and passwords, but it also uses factors such as device location, type of configuration, time of day, and so on.

☒ **A, B,** and **C** are incorrect. Single sign on (SSO) is an authentication configuration that enables users to sign in once and access multiple resources without having to re-enter authentication credentials. Multifactor authentication (MFA) uses multiple authentication categories together, such as something you know (username and password), something you are (fingerprint), and something you have (smartcard, key fob, unique authentication PIN derived from alternative device). Identity federation is an authentication configuration that links identity stores across administrative boundaries, such as between organizations. As an example, users in organization B may require access to resources in organization A. With identity federation, resources in organization A may be configured to "trust" successful authentication tokens from organization B. This means organization B user identities do not have to be duplicated in organization A to enable access to resources in organization A by organization B user accounts.

Chapter 8

Securing the Network Infrastructure

QUESTIONS

Planning the design of a secure network architecture is an ongoing task, as network requirements evolve over time. New technologies in network switches, firewalling, virtual private networks (VPNs), and threat mitigation present a need for periodic network security evaluations.

Network perimeter security can be achieved using hardware firewalls, proxy servers, network access control configurations, and VPNs. VPN solutions can require client-side VPN software or can be clientless, meaning existing common software such as a web browser can be used to access resources securely through an encrypted tunnel.

Comparing current network, host, and app performance to known baselines of normal activity can help you quickly identify anomalies. You can protect sensitive data by using hashing, encryption, data loss prevention, data masking, and data tokenization.

You can also use decoy hosts and networks (honeypots and honeynets) to monitor malicious user activity, which can help mitigate those threats against real production network assets. All of these network management and control options can be applied remotely from a network operations center (NOC).

1. Your manager has asked you to configure performance alert notifications for abnormal app performance conditions. What must you establish first?

   A. IP addressing schema

   B. Baseline

   C. Network diagrams

   D. Naming conventions

2. A security audit of your call center has revealed that callers' credit card numbers are shown on call center employees' screens while they are working with customer queries. What should be configured to conceal customer credit card numbers?

   A. Encryption

   B. Data loss prevention

   C. Data tokenization

   D. Data masking

3. Your organization stores sensitive medical data in the cloud. You must ensure that the data is not replicated outside of national boundaries for legal reasons. Which term best encompasses this scenario?

   A. Rights management

   B. API strategy

   C. Zero trust

   D. Data sovereignty

4. Users in your company use a VPN to connect to the corporate network. In terms of network placement, where should the VPN appliance be placed?

   A. Default VLAN

   B. Intranet

   C. Screened subnet

   D. Public cloud

5. You need to secure network traffic between clients and servers for multiple line of business apps running on your organization's private Microsoft Active Directory (AD) network. Which solution meets this requirement while minimizing the amount of technician effort?

   A. SSL/TLS

   B. L2TP

   C. Reverse proxy server

   D. IPSec

6. You are running virtual machines in the public cloud. For security reasons, you do not want each virtual machine to have a publicly accessible IP address. What should you configure to enable remote management of the virtual machines? Each answer is independent of the other. (Choose two).

   A. Jump box

   B. VPN

   C. Forward proxy server

   D. HSM

7. You need to limit which devices can be active when plugged into a network switch port. What should you configure?

   A. Broadcast storm prevention

   B. MAC filtering

   C. Bridging loop prevention

   D. BPDU guard

8. Your network intrusion detection system (NIDS) is configured to receive automatic updates for known malicious attacks. Which type of intrusion detection is used in this case?

A. Anomaly-based

B. Heuristic-based

C. Signature-based

D. Inline

9. Your firewall is configured to examine each individual packet without regard for network sessions. Which type of firewall being used?

A. Stateful

B. Web application firewall

C. Content filtering (aka URL filtering)

D. Stateless

10. Virtual machines in your public cloud are configured with private IP addresses. Each virtual machine requires access only to the Internet. Which of the following options is the best choice?

A. Web application firewall

B. NAT gateway

C. Unified threat management gateway

D. Intrusion prevention system

11. You run a small business and need an inexpensive, yet effective, network firewall solution. Which type of firewall should you consider? (Choose the best answer.)

A. Unified threat management

B. Proprietary

C. Open source

D. Next-generation

12. You need a fast, secure, and reliable multihomed network perimeter solution that is designed to prevent specific types of network traffic from entering your corporate network. Which solution should you deploy?

A. Software firewall

B. Virtual firewall

C. Host-based firewall

D. Hardware firewall

13. Due to changes in your network infrastructure, you have been tasked with modifying firewalls to allow and block network traffic. Which aspect of the firewalls will you be configuring?

A. File integrity monitoring

B. Port taps

C. Quality of service

D. Access control lists

14. To which of the following does SSL/TLS directly apply? (Choose two.)
    A. Data at rest
    B. Data in process
    C. Data in motion
    D. Data in transit

15. Currently in your organization, on-premises user app access is limited based on their security clearance and the type of mobile device they are using. You would like to extend this configuration to the cloud. Which security service should be enabled?
    A. Unified threat management
    B. Cloud access security broker
    C. DDoS mitigation
    D. Web application firewall

16. Which type of cryptographic operation serves as a one-way function resulting in a unique value?
    A. Hashing
    B. Encryption
    C. Data masking
    D. Tokenization

17. To attract and monitor malicious user activity, you need to deploy a single server with fake data that appears vulnerable. What should you configure?
    A. Honeynet
    B. Honeypot
    C. Honeyfile
    D. DNS sinkhole

18. Which term is used to describe network traffic within a data center?
    A. East-west traffic
    B. North-south traffic
    C. Honeynet traffic
    D. Honeypot traffic

19. VPN users complain that accessing Internet web sites when connected to the corporate VPN is very slow. Which VPN option should you configure to allow Internet access through the user's Internet connection when the corporate VPN is active?
    A. Always On VPN
    B. Split tunnel
    C. Full tunnel
    D. IPSec

20. You need to connect branch office networks securely over the Internet. Which type of VPN should you deploy?

    A. Always On VPN

    B. Split tunnel

    C. Site-to-site

    D. IPSec

21. You need to enable secure remote access to internal company HTTPS web applications as well as SSH connections to internal Linux hosts for users authenticating over the Internet. What should you enable?

    A. Always On VPN

    B. Split tunnel

    C. HTML5 VPN portal

    D. Full tunnel

22. You are configuring firewall ACLs. You need to allow DNS client queries to reach DNS servers hosted on different internal networks. Which details should exist in the rule to allow the DNS query traffic?

    A. TCP 53

    B. UDP 161

    C. TCP 80

    D. UDP 53

23. Which statement best embodies the purpose of Network Access Control (NAC) solutions?

    A. DDoS mitigation

    B. Firewall ACLs

    C. Data loss prevention

    D. Control device network access

24. Your network infrastructure team has recommended dedicated VLANs with dedicated management interfaces for servers and network equipment. Which term best embodies this configuration?

    A. Data loss prevention

    B. Out-of-band management

    C. Bridge looping

    D. Route security

25. Refer to Figure 8-1. You are configuring cloud storage and must enable confidentiality for data at rest. Which panel should you click?

    A. Versioning

    B. Server access logging

    C. Default encryption

    D. Object-level logging

FIGURE 8-1   Amazon Web Services S3 bucket properties

Versioning

Keep multiple versions of an object in the same bucket.

Learn more

✓ Enabled

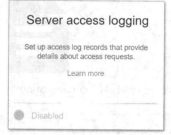

Server access logging

Set up access log records that provide details about access requests.

Learn more

● Disabled

Static website hosting

Host a static website, which does not require server-side technologies.

Learn more

● Disabled

Default encryption

Automatically encrypt objects when stored in Amazon S3

Learn more

● Disabled

Object-level logging

Record object-level API activity using the CloudTrail data events feature (additional cost).

Learn more

● Disabled

26. Which of the following is a cryptographic hashing algorithm?
- A. 3DES
- B. AES
- C. SHA
- D. RSA

27. Refer to Figure 8-2. A network technician has plugged in a network cable connecting ports 1 and 2 on SWITCH1. What will occur as a result of this configuration?
- A. Nothing
- B. DCHP broadcast storm
- C. DNS sinkhole
- D. Bridging loop

FIGURE 8-2

Network switch configuration

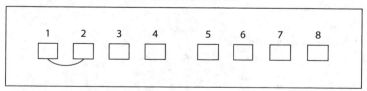

Network Switch: SWITCH1

IP address: 192.168.1.100
Spanning tree protocol: Disabled
Port MAC filtering: Disabled

28. Refer to Figure 8-3. What is being configured in this example?

   A. Web application firewall
   B. Proxy server
   C. Web application load balancer
   D. DDoS mitigation

FIGURE 8-3   Amazon Web Services cloud web ACL configuration

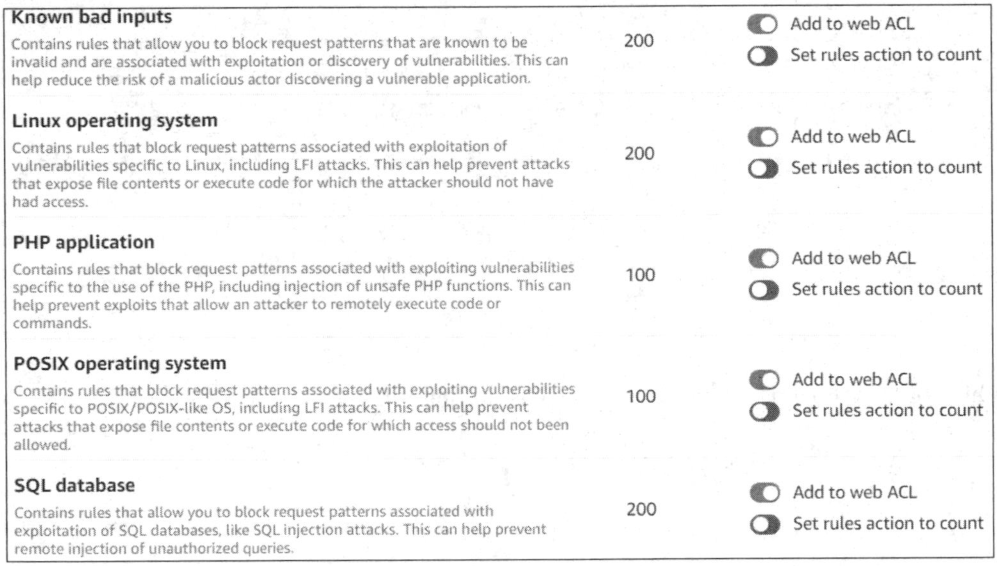

29. You need to analyze all network traffic within a network switch. What must be configured?

   A. DHCP snooping
   B. MAC filtering
   C. BPDU guard
   D. Port mirroring

30. Refer to Figure 8-4. Which term best describes the network security appliance in the diagram?

   A. Passive
   B. Port mirror
   C. Network aggregator
   D. Inline

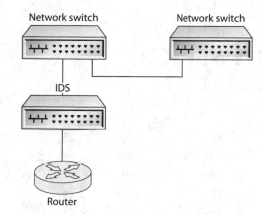

FIGURE 8-4

Network
infrastructure
device diagram

31. Refer to Figure 8-5. What type of network security appliance is in use?
    A. VPN concentrator
    B. NIDS
    C. NIPS
    D. HSM

FIGURE 8-5

Network security
appliance usage

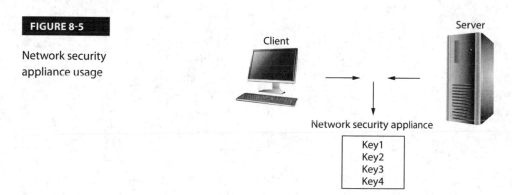

32. Which of the following is used by file integrity monitoring?
    A. Encryption
    B. Hashing
    C. Data loss protection
    D. Quality of service

QUICK ANSWER KEY

1.	B	**12.**	D	**23.**	D
2.	D	**13.**	D	**24.**	B
3.	D	**14.**	C, D	**25.**	C
4.	C	**15.**	B	**26.**	C
5.	D	**16.**	A	**27.**	D
6.	A, B	**17.**	B	**28.**	A
7.	B	**18.**	A	**29.**	D
8.	C	**19.**	B	**30.**	D
9.	D	**20.**	C	**31.**	D
10.	B	**21.**	C	**32.**	B
11.	C	**22.**	D		

IN-DEPTH ANSWERS

1. ☑ **B.** A performance baseline is established over time during normal application performance. Comparing the baseline to current performance conditions can identify performance problems, which could be indicative of malicious activity such as excessive CPU utilization resulting from Bitcoin mining malware or other malicious apps.

   ☒ **A, C,** and **D** are incorrect. The listed options are not related to application performance. Establishing an IP addressing schema is part of designing a network infrastructure to allocate specific IP address ranges to specific networks and to allocate specific IP addresses (such as those ending in 200) to the same type of device, such as network printers or routers. Network diagrams aid in designing, securing, and troubleshooting a network environment. Naming conventions provide consistency when naming network items such as end-points, servers, and network devices.

2. ☑ **D.** Data masking is used to hide, or "mask," some or all parts of sensitive data, such as hiding all but the last few credit card account numbers. This enables call center workers to verify customer details without exposing the customer's entire credit card number.

   ☒ **A, B,** and **C** are incorrect. Encryption is important for protecting sensitive data from unauthorized users, but it would not apply to this scenario. Data loss prevention is used to monitor and prevent sensitive data from being exfiltrated, or exposed outside of an organization or to unauthorized users, whether intentionally or unintentionally. Data tokenization substitutes sensitive data with something that cannot be traced back to that sensitive data (the token). The token can then be presented to apps instead of the original sensitive data (for example, credit card details).

3. ☑ **D.** Data sovereignty refers to managing sensitive data that is subject to the laws present at the storage location.

   ☒ **A, B,** and **C** are incorrect. Rights management, often called information rights management (IRM), strives to ensure that only authorized access is granted to specific types of data, such as ensuring that top secret information is accessible only by those with the appropriate security clearance. A secure API strategy includes ensuring authorized API access over encrypted connections as well as implementing controls such as API throttling to limit excessive API calls within a small amount of time. A zero-trust security framework does not assume internal users and devices are benign; instead zero trust relies on successful authentication details such as user credentials, device used, location, and so on. Zero trust also ensures end-to-end encryption and controls system and data access while adhering to the principle of least privilege, which states that only the required permissions to perform a task should be granted, and nothing more.

4. ☑ **C.** A screened subnet is a network that resides between a public network such as the Internet and an internal secured network. Publicly accessible services such as corporate VPN end-points should be placed in a screened subnet. Firewall rules are still used to control traffic into and out of the screened subnet.
☒ **A, B,** and **D** are incorrect. All ports in a network switch are configured to be in the same default VLAN, but this can be changed. If the VPN appliance port is configured as a DMZ port, it would then make sense for the VPN appliance. An intranet is a private network for use by employees of an organization. An intranet uses Internet protocols such as HTTPS for internal web applications, whereas an extranet allows limited access to users outside of the organization. While public cloud providers do support VPN configurations, placing a VPN appliance in the public cloud is a generic placement as compared to a DMZ, which can exist on-premises or in the cloud.

5. ☑ **D.** IPSec requires the least amount of administrative effort, because it can be configured centrally for Active Directory using Group Policy, and it can protect network traffic without having to configure individual applications specifically, unlike SSL/TLS.
☒ **A, B,** and **C** are incorrect. Transport layer security (TLS) is a network security protocol that supersedes the deprecated Secure Sockets Layer (SSL). Securing applications with TLS requires one or more PKI certificates that are configured with an HTTPS binding for each application. Layer 2 tunneling protocol (L2TP) enables OSI model layer 2 (the data link layer) traffic to traverse an OSI model layer 3 (the network layer) tunnel. While L2TP itself does not secure traffic, it is commonly used with security protocols such as IPSec to create an encrypted VPN tunnel. A reverse proxy server accepts client requests and forwards those requests to the respective backend server, which often resides on a private secured network.

6. ☑ **A** and **B.** A jump box is a host with connectivity to both a public network such as the Internet as well as to an internal network. By authenticating to a jump box, from there remote management sessions to internal devices and hosts can be initiated. Using a VPN to connect to a private network would also enable remote management of devices and hosts.
☒ **C** and **D** are incorrect. A forward proxy server accepts internal client requests for Internet content, fetches the content, potentially caches it for subsequent requests, and returns that content to the requesting internal client. A hardware security module (HSM) is an appliance that is used to securely store cryptographic secrets that can be accessed by multiple hosts.

7. ☑ **B.** Network interface cards are uniquely identified with a 48-bit hexadecimal Media Access Control (MAC) address. Network switch ports can be configured to allow only specific MAC addresses to be connected to a switch port and present on the network.
☒ **A, C,** and **D** are incorrect. Broadcast network transmissions are addressed to all devices on a network. Excessive broadcasts can be caused by faulty network equipment or configurations. Modern network devices such as network switches enable switch ports to block broadcast traffic after a configured threshold value has been met. Preventing a bridging loop can be as simple as ensuring that only a single link exists between network switches, or the Spanning Tree Protocol (STP) can be enabled on the network switch, which is often a default setting. Bridge Protocol Data Unit (BPDU) guard is a network switch feature that can be enabled to prevent BPDU traffic from switch ports connected to end-point devices such as user workstations, servers, network printers, and so on. Only network switches transmit BPDU traffic.

8. ☑ **C.** Updated signature databases of known malware and attack patterns can be compared against current activity to determine if a suspicious incident is taking place. Both network intrusion prevention system (IPS) and network intrusion detection system (IDS) sensors can be used to collect and monitor network activity. The primary difference is that an IPS can take response and recovery steps to block suspicious activity, while an IDS is more focused on reporting and alerting.

  ☒ **A, B,** and **D** are incorrect. Anomaly-based IDS and IPS solutions (aka heuristic-based) compare current activity to a known baseline of normal activity to detect anomalies. Inline network appliances are carefully placed such that the relevant network traffic is seen, analyzed, and potentially modified in some way (including traffic being dropped) before continuing on to the intended destination, as opposed to passive network appliances, which are primarily used for monitoring and do not modify network traffic.

9. ☑ **D.** To determine whether network traffic should be allowed or blocked, stateless firewalls examine each packet and treat each independently from the others with no regard for the relationship of packets in a network session.

  ☒ **A, B,** and **C** are incorrect. Stateful firewalls are aware of multiple related packets for a unique network session and can allow or block traffic based on session characteristics such as the order in which specific packet types should appear within a session. Web application firewalls (WAFs) protect web apps from known web app–specific attacks such as web server directory traversals or database injection attacks. Content filtering can allow or block access to items such as specific URLs; solutions can use website allow and block/deny lists to limit user access to Internet content.

10. ☑ **B.** Network address translation (NAT) gateways enable hosts with only private IP addresses to access Internet resources through the NAT gateway public IP address; this removes the need for all hosts to have public IP addresses.

  ☒ **A, C,** and **D** are incorrect. Web application firewalls (WAFs) protect web apps from known web app–specific attacks such as web server directory traversals or database injection attacks. Unified threat management (UTM) solutions combine IT security technologies such as intrusion detection and prevention, firewalling, and antimalware. While UTM could allow Internet access, NAT gateways are designed for this purpose. An IPS can take response-and-recovery steps to block suspicious activity.

11. ☑ **C.** Open source software such as firewall software is normally inexpensive (often free), compared to proprietary software solutions.

  ☒ **A, B,** and **D** are incorrect. Unified threat management (UTM) solutions combine IT security technologies such as intrusion detection and prevention, firewalling, and antimalware and would be suitable for large organizations with complex security requirements. Proprietary firewall solutions are closed-source, meaning the source code is not freely available to everybody, which usually results in a higher cost than open source equivalences. Next-generation firewalls (NGFW) go beyond standard stateful packet header inspection and are often referred to as "deep packet inspection" firewalls, because packet payloads can be examined and suspicious activity or malware can be detected and blocked, among other capabilities.

12. ☑ **D.** Because hardware firewall appliances use firmware that is designed for security purposes, they are generally considered more reliable and fast than most software firewalls, which run within multipurpose operating systems.

    ☒ **A, B,** and **C** are incorrect. Software firewalls run within a multipurpose operating system and are generally not considered to be as robust as hardware firewalls. Virtual firewall appliances are a software solution that usually come in the form of virtual machine guests that run on a hypervisor. Host-based firewalls are end-point firewalls often built into a multipurpose operating system, an example of which is Microsoft Defender Firewall, which is built into the Windows 10 operating system.

13. ☑ **D.** Firewall access control lists (ACLs) are collections of rules that contain transmission detail conditions such as source IP address, destination URL, port numbers, or protocol types that should be allowed or blocked.

    ☒ **A, B,** and **C** are incorrect. File integrity monitoring (FIM) is used to detect, notify, and report unauthorized changes to files on a host or across an entire network, including database and log files. Port taps (also called network taps) are devices that passively capture network traffic. Capturing network traffic can also be configured within a network switch using port spanning or mirroring, which copies all switch port network traffic to a designated monitoring port. In computer networking, quality of service (QoS) solutions manage network traffic to reduce network congestion or to ensure reliability of time-sensitive network usage, such as for Voice over IP (VoIP) calls.

14. ☑ **C and D.** Data in motion and data in transit are the same thing: data being transmitted over a network. Secure Sockets Layer (SSL) and Transport Layer Security (TLS) are network security protocols that can encrypt network communications. SSL has been deprecated in favor of using newer versions of TLS such as version 1.3. SSL and TLS require a PKI certificate to secure connections, such as requiring a PKI certificate on a web server to allow HTTPS communication.

    ☒ **A and B** are incorrect. Data at rest refers to stored data, which can be encrypted with disk volume or file-level encryption. Data in process refers to data being made available from storage devices or from across the network, both of which can be protected with disk or file encryption and network encryption.

15. ☑ **B.** A cloud access security broker (CASB) provides services to centrally manage IT security policies including encryption, data loss prevention, authentication, and authorization across on-premises and cloud environments. CASB solutions can greatly enhance an organization's ability to comply with data privacy regulations.

    ☒ **A, C,** and **D** are incorrect. Unified threat management (UTM) solutions combine security technologies such as intrusion detection and prevention, firewalling, and antimalware. Distributed denial of service (DDoS) attacks stem from malicious user control of infected computers (called zombies or bots); the bots receive commands to perform actions such as flooding a victim's machine with large amounts of useless network traffic in an attempt to prevent legitimate connections to the machine. Web application firewalls (WAFs) protect web apps from known web app–specific attacks such as web server directory traversal or database injection attacks.

16. ☑ **A.** Hashing feeds data as a one-way cryptographic hashing algorithm such as SHA-256, which results in a unique value representative of the original data. This is used for storing standard Unix and Linux passwords in the /etc/shadow file and to track changes to files or network transmissions.

☒ **B, C,** and **D** are incorrect. Encryption feeds data and an encryption key into a cryptographic encryption algorithm, resulting in cipher text, or encrypted data. Data masking is used to hide or "mask" some or all parts of sensitive data, such as hiding all but the last few numbers of a credit card account number on a screen or printed receipt. Data tokenization substitutes sensitive data with something that cannot be traced back to that sensitive data (the token). The token can then be presented to apps instead of the original sensitive data (for example, credit card information).

17. ☑ **B.** A honeypot is a decoy system configured to appear as a legitimate host that may contain legitimate sensitive data. The host is intentionally configured in this way to track malicious user activity. The resultant telemetry can provide insights to the security posture of the organization and indicate what must be done to harden the environment.

☒ **A, C,** and **D** are incorrect. A honeynet is a collection of honeypot decoy systems with one or more intentional vulnerabilities used to attract and monitor malicious user activity. Honeyfiles may contain what appear to be production data files that could contain sensitive information, when really these files are fake data. DNS sinkholing is a deliberate configuration that returns invalid results for DNS client queries for specific hosts or domains; this can prove useful in preventing infected bot computers from communicating with an attacker command and control (C&C) server.

18. ☑ **A.** East-west traffic refers to network transmissions occurring within the boundaries of a network environment, such as between physical and virtual devices and hosts within a single data center.

☒ **B, C,** and **D** are incorrect. North-south traffic refers to network transmissions occurring outside of a single network, such as between data center hosts and hosts outside of the data center. Honeynet traffic refers to network transmissions on a honeynet, which is a collection of honeypot decoy systems with one or more intentional vulnerabilities used to attract and monitor malicious user activity. A honeypot is a decoy system configured to appear as a legitimate host that may contain legitimate sensitive data, but the host has been intentionally configured in this way to track malicious user activity against the host.

19. ☑ **B.** Split tunneling can be configured for the VPN so that connections to corporate resources traverse the VPN and Internet connections go through the user's Internet connection.

☒ **A, C,** and **D** are incorrect. An Always On VPN configuration does not require the user to invoke the VPN tunnel manually; instead, this occurs as a device is turned on and connects to the Internet or when a specific app is launched on the user's device. With full tunnel VPN configurations, all network connections traverse the VPN when the VPN is active on a client device; this is often done for security reasons as all traffic can be centrally monitored and logged. IPSec is a network security protocol that can protect network traffic without having to configure individual applications specifically, unlike SSL/TLS. IPSec can also be used to secure a client-to-site or site-to-site VPN.

20. ☑ **C.** A site-to-site VPN can link networks, such as the networks at remote branch offices, together over the Internet. A VPN device must reside on each network. When the VPN tunnel is active, traffic between branch offices is encrypted as it traverses the VPN tunnel. Client end-point devices in each branch office do not need a VPN client configuration, as they would with a client-to-site VPN connection.

☒ **A, B,** and **D** are incorrect. An Always On VPN configuration does not require the user to create a VPN tunnel manually; instead, this occurs as a device is turned on and connects to the Internet or when a specific app is launched on the user's device. Split tunneling can be configured for the VPN so that connections to corporate resources traverse the VPN and Internet connections go through the user's Internet connection. IPSec is a network security protocol that can protect network traffic without having to configure individual applications specifically, unlike SSL/TLS.

21. ☑ **C.** An HTML5 VPN portal enables users to make secured connections to private network resources over the Internet using a only an HTML5 web browser. This is normally an option that must be enabled within a unified threat management (UTM) or next-generation firewall. HTML5 VPN portals are also called "clientless VPNs," since a separate VPN client is not required.

☒ **A, B,** and **D** are incorrect. An Always On VPN configuration does not require the user to invoke the VPN tunnel manually; instead, this occurs as a device is turned on and connects to the Internet or when a specific app is launched on the user's device. Split tunneling can be configured for the VPN so that connections to corporate resources traverse the VPN and Internet connections go through the user's Internet connection. With full tunnel VPN configurations, all network connections traverse the VPN when the VPN is active on a client device; this is often done for security reasons, as all traffic can be centrally monitored and logged.

22. ☑ **D.** Client DNS queries occur over UDP port 53.

☒ **A, B,** and **C** are incorrect. TCP port 53 is normally used for DNS zone transfers, or replication of DNS records among DNS servers as well as DNS replies larger than 512 bytes. UDP port 161 is used by the Simple Network Management Protocol (SNMP) used to remotely manage and view performance metrics of network devices and hosts. TCP port 80 is used for HTTP web server communication.

23. ☑ **D.** Network Access Control (NAC) solutions can control device network access by ensuring that connecting users and devices meet a variety of conditions before being granted network access, such as specific authentication method used, device type, up-to-date software patches, and so on. Some NAC solutions require an agent to be installed on connecting devices, whereas others are agentless.

☒ **A, B,** and **C** are incorrect. Distributed denial of service (DDoS) attacks stem from malicious user control of infected computers (called zombies or bots); the bots receive commands to perform actions such as flooding a victim's machine with large amounts of useless network traffic in an attempt to prevent legitimate connections to the machine. Firewall access control lists (ACLs) are collections of rules that contain transmission detail conditions such as source IP address, destination IP address, port numbers, or protocol types that should be allowed or blocked. Data loss prevention is used to monitor and prevent sensitive data from being exfiltrated, or exposed outside of an organization or to unauthorized users, whether intentionally or unintentionally.

24. ☑ **B.** Out-of-band management refers to using an alternative connection (not the standard network communication medium) to manage network devices and hosts. This provides a layer of security and reliability due to network isolation.

☒ **A, C,** and **D** are incorrect. Data loss prevention is used to monitor and prevent sensitive data from being exfiltrated, or exposed outside of an organization or to unauthorized users, whether intentionally or unintentionally. Bridging loops can results from having multiple paths linking network switches together, and this is mitigated by ensuring that the Spanning Tree Protocol (STP) is enabled on network switches. Route security can be achieved by ensuring that the exchange of routing information using routing protocols such as Open Shortest Path First (OSPFv3) is authenticated and encrypted.

25. ☑ **C.** Data confidentiality is achieved by enabling default encryption.

☒ **A, B,** and **D** are incorrect. Versioning is used to retain multiple versions of a file over time as it is modified. Server access logging tracks all activity related to requesting cloud-stored content. Object-level logging tracks cloud storage requests for specific stored items.

26. ☑ **C.** The Secure Hashing Algorithm (SHA-256) is a one-way cryptographic hashing algorithm that results in a unique value representative of the original data. This is used for storing standard Unix and Linux passwords in the /etc/shadow file and to track changes to files or network transmissions.

☒ **A, B,** and **D** are incorrect. Triple Digital Encryption Standard (3DES) provides 168-bit encryption and has been superseded by the Advanced Encryption Standard (AES) as the US government encryption standard. Rivest-Shamir-Adleman (RSA) is a cryosystem that uses public and private key pairs; data encryption occurs with the public key and decryption occurs with the mathematically related private key.

27. ☑ **D.** A bridging loop (also called switching loop) can occur when ports on the same switch are connected together. This can be prevented if the Spanning Tree Protocol (STP) is enabled on the switch.

☒ **A, B,** and **C** are incorrect. With the Dynamic Host Configuration Protocol (DHCP), clients and DHCP servers communicate so that clients receive their IP configurations from a DHCP host. The initial DHCP communication occurs as a network broadcast, so if enough DHCP clients broadcast at the same time, the network can become congested for a period of time. DNS sinkholing is a deliberate configuration that returns invalid results for DNS client queries for specific hosts or domains; this can prove useful in preventing infected bot computers from communicating with an attacker command and control (C&C) server.

28. ☑ **A.** Web application firewalls (WAFs) protect web apps from known web app–specific attacks such as database injection attacks.

☒ **B, C,** and **D** are incorrect. A forward proxy server accepts internal client requests for Internet content, fetches the content, potentially caches it for subsequent requests, and returns that content to the requesting internal client. A reverse proxy server accepts client requests and forwards them to the respective backend server, which often resides on a private secured network. Load balancers distribute incoming client requests to backend servers to increase app performance and availability. Distributed denial of service (DDoS) attacks stem from malicious user control of infected computers (called zombies or bots); the bots receive commands to perform actions such as flooding a victim's machine with large amounts of useless network traffic in an attempt to prevent legitimate connections to the machine. One way to mitigate DDoS attacks is to block abnormally excessive network traffic.

29. ☑ **D.** Capturing network traffic can be configured within a network switch using port spanning or mirroring, which copies all switch port network traffic to a designated monitoring port. The technician plugged into the monitoring port could then run network-capturing software such as Wireshark to analyze all switch network traffic.

☒ **A, B,** and **C** are incorrect. DHCP snooping protects the network from rogue DHCP servers that may exist on the network that can hand out incorrect IP configurations to DHCP clients. In a router or switch, ports connected to known legitimate DHCP servers are identified as trusted. Any DHCP server messages not originating from trusted ports are blocked. MAC filtering can allow or block connections based on the unique 48-bit hexadecimal addresses assigned to network interfaces. Bridge Protocol Data Unit (BPDU) guard is a network switch feature that can be enabled to prevent BPDU traffic from switch ports connected to end-point devices such as user workstations, servers, network printers, and so on. Only network switches transmit BPDU traffic.

30. ☑ **D.** Inline network appliances such as IDSs are carefully placed such that the relevant network traffic is seen, analyzed, and potentially modified in some way (including traffic being dropped) before continuing on the intended destination.

☒ **A, B,** and **C** are incorrect. Passive network appliances are primarily used for network traffic monitoring and do not modify network traffic. Capturing network traffic can be configured within a network switch using port spanning or mirroring, which copies all switch port network traffic to a designated monitoring port. The technician plugged into the monitoring port could then run network capturing software such as Wireshark to analyze all switch network traffic. Network aggregation combines different types of network traffic on the same network transmission medium.

31. ☑ **D.** A hardware security module (HSM) is an appliance that is used to securely store cryptographic secrets that can be accessed by multiple hosts.

☒ **A, B,** and **C** are incorrect. A VPN concentrator supports concurrent VPN connections; this is required on a network to enable client-to-site or site-to-site VPN connections. Both IPS and network IDS sensors can be used to collect and monitor network activity. The primary difference is that an IPS can take response and recovery steps to block suspicious activity while an IDS is more focused on reporting and alerting.

32. ☑ **B.** Hashing feeds data as a one-way cryptographic hashing algorithm such as SHA-256, which results in a unique value representative of the original data. This is used for storing standard Unix and Linux passwords in the /etc/shadow file and to track changes to files or network transmissions. File integrity monitoring can use hashing to detect changes to any type of file including database, office productivity, and operating system files.

☒ **A, C,** and **D** are incorrect. Encryption is important for protecting sensitive data from unauthorized users but would not apply to this scenario. Data loss prevention is used to monitor and prevent sensitive data from being exfiltrated, or exposed outside of an organization or to unauthorized users, whether intentionally or unintentionally. In computer networking, quality of service (QoS) solutions manage network traffic to reduce network congestion or to ensure reliability of time-sensitive network usage such as for Voice over IP (VoIP) calls.

Chapter 9

Wireless Networking and Security

QUESTIONS

Most of the modern business world uses wireless technologies in some form, from door access cards, to embedded dog ID chips, private and public Wi-Fi hotspots, and inventory tracking. Securing wireless networks requires an understanding of various wireless technology uses.

Short-range wireless technologies include Bluetooth, which is often used for hands-free connectivity for phone conversations while the user is driving or connecting to wireless speakers to listen to music. Near Field Communication (NFC) is commonly used for wireless ticketing in amusement parks and for wireless tap-and-go retail payments. Wi-Fi is common in many homes and business to enable convenient network access without the hassle associated with network cabling.

The first defense in securing a network is controlling network access, such as through network access control device authentication. Edge devices such as wireless access points (WAPs) or network switches can be configured to forward authentication requests to a centralized authentication server. Proper placement, configuration, and use of network security protocols go a long way in preventing security breaches.

1. You have discovered an unauthorized wireless router that a user plugged into a network jack in her office. Which term best describes this scenario?
   A. Evil twin
   B. Rogue access point
   C. Jamming
   D. Bluejacking

2. After reviewing device security logs, you learn that a malicious user in an airport terminal seating area was able to connect wirelessly to a traveling employee's smartphone and downloaded her contact list. Which type of attack has taken place?
   A. Bluejacking
   B. Bluesnarfing
   C. Disassociation
   D. Social engineering

3. Which of the following represents a weakness of the Wired Equivalent Privacy (WEP) protocol?
   A. 128-bit initialization vector
   B. Inability to secure connections with HTTPS
   C. Inability to secure connections with IPSec
   D. 24-bit initialization vector

4. You need to implement a network security solution that grants network access only after successful user authentication and device condition checks. What should you deploy?

   A. PSK

   B. WPS

   C. EAP

   D. IEEE 802.1x

5. You have been tasked with configuring WAPs in your organization so that authentication takes place on a secured server on a private network instead of directly on the WAP. What type of server should you implement?

   A. Forward proxy server

   B. Reverse proxy server

   C. RADIUS server

   D. VPN concentrator

6. Which authentication protocol requires the client and server to be configured with a PKI certificate?

   A. EAP-FAST

   B. IEEE 802.1x

   C. EAP-TTLS

   D. EAP-TLS

7. Which authentication protocols require only the server to be configured with a PKI certificate? (Choose two.)

   A. EAP-TTLS

   B. EAP-TLS

   C. EAP-FAST

   D. PEAP

8. Which authentication protocol does not require the use of PKI certificates?

   A. EAP-FAST

   B. PEAP

   C. EAP-TTLS

   D. EAP-TLS

9. During a network security audit, open WAPs are discovered on the corporate network. Which security protocols can be enabled to add a layer of security to the use of the WAPs? (Choose two.)

   A. WPA2

   B. NFC

   C. IV

   D. WPA3

10. When connecting to hotel Wi-Fi networks, employees are presented with a web page requiring further authentication before providing Internet access. What type of authentication method is in use?

    A. Wi-Fi protected setup
    B. Captive portal
    C. PSK
    D. Open

11. One of your remote users has begun working from home. The user lives in a building in a small, one-bedroom apartment. After installing a wireless router at the his home, the user complains about intermittent wireless network disruptions. What is the most likely cause of this problem?

    A. Wireless router placement
    B. Faulty wireless router
    C. Cell phone tower interference
    D. Overlapping Wi-Fi channels

12. Which standard port is used to authenticate with a RADIUS server?

    A. UDP 161
    B. UDP 1812
    C. TCP 80
    D. TCP 443

13. You are configuring wireless router WPA2 enterprise settings. Which items must be specified? (Choose two.)

    A. PSK
    B. Wireless channel
    C. Shared secret
    D. RADIUS server IP address

14. You are configuring MAC filtering rules on a wireless router. Which Windows command will display a station's wireless interface MAC address?

    A. **ipconfig /all**
    B. **ipconfig**
    C. **ipconfig /mac**
    D. **ipconfig /flushdns**

15. Refer to Figure 9-1. Log files from your wireless router must be sent via e-mail to your inbox. You need to ensure that the network firewall allows connectivity between the wireless router and your internal SMTP mail server. Which port must the firewall allow?

    A. UDP 25
    B. UDP 161
    C. TCP 80
    D. TCP 25

FIGURE 9-1

Wireless router
log file settings

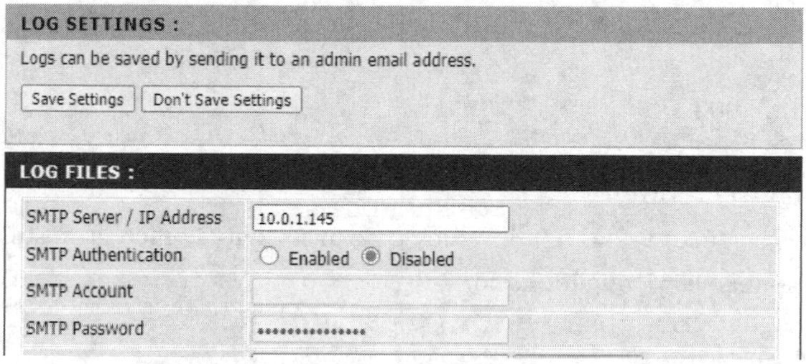

LOG SETTINGS :

Logs can be saved by sending it to an admin email address.

Save Settings   Don't Save Settings

LOG FILES :

SMTP Server / IP Address	10.0.1.145
SMTP Authentication	○ Enabled ⦿ Disabled
SMTP Account	
SMTP Password	•••••••••••••••

16. You need to connect an IoT device with a QR code to a wireless network. The wireless network uses WPA3 security. Which WPA3 feature will solve the problem in this scenario?

A. Always On VPN

B. Pre-shared key

C. RADIUS authentication

D. Wi-Fi Easy Connect

17. Which of the following security protocols is designed specifically for Wi-Fi networks?

A. IPSec

B. SSL

C. WPA

D. TLS

18. You are configuring EAP-TTLS for wireless network authentication. Which statements regarding your configuration are correct? (Choose two.)

A. Clients require a PKI certificate.

B. Servers require a PKI certificate.

C. Servers do not require a PKI certificate.

D. Clients do not require a PKI certificate.

19. Which of the following are symmetric block ciphers? (Choose two.)

A. CBC-MAC

B. RSA

C. AES

D. ECC

20. To which network security protocol does Simultaneous Authentication of Equals (SAE) apply?

A. WEP

B. IPSec

C. WPA2

D. WPA3

21. Which Wi-Fi component is used to manage multiple wireless routers?

    A. PSK

    B. IEEE 802.1x

    C. WAP

    D. WLAN controller

22. Refer to Figures 9-2 and 9-3. Which type of security breach is most likely taking place?

    A. None; everything looks normal

    B. Rogue access point

    C. Bluesnarfing

    D. DDoS

FIGURE 9-2

Windows TCP/
IP status on Wi-Fi
client

```
Wireless LAN adapter Wi-Fi:

   Connection-specific DNS Suffix  . :
   IPv4 Address. . . . . . . . . . : 192.168.4.24
   Subnet Mask . . . . . . . . . . : 255.255.252.0
   Default Gateway . . . . . . . . : 192.168.4.1

C:\>arp -a

Interface: 192.168.4.24 --- 0x2
   Internet Address      Physical Address      Type
   192.168.4.1           18-90-88-a0-36-32     dynamic
   192.168.4.20          f8-2d-c0-c4-f6-87     dynamic
   192.168.4.21          94-8f-cf-1f-8a-f2     dynamic
```

FIGURE 9-3

Corporate
network diagram

Network perimeter firewall
Public IP: 200.1.1.56
Private IP: 192.168.1.253
MAC address: 9c:5a:44:44:b3:72

Wireless router
IP: 192.168.4.1
MAC address: 18:90:88:a6:36:32

Ethernet switch
IP: 192.168.4.160
MAC address: 7c:42:82:e0:72:b2

Wireless client DHCP address range: 192.168.4.10 - 192.168.4.150

23. Penetration testers are executing Wi-Fi disassociation attacks as part of their mandate. What type of behavior can Wi-Fi users expect during the pen test?

   A. Wi-Fi users will not notice anything unusual.

   B. Wi-Fi users will notice wireless network performance degradation.

   C. Wi-Fi users will notice Wi-Fi network disruptions.

   D. Wi-Fi users will notice that their devices will randomly reboot.

24. During the IEEE 802.1x authentication process, which term is used to describe a user's smartphone device attempting to authenticate to the wired network through a wireless access point?

   A. Client

   B. Applicant

   C. Authenticator

   D. Supplicant

25. During the IEEE 802.1x authentication process, which network protocol is used between the supplicant and authenticator?

   A. EAPOL

   B. RADIUS

   C. TCP

   D. UDP

26. During the IEEE 802.1x authentication process, which network protocol is used between the authenticator and authentication server?

   A. EAPOL

   B. RADIUS

   C. TCP

   D. UDP

27. A malicious user, Ivan, is attempting to learn the Wi-Fi password for a protected wireless network by creating a fake wireless access point identical to the real one. Ivan is hoping that users will connect to his fake WAP and provide their Wi-Fi passwords. What type of attack is this?

   A. Jamming

   B. Evil twin

   C. Bluesnarfing

   D. Bluejacking

28. Which wireless protocol stack is used for contactless payments and ticketing applications?

   A. WPA3

   B. IEEE 802.1x

   C. NFC

   D. EAPOL

29. What is the relationship between NFC and RFID?

    A. There is no relationship.

    B. RFID uses NFC.

    C. Both operate at 900 MHz.

    D. NFC uses RFID.

30. A veterinary clinic implants chips into dogs so that information about each dog and owner can be read in case the dog gets loose. What types of technology are being used in this scenario? (Choose two.)

    A. EAPOL

    B. NFC

    C. RFID

    D. IEEE 802.1x

31. Which term is used to describe RFID chips that do not have their own power supply?

    A. Passive emitter

    B. Active emitter

    C. Passive receiver

    D. Active receiver

32. A hotel guest holds a room card near the door card reader to unlock her hotel room door. What type of system is being used?

    A. EAPOL

    B. RFID

    C. IEEE 802.1x

    D. WPA3

QUICK ANSWER KEY

1.	B	**12.**	B	**23.**	C
2.	B	**13.**	C, D	**24.**	D
3.	D	**14.**	A	**25.**	A
4.	D	**15.**	D	**26.**	B
5.	C	**16.**	D	**27.**	B
6.	D	**17.**	C	**28.**	C
7.	A, D	**18.**	B, D	**29.**	D
8.	A	**19.**	A, C	**30.**	B, C
9.	A, D	**20.**	D	**31.**	A
10.	B	**21.**	D	**32.**	B
11.	D	**22.**	B		

IN-DEPTH ANSWERS

1. ☑ **B.** A rogue access point is an active unauthorized wireless access point (WAP). Unknowing users may use an unauthorized WAP for their own convenience at work, without realizing that the configuration could compromise network security. Malicious users can also deploy this to gain wireless access to a network if the access point is connected to a wired network, or their intent may be to trick users into connecting to the access point, because it has the same extended service set identifier (ESSID), or wireless network name, as a valid access point, so that they can capture user traffic.

   ☒ **A, C,** and **D** are incorrect. A rogue access point specifically configured to appear as a known legitimate access point is known as an evil twin. Malicious users deploy evil twins to trick users into connecting to their access point with the intent of stealing sensitive user information, often through fake web pages asking users to enter personal information or passphrase confirmations. Users connected to a legitimate access point can be forcibly disconnected (disassociated) from the access point to trigger a connection to the evil twin. In the radio-frequency (RF) realm, jamming is the intentional creation of interference in an attempt to disrupt normal wireless RF communications. The act of sending unsolicited messages to Bluetooth-enabled devices without using device pairing is referred to as bluejacking, even if the perpetrator is not actually hijacking the target Bluetooth device.

2. ☑ **B.** The theft of sensitive information using Bluetooth wireless technology is referred to as bluesnarfing. This technique does not require the target victim's device to have Bluetooth discovery enabled, although Bluetooth itself must be turned on. Freely available tools can be used to discover and connect to a victim's Bluetooth device to retrieve and delete contact lists, view phone call logs, make phone calls on the target device, and perform other nefarious deeds.

   ☒ **A, C,** and **D** are incorrect. The act of sending unsolicited messages to Bluetooth-enabled devices without using device pairing is referred to as bluejacking, even though the perpetrator is not actually hijacking the target Bluetooth device. Attackers can forcibly disconnect Wi-Fi users from a WAP through disassociation, which forces the victim's device to disconnect from the WAP, similar to unplugging a host from a network switch, thus preventing the victim's wireless networking connectivity until the victim reconnects to the WAP. Social engineering is the act of intentionally manipulating and tricking people so that they do what you want them to do, such as disclosing sensitive personal information. An example of social engineering is a scammer calling taxpayers and posing as a legitimate tax authority demanding outstanding tax payments be made to avoid jail time; the payments are received by the scammer through methods such as money wire transfers.

3. ☑ **D.** Using a 24-bit value for the WEP initialization vector (IV) provides 16.7 million possible values, so reusing IVs is inevitable on busy Wi-Fi networks since very packet contains an IV. Given the capture of enough clear text IVs on a Wi-Fi network and WEP's weak implementation of the RC4 cryptographic algorithm, attackers can easily determine the network encryption key (they already know 24 bits of it) using freely available tools.

☒ **A, B,** and **C** are incorrect. The WEP IV itself is only 24 bits, not 128 bits. The use of WEP does not prevent the use of HTTPS secured web server communications or IPSec. WEP was designed in the 1990s to protect Wi-Fi transmissions, not limit which higher level protocols can be used.

4. ☑ **D.** IEEE 802.1x is the port based network access control (NAC) standard. This solution requires that devices be authenticated before being granted wired or wireless network access. NAC can require that devices meet certain conditions such as device type and configuration, updates having been installed, and so on.

☒ **A, B,** and **C** are incorrect. Network security for IPSec and Wi-Fi networks can use a pre-shared key (PSK), which must be known on both ends of a connection to secure transmissions over a network. Wi-Fi networks can also be open, which means no key is required to establish a connection. The Wi-Fi Protected Access (WPA) standard, in addition to a PSK, can also use enterprise security in the form a centralized authentication server hosted on a secured network. Wi-Fi Protected Setup (WPS) was designed to facilitate secure Wi-Fi connectivity by requiring users either to press a WPS button on the WAP and connecting device or to enter a PIN displayed on the WAP. The Extensible Authentication Protocol (EAP) is a framework that allows for the use of many different types of wired and wireless network authentication methods, such as EAPTLS and EAPTTLS.

5. ☑ **C.** A Remote Authentication Dial-In User Service (RADIUS) server is a centralized authentication server that receives authentication requests on behalf of supplicants such as user devices, from RADIUS clients such as WAPs, and VPN concentrators of network switches. This prevents authentication from occurring on edge devices such as network switches, thus increasing security. RADIUS authentication traffic normally occurs over UDP port 1812.

☒ **A, B,** and **D** are incorrect. A forward proxy server retrieves Internet content on behalf of internal requesting clients, thus hiding the identity of the internal clients. The proxy server can also cache retrieved content to speed up subsequent requests for that content. A reverse proxy server enables connectivity from a public network to internal servers, where the proxy server listens on specific IP addresses and port numbers and forwards requests to the backend host, thus hiding their true identities. A VPN concentrator is a dedicated hardware device designed to support multiple concurrent VPN connections.

6. ☑ **D.** Extensible Authentication Protocol – Transport Layer Security (EAP-TLS) is a network authentication protocol that requires a PKI certificate on both sides of a network connection, such as on a user's smartphone and on a WAP.

   ☒ **A, B,** and **C** are incorrect. EAP – Flexible Authentication via Secure Tunneling (EAP-FAST) is a network authentication protocol that uses a shared secret (PKI certificates are not required) to establish a secured encrypted tunnel between two end-points through which authentication then occurs. IEEE 802.1x is the port-based NAC standard. This requires devices to be authenticated before being granted wired or wireless network access. EAP – Tunneled Transport Layer Security (EAP-TTLS) enhances EAP-TLS in that authentication occurs through an encrypted tunnel as opposed to over the network without a secure tunnel (EAP-TLS).

7. ☑ **A** and **D.** EAP-TTLS enhances EAP-TLS in that authentication occurs through an encrypted tunnel as opposed to over the network without a secure tunnel. Protected Extensible Authentication Protocol (PEAP) is commonly used for IEEE 802.1x authentication; it uses a server-side PKI certificate to create an encrypted connection through which password authentication occurs, after which network access is granted.

   ☒ **B** and **C** are incorrect. EAP-TLS is a network authentication protocol that requires a PKI certificate on both sides of a network connection, such as on a user's smartphone and on a WAP. EAP-TTLS enhances EAP-TLS in that authentication occurs through an encrypted tunnel as opposed to over the network without a secure tunnel.

8. ☑ **A.** EAP-FAST is a network authentication protocol that uses a shared secret (PKI certificates are not required) to establish a secured encrypted tunnel between two end-points through which authentication then occurs.

   ☒ **B, C,** and **D** are incorrect. PEAP is commonly used for IEEE 802.1x authentication; it uses a server-side PKI certificate to create an encrypted connection through which password authentication occurs, after which network access is granted. EAP-TTLS enhances EAP-TLS in that authentication occurs through an encrypted tunnel as opposed to over the network without a secure tunnel. EAP-TLS is a network authentication protocol that requires a PKI certificate on both sides of a network connection, such as on a user's smartphone and on a WAP.

9. ☑ **A** and **D.** WPA versions 2 and 3 provide security beyond open Wi-Fi networks by encrypting connections using either WPA2 PSKs or WPA3 Simultaneous Authentication of Equals (SAE) keys configured on both ends of the connection, or by requiring authentication to a centralized RADIUS server (often called WPA enterprise) hosted on a protected network.

   ☒ **B** and **C** are incorrect. NFC is a low-speed, close proximity (approximately 4 centimeters, or 1.6 inches) wireless transmission standard often used for ticketing, inventory, or as a payment method. An initialization vector (IV), in the context of Wi-Fi, is a 24-bit value that is different for each wireless packet transmission that is part of the deprecated WEP Wi-Fi security standard. IVs are transmitted in clear text, and because they are only 24 bits long, there are 16.7 million possible unique IV values.

10. ☑ **B.** Captive portals control Internet access, usually with a web page that displays automatically upon connecting to a network. The portal requires that the user enter a username, password, voucher number, or hotel room code, and the user must agree to the terms of use to access the Internet.

☒ **A, C,** and **D** are incorrect. Wi-Fi Protected Setup (WPS) was designed to facilitate secure Wi-Fi connectivity by requiring users either to press a WPS button on the WAP and connecting device or to enter a PIN displayed on the WAP. Network security for IPSec and Wi-Fi networks can use a PSK, which must be known on both ends of a connection to secure transmissions over a network. Open Wi-Fi networks do not require network authentication.

11. ☑ **D.** Multiple WAPs in close proximity to one another increase the possibility of overlapping Wi-Fi channels. One way to counter this is to change the channel used by the WAP, so if WAP1 is using channel 3, instead of using the next channel for WAP2, you would choose the furthest frequency band possible, such as channel 11. A Wi-Fi analysis tool can be used to conduct a site survey to determine local WAPs and their channel usage, as well as to provide a heat map, or visualization, of WAP signal coverage.

☒ **A, B,** and **C** are incorrect. The placement of a wireless router will most likely not make as big a difference as changing the channel, since the apartment is very small. There is a greater likelihood of signal interference than of the router being faulty. Cell phone tower frequency ranges vary based on location and provider, but they do not overlap with Wi-Fi frequencies such as 2.4 GHz or 5 GHz.

12. ☑ **B.** RADIUS server authentication uses a standard port number of UDP 1812.

☒ **A, C,** and **D** are incorrect. UDP port 161 is used by the Simple Network Management Protocol (SNMP), which is used to remotely manage and view performance metrics of network devices and hosts. TCP port 80 is used for HTTP web server communication, and TCP port 443 is used for secure HTTPS web server communication.

13. ☑ **C and D.** WPA2 enterprise settings use a RADIUS server for centralized authentication; thus a RADIUS shared secret used to authenticate the wireless router to the RADIUS server is required, and the RADIUS server IP address is required so the wireless router knows where to forward supplicant authentication requests.

☒ **A and B** are incorrect. Network security for IPSec and Wi-Fi networks can use a PSK, which must be known on both ends of a connection to secure transmissions over a network. Wi-Fi communications occur over a specific channel; Wi-Fi routers configured on the same channel that are in close proximity to one another can sometimes cause interference.

14. ☑ **A.** The Windows **ipconfig /all** command as depicted in Figure 9-4 shows the 48-bit physical (MAC) address for each enabled network interface on the host.

☒ **B, C,** and **D** are incorrect. The **ipconfig** command will show the IP address, subnet mask, and default gateway, but not the physical, or MAC, address. The **ipconfig /mac** command is an invalid command line switch. The **ipconfig /flushdns** command clears the local host DNS name resolution cache.

FIGURE 9-4 Output of the ipconfig /all command

```
Connection-specific DNS Suffix  . :
Description . . . . . . . . . . . : Intel(R) Wireless-AC 9560 160MHz
Physical Address. . . . . . . . . : 18-56-80-C3-68-BA
DHCP Enabled. . . . . . . . . . . : Yes
Autoconfiguration Enabled . . . . : Yes
IPv4 Address. . . . . . . . . . . : 192.168.4.24(Preferred)
Subnet Mask . . . . . . . . . . . : 255.255.252.0
Lease Obtained. . . . . . . . . . : August 15, 2020 5:44:00 PM
Lease Expires . . . . . . . . . . : August 16, 2020 2:25:22 PM
Default Gateway . . . . . . . . . : 192.168.4.1
DHCP Server . . . . . . . . . . . : 192.168.4.1
DNS Servers . . . . . . . . . . . : 24.222.0.94
```

15. ☑ **D.** SMTP exchanges mail messages between SMTP servers over TCP port 25.
☒ **A, B,** and **C** are incorrect. UDP port 161 is used by the SNMP, which is used to remotely manage and view performance metrics of network devices and hosts. TCP port 80 is used for HTTP web server communication. SMTP exchanges mail messages between SMTP servers over TCP port 25, not UDP port 25.

16. ☑ **D.** The Wi-Fi Easy Connect standard enables wireless network connectivity by simply scanning the WAP and IoT device quick response (QR) codes with a smartphone. The WAP QR code can be generated using a Wi-Fi Easy Connect app, while some phones have this capability built into their Wi-Fi settings.
☒ **A, B,** and **C** are incorrect. An Always On VPN configuration does not require the user to manually invoke the VPN tunnel; instead, this occurs as a device is turned on and connects to the Internet or when a specific app is launched on the user device. Network security for Wi-Fi networks can use a PSK, which must be known on both ends of a connection to secure transmissions over a network, but PSKs are used by WPA2. WPA3 uses SAE keys, which must be configured on both sides of the wireless connection to enable Wi-Fi security. Wi-Fi networks can use a RADIUS server for centralized authentication, but RADIUS does not determine client-to-WAP connectivity.

17. ☑ **C.** Wi-Fi protected access (WPA), of which the current version is 3, supersedes WEP and WPA2 to provide Wi-Fi network security.
☒ **A, B,** and **D** are incorrect. IPSec is a network security protocol that can protect network traffic without having to configure individual applications specifically, unlike SSL/TLS. IPSec can also be used to secure a client-to-site or site-to-site VPN. Secure Sockets Layer (SSL) is a network security protocol that uses PKI certificates and is superseded by Transport Layer Security (TLS).

18. ☑ **B** and **D.** EAP-TTLS enhances EAP-TLS in that authentication occurs through an encrypted tunnel, as opposed to over the network without a secure tunnel. EAP-TLS is a network authentication protocol that requires a PKI certificate on both sides of a network connection, such as on a user's smartphone and on a WAP; EAP-TTLS, however, requires only a server-side PKI certificate.

☒ **A** and **C** are incorrect. EAP-TTLS requires an installed PKI certificate on servers, not clients.

19. ☑ **A** and **C.** Cipher block chaining message authentication code (CBC-MAC) uses a symmetric block cipher such as AES with a shared secret key to encrypt message hashes (not the message itself) to authenticate messages.

☒ **B** and **D** are incorrect. Rivest-Shamir-Adleman (RSA) is a cryposystem that uses public and private key pairs; data encryption occurs with the public key and decryption occurs with the mathematically related private key. AES is the U.S. government encryption standard that supersedes DES and 3DES; it is a symmetric cryptographic algorithm used to encrypt data. Elliptic-curve cryptography (ECC) is a technique used to generate public and private key pairs based on elliptic curve mathematical theory, which makes it much more difficult to determine what the private key is than it would be for the same bit length used by other algorithms such as RSA.

20. ☑ **D.** WPA3 can be configured to use SAE keys configured on both ends of the connection to provide Wi-Fi security. SAE keys are not susceptible to offline dictionary attacks due to how both connecting devices generate and agree upon group domain parameters during session setup. Parameters are never sent over the network, thus rendering SAE network conversation captures useless for dictionary attacks.

☒ **A, B,** and **C** are incorrect. WPA2 uses PSKs, not SAE keys, configured on both ends of the connection to provide Wi-Fi security. WEP is a 1990s deprecated Wi-Fi security protocol that is known to be easily defeated using freely available tools. IPSec is a network security protocol that can protect network traffic without having to specifically configure individual applications, unlike SSL/TLS. IPSec can also be used to secure a client-to-site or site-to-site VPN.

21. ☑ **D.** Wireless local area network (WLAN) controllers are used in larger network environments where managing the settings of individual WAPs is not feasible. Each WAP has its own unique basic service set identifier (BSSID), which is the WAP MAC address.

☒ **A, B,** and **C** are incorrect. WPA2 uses PSKs configured on both ends of the connection to provide Wi-Fi security; PSKs are not used to manage routers. IEEE 802.1x is the port-based NAC standard that requires devices to be authenticated before being granted wired or wireless network access. A WAP allows Wi-Fi client connectivity to a Wi-Fi network and can also include routing functionality to other networks, at which point the device is referred to as a wireless router.

22. ☑ **B.** The correct MAC address for the wireless router according to the network diagram in Figure 9-3 is 18:90:88:a6:36:32, but Figure 9-2 shows the MAC address for 192.168.4.1 as 18-90-88-a0-36-32 (in other words, the MAC addresses are not the same). This could indicate that a rogue access point is masquerading as a legitimate access point.

    ☒ **A, C,** and **D** are incorrect. The IP-to-MAC address mapping in Figure 9-2 is not consistent with the corporate network diagram and this is not normal. The theft of sensitive information using Bluetooth wireless technology is referred to as bluesnarfing. DDoS attacks stem from malicious user control of infected computers (called zombies or bots); the bots receive commands to perform actions such as flooding a victim's machine with large amounts of useless network traffic in an attempt to prevent legitimate connections to the victim's machine.

23. ☑ **C.** Disassociating a device from a wireless network is equivalent to unplugging a wired network computer from a network switch port. Wireless users will experience sporadic wireless network disruptions.

    ☒ **A, B,** and **D** are incorrect. Wireless users will notice periodic network disruptions, not performance degradation, when they manage to stay connected. They will not experience device reboots.

24. ☑ **D.** Supplicant is the term used to describe an end-point client device attempting to authenticate to the network.

    ☒ **A, B,** and **C** are incorrect. In a RADIUS authentication configuration, clients are network infrastructure devices that forward end-point client device (supplicant) authentication requests to the RADIUS server. Applicant is an invalid term in this context, and the WAP would be considered the authenticator in this example, not the smartphone.

25. ☑ **A.** The initial connection between a supplicant and an IEEE 802.1x authenticator such as an Ethernet network switch occurs using the Extensible Authentication Protocol over LAN (EAPOL). After successful authentication, the authenticator flags the connected supplicant port as being authorized.

    ☒ **B, C,** and **D** are incorrect. A RADIUS server is a centralized authentication server that receives authentication requests on behalf of supplicants, such as user devices, from RADIUS clients, such as WAPs, VPN concentrators, or network switches. TCP establishes "sessions" between hosts before transmissions can occur. After session establishment, transmitted data receipt must be acknowledged by the recipient; otherwise, the data is re-sent by the sender. Many network services use TCP, and each network service on a host is uniquely identified by a port number. User Datagram Protocol (UDP) does not use sessions; instead, it simply transmits data to a target with no receipt acknowledgements. Network services that use the UDP transport also use port numbers.

26. ☑ **B.** RADIUS is used between an authenticator such as a WAP and an authentication server. RADIUS traffic normally uses UDP port 1812.

    ☒ **A, C,** and **D** are incorrect. The initial connection between a supplicant and an IEEE 802.1x authenticator such as an Ethernet network switch occurs using EAPOL. Many network services use TCP, and each network service on a host is uniquely identified by a port number. UDP does not use sessions; instead, it simply transmits data to a target with no receipt acknowledgments. Network services that use the UDP transport also use port numbers.

27. ☑ **B.** A rogue access point specifically configured to appear as a known legitimate access point is known as an evil twin. Malicious users deploy evil twins to trick users into connecting to their access point with the intent of stealing sensitive user information.

    ☒ **A, C,** and **D** are incorrect. In the radio-frequency (RF) realm, jamming is the intentional creation of interference in an attempt to disrupt normal wireless RF communications. The theft of sensitive information using Bluetooth wireless technology is referred to as bluesnarfing. This technique does not require the target victim device to have Bluetooth discovery enabled, although Bluetooth itself must be turned on. The act of sending unsolicited messages to Bluetooth-enabled devices without device pairing is referred to as bluejacking, even though the perpetrator is not actually hijacking the target Bluetooth device.

28. ☑ **C.** Near Field Communication (NFC) is a low-speed, close-proximity (approximately 4 centimeters, or 1.6 inches) wireless transmission standard often used for ticketing, inventory, or as a payment method.

    ☒ **A, B,** and **D** are incorrect. Wi-Fi Protected Access (WPA), of which the current version is 3, supersedes WEP and WPA2 to provide Wi-Fi network security. IEEE 802.1x is the port-based NAC standard. This requires devices to be authenticated before being granted wired or wireless network access. NAC can require that devices meet certain conditions such as device type and configuration, updates having been installed, and so on. The initial connection between a supplicant and an IEEE 802.1x authenticator such as an Ethernet network switch occurs using EAPOL.

29. ☑ **D.** NFC is a low-speed, close-proximity (approximately 4 centimeters, or 1.6 inches) wireless transmission standard often used for ticketing, inventory, or as a payment method. NFC falls under the RFID protocol, which is normally used as method of uniquely identifying items (think inventory control) over radio waves.

    ☒ **A, B,** and **C** are incorrect. NFC exists within the RFID standards hierarchy, not the other way around. Both related standards use the 13.56 MHz frequency range.

30. ☑ **B** and **C.** NFC is a low-speed, close-proximity (approximately 4 centimeters, or 1.6 inches) wireless transmission standard often used for ticketing, inventory or as a payment method. NFC is a type of RFID protocol, which is normally used as method of uniquely identifying items over radio waves. NFC exists within the RFID standards hierarchy. NFC dog chips can be read by anybody with an NFC-enabled smartphone to retrieve owner information.

☒ **A** and **D** are incorrect. The initial connection between a supplicant and an IEEE 802.1x authenticator such as an Ethernet network switch occurs using EAPOL. IEEE 802.1x is the port-based NAC standard. This requires devices to be authenticated before being granted wired or wireless network access. NAC can require that devices meet certain conditions, such as device type and configuration, or updates having been installed.

31. ☑ **A.** RFID is a standard method of uniquely identifying items over radio waves, such as for tracking inventory or building access cards. Passive emitters do not have their own power but wait for connections from an RFID reading device.

☒ **B, C,** and **D** are incorrect. The listed terms do not describe RFID chips lacking their own power source.

32. ☑ **B.** RFID is a standard method of uniquely identifying items over radio waves and is used in hotel room access cards.

☒ **A, C,** and **D** are incorrect. The initial connection between a supplicant and an IEEE 802.1x authenticator such as an Ethernet network switch occurs using EAPOL. IEEE 802.1x is the port-based NAC standard. This requires devices to be authenticated before being granted wired or wireless network access. NAC can require that devices meet certain conditions, such as device type and configuration, or updates having been installed. WPA3 supersedes WEP and WPA2 to provide Wi-Fi network security.

Chapter 10

Authentication

QUESTIONS

Authentication proves the identity of a user, device, or software, after which authorization to access resources is granted. Identity and access management (IAM) ensures the proper creation and configuration of entities requiring resource access. Many authentication and authorization standards such as OpenID and OAuth make it easy and secure for users to access multiple applications without setting up separate user accounts for each service or web site.

Single sign-on (SSO) prevents users from having to keep reentering credentials as they access additional applications. Password vaults provide a secure solution to users otherwise having to remember multiple sets of credentials when accessing multiple applications or web sites.

Multifactor authentication (MFA) enhances user sign-in security by requiring authentication factors from multiple categories and can also use unique codes that expire. Biometric authentication proves user identity by using a unique physical characteristic such as facial recognition.

1. Which authentication protocol is used by Microsoft Active Directory Domain Services?
    A. 802.1x
    B. Kerberos
    C. RADIUS
    D. OAuth

2. Your organization requires a method for desktop computers to verify that the machine boots only with trusted operating systems. Which firmware components must be present to meet this requirement? (Choose two.)
    A. EAP
    B. HSM
    C. UEFI
    D. TPM

3. Which configuration option enhances the user authentication process?
    A. TPM
    B. HSM
    C. SSO
    D. MFA

4. Which term best embodies a centralized network database containing user account information?
   A. SSO
   B. OpenID
   C. SAML
   D. Directory service

5. Which authentication example is considered multifactor authentication?
   A. Username, password
   B. Smartcard, key fob
   C. Username, password, fingerprint scan
   D. Username, password, security question

6. When authenticating to your cloud account, you must supply a username, password, and a unique numeric code supplied from a smartphone app that changes every 30 seconds. Which term is used to describe the changing numeric code?
   A. SMS
   B. TOTP
   C. Virtual smartcard
   D. Push notification

7. Which authentication protocol transmits user sign-in credentials in plain text over the network?
   A. CHAP
   B. TACACS+
   C. PAP
   D. Kerberos

8. Your organization is creating a web application that generates animated video from story text. Instead of requiring users to create an account with your organization before using the app, you want to enable users to sign in using their existing Google or Facebook accounts. What type of authentication is this?
   A. Attested
   B. Token key
   C. Federated
   D. Kerberos

9. Which security hardware can be used for multifactor authentication?
   A. Token key
   B. TPM
   C. HSM
   D. Password vault

10. Which term best describes a user authenticating to a service and receiving a unique authentication code via a phone call?
    A. Token key
    B. Out-of-band authentication
    C. Federation
    D. SAML

11. Which type of authentication method measures the motion patterns of a person's body movement?
    A. SAML
    B. Biometric
    C. Gait analysis
    D. TOTP

12. A user complains that her new laptop occasionally does not allow fingerprint authentication. Which term best describes this situation?
    A. Crossover error rate
    B. False acceptance
    C. False rejection
    D. Efficacy rate

13. A travelling employee is unable to authenticate to a corporate custom web application that is normally accessible when he's at home. What type of authentication is in place or the custom web application?
    A. Biometric
    B. Federated
    C. Geolocation
    D. Attested

14. Which of the following represents the correct sequence in which AAA occurs?
    A. All AAA items occur simultaneously
    B. Authorization, authentication, accounting
    C. Authentication, authorization, accounting
    D. Accounting, authentication, authorization

15. You have configured your smartphone authentication such that, using your finger, you connect points on a picture. Which type of authentication category does this apply to?
    A. Something you are
    B. Somewhere you are
    C. Something you know
    D. Something you do

16. You have forgotten your login credentials for a secure web site. The forgotten password mechanism on the site prompts you to enter your PIN before selecting a help desk user that will supply you with a reset code. Which type of forgotten password authentication mechanism is at work here?

   A. Something you are
   B. Somewhere you are
   C. Something you exhibit
   D. Someone you know

17. Cloud technicians in your organization have linked your on-premises Microsoft Active Directory domain to a cloud-based directory service. What benefit is derived from this configuration?

   A. Multifactor authentication can be enabled.
   B. User authentication will occur faster.
   C. Users can authenticate to cloud apps using their on-premises credentials.
   D. User authorization will occur faster.

18. Which type of authentication environment is depicted in Figure 10-1?

   A. SSO
   B. Federated
   C. Kerberos
   D. Multifactor

FIGURE 10-1

Network
authentication
diagram

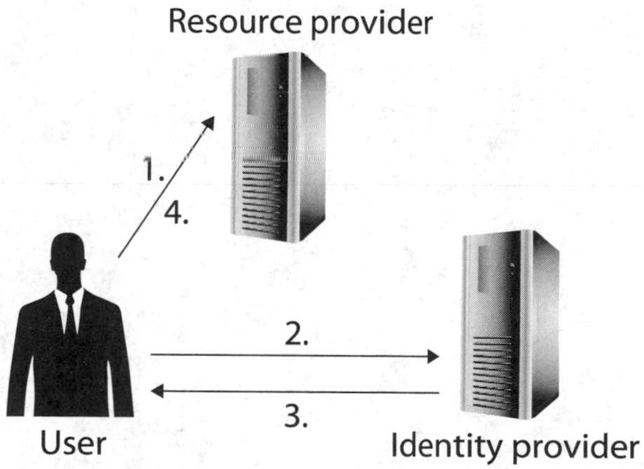

19. Which type of authentication is depicted in Figure 10-2?
    A. Biometric
    B. Geolocation
    C. SSO
    D. TOTP

FIGURE 10-2

Mobile
device cloud
authentication

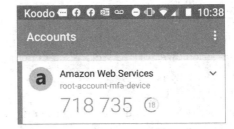

20. Which type of authentication is depicted in Figure 10-3?
    A. Biometric
    B. Gesture-based
    C. Location-based
    D. TOTP

FIGURE 10-3

Mobile device
unlock pattern

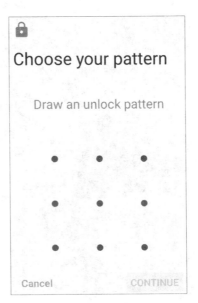

21. Which of the following is an example of authentication?
    A. Accessing a secured part of a web site
    B. Writing a log entry when users access sensitive files
    C. Verifying that files have not been modified by unauthorized users
    D. Supplying a username and password

22. Users complain that they cannot use different usernames and passwords for all of the web applications they use because there are too many to remember, so they use the same username and password for all of the web apps. You need to ensure that users maintain unique usernames and complex passwords for all web apps while minimizing user frustration. What should you deploy for users?
    A. HSM
    B. TPM
    C. Token key
    D. Password vault

23. A malicious user has removed an encrypted drive from a TPM-enabled system and connected it to his own TPM-enabled computer. What will the outcome be?
    A. The malicious user will have full access to the drive contents.
    B. The malicious user will be unable to access the drive contents.
    C. The drive contents will be erased automatically.
    D. The drive contents will be accessible in read-only mode.

24. Which fact is specific to the Challenge Handshake Authentication Protocol (CHAP)?
    A. Passwords are sent over the network in encrypted form.
    B. Passwords are sent over the network in plaint text.
    C. Passwords are never sent over the network.
    D. Passwords are combined with a one-time password to complete authentication.

25. How does OAuth determine whether a user is permitted to access a resource?
    A. Username, password
    B. PKI certificate
    C. One-time password
    D. Access token

26. Which term is the most closely associated with Figure 10-4?
    A. OAuth
    B. MFA
    C. OTP
    D. TPM

FIGURE 10-4

Web site sign-in

27. After successful authentication, which method can be used to transmit authorization details to a resource provider to grant resource access?

A. Kerberos

B. SAML

C. MFA

D. OTP

28. Which statements regarding OAuth are correct? (Choose two.)

A. OAuth passes encrypted user credentials to a resource provider.

B. OAuth tokens are issued by a resource provider.

C. OAuth tokens are consumed by a resource provider.

D. OAuth does not handle authentication.

29. You need to configure VPN authentication methods that use PKI certificates. Which VPN configuration option should you choose?

A. PAP

B. CHAP

C. OAuth

D. EAP

30. To secure VPN access, you need a solution that will first authenticate devices before allowing network access. Which authentication standard does this apply to?

A. OAuth

B. MFA

C. IEEE 802.1x

D. SSO

31. You do not want authentication handled by wireless access points in your network. What should you configure?

    A. RADIUS server

    B. OAuth

    C. SSO

    D. Identity federation

32. Which authentication standard is directly related to identity federation?

    A. Kerberos

    B. CHAP

    C. OpenID

    D. IEEE 802.1x

QUICK ANSWER KEY

1. B
2. C, D
3. D
4. D
5. C
6. B
7. C
8. C
9. A
10. B
11. C

12. C
13. C
14. C
15. D
16. D
17. C
18. B
19. D
20. B
21. D
22. D

23. B
24. C
25. D
26. A
27. B
28. C, D
29. D
30. C
31. A
32. C

IN-DEPTH ANSWERS

1. ☑ **B.** The Kerberos network authentication protocol is used by Microsoft Active Directory Domain Services (AD DS).

    ☒ **A, C,** and **D** are incorrect. IEEE 802.1x is the port-based network access control (NAC) standard. This requires devices to be authenticated before being granted wired or wireless network access. Remote Authentication Dial-In User Service (RADIUS) is a protocol that uses a centralized authentication server to grant network access. Edge devices such as wireless access points and network switches are configured to forward network connection requests to the RADIUS server. Upon successful authentication, the Open Authorization (OAuth) protocol uses a token (not the original credentials) that represents an authenticated user or device to grant resource access, such as access to a web application.

2. ☑ **C** and **D.** When a computer system is turned on, the first firmware instructions executed are either the Basic Input Output System (BIOS) or the newer Unified Extensible Firmware Interface (UEFI) standard that supports security features such as secure boot and larger storage devices. When secure boot is enabled, only trusted operating systems (OSs) that have not been tampered with, such as with malware infected OS boot files, are allowed to start on the computer. Trusted Platform Module (TPM) is a firmware chip within a computing device that ensures device boot integrity as well as storing cryptographic keys used to encrypt storage devices.

    ☒ **A** and **B** are incorrect. The Extensible Authentication Protocol (EAP) is a framework that allows for the use of many different types of wired and wireless network authentication methods. A hardware security module (HSM) is a dedicated tamper-resistant device designed to store and manage cryptographic keys securely.

3. ☑ **D.** Multifactor authentication (MFA) uses two or more identity validation methods, each from different categories, such as a username and password (something you know) and a key fob (something you have).

    ☒ **A, B,** and **C** are incorrect. TPM is a firmware chip within a computing device that ensures device boot integrity as well as storing cryptographic keys used to encrypt storage devices. A HSM is a dedicated tamper-resistant device designed to store and manage cryptographic keys securely. SSO is an authentication standard that, after successful initial authentication, does not require the user to keep entering her credentials to access additional applications.

4.   ☑   **D.** A directory service, such as Microsoft Active Directory, serves as a central network database containing objects such as users, groups, applications, and various network configurations. In the current era of cloud computing, directory services can be hosted in the cloud without having to configure servers manually to support the directory service, and the cloud-based directory service can be synchronized with an on-premises directory service.

☒   **A, B,** and **C** are incorrect. SSO is an authentication standard that, after successful initial authentication, does not require the user to keep entering his credentials to access additional applications. The OpenID standard is an identity federation solution that uses a centralized user identity store, eliminating the need for users to create and maintain user accounts for multiple web sites. With OpenID, you could use your existing Google, Microsoft, or Facebook account (to name just a few) to authenticate to third-party web sites. The Security Assertion Markup Language (SAML) standard is used to transmit authentication and authorization messages between users, centralized identity providers, and resource providers that trust the identity providers.

5.   ☑   **C.** Multifactor authentication uses two or more identity validation methods, each from different categories, such as a username and password (something you know) and a fingerprint scan (something you are). "Something you are" refers to biometric authentication, which can also include authentication through other unique personal characteristics related to face geometry, voice pattern, retinal and iris scans, as well as unique palm or finger vein patterns.

☒   **A, B,** and **D** are incorrect. Username and password are both "something you know," smartcard and key fob are both "something you have," and username, password and security question are "something you know"; none of these options uses more than a single authentication category and as a result does not constitute multifactor authentication.

6.   ☑   **B.** A time-based one-time password (TOTP) derives randomness from the current time in which it is generated and normally expires within a short period of time such as 30 seconds, as opposed to a static, unchanging code that does not expire. The closely related HMAC-based one-time password (HTOP) is technique whereby a client device is synchronized with a server and uses this to generate a unique code instead of the current time. TOTPs are normally transmitted out-of-band on a different device such as through a smartphone app (something you have) when a user attempts to authenticate with a username and password (something you know) using a different device such as a laptop thus constituting multifactor authentication.

☒   **A, C,** and **D** are incorrect. Short message service (SMS) is used for sending text messages between mobile devices over a phone carrier network. SMS texting is commonly used for receiving authentication codes; this is referred to out-of-band transmission because the user will normally be attempting to authenticate using a different communication channel such as a web browser. TPM firmware allows for the use of a virtual smartcard for multifactor authentication as opposed to using a physical smartcard and smartcard reader. Push notifications are message transmissions to end user devices initiated by an application server, such as notifying users about current sale items when they enter a shopping mall.

7. ☑ **C.** The Password Authentication Protocol (PAP) is an older authentication standard that passes credentials over the network in clear text format, meaning that capturing those network transmissions reveals user credentials. PAP was often used for remote authentication such as for Point-to-Point Protocol (PPP) and virtual private network (VPN) connections.

☒ **A, B,** and **D** are incorrect. Challenge Handshake Authentication Protocol (CHAP) is an authentication standard that uses a three-way handshake whereby the hashing of a secret known on both ends of the connection is verified without ever sending that secret over the network. Microsoft's implementation of CHAP is known as MS-CHAP. Terminal Access Controller Access Control System (TACACS+) is a Cisco network security protocol that was designed to replace RADIUS to centrally authenticate network access. The Kerberos network authentication protocol is used by Microsoft AD DS.

8. ☑ **C.** Identity federation solutions use a centralized user identity store, eliminating the need for users to create and maintain user accounts for multiple web sites.

☒ **A, B,** and **D** are incorrect. With IT security, attestation is used to verify the validity of an entity, such as ensuring a machine's boot process has not been tampered with, or trusting a PKI certificate issued from a specific certification authority. A token key refers to a hardware device or a special software app used for IT system authentication (something you have) that generates a unique value used in addition to other authentication factors such as a username and password (something you know). The Kerberos network authentication protocol is used by Microsoft AD DS.

9. ☑ **A.** A token key refers to a hardware device used for IT system authentication (something you have) that generates a unique value used in addition to other authentication factors such as a username and password (something you know).

☒ **B, C,** and **D** are incorrect. TPM is a firmware chip within a computing device that ensures device boot integrity as well as storing cryptographic keys used to encrypt storage devices. A HSM is a dedicated tamper-resistant device designed to store and manage cryptographic keys securely. A password vault is an encrypted password store used by password manager software.

10. ☑ **B.** Out-of-band authentication is used with multifactor authentication. An example is a user initiating logging in to a web site using a laptop computer where an authentication code is sent to the user's smartphone and is required to complete authentication.

☒ **A, C,** and **D** are incorrect. A token key refers to a hardware device used for IT system authentication (something you have) that generates a unique value used in addition to other authentication factors such as a username and password (something you know). Identity federation solutions use a centralized user identity store, eliminating the need for users to create and maintain user accounts for multiple web sites. The SAML standard is used to transmit authentication and authorization messages between users, centralized identity providers, and resource providers that trust the identity providers.

11. ☑ **C.** Gait analysis measures the way a person moves and can be used as an authentication measure.

☒ **A, B,** and **D** are incorrect. The SAML standard is used to transmit authentication and authorization messages between users, centralized identity providers, and resource providers that trust the identity providers. Biometric authentication uses unique personal characteristics such as a fingerprint or a voice or retinal scan to uniquely identify, or authenticate, an individual. A TOTP derives randomness from the current time in which it is generated and normally expires within a short period of time such as 30 seconds.

12. ☑ **C.** An authentication system's rejection of legitimate authentications is referred to as a false rejection rate (FRR). An example would be a 5 percent rejection rate, based on facial recognition authentication that does not correctly identify a user's face.

☒ **A, B,** and **D** are incorrect. The junction of a false rejection and false acceptance rate is the crossover error rate (CER); in other words, the false rejection and false acceptance rates are both equal. The false acceptance rate (FAR) is the probability of a biometric authentication system's propensity to incorrectly allow access to an illegitimate system user. The efficacy rate measures how effective an authentication system is; lower false acceptance and rejection rates mean the solution will have a higher efficacy rate.

13. ☑ **C.** Geolocation is a form of authentication (where you are) that checks where a connection is originating from. Some web sites will not allow access to users who travel to foreign countries and attempt to log in to a web site.

☒ **A, B,** and **D** are incorrect. Biometric authentication uses unique personal characteristics such as a fingerprint or a voice or retinal scan to uniquely identify, or authenticate, an individual. Identity federation solutions use a centralized user identity store, eliminating the need for users to create and maintain user accounts for multiple web sites. With IT security, attestation is used to verify the validity of an entity, such as ensuring a machine's boot process has not been tampered with, or trusting a PKI certificate issued from a specific certification authority.

14. ☑ **C.** AAA refers to authentication (proving of one's identity) which occurs first, followed by authorization (being granted resource access), and finally accounting (logging and auditing resource access). Centralized authentication systems such as RADIUS are AAA systems.

☒ **A, B,** and **D** are incorrect. The listed items represent the incorrect AAA order.

15. ☑ **D.** "Something you do" is an authentication category that includes actions such as drawing points on a picture using your finger.

☒ **A, B,** and **C** are incorrect. The listed authentication categories are not related to using a finger to draw points on a picture. "Something you are" refers to biometric authentication, such as with fingerprint scans. "Somewhere you are" is a geolocation mechanism that limits where you can be to authenticate successfully to a system. "Something you know" includes common authentication factors such as knowing a username and password.

16. ☑ **D.** "Someone you know" is an authentication mechanism often used when resetting forgotten passwords, whereby a user must selecting a "helper" user that is trusted by the system to supply some kind of authentication detail, such as a unique user PIN, to enable password resets.

☒ **A, B,** and **C** are incorrect. "Something you are" refers to biometric authentication, such as with fingerprint scans. "Somewhere you are" is a geolocation mechanism that limits where you can be to authenticate successfully to a system. Authentication that uses a unique personal behavior or characteristic trait is referred to as "something you exhibit."

17. ☑ **C.** Cloud directory synchronization solutions such as Microsoft Azure's AD Connect link to an on-premises directory service such as Microsoft Active Directory. This enables users to sign in to cloud apps using their familiar on-premises credentials.

☒ **A, B,** and **D** are incorrect. Linking a cloud directory service to an on-premises directory service is not required to enable multifactor authentication, nor does it speed up authentication or authorization.

18. ☑ **B.** Identity federation solutions use a centralized user identity store, eliminating the need for users to create and maintain user accounts for multiple web sites.

☒ **A, C,** and **D** are incorrect. SSO is an authentication standard that, after successful initial authentication, does not require the user to keep entering his or her credentials to access additional applications. The Kerberos network authentication protocol is used by Microsoft AD DS. Multifactor authentication (MFA) uses two or more identity validation methods, each from different categories, such as a username and password (something you know) and a key fob (something you have).

19. ☑ **D.** A time-based one-time password (TOTP) derives randomness from the current time in which it is generated and normally expires within a short period of time such as 30 seconds, as opposed to a static, unchanging code that does not expire.

☒ **A, B,** and **C** are incorrect. Biometric authentication uses unique personal characteristics such as a fingerprint or facial recognition to authentication users. Geolocation is a form of authentication (where you are) that checks where a connection is initiated from. Some web sites will not authenticate users who travel to foreign countries and attempt to log in to a web site. SSO is an authentication standard that, after successful initial authentication, does not require the user to keep entering his or her credentials to access additional applications.

20. ☑ **B.** Gesture-based authentication authenticates users based on unique gestures, such as device unlock patterns on a smartphone.

☒ **A, C,** and **D** are incorrect. Biometric authentication uses unique personal characteristics such as a fingerprint or facial recognition to authentication users. Location-based authentication is a form of authentication (where you are) that checks where a connection is initiated from. Some web sites will not authenticate users who travel to foreign countries and attempt to log in to a web site. A TOTP derives randomness from the current time in which it is generated and normally expires within a short period of time such as 30, seconds as opposed to a static, unchanging code that does not expire.

21. ☑ **D.** Username and password (something you know) can be provided to authenticate a user and grant resource access.
    ☒ **A, B,** and **C** are incorrect. Accessing resources occurs through authorization, which is possible only after successful authentication. Writing log entries resulting from user activity is auditing. Hashing is a cryptographic operation that can be used to detect unauthorized changes to files.

22. ☑ **D.** A password vault is an encrypted password store used by password manager software that can store usernames and passwords for applications and web sites the user accesses.
    ☒ **A, B,** and **C** are incorrect. A HSM is a dedicated tamper-resistant device designed to store and manage cryptographic keys securely. A TPM is a firmware chip within a computing device that ensures device boot integrity as well as storing cryptographic keys used to encrypt storage devices. A token key refers to a hardware device used for IT system authentication (something you have) that generates a unique value used in addition to other authentication factors such as a username and password (something you know).

23. ☑ **B.** TPM is firmware that can store cryptographic keys used to protect data at rest. If the encrypted drive is moved to a different computer, then the correct decryption key is unavailable, resulting in the user being unable to access the drive contents.
    ☒ **A, C,** and **D** are incorrect. None of the listed outcomes will result when placing a TPM-encrypted storage device in a different computer.

24. ☑ **C.** CHAP is an authentication standard that uses a three-way handshake whereby the hashing of a secret known on both ends of the connection is verified without ever sending that secret over the network.
    ☒ **A, B,** and **D** are incorrect. CHAP authentication does not exhibit any of the listed characteristics.

25. ☑ **D.** Upon successful authentication, the OAuth protocol uses a token (and not the original credentials) generated by a trusted identity provider that represents an authenticated user or device to grant resource access, such as to a web application.
    ☒ **A, B,** and **C** are incorrect. None of the listed items is directly used by OAuth to grant resource access; instead, a representative token is used.

26. ☑ **A.** Upon successful authentication, the OAuth protocol uses a token (and not the original credentials) generated by a trusted identity provider that represents an authenticated user or device to grant resource access, such as to a web application.
    ☒ **B, C,** and **D** are incorrect. MFA uses two or more identity validation methods, each from different categories, such as a username and password (something you know) and a key fob (something you have). A one-time password (OTP) is a unique code generated for use only once, an example of which would be a code sent via e-mail or SMS text when resetting a forgotten password. TPM is firmware that can store cryptographic keys used to protect data at rest.

27. ☑ **B.** The Security Assertion Markup Language (SAML) standard is used to transmit authentication and authorization messages between users, centralized identity providers, and resource providers that trust the identity providers.

    ☒ **A, C,** and **D** are incorrect. The Kerberos network authentication protocol is used by Microsoft AD DS. MFA uses two or more identity validation methods, each from different categories. An OTP is a unique code generated for use only once, an example of which would be a code sent via e-mail or SMS text when resetting a forgotten password.

28. ☑ **C and D.** After successful authentication, the OAuth protocol uses a token (and not the original credentials) generated by a trusted identity provider that represents an authenticated user or device to grant resource access, such as to a web application. The web application is a resource provider that would consume the token to grant access.

    ☒ **A and B** are incorrect. OAuth uses tokens and does not transmit the user credentials to resource providers. OAuth tokens are generated by a trusted identity provider.

29. ☑ **D.** The Extensible Authentication Protocol (EAP) is a framework that allows for the use of many different types of wired and wireless network authentication methods, including for VPN access.

    ☒ **A, B,** and **C** are incorrect. The Password Authentication Protocol (PAP) is an older authentication standard that passes credentials over the network in the clear, meaning that capturing those network transmissions reveals user credentials. CHAP is an authentication standard that uses a three-way handshake, whereby the hashing of a secret known on both ends of the connection is verified without ever sending that secret over the network. OAuth uses tokens and does not transmit the user credentials to resource providers. OAuth tokens are generated by a trusted identity provider.

30. ☑ **C.** IEEE 802.1x is the port-based NAC standard. This requires devices to be authenticated before being granted wired or wireless network access.

    ☒ **A, B,** and **D** are incorrect. OAuth uses tokens and does not transmit the user credentials to resource providers. MFA uses two or more identity validation methods, each from different categories. SSO is an authentication standard that, after successful initial authentication, does not require the user to keep entering his credentials to access additional applications.

31. ☑ **A.** RADIUS is a protocol that uses a centralized authentication server to grant network access. Edge devices such as wireless access points and network switches are configured to forward network connection requests to the RADIUS server.

    ☒ **B, C,** and **D** are incorrect. OAuth uses tokens and does not transmit the user credentials to resource providers. SSO is an authentication standard that, after successful initial authentication, does not require the user to keep entering her credentials to access additional applications. Identity federation solutions use a centralized user identity store, eliminating the need for users to create and maintain user accounts for multiple web sites.

32. ☑ **C.** The OpenID standard is an identity federation solution that uses a centralized user identity store, eliminating the need for users to create and maintain user accounts for multiple web sites.

☒ **A, B,** and **D** are incorrect. The Kerberos network authentication protocol is used by Microsoft AD DS. CHAP is an authentication standard that uses a three-way handshake, whereby the hashing of a secret known on both ends of the connection is verified without ever sending that secret over the network. IEEE 802.1x is the port-based NAC standard. This requires devices to be authenticated before being granted wired or wireless network access.

Chapter 11

Authorization
and Access Control

QUESTIONS

Modern web applications have the ability to authenticate users directly with a username and password or by trusting providers such as Google and Facebook, where users may already have login credentials and potentially multifactor authentication settings.

Granting permissions to access resources can be done using many methods, including role membership, conditional rule access, or security policies, and can be enforced by a specialized, secure operating system.

IT technicians can use a variety of security control types to protect assets. Some controls are preventative in nature, such as firewalls, whereas others are detective in nature, such as log file analysis. The proper security control must be put in place and its efficacy periodically assessed, especially if security controls are required by laws or regulations.

1. Which identity federation component authenticates users?
   A. Identity provider
   B. Resource provider
   C. OAuth
   D. SAML

2. After successful authentication, which SAML component contains claim information?
   A. Resource provider
   B. Security token service
   C. PKI certificate
   D. Token

3. You are configuring file system security such that Microsoft Active Directory user accounts with a specific manager configured in their user account properties are granted file system access. What type of access control configuration is this?
   A. Role-based
   B. Discretionary
   C. Attribute-based
   D. Time-based

4. Which of the following constitutes multifactor authentication?

    A. Username, password

    B. Username, PIN

    C. Smartcard, PIN

    D. Smartcard, key fob

5. You are configuring SSH public key authentication for a Linux host. Which statements about this configuration are correct? (Choose two.)

    A. The public key is stored with the user.

    B. The private key is stored with the user.

    C. The public key is stored with the Linux host.

    D. The private key is stored with the Linux host.

6. After configuring SSH public key authentication for a Linux host, users complain that they are prompted for a passphrase when using SSH to connect to the host. Why is this happening?

    A. SSH is configured incorrectly on the Linux host.

    B. SSH is configured incorrectly on the client device.

    C. A passphrase has been configured to protect the private key.

    D. A passphrase has been configured to protect the public key.

7. Which configuration limits the use of a mobile device to a specific area?

    A. Geotagging

    B. Geolocation

    C. GPS

    D. Geofencing

8. While scrolling through social media posts, you come across a friend's post stating that he had recently boarded a flight from Las Vegas en route to Toronto. What is this an example of?

    A. Geotagging

    B. Geolocation

    C. GPS

    D. Geofencing

9. Which user password setting will prevent the reuse of old passwords?

    A. Password complexity

    B. Account lockout

    C. Password history

    D. Time-based login

10. You have configured user workstations so that upon a user's login, a message states that the system may be used only to conduct business in accordance with organizational security policies, and that noncompliance could result in disciplinary action. Which type of security control is this?

    A. Detective
    B. Corrective
    C. Deterrent
    D. Compensating

11. Which type of access control model uses a hardened specialized operating system with resource labeling and security clearance levels to control resources access?

    A. Discretionary access control
    B. Role-based access control
    C. Attribute-based access control
    D. Mandatory access control

12. Your cloud-based virtual machine runs a custom application workload that requires access to resources running within on-premises virtual machines. What should you do to enable secure connectivity between the virtual machines? (Choose two.)

    A. Configure HTTP connectivity between the virtual machines.
    B. Configure a guest account for the application.
    C. Configure a service account for the application.
    D. Configure a VPN tunnel between the virtual machines.

13. Which term is the most closely related to the "impossible travel time" security feature?

    A. Chain of trust
    B. Security token
    C. Geofencing
    D. Anomaly detection

14. You are configuring file servers in the enterprise to allow read-only access to files labeled as "PII" for users accessing files from the corporate network if they have been assigned to a project named "ProjectA." Which type of access control mechanism is being used?

    A. Discretionary
    B. Conditional
    C. Mandatory
    D. Role-based

15. The IT department has been tasked with conducting a risk assessment related to the migration of a line-of-business app to the public cloud. To which security control category does this apply?

    A. Operational
    B. Managerial
    C. Technical
    D. Physical

16. You have been tasked with the weekly tape backup rotation for backing up on-premises database servers. To which security control category does this apply?
    A. Operational
    B. Managerial
    C. Technical
    D. Physical

17. Organizational security policies require that customers' personal information be encrypted when stored. To which security control category does this apply?
    A. Operational
    B. Managerial
    C. Technical
    D. Physical

18. You are configuring a hardware firewall to allow traffic only from a jump box in the DMZ to internal Linux hosts. Which type of security control is this?
    A. Physical
    B. Compensating
    C. Preventative
    D. Detective

19. To achieve regulatory compliance, your organization must encrypt all fixed disks to protect data at rest on each station. Your company plans on using the Microsoft Windows BitLocker drive encryption feature. None of your computers has a TPM chip, so you have configured Group Policy such that decryption keys can be stored on a removable USB thumb drive. Which type of security control is this?
    A. Physical
    B. Compensating
    C. Detective
    D. Corrective

20. You have configured a network-based intrusion prevention system (NIPS) hardware appliance to block traffic from IP addresses that send excessive traffic to your network. Which type of security control is this?
    A. Physical
    B. Compensating
    C. Deterrent
    D. Corrective

21. You are a consultant helping a retail client with app geofencing. Which type of tracking mechanisms can you use to enable geofencing for customers with the retail app installed on their smartphones?

    A. GPS, Wi-Fi
    B. Wi-Fi, NFC
    C. GPS, NAC
    D. NAC, Bluetooth

22. Your identity federation configuration creates digitally signed tokens for authenticated users that contain the user date of birth and security clearance level. Which term is used to describe this extra data added to the token?

    A. PKI certificate
    B. Cookie
    C. SAML
    D. Claim

23. Why is the SSH authentication error in Figure 11-1 occurring?

    A. The incorrect public key is being used.
    B. The incorrect private key is being used.
    C. The username is incorrect.
    D. The password is incorrect.

FIGURE 11-1

SSH
authentication
error

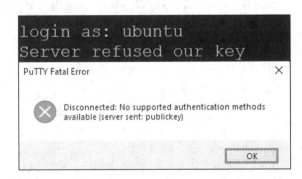

24. You are viewing the contents of the Linux authorized_keys file. Which type of key is stored here?

    A. Public
    B. Private
    C. Secret
    D. Symmetric

25. You need to assess whether Linux servers in the screened subnet need to be hardened. The servers are currently configured with SSH public key authentication. What should you check that should be in place? (Choose two.)

    A. Password protection for the public key

    B. Private key password protection

    C. Default SSH port number TCP 22 has been changed to an unreserved port number

    D. Default SSH port number TCP 25 has been changed to an unreserved port number

26. Which statements regarding SSH public key authentication are correct? (Choose two.)

    A. A user password is not required.

    B. A user password is required.

    C. A public and private key pair is required.

    D. A symmetric key is required.

27. You are an IT technician for FakeCorp1. You have configured your on-premises Microsoft Active Directory domain controller server, Dc1, as a federated identity provider during the acquisition phase of a competitor, FakeCorp2. The IT team at FakeCorp2 must configure web app servers to trust tokens issued by FakeCorp1. What should you provide to the technicians?

    A. The private key for DC1

    B. The administrative username for DC1

    C. The public key for DC1

    D. The administrative password for DC1

28. What is normally required when using smartcard authentication? (Choose two.)

    A. Smartcard reader

    B. PIN

    C. TPM

    D. HSM

29. Where are virtual smartcards stored?

    A. Windows registry

    B. RADIUS server

    C. Identity provider

    D. TPM

30. Your organization plans on issuing smartcards to users for the purposes of digitally signing and decrypting e-mail messages. What must be deployed to the smartcards?

    A. Server public key

    B. User public key

    C. Server private key

    D. User private key

31. What is one disadvantage of using a virtual smartcard in a Microsoft Windows environment?

    A. It is available only on a single Android smartphone at a time.

    B. It cannot be used for remote management.

    C. It requires a virtual smartcard reader.

    D. It is available only on a host with TPM.

32. A user account lockout configuration helps mitigate which type of attack?

    A. Denial of service

    B. Ransomware

    C. Phishing

    D. Brute-force password attacks

A QUICK ANSWER KEY

1.	A	**12.**	C, D	**23.**	B
2.	D	**13.**	D	**24.**	A
3.	C	**14.**	B	**25.**	B, C
4.	C	**15.**	B	**26.**	A, C
5.	B, C	**16.**	A	**27.**	C
6.	C	**17.**	C	**28.**	A, B
7.	D	**18.**	C	**29.**	D
8.	A	**19.**	B	**30.**	D
9.	C	**20.**	D	**31.**	D
10.	C	**21.**	A	**32.**	D
11.	D	**22.**	D		

IN-DEPTH ANSWERS

1. ☑ **A.** Identity providers (IdPs) contain user accounts and perform authentication, and along with federated identify environments, they will generate a security token that may contain assertions (claims) about the user such as date of birth, department, and so on. The security token is then digitally signed by the IdP with its private key. Applications that trust the IdP signature (using the IdP public key) accept tokens and allow user access.

    ☒ **B, C,** and **D** are incorrect. Resource providers accept security tokens from trusted IdPs and allow access, such as to a web application. Upon successful authentication, the Open Authorization (OAuth) protocol uses a token (and not the original credentials) that represents an authenticated user or device to grant resource access, such as to a web application. The Security Assertion Markup Language (SAML) standard is used to transmit authentication and authorization messages between users, IdPs, and resource providers that trust the IdPs.

2. ☑ **D.** The SAML standard is used to transmit authentication and authorization messages between users, IdPs, and resource providers. IdPs digitally sign security tokens, which can contain claims, or assertions, about a user or device, such as a date of birth, cost center, subnet address range, and so on. Claims are often derived from user or device attributes stored with the user or device account.

    ☒ **A, B,** and **C** are incorrect. Resource providers accept security tokens from trusted IdPs and allow access, such as to a web application. IdPs in a federated identity configuration run as a security token service (STS), which digitally signs tokens upon successful user or device authentication; the token is then used to grant resource access. A Public Key Infrastructure (PKI) certificate is a security certificate that can be stored in a file, a network directory service, or a smartcard. It uniquely identifies a subject such as a device or user.

3. ☑ **C.** User accounts contain many attributes (properties) such as manager name, group membership, last login time, city, and so on. These attributes can be compared to conditional access policies to allow or block file system access.

    ☒ **A, B,** and **D** are incorrect. Role-based access control (RBAC) assigns permissions to a role, such as "Virtual Machine Manager," and users assigned to that role inherit the role permissions. Discretionary access control (DAC) places control of permissions assignments in the hands of the data custodian (the person responsible for managing data). Time-based access control uses policies to allow or deny resource access based on the date and time.

4. ☑ **C.** A smartcard (something you have) is the size of a credit card and is commonly used for authenticating to IT systems. Smartcards can be used for other applications such as building access or as a credit card. Modern credit cards contain an embedded microprocessor that can perform cryptographic operations. Using a smartcard normally requires entering a PIN (something you know).

☒ **A, B,** and **D** are incorrect. The listed items are examples of single-factor authentication (something you know, something you have). Multifactor authentication must use two or more authentication categories such as something you have (smartcard) and something you know (PIN).

5. ☑ **B** and **C.** SSH public key authentication uses a public and private key pair for each user that will authenticate to the Linux host. The public key is stored in the user's home directory in a hidden directory named .ssh (the leading dot in Linux means the file or directory is hidden). The private key is stored on the user management device and should be protected with a passphrase. When users authenticate to the Linux host, they must know the username and the passphrase for the private key.

☒ **A** and **D** are incorrect. The public key is not stored with the user; it is stored on the Linux host. The private key is stored on the device the user will use to remotely manage the Linux host via SSH.

6. ☑ **C.** With SSH public key authentication, the private key is stored on the user management device. Standard security best practices dictate that private key files must be protected with a passphrase. Users are being prompted for the private key passphrase, not their user account password.

☒ **A, B,** and **D** are incorrect. SSH is not configured incorrectly on the client or server since the user is being prompted for a private key passphrase (not a public key passphrase).

7. ☑ **D.** Geofencing uses device location tracking to present mobile device users with a message when they are within a specific geographic boundary.

☒ **A, B,** and **C** are incorrect. Geotagging is used to provide detailed location information metadata to files such as photos. Geolocation uses methods such as GPS or IP addressing to determine the location of a device. The global positioning system (GPS) uses a network of satellites orbiting the Earth to track device locations using longitude and latitude coordinates.

8. ☑ **A.** Geotagging is used to provide detailed location information metadata to files such as photos or social media posts.

☒ **B, C,** and **D** are incorrect. Geolocation uses methods such as GPS or IP addressing to determine the location of a device. GPS uses a network of satellites orbiting the Earth to track device locations using longitude and latitude coordinates. Geofencing uses device location tracking to present mobile device users with message when they are within a specific geographic boundary.

9. ☑ **C.** Configuring password history for user accounts prevents users from reusing passwords; this option can be configured according to how many passwords should be remembered.

☒ **A, B,** and **D** are incorrect. These options will not prevent the use of old passwords. Requiring complex passwords makes it more difficult for malicious users to break into user accounts using dictionary attacks, for example. Configuring user account lockout temporarily locks (and does not permanently disable) an account after a configured number of successive failed login attempts takes place during a specific timeframe and helps mitigate against brute-force password attacks. Time-based login allows user login only during specified days and times, and user activity can be tracked through user account auditing.

10. ☑ **C.** Deterrent controls such as device login messages are designed to deter or discourage illegal or malicious behaviors.

☒ **A, B,** and **D** are incorrect. Detective controls are designed to identify security incidents such as identifying suspicious activity through log analysis. Corrective controls take active steps to contain or block suspicious activity, such as a security appliance blocking IP addresses from which excessive network traffic originates. Compensating controls are used when a preferred security control cannot be implemented because it is impractical or prohibitively expensive; compensating controls must still satisfy the stated security requirement.

11. ☑ **D.** Specialized security operating systems such as security enhanced (SE) Linux use mandatory access control (MAC) to control resource access. With MAC, administrators label items such as files, network ports, or running processes and create security levels that are assigned to users or remote network devices to allow or block access to labeled items. The operating system enforces MAC.

☒ **A, B,** and **C** are incorrect. DAC places control of permissions assignments in the hands of the data custodian (the person responsible for managing data). RBAC assigns permissions to a role, such as "Virtual Machine Manager," and users assigned to that role inherit the role permissions. User and device accounts contain many attributes (properties) such as manager name, group membership, last login time, city, and so on. These attributes can be compared to conditional access policies to allow or deny access to resources.

12. ☑ **C and D.** Service accounts can be assigned only the permissions required for software to function correctly, and the software is then configured to use the service account. Secure connectivity between virtual machines in the cloud and on-premises can be achieved with a site-to-site VPN between the on-premises network and the public cloud provider.

☒ **A and B** are incorrect. HTTP is not a secure network protocol, though HTTPS would meet the stated requirements. Using a guest account that could be shared among multiple people is not appropriate for this scenario; guest accounts should provide very restricted access to resources.

13. ☑ **D.** The impossible travel time security feature monitors user activity from different locations to identity anomalies or risky login. As an example, logging in from New York City at 10 a.m. EST and then Paris at 11 a.m. EST would mean traveling between those locations within one hour, which is not possible. If network proxy servers or personal VPN anonymizing software are used, this type of situation might be valid and must be considered when configuring this type of feature.

    ☒ **A, B,** and **C** are incorrect. A chain of trust is established in a PKI hierarchy, where devices would trust certificates issued from a trusted issuing certification authority. Security tokens are issued by IdPs, which contain user accounts and perform authentication, and with federated identify environments, IdPs generate a security token that may contain assertions (claims) about the user such as date of birth, department, and so on. The security token is then digitally signed by the identity provider with its private key. Applications that trust the IdP signature (using the IdP public key) accept tokens and allow user access. Geofencing uses device location tracking to present mobile device users with a message when they are within a specific geographic boundary.

14. ☑ **B.** Conditional access control uses rules (rule-based access control) in conditional access policies to allow or deny access to labeled resources such as files. In this example, files labeled as PII, the corporate network location, and project assignment attributes are the conditions.

    ☒ **A, C,** and **D** are incorrect. DAC places control of permissions assignments in the hands of the data custodian (the person responsible for managing data). With MAC, administrators label items such as files, network ports, or running processes and create security levels that are assigned to users or remote network devices to allow or block access to labeled items. The operating system enforces MAC. RBAC assigns permissions to a role, such as "Virtual Machine Manager," and users assigned to that role inherit the role permissions.

15. ☑ **B.** Managerial security controls are administrative in nature, from a business perspective, and include activities such as risk assessments and personnel management.

    ☒ **A, C,** and **D** are incorrect. Operational security controls are the day-to-day activities related to IT management security such as configuration and update management. Technical security controls are processed by computing devices, such as configuring firewall access control lists (ACLs) to control network access or encrypting storage media. Physical security controls address physical security issues and include mitigations such as door locks and motion detection sensors.

16. ☑ **A.** Operational security controls are the day-to-day activities related to IT management security such as the execution of daily or weekly backups.

    ☒ **B, C,** and **D** are incorrect. Managerial security controls are administrative in nature from a business perspective and include activities such as risk assessments and personnel management. Technical security controls are processed by computing devices, such as configuring firewall access control lists (ACLs) to control network access. Physical security controls address physical security issues and include mitigations such as door locks and motion detection sensors.

17.   ☑   **C.** Technical security controls are processed by computing devices, such as encrypting sensitive data.
☒   **A, B,** and **D** are incorrect. Operational security controls are the day-to-day activities related to IT management security such as the execution of daily or weekly backups. Managerial security controls are administrative in nature from a business perspective and include activities such as risk assessments and personnel management. Physical security controls address physical security issues and include mitigations such as door locks and motion detection sensors.

18.   ☑   **C.** Preventative controls are configured to avoid security incidents from occurring, such as allowing unnecessary traffic through a firewall destined for an internal network.
☒   **A, B,** and **D** are incorrect. Physical security controls address physical security issues and include mitigations such as door locks and motion detection sensors. Compensating controls are used when a preferred security control cannot be implemented because it is impractical or prohibitively expensive; compensating controls must still satisfy the stated security requirement. Detective controls are designed to identify security incidents such as identifying suspicious activity through log analysis.

19.   ☑   **B.** Compensating controls are used when a preferred security control, such as TPM-enabled computers, cannot be implemented because it is impractical or prohibitively expensive; compensating controls, such as decryption keys on removable storage, must still satisfy the stated security requirement.
☒   **A, C,** and **D** are incorrect. Physical security controls address physical security issues and include mitigations such as door locks and motion detection sensors. Detective controls are designed to identify security incidents such as identifying suspicious activity through log analysis. Corrective controls take active steps to contain or block suspicious activity, such as a security appliance blocking IP addresses from which excessive network traffic originate.

20.   ☑   **D.** Corrective controls take active steps to contain or block suspicious activity, such as a security appliance blocking IP addresses from which excessive network traffic originate.
☒   **A, B,** and **C** are incorrect. Physical security controls address physical security issues and include mitigations such as door locks and motion detection sensors. Compensating controls are used when a preferred security control cannot be implemented because it is impractical or prohibitively expensive; compensating controls must still satisfy the stated security requirement. Deterrent controls such as device login messages are designed to deter or discourage illegal or malicious behavior.

21.   ☑   **A.** The GPS uses a network of satellites orbiting the Earth to track device locations using longitude and latitude coordinates. Wi-Fi can also be used to track devices through either their IP address or their presence on a specific Wi-Fi network.
☒   **B, C,** and **D** are incorrect. Near field communication (NFC), Bluetooth, and network access control (NAC) are not used to track device location. NFC is commonly used for "tap" contactless payment systems from smartphones or payment cards over very small distances of approximately 4 centimeters (1.6 inches). Bluetooth allows for wireless connectivity such as for transferring files between devices at close range, which is normally up to approximately 10 meters (33 feet). NAC solutions can limit device network access by checking that connecting users and devices meet a variety of conditions before being granted network access.

22. ☑ **D.** Federated IdPs generate a security token that may contain assertions (claims) about the user such as date of birth, security clearance level, and so on.

☒ **A, B,** and **C** are incorrect. A PKI certificate is a security certificate that can be stored in a file, a network directory service, or a smartcard, that uniquely identifies a subject such as a device or user. A cookie is a small text file that can contain web site session or preference information and is used by a web browser. The SAML standard is used to transmit authentication and authorization messages between users, IdPs, and resource providers.

23. ☑ **B.** The error message states that the public key was sent by the server but that the server refused "our" key; in this context, that would be the private key. The public and private key are a pair. What probably happened is the wrong private key was used to connect to the Linux host.

☒ **A, C,** and **D** are incorrect. The listed possibilities do not reflect why the SSH public key authentication failed.

24. ☑ **A.** SSH public keys are stored in the Linux authorized_keys file.

☒ **B, C,** and **D** are incorrect. None of the listed keys is stored in the authorized_keys file on a Linux server.

25. ☑ **B** and **C.** Because private keys uniquely identify a user, a private key file should be password protected. Changing default settings, such as port numbers, is a part of hardening. A port between 49,152 and 65,535 should be used, since ports 0–1023 are reserved for well-known TCP/IP network services and ports 1,020–49,151 are reserved as registered ports.

☒ **A** and **D** are incorrect. Public keys do not have to be kept private. TCP port 25 is not the standard SSH port number; port 22 is.

26. ☑ **A** and **C.** SSH public key authentication replaces standard username and password authentication. A username is required in addition to a private key (and possibly private key file passphrase). The private key must be part of the public/private key pair where the public key is stored on the server.

☒ **B** and **D** are incorrect. User passwords are not required with SSH public key authentication, nor is a symmetric key required.

27. ☑ **C.** With identity federation, one common requirement to allow resource providers (FakeCorp2 web app servers) to trust IdPs (Dc1) is to install the public key certificate for the identity provider on the resource provider host. This enables the resource provider to validate security tokens digitally signed by the identity provider with its private key.

☒ **A, B,** and **D** are incorrect. Only Dc1 should have access to its own private key, to digitally sign security tokens after successful user authentication. The administrative username or password should not be supplied to resource provider technicians.

28. ☑ **A** and **B.** Smartcards require a reader for authentication, and the owner of the smartcard must enter a personal identification number (PIN) to use the card.

☒ **C** and **D** are incorrect. TPM is a firmware chip within a computing device that ensures device boot integrity and stores cryptographic keys used to encrypt storage devices. A HSM appliance is used to securely store cryptographic secrets that can be accessed by multiple hosts.

29. ☑ **D.** TPM is a firmware chip within a computing device that ensures device boot integrity and stores cryptographic keys used to encrypt storage devices. Virtual smartcards are a feature of TPM whereby, to the operating system on the TPM host, the smartcard always appears to be inserted.

    ☒ **A, B,** and **C** are incorrect. The listed locations are not used to store virtual smartcards. The Windows registry stores Windows configuration settings, RADIUS servers are centralized authentication servers in a network access control environment, and identity providers contain user and device accounts.

30. ☑ **D.** The user private key is used to create a digital signature. Decrypting messages requires the related private key from the key pair.

    ☒ **A, B,** and **C** are incorrect. User smartcards do not store server keys. The public key is not used to create digital signatures or to decrypt messages. The user's public key is used by recipients to verify the integrity of the message, and encrypting messages requires the public key of the recipient.

31. ☑ **D.** Using a physical smartcard is possible on a device with a smartcard reader. A virtual smartcard is tied to the TPM within a specific host.

    ☒ **A, B,** and **C** are incorrect. TPM, and by extension, virtual smartcards, are not available on Android-based smartphones. Virtual smartcards can be used for remote management because the target system smartcard service redirects to the system the user is using for remote management, so as long as the user system supports virtual smartcards via TPM, remote smartcard authentication will work. There is no such thing as virtual smartcard reader other than the notion of standard smartcard APIs reading a virtual smartcard as if it were a physical smartcard.

32. ☑ **D.** Configuring user account lockout to temporarily lock an account after consecutive login failures can help mitigate brute-force password attacks because after the account is locked, additional passwords cannot be tested against it.

    ☒ **A, B,** and **C** are incorrect. A denial of service (DoS) attack prevents legitimate access to a service and comes in many forms, such as flooding a network with useless network traffic or crashing a server intentionally. A ransomware attack encrypts user data files and promises to provide a decryption key upon user payment, often anonymously via Bitcoin, but there is never a guarantee that decryption keys will be provided. Phishing attacks attempt to trick victims into divulging sensitive information and can be perpetrated in many ways, including fraudulent phone calls or e-mail messages.

Chapter 12

Introduction to Cryptography

CERTIFICATION OBJECTIVES

QUESTIONS

IT security specialists implement cryptographic solutions to protect sensitive data and to ensure the trustworthiness of data including network transmissions.

Hashing is used to verify the integrity of data such as ensuring that files or network messages have not been altered by unauthorized parties. Encryption provides data confidentiality and can use either a single key for encryption and decryption or a related public and private key pair.

IPSec can be used to secure network traffic through authentication and encryption and to establish a VPN tunnel. Other network security protocols such as Transport Layer Security (TLS) are specific to an application and require host-specific configurations. A strong knowledge of when to use specific cryptographic algorithms goes a long way in enhancing your organization's security posture.

1. Which cryptographic operations use an asymmetric private key? (Choose two.)
   A. Creating a digital signature
   B. Verifying a digital signature
   C. Encrypting a message
   D. Decrypting messages

2. Which cryptographic operation does not use a cryptographic key?
   A. Encrypting
   B. Hashing
   C. Decrypting
   D. Creating digital signatures

3. Which type of key is used by an IPSec VPN configured with a pre-shared key (PSK)?
   A. Public
   B. Private
   C. Asymmetric
   D. Symmetric

4. You are evaluating a secure network management solution that will be used to monitor and configure network infrastructure devices remotely. Which of the following is the best choice?
   A. SFTP
   B. FTPS
   C. SNMPv3
   D. HTTPS

5. Your company provides remote word processing and spreadsheet file access using FTP. After a security audit, the findings suggest employing TLS to harden FTP access. Which protocol should you configure to address this concern?

   A. SFTP

   B. FTPS

   C. SNMPv3

   D. HTTPS

6. You are reviewing network perimeter firewall rules for the firewall public interface and notice allowances for incoming UDP port 161 and TCP port 443 traffic. What type of traffic will be allowed through the firewall public interface, assuming default ports are being used? (Choose two.)

   A. SFTP

   B. SNMPv3

   C. FTPS

   D. HTTPS

7. Which encryption algorithms can SNMPv3 use?

   A. AES, MD5

   B. SHA-256, 3DES

   C. 3DES, AES

   D. MD5, 3DES

8. You are configuring SNMPv3 authentication. Which of the following hashing algorithms are available?

   A. MD5, RSA

   B. MD5, SHA

   C. SHA, AES

   D. AES, 3DES

9. You have configured LDAP over SSL (LDAPS) with default settings to secure directory service queries across subnets. Which port must be open on the subnet firewall?

   A. TCP 389

   B. TCP 22

   C. TCP 25

   D. TCP 636

10. Refer to Figure 12-1. Which security option is enabled?

    A. IPSec

    B. VPN

    C. DNSSEC

    D. HTTPS

FIGURE 12-1

Microsoft
Windows DNS
zone records

(same as parent folder)	RR Signature (RRSIG)	[DNSKEY][Inception(UTC):...	static
(same as parent folder)	RR Signature (RRSIG)	[NSEC3PARAM][Inception...	static
(same as parent folder)	DNS KEY (DNSKEY)	[256][DNSSEC][RSA/SHA-...	static
(same as parent folder)	DNS KEY (DNSKEY)	[256][DNSSEC][RSA/SHA-...	static
(same as parent folder)	DNS KEY (DNSKEY)	[257][DNSSEC][RSA/SHA-...	static
(same as parent folder)	DNS KEY (DNSKEY)	[257][DNSSEC][RSA/SHA-...	static
(same as parent folder)	Next Secure 3 Parameter...	[SHA-1][0][50][C3F1779A9...	static
028ub3gosba3qhanumu5h...	RR Signature (RRSIG)	[NSEC3][Inception(UTC): 7...	static

11. Secure POP mail transmissions use which standard port number?

   A. 995

   B. 110

   C. 993

   D. 443

12. You are reviewing captured network traffic shown in Figure 12-2. Which network security protocol is in use on the network?

   A. SSL

   B. TLS

   C. HTTPS

   D. IPSec

FIGURE 12-2

Network packet
capture

No.	Time	Source	Destination	Protocol
721	11.779097	192.168.0.21	192.168.0.231	ESP
727	11.804623	192.168.0.231	192.168.0.21	ESP
1083	23.067493	192.168.0.21	192.168.0.231	ESP
1084	23.067593	192.168.0.231	192.168.0.21	ESP
1208	27.408648	192.168.0.21	192.168.0.231	ESP
1212	27.426431	192.168.0.231	192.168.0.21	ESP
1531	38.352586	192.168.0.21	192.168.0.231	ESP

13. Which IPSec configuration mode encapsulates origin IP packets?

   A. ESP

   B. AH

   C. Tunnel

   D. Transport

14. You are planning your SMTP mail system so that mail transfers are encrypted. Which protocol should you use?

   A. NTS

   B. SRTP

   C. S/MIME

   D. LDAPS

15. Which term refers to providing random data as additional input to a hashing algorithm?
  A. Key stretching
  B. Salting
  C. Perfect forward secrecy
  D. Ephemeral

16. Which cryptographic operations use a public key? (Choose two.)
  A. Verifying digital signatures
  B. Encrypting messages
  C. Creating digital signatures
  D. Decrypting messages

17. Which technology is described as "a secure distributed public ledger of transactions"?
  A. Quantum communications
  B. Quantum computing
  C. Steganography
  D. Blockchain

18. A government informant embeds sensitive drug cartel data in an e-mail attachment. The attachment appears to be a picture of a dog. Which data secrecy technique is being used?
  A. Steganography
  B. Encryption
  C. Hashing
  D. Blockchain

19. Which cryptographic attribute mitigates brute-force key attacks?
  A. Key length
  B. Key exchange
  C. Authentication
  D. Encryption

20. Which of the following is a cryptographic stream cipher?
  A. AES
  B. DES
  C. Blowfish
  D. RC4

21. Which of the following are symmetric encryption block ciphers? (Choose two.)
  A. AES
  B. CBC
  C. RC5
  D. RC4

22. Which public key cryptographic design can use smaller keys while maintaining cryptographic strength?
    A. CBC
    B. S/MIME
    C. ECC
    D. IPSec

23. Which encryption technique is designed to run on devices with constraints such as low power and low processing capabilities?
    A. Homomorphic encryption
    B. Lightweight cryptography
    C. Entropy
    D. Blockchain

24. Which cryptographic technique allows the analysis of data without first decrypting it?
    A. Lightweight encryption
    B. Homomorphic encryption
    C. Entropy
    D. Blockchain

25. You are using the free PuTTY Key Generator tool to create a public and private key pair. Which term best describes what is happening in Figure 12-3?
    A. Salting
    B. Obfuscation
    C. Hashing
    D. Entropy

FIGURE 12-3

Key pair
generation
using PuTTY Key
Generator

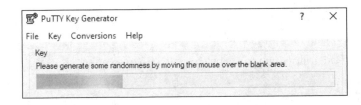

26. Which benefit is derived from using a HSM to carry out cryptographic operations as opposed to a standard operating system such as Microsoft Windows?
    A. Ability to store cloud-generated certificates
    B. Ability to enable IPSec tunnel mode
    C. Lower cost
    D. Lower computational latency

27. Which statements regarding PKI certificates are correct? (Choose two.)
    A. A certificate can be used for more than one cryptographic purpose.
    B. A 2048-bit key is considered weak.
    C. Certificates cannot be issued to routers.
    D. Certificates have an expiry date.

28. For security and performance reasons, you would like IP phone VoIP traffic to be isolated from regular TCP/IP network traffic. Which network protocol will allow this end result?
    A. IPSec
    B. S/MIME
    C. SSH
    D. DHCP

29. You plan on using a web browser secured connection to manage your public cloud subscription. Which outbound port number must be allowed on your network firewall?
    A. 636
    B. 995
    C. 993
    D. 443

30. Which service is provided by DNSSEC?
    A. Confidentiality
    B. Integrity
    C. Network address allocation
    D. Availability

31. Which network security protocol can encrypt all network traffic using a single configuration?
    A. TLS
    B. SSL
    C. IPSec
    D. HTTPS

32. Which cryptographic technique is often referred to as "hiding in plain sight"?
    A. Entropy
    B. Quantum computing
    C. Hashing
    D. Steganography

QUICK ANSWER KEY

1. A, D
2. B
3. D
4. C
5. B
6. B, D
7. C
8. B
9. D
10. C
11. A

12. D
13. C
14. C
15. B
16. A, B
17. D
18. A
19. A
20. D
21. A, C
22. C

23. B
24. B
25. D
26. D
27. A, D
28. D
29. D
30. B
31. C
32. D

IN-DEPTH ANSWERS

1. ☑ **A** and **D.** Digital signatures assure the recipient of a message that it is authentic and has not been modified. The message sender's private key is used to create a digital signature thus constituting nonrepudiation; the sender cannot deny having sent and signed the message because only the sender has access to their private key. Private keys are also used to decrypt messages, such as e-mail messages.

    ☒ **B** and **C** are incorrect. Private keys create a digital signature and the related public key is used to verify the signature. The sender of an encrypted message must have access to the public key of message recipients in order to encrypt the message for them.

2. ☑ **B.** Hashing is used to verify that a file or message has not changed. The origin data is fed into a one-way cryptographic algorithm resulting in a unique value called a hash; a cryptographic key is not used. One-way algorithms are easy to compute given input, but it is very difficult to take a hash and determine the original value.

    ☒ **A, C,** and **D** are incorrect. Encryption uses a cryptographic key and algorithm to convert plain text into encrypted data or cipher text to provide data confidentiality. Decryption requires a cryptographic key and algorithm to convert cipher text back to the original plain text. With symmetric encryption, the same key is used for encryption and decryption. With asymmetric encryption, the public key encrypts and the related private key decrypts. Digital signatures assure the recipient of a message that it is authentic and has not been modified. The message sender's private key is used to create a digital signature.

3. ☑ **D.** With symmetric encryption, the same key is used for encryption and decryption. The IPSec VPN PSK must be configured on both ends of the VPN tunnel.

    ☒ **A, B,** and **C** are incorrect. PSKs do not use asymmetric encryption, which uses public and private key pairs. With asymmetric encryption, the public key encrypts and the related private key decrypts.

4. ☑ **C.** The Simple Network Management Protocol (SNMP) version 3 supports authenticated and encrypted messages when remotely monitoring and managing devices running an SNMP agent such as routers, switches, and server operating systems. SNMP normally uses UDP port 161.
☒ **A, B,** and **D** are incorrect. SSH File Transfer Protocol (SFTP) uses remote encrypted SSH sessions to transfer files securely between SSH hosts, which normally listen on TCP port 22. File Transfer Protocol Secure (FTPS) uses Transport Layer Security (TLS) to enable the secure transfer of files between FTP hosts over TCP port 21 (explicit FTPS) or 990 (implicit FTPS); traditional FTP passes credentials and data over the network in clear text. Hypertext Transfer Protocol Secure (HTTPS) secures transmissions between clients and web servers using the TLS network security protocol. Due to security vulnerabilities, Secure Sockets Layer (SSL) has been deprecated and superseded by TLS (with the latest version being 1.3).

5. ☑ **B.** FTPS uses TLS to enable the secure transfer of files between FTP hosts over TCP port 21 (explicit FTPS) or 990 (implicit FTPS); traditional FTP passes credentials and data over the network in clear text.
☒ **A, C,** and **D** are incorrect. SFTP uses remote encrypted SSH sessions to transfer files securely between SSH hosts, which normally listen on TCP port 22. SNMP version 3 supports authenticated and encrypted messages when remotely monitoring and managing devices running an SNMP agent such as routers, switches, and server operating systems. HTTPS secures transmissions between clients and web servers using the TLS network security protocol.

6. ☑ **B** and **D.** SNMP uses UDP port 161 and HTTPS uses TCP 443.
☒ **A** and **C** are incorrect. SFTP uses remote encrypted SSH sessions to transfer files securely between SSH hosts. FTPS uses TLS to enable the secure transfer of files between FTP hosts over TCP port 21 (explicit FTPS) or 990 (implicit FTPS).

7. ☑ **C.** SNMPv3 can use Triple Digital Encryption Standard (3DES) or the newer Advanced Encryption Standard (AES) algorithm to encrypt SNMP data sent over the network.
☒ **A, B,** and **D** are incorrect. The listed combinations are not encryption algorithms; Message Digest 5 (MD5) and Secure Hashing Algorithm (SHA) are hashing algorithms that are used to verify the integrity of data, not to encrypt it.

8. ☑ **B.** MD5 and SHA are hashing algorithms that are used to verify the integrity of data and can be used for authentication SNMPv3 connections over the network.
☒ **A, C,** and **D** are incorrect. These items contain encryption algorithms that are not used for authentication. Rivest Shamir Adleman (RSA) is an asymmetric encryption standard, the AES algorithm is a symmetric block cipher, and 3DES is an older encryption standard whose use has diminished in favor of AES.

9. ☑ **D.** Lightweight Directory Access Protocol Secure (LDAPS) uses a PKI certificate to secure LDAP connections over the network and uses TCP port 636. LDAP is used to connect to and query a centralized network directory service database such as Microsoft Active Directory.
☒ **A, B,** and **C** are incorrect. LDAP uses TCP and UDP ports 389, SSH uses TCP port 22, and SMTP uses TCP port 25.

10. ☑ **C.** Domain Name System Security Extensions (DNSSEC) protects DNS clients from forged DNS answers in response to client DNS queries. With DNSSEC, DNS zone records are digitally signed. DNS clients verify the signature of DNS query results using a public key to ensure the response is valid. (DNS clients trust the private key used to sign the DNS zone.) Figure 12-1 shows resource record (RR) signatures and DNS KEY records, which exist in the zone only when DNSSEC is enabled.
☒ **A, B,** and **D** are incorrect. The listed items do not make changes to DNS zone records. IPSec is a network security protocol that can be configured to authenticate and encrypt network traffic, including establishing a VPN tunnel. IPSec can use a variety of methods to secure connections including PSKs and PKI security certificates. A virtual private network creates an encrypted tunnel between two end-points to enable secure access to a remote host or network over an untrusted network such as the Internet. HTTPS secures transmissions between clients and web servers using the TLS network security protocol.

11. ☑ **A.** The Post Office Protocol (POP) is a client mail retrieval standard and can be secured using a PKI certificate. Secure POP uses a standard port number of TCP 995.
☒ **B, C,** and **D** are incorrect. POP mail transmissions (and not secure POP) use a standard port number of TCP 110. The Internet Message Access Protocol over SSL (IMAPS) is a client to mail server message retrieval standard that normally uses TCP port 993 (standard IMAP uses TCP port 143). TCP port 443 is used for secured HTTPS web server communication.

12. ☑ **D.** We know that IPSec is in use because of the Encapsulating Security Payload (ESP) traffic. In addition to message authentication, ESP tunnel mode can place an entire IP packet within another IP packet (encapsulation) and encrypt that payload, or in transport mode, ESP can encrypt the original packet IP payload (no encapsulation).
☒ **A, B,** and **C** are incorrect. SSL is a deprecated network security protocol superseded by TLS. Both SSL and TLS use a PKI certificate to secure network transmissions for higher level protocols such as FTP and HTTP. HTTPS stems from securing HTTP communications with a PKI certificate.

13. ☑ **C.** IPSec tunnel mode can place an entire IP packet within another IP packet (encapsulation) and encrypt that payload.
☒ **A, B,** and **D** are incorrect. ESP can be used in both IPSec tunnel and transport modes to provide message authentication and confidentiality through encryption. Authentication Header provides only message authentication and not encryption. IPSec tunnel mode is used for IPSec VPNs where packet encapsulation is use, whereas transport mode encrypts the IP packet payload and does not use encapsulation.

14. ☑ **C.** Mail traffic can be encrypted and digitally signed through the Secure/Multipurpose Internet Mail Extensions (S/MIME) protocol, which requires SMTP hosts to be configured with a PKI certificate.
☒ **A, B,** and **D** are incorrect. Network Time Security (NTS) uses TLS to secure Network Time Protocol (NTP) network time synchronization traffic. The Secure Real-Time Transport Protocol (SRTP) is used to secure video and audio transmissions such as Voice over IP (VoIP). Lightweight Directory Access Protocol Secure (LDAPS) uses a PKI certificate to secure LDAP connections over the network and used TCP port 636.

15.   ☑   **B.** Salting enhances hashing security using random bits in addition to origin data, such as a passphrase that is fed into a one-way hashing algorithm. To calculate the original passphrase value, the salt value must be known. Salting makes dictionary attacks much less likely to succeed.
☒   **A, C,** and **D** are incorrect. Key stretching is a cryptographic technique used to make weak keys, passwords, or even hashes more secure (more complex to reverse-engineer) by executing multiple rounds of encryption against previous encryption results. Perfect forward secrecy uses unique session keys that have a limited lifetime so that a compromised session key can be used for a specific session only. In cryptography, ephemeral keys are temporary, such as unique session keys that are valid for a specific network session only.

16.   ☑   **A and B.** Private keys create a digital signature and the related public key is used to verify the signature. The sender of an encrypted message must have access to the public key of message recipients to encrypt the message for them.
☒   **C and D** are incorrect. Digital signatures assure the recipient of a message that it is authentic and has not been modified. The message sender's private key is used to create a digital signature. Private keys are also used to decrypt messages, such as e-mail messages.

17.   ☑   **D.** Blockchain provides a distributed public ledger of transactions that cannot be modified. Because the blockchain of transactions is managed by thousands of computers, it is not controlled by a single central organization or government. Bitcoin digital currency transactions are one example of how blockchain can be used. Bitcoin transactions are considered anonymous, since the transactions are linked to a digital identity.
☒   **A, B,** and **C** are incorrect. Quantum communications use characteristics of quantum physics to keep network transmissions private. The simple act of eavesdropping on a transmission alters the transmission, which cannot be hidden. Quantum computing is based on the premise of manipulating quantum bits (qbits), which can exhibit multiple states simultaneously as opposed to current-day computing, which uses bits (0's and 1's) to represent the state of data (only two possibilities). Quantum computing results in the ability to perform multiple calculations quickly, thus increasing compute power. Post-quantum cryptographic algorithms are considered to be safe even from quantum computers in the future. Steganography is a technique used to hide sensitive data within other nonsensitive items, such as hiding a secret message within a photo.

18.   ☑   **A.** Steganography is a technique used to hide sensitive data within other nonsensitive items, such as hiding a secret message within a photo of a dog, which often requires special software to hide and unhide the message. Messages can he hidden in many types of files, including audio and video.
☒   **B, C,** and **D** are incorrect. Encryption uses a cryptographic key and algorithm to convert plain text into encrypted data, also known as cipher text, to provide data confidentiality. Hashing is used to verify that a file or message has not changed. The origin data is fed into a one-way hashing algorithm, resulting in a unique value called a hash. Blockchain provides a distributed public ledger of transactions that cannot be modified. Because the blockchain of transactions is managed by thousands of computers, it is not controlled by a single central organization or government.

19. ☑ **A.** In general, the longer a cryptographic key (number of bits), the more difficult it becomes to brute-force key values due to the increased number of possible key combinations. The strength and implementation of an encryption algorithm (and not only the key size) determine its resilience to attacks.

☒ **B, C,** and **D** are incorrect. Key exchange refers to two end-points communicating over a network to generate a unique session key. Diffie-Hellman is a key exchange algorithm used by network security protocols such as Internet Key Exchange (IKE). Authentication proves the identity of a user or device, and it is also used to ensure that a message has not been forged or altered. Encryption uses a cryptographic key and algorithm to convert plain text into encrypted data, or cipher text, to provide data confidentiality.

20. ☑ **D.** The Rivest Cipher 4 (RC4) algorithm is a stream cipher, meaning that data is encrypted 1 byte at a time instead of an entire data block (more than 1 byte) being encrypted at once.

☒ **A, B,** and **C** are incorrect. Advanced Encryption Standard (AES), Digital Encryption Standard (DES), and Blowfish are all block ciphers.

21. ☑ **A and C.** AES and RC5 are symmetric block encryption ciphers. Block ciphers encrypt entire data blocks as opposed to individual bytes of data.

☒ **B and D** are incorrect. Cipher block chaining (CBC) is a mode of operation that can be used by a block cipher; the current plain text data block being processed is added to the previous encrypted block, and the combined items are then encrypted; then this is repeated. The RC4 algorithm is a stream cipher, meaning that data is encrypted 1 byte at a time instead of an entire data block (more than 1 byte) being encrypted at once.

22. ☑ **C.** Elliptic curve cryptography uses a set of points for a curve over a finite field instead of using prime number factoring for encryption. This allows for smaller key lengths, which minimizes required compute power. ECC small keys have the strength of much longer keys. For example, a 256-bit ECC key is equivalent to a 3072-bit RSA key.

☒ **A, B,** and **D** are incorrect. CBC is a mode of operation that can be used by a block cipher; the current plain text data block being processed is added to the previous encrypted block and the combined items are then encrypted. SMTP mail transfer traffic can be encrypted and digitally signed through the S/MIME protocol, which requires SMTP hosts to be configured with a PKI certificate. IPSec is a network security protocol.

23. ☑ **B.** Lightweight encryption requires less compute power than traditional encryption algorithms and is well suited for mobile devices. ECC is a lightweight encryption technique that uses small keys to achieve strong security. A small key size means less computational requirements.

☒ **A, C,** and **D** are incorrect. Homomorphic encryption is a computationally expensive cryptographic technique that enables encrypted data to be analyzed without fully decrypting it. In cryptography, entropy provides randomness, such as when generating key pairs. Blockchain provides a distributed public ledger of transactions that cannot be modified. Because the blockchain of transactions is managed by thousands of computers, it is not controlled by a single central organization or government.

24. ☑ **B.** Homomorphic encryption provides data confidentiality and is a computationally expensive cryptographic technique that allows encrypted data to be analyzed without fully decrypting it. Decrypting data, while it is accessed, presents a risk of unauthorized access while in a decrypted state.

    ☒ **A, C,** and **D** are incorrect. Lightweight encryption requires less compute power than traditional encryption algorithms and is well suited for mobile devices. In cryptography, entropy provides randomness, such as when generating key pairs. Blockchain provides a distributed public ledger of transactions that cannot be modified. Because the blockchain of transactions is managed by thousands of computers, it is not controlled by a single central organization or government.

25. ☑ **D.** Figure 12-3 is prompting the user to move the move to generate randomness, which is what entropy means. Entropy reduces the likelihood of predicting cryptographic key values.

    ☒ **A, B,** and **C** are incorrect. Salting enhances hashing security using random bits in addition to origin data such as a passphrase that are fed into a one-way hashing algorithm. To calculate the original passphrase value, the salt value must be known. Salting makes dictionary attacks much less likely to succeed. Obfuscation is used to make it more difficult to read or understand something such as programming code or sensitive data. Hashing is used to verify that a file or message has not changed. The origin data is fed into a one-way hashing algorithm, resulting in a unique value called a hash.

26. ☑ **D.** A hardware security module (HSM) is a tamper-proof dedicated appliance that can securely store cryptographic keys and perform cryptographic operations. Offloading these tasks from a Microsoft Windows computer results in lower computational latency, since dedicated firmware is generally faster and more reliable than a general purpose operating system.

    ☒ **A, B,** and **C** are incorrect. Both a HSM and a Windows host can store cloud-generated certificates. IPSec tunnel mode is more a function of a VPN appliance than a HSM. HSMs will not lower cost since they are a separate dedicated hardware security appliance.

27. ☑ **A** and **D.** PKI certificates can be used for multiple purposes such as message encryption, digital signatures, and file encryption. Certificates have an expiry date upon which the certificate is no longer valid.

    ☒ **B** and **C** are incorrect. Although key length is not the only factor determining encryption strength, a 2048-bit key is not considered weak. Certificates can be issued to network infrastructure devices such as switches and routers for the purpose of client-to-network authentication, device-to-device authentication, or the decryption of network traffic.

28. ☑ **D.** You can configure DHCP vendor-class options to identity the type of device making a DHCP request (IP phone), and then assign IP settings such as IP address range and default gateway.

    ☒ **A, B,** and **C** are incorrect. IPSec is a network security protocol that can be configured to authenticate and encrypt network traffic, including establishing a VPN tunnel. SMTP mail transfer traffic can be encrypted and digitally signed through the S/MIME protocol, which requires SMTP hosts to be configured with a PKI certificate. SSH is an encrypted remote management protocol that uses TCP port 22.

29. ☑ **D.** HTTPS secured connections use TCP port 443.
☒ **A, B,** and **C** are incorrect. LDAPS uses TCP port 636, secure POP uses TCP port 995, and IMAPS servers use TCP port 993.

30. ☑ **B.** DNSSEC protects DNS clients from forged DNS answers in response to client DNS queries. With DNSSEC, DNS zone records are digitally signed. DNS clients verify the signature of DNS query results using a public key to ensure that the response is valid. (DNS clients trust the private key used to sign the DNS zone.)
☒ **A, C,** and **D** are incorrect. The listed items are not provided by DNSSEC. Data confidentiality is achieved through encryption. DHCP provides IP configuration settings to clients from a central configuration. Availability ensures that IT systems and data are accessible when needed and includes items such as data backups and high availability server clusters.

31. ☑ **C.** IPSec can be configured to secure some or all network traffic using a single configuration, unlike application security protocols like HTTPS, which apply only to web servers, where each server requires a PKI certificate.
☒ **A, B,** and **D** are incorrect. TLS supersedes the deprecated SSL network security protocol. TLS requires services to be configured with a PKI certificate, such as web servers or mail servers. Web servers using TLS use HTTPS to exchange messages with clients. Unlike IPsec, the listed protocols cannot secure all network traffic.

32. ☑ **D.** Steganography is a technique used to hide sensitive data within other nonsensitive items, such as hiding a secret message within a photo of a dog, which requires special software to hide and unhide the message.
☒ **A, B,** and **C** are incorrect. In cryptography, entropy provides randomness, such as when generating key pairs. Quantum computing is based on the premise of manipulating quantum bits (qbits), which can exhibit multiple states simultaneously, as opposed to current-day computing, which uses bits (0's and 1's) to represent the state of data (only two possibilities). Hashing is used to verify that a file or message has not changed. The origin data is fed into a one-way cryptographic algorithm, resulting in a unique value called a hash; a cryptographic key is not used. One-way algorithms are easy to compute given input, but it is very difficult to take a hash and determine the original value.

Chapter 13

Managing a Public Key Infrastructure

QUESTIONS

Sensitive data exchange on any network will benefit from a public key infrastructure (PKI). A PKI provides security using digital certificates. Certificate authorities (CAs) issue certificates to valid parties for the purpose of confidentiality (encryption), integrity (digital signatures and hashing), authentication (user or device), and nonrepudiation (no disputing of an entity performing an action).

Each certificate consists of a unique, mathematically related public and private key pair in addition to other data such as the certificate expiration date. Compromised certificates can be revoked and their serial numbers published with a certificate revocation list (CRL).

1. Which of the following items are stored within a user PKI certificate? (Choose two.)
   A. Public key
   B. Intermediary CA
   C. CRL
   D. Expiration date

2. Which component sits at the top of a PKI hierarchy?
   A. Intermediate CA
   B. Root CA
   C. CRL
   D. Device certificate

3. What is established when a device trusts a pubic CA root certificate?
   A. Certificate revocation
   B. Registration authority
   C. Certification authority
   D. Chain of trust

4. Users complain that they receive an untrusted web site warning in their web browsers when connecting to a HTTPS-enabled intranet web server, but not when they connect over HTTP. What is the most likely reason this is happening?
   A. Users have not yet authenticated to the web site.
   B. The web site is blocked by a content-filtering firewall.
   C. The web server is using a self-signed certificate.
   D. User devices do not have a client certificate installed.

5. You are a Windows administrator that uses PowerShell scripts to manage Windows devices over the network. Only trusted scripts should run on hosts. What should you configure?

A. Intermediate CA

B. Code-signing certificate

C. Certificate signing request

D. Registration authority

6. What should you do to harden your PKI? (Choose two.)

A. Ensure that public key files are password protected.

B. Ensure that the root CA is online.

C. Ensure that the root CA is offline.

D. Ensure that private key files are password protected.

7. Which of the following is never stored with a digital certificate?

A. Public key

B. Private key

C. Digital signature of issuing CA

D. IP address of CA server

8. You are providing consulting services to a legal firm that has a PKI. The firm would like to enable document workflow where documents are sent electronically to the appropriate internal employees. You are asked whether there is a way to prove that documents were sent from the user listed in the FROM field. Of the following, what would you recommend?

A. File encryption

B. Digital signatures

C. E-mail encryption

D. Certificate revocation list

9. Which of the following best describes the term *key escrow*?

A. A trusted third party with decryption keys in case the original keys have expired

B. A trusted third party with copies of decryption keys in addition to existing original keys

C. An account that can be used to encrypt private keys

D. An account that can be used to encrypt data for any user

10. Which PKI component verifies the identity of certificate requestors before a certificate is issued?

A. Public key

B. RA

C. Private key

D. CRL

11. A user reports that she is unable to authenticate to the corporate VPN while traveling. You have configured the VPN to require user certificate authentication. After investigating the problem, you learn that the user certificate has expired. Which of the following presents the quickest secure solution?

    A. Create a new user certificate and configure it on the user's computer.

    B. Disable certificate authentication for your VPN.

    C. Reduce the CRL publishing frequency.

    D. Set the date back on the VPN appliance to before the user certificate expired.

12. When users connect to an intranet server by typing **https://intranet.corp.local**, their web browser displays a warning message stating the site is not to be trusted. How can this warning message be removed while maintaining security?

    A. Configure the web server to use HTTP instead of HTTPS.

    B. Install the intranet server private key on all client workstations.

    C. Use TCP port 443 instead of TCP port 80.

    D. Install the trusted root certificate in the client web browser for the issuer of the intranet server certificate.

13. An HTTPS-secured web site requires that you restrict some workstations from making a connection. Which option is the most secure?

    A. Configure the web site to allow connections only from the IP addresses of valid workstations.

    B. Configure the web site to allow connections only from the MAC addresses of valid workstations.

    C. Configure the web site to use user authentication.

    D. Configure the web site to require client-side certificates.

14. You are responsible for enabling TLS on a newly installed e-commerce web site. What should you do first? (Choose the best answer.)

    A. Install the web server digital certificate.

    B. Enable TLS on the web server.

    C. Create a CSR and submit it to a CA.

    D. Configure HTTPS on the web server to use port 443.

15. While generating a CSR for a web site, you enter the information listed here. Users will connect to the web site by typing https://www.corp.com. Identify the configuration error.

Expires: Wednesday, 4 August 2021 at 11:04:38 Eastern
Bit length: 2048
Common Name: 10.10.10.10
Organization: Corp Inc.
OU: Sales
Country: US
State: TN
City: Memphis

   A.   The expiry date is less than a year away.

   B.   The bit length should be 128.

   C.   The common name should be www.corp.com.

   D.   The State field must not be abbreviated.

16. A large national company with headquarters in Dallas, Texas, is implementing a PKI for thousands of users. There are corporate locations in 12 other major U.S. cities. Each of those locations has a senior network administrator that should retain control of IT for the location's user base. User devices in all locations must trust all certificates issued within the company. Which option presents the PKI solution that reflects best practices?

   A.   Install a root CA in Dallas. Create intermediate CAs for each city, and use these to issue certificates for users and computers in each city. Take the root CA offline.

   B.   Install a root CA in Dallas. Issue certificates for users and computers in all locations.

   C.   Install a root CA in Dallas. Issue certificates for users and computers in all locations. Take the root CA offline.

   D.   Install a root CA in Dallas and each city. Issue certificates for users and computers using each city root CA. Take the root CAs offline.

17. Which types of keys are all commonly required when connecting via HTTPS to an e-commerce web site?

   A.   Public, private, and session

   B.   Public and private

   C.   Public only

   D.   Private only

18. Which PKI component does the CA use to digitally sign issued certificates?

   A.   Private key

   B.   Public key

   C.   CRL

   D.   OCSP

19. In a PKI, what role does the CA play? (Choose two.)

   A.   Revokes certificates

   B.   Uses its private key to digitally sign certificates

   C.   Uses its public key to digitally sign certificates

   D.   Controls access to the network using certificates

20. You are developing Microsoft PowerShell scripts to automate network administration tasks. The .PS1 script files need to be digitally signed and trusted to run on computers in your environment. You have already acquired a code-signing PKI certificate. You need to back up your private key. Which file format should you choose during export? (Choose two.)

    A. DER
    B. PEM
    C. PFX
    D. CER
    E. P12
    F. P7B

21. Which security technique associates a host with its related public key?

    A. CRL
    B. OSCP
    C. Certificate pinning
    D. FQDN

22. Your web server hosts the www.corp.com and info.corp.com DNS names. Both sites require HTTPS. Which configuration meets the stated requirement while requiring the least amount of administrative effort?

    A. Install two certificates; one for each DNS name.
    B. Install a certificate revocation list on the web server host.
    C. Install a subject alternative name certificate on the web server host.
    D. Configure IPSec for the web server host.

23. Which PKI verification processes can best mitigate the creation of phishing web sites by scammers? (Choose two.)

    A. Extended validation
    B. Domain validation
    C. CRL
    D. OSCP

24. You need to reduce the amount of network traffic directed at CAs by OSCP clients. What should you configure?

    A. CSR
    B. Stapling
    C. CRL
    D. Pinning

25. How do client devices trust the TLS certificate used by an HTTPS web server?
    A. Key escrow
    B. Stapling
    C. Pinning
    D. Certificate chaining

26. Your company has registered DNS domains such as corp.com and info.corp.com. You need to ensure that web servers for these DNS domains use secured HTTPS, and you must also ensure that future subdomains of corp.com are supported for HTTPS with the least amount of administrative effort. What should you deploy?
    A. A certificate for each current and future web site
    B. RA
    C. SAN certificate
    D. Wildcard certificate

27. Refer to Figure 13-1. Under which circumstance might you click the Yes button?
    A. You require the ability to digital sign e-mail messages.
    B. You require the ability to encrypt e-mail messages.
    C. The RootCert CA has issued certificates to intranet web servers.
    D. The RootCert CA certificate is about to expire.

FIGURE 13-1

Windows security warning

28. Identify the problem in Figure 13-2.

    A. The RootCert CA certificate is not trusted.

    B. The ClientCert certificate is not trusted.

    C. The RootCert CA is offline.

    D. Certificate stapling is not enabled for the RootCert CA.

FIGURE 13-2

Windows
certificate
certification path

29. Which statements regarding Figure 13-3 are correct? (Choose two.)

    A. Encrypted e-mail messages can be decrypted.

    B. Encrypted e-mail messages can be sent.

    C. Digital signatures can be verified.

    D. Digital signatures can be created.

FIGURE 13-3

Windows general certificate details

30. Which PKI options can be used check for certificate validity? (Choose two.)
    A. Stapling
    B. CRL
    C. RA
    D. OSCP

31. Which of the following is a valid CA signing algorithm?
    A. SHA 256
    B. AES
    C. DES
    D. IKE

32. Which naming prefix identifies a PKI certificate subject name?
    A. Domain component
    B. Component name
    C. Common name
    D. DNS component

33. After importing a user certificate file to an e-mail program, a user finds she cannot digitally sign sent e-mail messages. What are some possible reasons for this? (Choose two.)
    A. The certificate was not created for e-mail usage.
    B. The private key is not in the certificate.
    C. The public key is not in the certificate.
    D. The CA signature is not in the certificate.

A

QUICK ANSWER KEY

1.	A, D	**12.**	D	**23.**	A, B
2.	B	**13.**	D	**24.**	B
3.	D	**14.**	C	**25.**	D
4.	C	**15.**	C	**26.**	D
5.	B	**16.**	A	**27.**	C
6.	C, D	**17.**	A	**28.**	A
7.	D	**18.**	A	**29.**	A, D
8.	B	**19.**	A, B	**30.**	B, D
9.	B	**20.**	C, E	**31.**	A
10.	B	**21.**	C	**32.**	C
11.	A	**22.**	C	**33.**	A, B

IN-DEPTH ANSWERS

1. ☑ **A** and **D**. Among many other items, a PKI certificate contains a public key used for cryptographic purposes such as encryption and verifying digital signatures. Certificates have an expiration date after which the certificate is no longer valid and cannot be used.
   ☒ **B** and **C** are incorrect. Intermediary certification authorities (CAs) issue certificates and are not stored within issued certificates, although their signatures are. A certificate revocation list (CRL) is a list of certificate serial numbers that have been revoked (not expired) for reasons such as a user leaving the organization or a lost or stolen user smartphone containing a certificate.

2. ☑ **B**. The root CA resides at the top of the PKI hierarchy, followed by issued certificates and registration authorities (RAs), which can issue certificates and subordinate registration authorities if required.
   ☒ **A, C,** and **D** are incorrect. Intermediate CAs exist under the Root CA and can issue certificates, in which case the root CA should be kept offline for security purposes; a compromised root CA means all certificates in the entire hierarchy are compromised. A CRL is a list of certificate serial numbers that have been revoked (not expired) for reasons such as a user leaving the organization or a lost or stolen user smartphone containing a certificate. A device certificate is issued to a device such as a smartphone and can be used for purposes such as authenticating to a VPN.

3. ☑ **D**. The PKI chain of trust is based on digital signatures written to issued certificates by a root or intermediary CA. For example, if a user device trusts RootCA1, then the user device trusts all certificates issued directly or indirectly by RootCA1.
   ☒ **A, B,** and **C** are incorrect. Certificate revocation renders certificates unusable and is done for reasons such as a user leaving the organization or a lost or stolen user smartphone containing a certificate. Registration authorities (RAs) are often referred to as intermediate CAs; they have the ability to accept certificate requests and either issue certificates or validate the request for issuance by another CA. CAs issue certificates. If your PKI hierarchy consists of only Root CA, then it also fulfills the role of the RA.

4. ☑ **C.** HTTPS web server connectivity requires a PKI certificate installed on the server; HTTP does not. If the certificate is self-signed, meaning not issued by a trusted third-party issuer, then web browsers will present a security warning to users when they attempt to connect to the site.
☒ **A, B,** and **D** are incorrect. Untrusted web site warnings are not related to user authentication; it is solely a PKI chain of trust issue. If users can connect to the web site over HTTP but not HTTPS, it is not likely a firewall issue. (Although it's technically feasible for a firewall to block HTTPS access to the web server, that would be the case only if a misconfiguration was present, as no admin would willingly block HTTPS and allow only HTTP access to a web server.) While client certificates can be required for a secure web site, the warning message does not indicate this issue; it seems to be related to an untrusted web site (pointing to a web server certificate issue, in comparison to a client one).

5. ☑ **B.** Script writers and software developers use code-signing certificates to digitally sign scripts or software files using a private key. Devices can be configured to run only trusted scripts or software, meaning that the signature can be verified with the correct public key.
☒ **A, C,** and **D** are incorrect. RAs are often referred to as intermediate CAs; they have the ability to accept certificate requests and either issue certificates or validate the request for issuance by another CA. A certificate signing request (CSR) is generated by a subject that would like an issued certificate. It contains information about the requestor, such as company name, user contact information, web site URL, and user e-mail address, as well as a public key. The CSR is normally e-mailed or copied to a certification authority web form to proceed with certificate issuance.

6. ☑ **C and D.** If the root CA is compromised, all certificates in the hierarchy are compromised, so it should be kept offline unless it is needed, such as to create a new intermediate CA. While a key pair public key can be shared with anyone, private keys must be available only to the key pair owner, since private keys are used to decrypt messages and create digital signatures.
☒ **A and B** are incorrect. Public keys do not have to be kept secret and the root CA should not be left online since this increases the risk of it being compromised.

7. ☑ **D.** The IP address of the issuing CA server is not stored in an issued certificate.
☒ **A, B,** and **C** are incorrect. The listed items are all valid items that can be stored with a certificate. With a PKI, public and private key pairs are associated with a specific certificate. With some CA issued certificates, installing a certificate, such as one used for HTTPS on a web server, also installs the related private key automatically. Sharing a certificate with others for purposes such as e-mail encryption means only the public key is included.

8. ☑ **B.** A digital signature is created from a private key and is used to verify the authenticity and integrity of the message using the related public key.
☒ **A, C,** and **D** are incorrect. File and e-mail encryption provide confidentiality but not message authenticity and integrity. A CRL is a list of certificate serial numbers that have been revoked (not expired) for reasons such as a user leaving the organization or a lost or stolen user smartphone containing a certificate.

9. ☑ **B.** Key escrow places private or secret keys in the possession of a trusted third party for safekeeping.
    ☒ **A, C,** and **D** are incorrect. Expired keys are invalid whether stored within a key escrow or not. Key escrow does not relate to encrypting data.

10. ☑ **B.** RAs are often referred to as intermediate CAs; they have the ability to accept certificate requests and either issue certificates or validate the request for issuance by another CA.
    ☒ **A, C,** and **D** are incorrect. Public and private key pairs are associated with a specific certificate and are usable for PKI security purposes after the certificate is issued. A CRL is a list of certificate serial numbers that have been revoked (not expired) for reasons such as a user leaving the organization or a lost or stolen user smartphone containing a certificate.

11. ☑ **A.** Expired certificates can no longer be used. A new certificate must be issued for the user.
    ☒ **B, C,** and **D** are incorrect. The problem is isolated to a single user certificate, so changing VPN and certificate options affecting multiple users does not make sense. Disabling VPN certificate authentication, reducing how often revoked certificate details are published, and setting the date back on the VPN appliance are not secure solutions or best practices.

12. ☑ **D.** If users' devices are configured with the correct trusted certificate for the intranet server certificate issuer, then user devices will trust certificates issued by that authority.
    ☒ **A, B,** and **C** are incorrect. Switching from HTTPS to HTTP does not maintain security; it reduces it. Server private keys must be in the possession of only the server. HTTPS already uses TCP port 443, so this will not solve the problem.

13. ☑ **D.** Mutual authentication requires both sides of a secured connection to authenticate with each other. Normally an HTTPS web site secures connections for anybody who has permissions to use the web site. To enhance security further, connecting devices can be required to have an installed and trusted certificate, which enables each party to validate the other's identity.
    ☒ **A, B,** and **C** are incorrect. The listed options are not as secure as client-side PKI certificates. IP addresses and MAC addresses are much easier to spoof than a certificate, and the requirement is to restrict workstations, not users, to the web site.

14. ☑ **C.** Depending on which tool is used, acquiring a publicly trusted server certificate for an e-commerce site begins with generating a public/private key pair, filling out information such as company name and web server URL, and providing the public key to the CA; this is a certificate signing request (CSR).
    ☒ **A, B,** and **D** are incorrect. If the site is new, the web server certificate will not yet exist. Most web servers will already have TLS support enabled, but even if this web server doesn't, enabling it will not achieve anything if a certificate isn't available to be used during a connection request. The web server cannot be configured to use port 443 for HTTPS until a server certificate is installed.

15. ☑ **C.** The common name in the CSR must match the organization's URL, in this case, the URL that will be used for HTTPS connections to https://www.corp.com. If the common name in the certificate does not match the URL users are connecting to, they will receive a warning that the certificate does not match the site.

    ☒ **A, B,** and **D** are incorrect. None of the listed items is correct, and none would cause a problem with the CSR or certificate issuance or usage.

16. ☑ **A.** In larger enterprises, intermediate CAs can be deployed for cities, departments, subsidiary companies, and so on. Intermediate CA technicians then have control of that part of the PKI hierarchy. The root CA should be taken offline to enhance security; a compromised root CA means all certificates in the hierarchy are compromised. A compromised intermediary CA mean only its issued certificates are compromised.

    ☒ **B, C,** and **D** are incorrect. Larger organizations with senior IT personnel in each city should have intermediate CAs deployed for each city. Using multiple root CAs for each city means user devices must trust multiple CAs, which requires more configuration effort than is necessary.

17. ☑ **A.** An HTTPS-enabled web site requires a PKI certificate containing a public and private key pair. In simple terms, when the client initially connects to the server and negotiates session details, the server sends the client its public key. The client generates a unique session key, which is encrypted with the server's public key and sent back to the server. The server then uses its private key to decrypt the message and reveal the session key. The session key, or shared secret key, is then used to encrypt transmissions throughout the session.

    ☒ **B, C,** and **D** are incorrect. The listed variations of keys used with HTTPS are not complete. That's because they don't depict the full list of keys used during a TLS handshake (which uses the public, private, and session keys).

18. ☑ **A.** Private keys are used to create digital signatures. In this example, the CA signature allows for the chain of trust, meaning clients that trust the CA will trust any certificates issued by that CA.

    ☒ **B, C,** and **D** are incorrect. A CRL is a list of certificate serial numbers that have been revoked (not expired) for reasons such as a user leaving the organization or a lost or stolen user smartphone containing a certificate. The Online Certificate Status Protocol (OCSP) enables verification of the validity of a single certificate instead of an entire list of all expired certificates.

19. ☑ **A and B.** CAs digitally sign certificates to establish the chain of trust; they can also revoke certificates, rendering those certificates unusable.

    ☒ **C and D** are incorrect. CA private keys create digital signatures, not public keys. While network infrastructure devices can use certificates to control network access, the CA is not involved other than issuing the certificates.

20. ☑ **C** and **E.** The personal information exchange format (PFX) and P12 file formats (same data, different file extensions) are often used to store private keys and should be password protected.
☒ **A, B, D,** and **F** are incorrect. There are many ways of storing the same PKI certificate information in a file. The Distinguished Encoding Rules (DER) file format contains a PKI certificate in binary form, whereas the Privacy-Enhanced Mail (PEM) file format contains one or more certificates, including a certificate chain in base64-encoded text form. CER files store certificate information in either binary or base64-encoded format. P7B format is a variation of PEM and is used to store root and intermediary certificate data; P7B and PEM files do not contain private keys.

21. ☑ **C.** Pinning is a technique used to associate hosts with their public keys. This can be done by client-side applications, including web browsers, that keep a copy, or a hash, of a host's public key. This is checked by the client app when server connectivity is initiated.
☒ **A, B,** and **D** are incorrect. A CRL provides expired certificate serial numbers to ensure that expired certificates are not trusted. The OCSP enables verification of the validity of a single certificate instead of an entire list of all expired certificates. Fully qualified domain names (FQDNs) are friendly names such as http://www.mheducation.ca/ that map to their associated IP addresses.

22. ☑ **C.** A subject alternative name (SAN) certificate enables you use one certificate to secure hosts with different names, such as www.corp.com and info.corp.com.
☒ **A, B,** and **D** are incorrect. Acquiring, installing, and managing two certificates require more effort than using a single certificate. A CRL provides expired certificate serial numbers to ensure that expired certificates are not trusted and is not related to securing multiple DNS names for web sites. IPSec is a network security protocol that can be configured to authenticate and encrypt network traffic, including establishing a VPN tunnel. IPSec can use a variety of methods to secure connections including PSKs and PKI security certificates.

23. ☑ **A** and **B.** Certification authorities perform various degrees of verification against CSRs. Domain validation certificates are easy to acquire. CAs require only that you prove DNS domain ownership such as through creating a DNS record in your domain with CA specified values, or through receipt of an e-mail message sent to the DNS domain owner. Before issuing extended validation certificates, CAs perform more tasks to ensure that the organization is genuine, such as by verifying organization details, whether the business is registered, and so on. Both types of certificates provide HTTPS security.
☒ **C** and **D** are incorrect. A CRL provides expired certificate serial numbers to ensure that expired certificates are not trusted. The OCSP enables the verification of the validity of a single certificate instead of an entire list of all expired certificates.

24. ☑ **B.** To reduce the amount of queries sent directly to CAs, OCSP stapling is initiated by a certificate holder to the CA, and the response is cached and then provided to client queries.
    ☒ **A, C,** and **D** are incorrect. A CSR is generated by a subject that would like an issued certificate, and it contains information about the requestor such as company name, user contact information, web site URL, and user e-mail address, as well as a public key. A CRL provides expired certificate serial numbers to ensure that expired certificates are not trusted. Pinning is a technique used to associate hosts with their public keys. This can be done by client-side applications, including web browsers that keep a copy, or a hash, of a host's public key. This is checked by the client app when server connectivity is initiated.

25. ☑ **D.** The PKI chain of trust, also referred to as certificate chaining, is based on digital signatures written to issued certificates by a root or intermediary CA. For example, if a user device trusts RootCA1, then the user device trusts all certificates issued directly or indirectly by RootCA1.
    ☒ **A, B,** and **C** are incorrect. Key escrow places private or secret keys in the possession of a trusted third party for safekeeping. To reduce the amount of queries sent directly to CAs, OCSP stapling is initiated by a certificate holder to the CA and the response is cached and then provided to client queries. Pinning is a technique used to associate hosts with their public keys.

26. ☑ **D.** Wildcard certificates are similar to SAN certificates in that a single certificate can be used to secure multiple DNS domain names, such as www.corp.com and info.corp.com.
    ☒ **A, B,** and **C** are incorrect. Acquiring and managing multiple certificates requires more administrative effort than using a single wildcard certificate. RAs receive CSRs and can either issue certificates or task a CA with actually issuing the certificate, if the CA is separate. The primary difference between wildcard certificates and SAN certificates is that wildcard certificates, such as for *.corp.com, would allow future subdomains under corp.com to be secured. SAN certificates use hard-coded DNS domain names.

27. ☑ **C.** If devices must trust web server certificates issued by RootCert for HTTPS connectivity, devices will have to install the trusted root certificate for RootCert.
    ☒ **A, B,** and **D** are incorrect. A user certificate is required for digitally signing or encrypting mail messages. There is no indication of the RootCert CA expiring.

28. ☑ **A.** The circle containing an X next to RootCert indicates that the chain of trust is broken; RootCert is not trusted on this device. Installing the trusted root certificate for the RootCert CA on the device would solve this problem.
    ☒ **B, C,** and **D** are incorrect. The circle containing an X is next to RootCert, not ClientCert; it is RootCert that is not trusted. The circle containing an X does not indicate that a CA is offline; neither does it reflect whether or not certificate stapling is enabled for the CA.

29. ☑ **A** and **D.** Because a private key is present in the certificate, encrypted e-mail messages for this user can be decrypted, and the user can digitally sign messages.
☒ **B** and **C** are incorrect. Sending encrypted messages means the sender must have access to the recipient public keys. Digital signature verification requires a public key, not a private key.

30. ☑ **B** and **D.** A CRL provides expired certificate serial numbers to ensure that expired certificates are not trusted. The OCSP enables verification of the validity of a single certificate instead of an entire list of all expired certificates as CRLs do.
☒ **A** and **C** are incorrect. To reduce the amount of queries sent directly to CAs, OCSP stapling is initiated by a certificate holder to the CA and the response is cached and then provided to client queries. RAs receive CSRs and can either issue certificates or task a CA with actually issuing the certificate, if the CA is separate.

31. ☑ **A.** SHA 256 bits can be used by CAs to digitally sign certificates they issue, thus establishing a chain of trust.
☒ **B, C,** and **D** are incorrect. The listed algorithms are encryption or key exchange algorithms, not algorithms used specifically for digital signatures. AES is a symmetric block encryption cipher. Block ciphers encrypt entire data blocks as opposed to individual bytes of data. The older DES is rarely used these days because of its small key length (64 bits); instead AES 128 or 256 is used. Key exchange refers to two end-points communicating over a network to generate a unique session key. Diffie-Hellman is a key exchange algorithm used by network security protocols such as Internet key exchange (IKE).

32. ☑ **C.** The common name property in a certificate identifies the subject, such as a user e-mail address or an FQDN for a web site. An example is CN=user1@corp.com.
☒ **A, B,** and **D** are incorrect. The domain component is used to further identify a network directory service hierarchy, such as DC=corp,DC=com. Component name and DNS component are not valid certificate properties.

33. ☑ **A** and **B.** User certificates are issued with specific usage constraints, so one possible explanation is that this certificate does not support digitally signing e-mail messages. Or the certificate does not contain the sender's private key, which is required to create a digital signature.
☒ **C** and **D** are incorrect. Public keys are not to create signatures; they are used to verify signatures. The issuing CA signature is always present in all certificates.

Chapter 14

Physical Security

CERTIFICATION OBJECTIVES

QUESTIONS

Security breaches can be perpetrated remotely across a network or physically on the premises. The effects of physical security, such as barricades, locks, and guards, must not be underestimated.

Many security breaches today are the result of poor physical security, including sensitive data stored on unencrypted storage media and the unsecure disposal of decommissioned computer equipment.

1. What can be done to protect switches and routers from physical security vulnerabilities? (Choose two.)
   A. Use a cable lock.
   B. Use SSH instead of Telnet.
   C. Set a strong console port password.
   D. Disable unused ports.

2. What can limit the data emanation from electromagnetic radio frequencies?
   A. Faraday cage
   B. Antistatic wrist strap
   C. ESD mat
   D. ESD boots

3. What methods are most commonly used by physical security teams to verify whether somebody is authorized to access a facility? (Choose two.)
   A. Employee ID badge
   B. Username and password
   C. Access list
   D. Smartcard

4. While reviewing facility entry points, you decide to replace existing doors with ones that will stay locked during power outages. Which term best describes this feature?
   A. Fail-secure
   B. Fault-tolerant
   C. Fail-safe
   D. UPS

5. A data center IT director requires the ability to analyze facility physical security breaches after they have occurred. Which of the following present the best solutions? (Choose two.)
   A. Motion sensor logs
   B. Laser security system
   C. Access control vestibule
   D. Software video surveillance system

6. Which of the following physical access control methods do not normally identify who has entered a secure area? (Choose two.)
   A. Access control vestibule
   B. Hardware lock
   C. Fingerprint scan
   D. Smartcard with PIN

7. Your company has moved to a new location where a server room is being built. The server room currently has a water sprinkler system in case of fire. Regarding fire suppression, what should you suggest?
   A. Keep the existing water sprinkler system.
   B. Purchase a smoke-detection, waterless fire suppression system.
   C. Keep the existing water sprinkler system and install a raised floor.
   D. Place a fire extinguisher in the server room.

8. A data center administrator uses thermal imaging to identify hot spots in a large data center. She then arranges rows of rack-mounted servers such that cool air is directed to server fan inlets and hot air is exhausted out of the building. Which of the following terms best defines this scenario?
   A. HVAC
   B. Form factoring
   C. Hot and cold aisles
   D. Data center breathing

9. Which access control method electronically logs entry into a facility?
   A. Picture ID card
   B. Security guard and log book
   C. IPSec
   D. Proximity card

10. You are consulting with a client regarding a new facility. Access to the building must be restricted only to those who know an access code. What might you suggest?
    A. Cipher lock
    B. Deadbolt lock
    C. Store the code in a safe
    D. Biometric authentication

11. Over the last month, you have added new rack-mount servers in your server room, and servers have begun mysteriously shutting down for no apparent reason. Servers restart normally only to shut down again eventually. Servers are fully patched, and virus scanners are up to date. Which of the following is the most likely reason for these failures?

    A. The server room temperature is too hot.

    B. The server room temperature is too cool.

    C. The servers are infected with a virus.

    D. The server operating systems contain programming flaws.

12. What should be done in facility parking lots to ensure employee safety?

    A. Install a barricade.

    B. Install proper lighting.

    C. Install an exit sign.

    D. Install a first-aid kit.

13. Which type of threat is mitigated by shredding paper documents?

    A. Rootkit

    B. Spyware

    C. Shoulder surfing

    D. Physical

14. You are writing code for a custom mobile device app, and for security reasons, you want to prevent tampering and the ability of others to read the code. Which technique will accomplish the requirement?

    A. Obfuscation

    B. Encryption

    C. Hashing

    D. Air gapping

15. Which of the following represent valid storage media destruction techniques? (Choose two.)

    A. Air gapping

    B. Shredding

    C. Burning

    D. Pulping

16. You are responsible for acquiring new laptop computers for employees in a branch office. What should you do to prevent sensitive data retrieval from discarded storage media used by the old laptops? (Choose two.)

    A. Pulverizing

    B. Degaussing

    C. Air gapping

    D. Reformatting of the old laptop hard disks

17. Currently, employees use a text file to store usernames and passwords they need to authenticate to a variety of web sites. You need to address this issue with a secure solution. What should you implement?
    A. HTTPS
    B. PKI
    C. Air gap
    D. Password vault

18. A private company conducting top-secret research for the military has headquarters in a rural location, with multiple buildings spread across a 30-acre property. Which solutions should be put in place to monitor and secure the property? (Choose two).
    A. DMZ
    B. Air gap
    C. Fencing
    D. Drones

19. In Figure 14-1, match the terms on the left with the descriptions on the right. Note that not all terms on the left have a matching description on the right.

FIGURE 14-1

Physical security terms and definitions

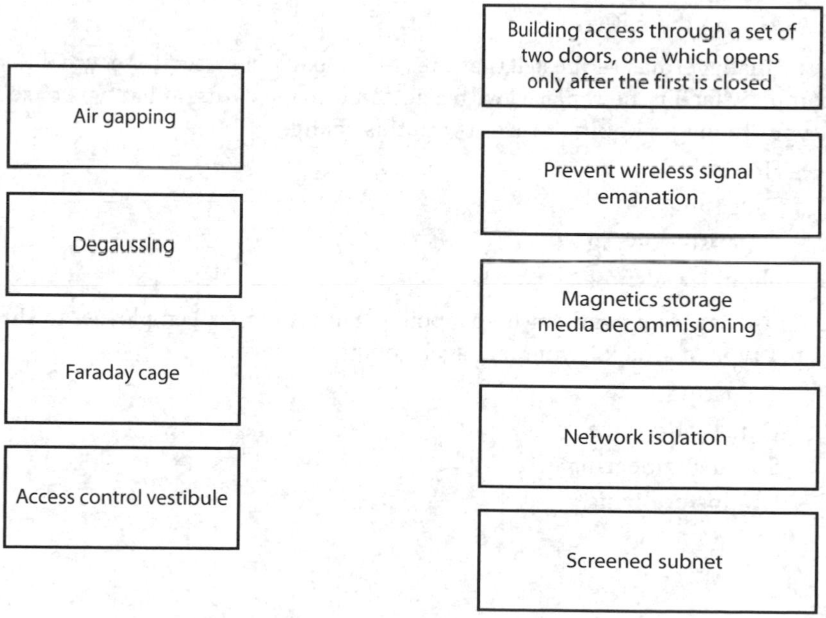

| Air gapping |
| Degaussing |
| Faraday cage |
| Access control vestibule |

| Building access through a set of two doors, one which opens only after the first is closed |
| Prevent wireless signal emanation |
| Magnetics storage media decommisioning |
| Network isolation |
| Screened subnet |

20. Computers in your organization's finance department are equipped with a TPM chip, and TPM-enabled full disk encryption of all disks attached to each computer has been enabled. How does this configuration mitigate physical security threats?

   A.   The contents of stolen encrypted disks are read-only.

   B.   When removed from the TPM-enabled device, the disks' contents are securely deleted.

   C.   The stolen disks cannot be placed in Faraday cages.

   D.   The contents of stolen encrypted disks are inaccessible.

21. Which class of fire extinguisher should be used to extinguish fires related to electrical equipment?

   A.   Class A

   B.   Class B

   C.   Class C

   D.   Class D

22. A top-secret local network must not allow connectivity from any other network. What can be done to address this security concern?

   A.   Deploy a NAT router at the network perimeter.

   B.   Configure a screened subnet.

   C.   Configure ACL rules to block traffic on the network perimeter router.

   D.   Air gap the network.

23. Your manager has requested that the combo padlocks used to secure different areas of the company facility be replaced with electronic swipe cards. What type of social-engineering attack is your manager hoping to avoid with this change?

   A.   Hoaxes

   B.   Tailgating

   C.   Dumpster diving

   D.   Shoulder surfing

24. Your manager has implemented a policy that requires all employees to shred sensitive documents. What type of attack is your manager hoping to prevent?

   A.   Tailgating

   B.   Denial of service

   C.   Social engineering

   D.   Dumpster diving

25. Trinity uses her building access card to enter a work facility after hours. She has access to only the second floor. What is this an example of?

A. Authorization

B. Authentication

C. Accountability

D. Confidentiality

26. You are installing an IP-based CCTV surveillance system throughout your company's facilities. What should you do to harden the CCTV environment? (Choose two).

A. Change default credentials.

B. Place CCTV equipment on an air-gapped network.

C. Configure a hot aisle.

D. Configure a cold aisle.

27. Which technology enables security robot sentries to interpret their environments to make security decisions?

A. Faraday cages

B. Degaussing

C. Air gapping

D. Artificial intelligence

28. You are planning the network cable distribution for one floor of your office building. What should you do to minimize the risk of wiretaps reading network transmissions?

A. Deploy Network Access Control switches.

B. Deploy twisted-pair copper wiring.

C. Deploy IPSec.

D. Deploy fiber-optic cabling.

29. After reviewing facility access logs, you notice that two on-duty security guards worked together to allow late-night building access to thieves. Which term best describes this situation?

A. Collusion

B. Access control vestibule

C. Degaussing

D. Shredding

30. Which solution prevents malware infections through charging mobile devices?

A. Air gapping

B. USB data blocker

C. Degaussing

D. Faraday cage

31. What is being depicted in Figure 14-2?
   A. Hot aisle
   B. Air gap
   C. Cold aisle
   D. Degaussing

FIGURE 14-2

Data center
layout

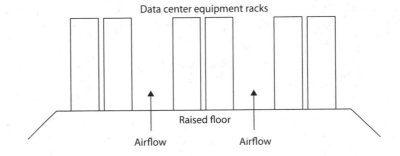

Data center equipment racks

Raised floor

Airflow   Airflow

32. Degaussing is a secure disposal mechanism that applies to _____.
   A. Faraday cages
   B. Paper documents
   C. Hard disks
   D. Solid state drives

A

QUICK ANSWER KEY

1.	C, D	**12.**	B	**22.**	D
2.	A	**13.**	D	**23.**	D
3.	A, C	**14.**	A	**24.**	D
4.	A	**15.**	B, C	**25.**	A
5.	A, D	**16.**	A, B	**26.**	A, B
6.	A, B	**17.**	D	**27.**	D
7.	B	**18.**	C, D	**28.**	D
8.	C	**19.**	See "In-Depth Answers."	**29.**	A
9.	D			**30.**	B
10.	A	**20.**	D	**31.**	C
11.	A	**21.**	C	**32.**	C

IN-DEPTH ANSWERS

1. ☑ **C and D.** A console port enables a local user to plug a cable into the router or switch to administer the device locally, so a strong password is recommended. Disabling unused switch ports and router interfaces prevents unauthorized people from plugging devices into those ports and gaining access to the device or the network.

   ☒ **A and B** are incorrect. Cable locks are used to secure devices such as laptops or projection units and not switches and routers, which should be in locked server rooms or locked data center equipment racks. Secure Shell (SSH) is an encrypted remote command line administrative tool. Telnet passes data across the network in clear text.

2. ☑ **A.** Data emanation results from the electromagnetic field generated by a network cable or network device, which can be manipulated to eavesdrop on conversations or to steal data. Faraday cages are used to enclose electronic equipment to prevent data emanation and to protect components from external static charges.

   ☒ **B, C, and D** are incorrect. The listed items are designed to put the user and the equipment at equal electrical charge to prevent the flow of electrons from causing personal injury and equipment damage, but they do not prevent data emanation.

3. ☑ **A and C.** An employee ID badge enables physical verification that somebody is allowed to access a building. An access list defines who is allowed to access a facility or office space and should be consulted by reception when anyone arrives.

   ☒ **B and D** are incorrect. Username and password can authenticate a user to a computer system, as can a smartcard, but these do not get verified by a security guard. Smartcards contain an embedded microchip. The user enters a PIN in conjunction with using his or her smartcard, which constitutes multifactor authentication.

4. ☑ **A.** Fail-secure systems ensure that a component failure (such as a power source) will not compromise security; in this case, the doors will stay locked.

   ☒ **B, C, and D** are incorrect. Fault tolerance (also referred to as fail-safe) ensures that a system can continue functioning despite a failure of some type. For example, a server may spread file and error recovery data across multiple disks in a RAID 5 disk configuration. In the event of a disk failure, data can be reconstructed from the remaining disks. An uninterruptible power supply (UPS) provides temporary power to devices when a power outage occurs.

5. ☑ **A** and **D.** Motion sensor logs can track a perpetrator's position more accurately than most video surveillance camera systems; however, closed-circuit television (CCTV) software video surveillance system footage can be played back and used to physically identify unauthorized people. To conserve disk space, most solutions record only when there is motion.

☒ **B** and **C** are incorrect. Laser security systems rely on laser beams being interrupted and do not work well with detailed analysis after the fact. Access control vestibule are small rooms controlling access to a building, where the first door must be closed before the second one will open. They offer little in terms of post-analysis.

6. ☑ **A** and **B.** Access control vestibule are designed to prevent tailgating and gaining access to a restricted area. Some access control vestibule variations use two sets of doors, one of which must close before the second one opens. Traditional access control vestibule do not require access cards. Hardware locks simply require possession of a key, although proper physical key management is necessary to track key issuance and return. Neither reveals a person's identity.

☒ **C** and **D** are incorrect. Fingerprints identify the user via biometric authentication. Doors can also be equipped with biometric locks. Smartcard authentication identifies the user through a unique code or Public Key Infrastructure (PKI) certificate contained within the smartcard. In this case, whoever is in possession of the smartcard must also know the PIN to use it.

7. ☑ **B.** Assuming local building codes allow waterless fire suppression systems, you should suggest these be used, because they will not damage or corrode computer systems or components like water will.

☒ **A, C,** and **D** are incorrect. Water sprinkler systems will damage or destroy computer equipment and data and should be avoided when possible. While important, placing a Class C fire extinguisher in the server room to mitigate electrical fires is not the only thing you should recommend; water damage devastates computer systems.

8. ☑ **C.** In a data center, cold aisles optimize cold airflow to equipment intake fans, while hot aisles optimize hot air equipment exhaust flow by directing it away from equipment to the outside. Cool air is often fed under raised floors with perforated vents to feed equipment. Panels are installed between equipment racks to keep the cool and warm air from mixing, resulting in greater cooling efficiency.

☒ **A, B,** and **D** are incorrect. Heating, ventilation, and air conditioning (HVAC) systems are generally in place to control for airflow and environmental controls within a room or building. Form factoring and data center breathing are fictitious terms.

9. ☑ **D.** Proximity cards must be positioned within a few centimeters of the reader to register the card and either allow or deny access to a facility. All access is logged electronically without the need of a physical log book or security guard.

☒ **A, B,** and **C** are incorrect. Picture ID cards identify people but don't relate to electronic log entry. Security guards also do not log facility access electronically. IP Security (IPSec) is a mechanism by which packets are authenticated and encrypted; there is no correlation to physical site security.

10. ☑ **A.** Cipher locks are electronic keypads that enable authorized people to enter an access code to gain access to a room or a building. All the user needs to know is the access code; no physical card is required.

    ☒ **B, C,** and **D** are incorrect. The listed items do not meet the client requirement of users knowing an access code. A deadbolt lock requires possession of a key. Although storing sensitive paper documents in a safe is recommended, it is not required for a cipher lock, which requires an access code. Biometric authentication methods such as a unique fingerprint do not require knowledge of an access code.

11. ☑ **A.** A hot server room is most likely the problem since new equipment has been added, which adds to the room temperature. An HVAC technician should be consulted, which could result in the implementation of hot and cold aisles if necessary.

    ☒ **B, C,** and **D** are incorrect. The listed items are not likely responsible for servers shutting down, since servers are patched and the problem began after adding new equipment to the server room.

12. ☑ **B.** Proper lighting in parking lots reduces the likelihood of attacks or muggings perpetrated against employees.

    ☒ **A, C,** and **D** are incorrect. Installing a barricade such as bollards in front of or around a building could prevent damage from vehicles, but it does not ensure employee safety in parking lots. Signage, such as exit signs, helps ensure user safety, along with valid escape routes and regular fire drills. Unless this is an interior parking lot, exit signs would not be needed. A first-aid kit is not standard practice for parking lot safety.

13. ☑ **D.** Shredding documents prevents physical threats such as theft of those documents or acquiring information from them.

    ☒ **A, B,** and **C** are incorrect. Rootkits hide themselves from the OS while commonly allowing access to a malicious user. Spyware gathers a user's computing habits without the user's knowledge. This information can be valuable to marketing firms. The direct observation of somebody accessing sensitive information is an example of shoulder surfing.

14. ☑ **A.** Obfuscating programming code, often called code camouflaging, is done using a software development plug-in. The result is an unreadable variation of the original readable text.

    ☒ **B, C,** and **D** are incorrect. Encryption feeds data and an encryption key into a cryptographic encryption algorithm, resulting in cipher text, or encrypted data. Hashing feeds data in a one-way cryptographic hashing algorithm such as SHA-256, which results in a unique value representative of the original data. Air gapping isolates a sensitive network through a lack of connectivity to other networks.

15. ☑ **B** and **C.** Shredding is used to cut paper documents into tiny pieces to ensure that the data included on the documents cannot be retrieved. Burning is also effective in destroying electrical equipment, where allowed by law, and reduces paper documents, thus making data retrieval impossible.

☒   **A** and **D** are incorrect. Air gapping isolates a sensitive network through a lack of connectivity to other networks. Pulping renders paper documents to a thick paste by adding a liquid compound; this is a rarely used as a secure document destruction method.

16.   ☑   **A** and **B.** Pulverizing is used to reduce documents or electrical components into small fragments, making them useless for information gathering. Degaussing uses a powerful magnet to erase data from magnetic storage media, such as conventional spinning hard disks.
☒   **C** and **D** are incorrect. Air gapping isolates a sensitive network through a lack of connectivity to other networks. Reformatting a disk resets the file system, but the old data still resides on the device and can be easily retrieved using freely available tools.

17.   ☑   **D.** Password vaults provide a centralized, secure credential storage solution to users otherwise having to remember multiple sets of credentials when accessing multiple applications or web sites. Normally a passphrase or smartcard is required to unlock the vault, similar to entering a code to unlock a safe.
☒   **A, B,** and **C** are incorrect. Hypertext Transfer Protocol secure (HTTPS) uses PKI certificates to secure network transmissions between a client and a web server, and it can protect credentials sent over the network, but it does not address the problem of securely retaining multiple usernames and passwords. A PKI is a hierarchy of security certificates use to secure computing environments such as through disk encryption and network authentication and encryption. Air gapping isolates a sensitive network through a lack of connectivity to other networks.

18.   ☑   **C** and **D.** Physical fencing can deter unauthorized access to the property and can also display signage regarding trespassing on private property. Many firms specializing in security fencing recommend a minimum height of 2.1 meters (7 feet). Security drones, also called unmanned aerial vehicles, are remote-controlled flying vehicles that can monitor large areas by flying over them. This type of drone is usually equipped with night vision motion detection video capabilities.
☒   **A** and **B** are incorrect. A screened subnet is a network that resides between a public network such as the Internet and an internal secured network. Publicly accessible services such as corporate VPN gateways should be placed in a screened subnet. Air gapping isolates a sensitive network through a lack of connectivity to other networks.

19.   ☑   Figure 14-3 shows the terms matched to the correct answers. An air-gapped network is physically isolated from all other networks; there are no external network connections. Degaussing is a process using a magnet to erase data stored on magnetic media such as hard disks. A Faraday cage is a small enclosure in which wireless devices are placed to prevent the receipt or transmission of wireless signals. To control facility access and prevent tailgating, a access control vestibule is a small room with two doors at the building entrance; the second inner door opens only after the first external door closes. The unused answer, a screened subnet, is a network that resides between a public network such as the Internet and an internal secured network. Publicly accessible services such as corporate VPN end-points should be placed in a screened subnet.

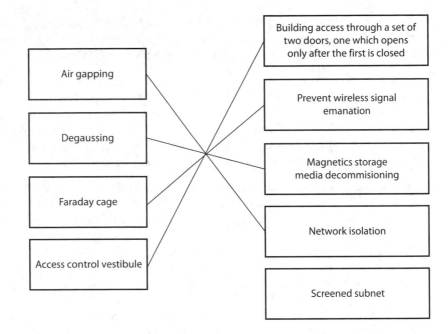

FIGURE 14-3

Physical security
terms and
definitions—the
answers

20. ☑ **D.** Trusted Platform Module (TPM) is cryptographic firmware designed to store cryptographic keys for disk encryption as well as to ensure the machine boot process has not been tampered with, including the malware infection of operating system boot files. The contents of a TPM-encrypted disk removed from a system where the disk was encrypted are inaccessible because the decryption key is not available.
☒ **A, B,** and **C** are incorrect. TPM-encrypted disks do not become read-only when moved to different systems, nor are the disk contents deleted. Faraday cages enclose electronic equipment to prevent data emanation and to protect components from external static charges; they are not related to disk encryption.

21. ☑ **C.** Class C fire extinguishers are designed to put out electrical fires.
☒ **A, B,** and **D** are incorrect. Class A fire extinguishers are designed to put out standard combustible material, such as wood or rubber, fires. Class B extinguishers are designed to put out fires resulting from flammable liquids such as gasoline. Class D fire extinguishers are designed to put out metal-based fires related to elements such as magnesium or potassium.

22. ☑ **D.** Air gapping isolates a sensitive network through a lack of connectivity to other networks.
☒ **A, B,** and **C** are incorrect. The listed items are not the best ways to block all network connectivity. A Network Address Translation (NAT) router is used to allow internal devices with only private IP addresses to gain access to a public network such as the Internet through the NAT devices using its public IP address. A screened subnet is a network that resides between a public network such as the Internet and an internal secured network. Publicly accessible services such as corporate VPN end-points should be placed in a screened subnet. Access control lists (ACLs) are firewall rules that determine what type of traffic is allowed or blocked; this is not as effective as air gapping a network when all network connectivity must be blocked.

23. ☑ **D.** Shoulder surfing involves a malicious user secretly looking over somebody's shoulder to acquire sensitive information. Using swipe cards requires possession of the card and swiping the card through a reader; there is no sensitive code that can be viewed by watching somebody swipe a card.

☒ **A, B,** and **C** are incorrect. Electronic swipe cards would not avoid any of these answers. Hoaxes are e-mail messages that present false stories and ask readers to take some form of action, such as forwarding a message on to others. Tailgating occurs when an unauthorized person tries to follow behind an authorized person to sneak through a locked door. Dumpster diving occurs when a malicious user seeking sensitive information rifles through the garbage of the intended target.

24. ☑ **D.** Dumpster diving is the act of going through a target's garbage trying to locate information that can help the hacker perform an attack or gain access to the company assets. Shredding paper documents helps to prevent this from happening.

☒ **A, B,** and **C** are incorrect. Shredding documents will not prevent any of these from occurring. Tailgating occurs when an unauthorized person tries to follow behind an authorized person to sneak through a locked door. Denial of service occurs when an attacker overloads a system, causing it to become unresponsive or crash. In social engineering, the attacker tries to trick someone into compromising security through social contact, such as phone call, text, or e-mail.

25. ☑ **A.** This is an example of authorization, which involves having legitimate access to specific resources such as web sites, files on a file server, or, in this case, access to a specific floor in a building.

☒ **B, C,** and **D** are incorrect. Authentication occurs when a user or computer correctly identifies the user's/computer's credentials. In this example, Trinity has authenticated herself by using an access card (an authorization credential). Accountability ensures that people are accountable for their actions, such as modifying a file. This is accomplished most often with auditing. Confidentiality ensures that data is accessible only to those parties that should be authorized to access the data.

26. ☑ **A and B.** Default credentials should never remain enabled for any type of device. To reduce the risk of network infiltration, CCTV equipment should be placed on an isolated air-gapped network that has no physical connection to other networks.

☒ **C and D** are incorrect. In a data center, cold aisles optimize cold airflow to equipment intake fans, while hot aisles optimize hot air equipment exhaust flow by directing it away from equipment to the outside. These configurations are unrelated to CCTV.

27. ☑ **D.** Artificial intelligence (AI) is the imitation of human behavior by technology, such as robot sentries used for security. Successful AI implementations are fed data such as environmental sensor data (temperature, humidity) from built-in firmware or expansion cards or video and audio surveillance feeds on which decision-making is learned within the confines of configured parameters.

☒ **A, B,** and **C** are incorrect. Faraday cages enclose electronic equipment to prevent data emanation and to protect components from external static charges. Degaussing uses a powerful magnet to erase data from magnetic storage media such as conventional spinning hard disks. Air gapping isolates a sensitive network through a lack of connectivity to other networks.

28. ☑ **D.** Fiber-optic cabling transmits light pulses instead of electrical signals on copper wires and is thus not susceptible to traditional wiretapping.
☒ **A, B,** and **C** are incorrect. Network Access Control (NAC) switches require user authentication before allowing full network access. Twisted-pair copper wiring and related equipment are cheaper than fiber-optic cabling but are susceptible to external electrical interference and wiretapping. IPSec can protect network traffic without having to specifically configure individual applications, unlike SSL/TLS. It is not related to cable distribution.

29. ☑ **A.** Collusion occurs when multiple parties work together to engage in dishonest or fraudulent behavior. In this case, having two people working together did not prevent the illegal activity from occurring.
☒ **B, C,** and **D** are incorrect. Access control vestibule are small rooms controlling access to a building, where the first door must be closed before the second one will open. Degaussing uses a powerful magnet to erase data from magnetic storage media such as conventional spinning hard disks. Shredding documents prevents physical threats such as theft of those documents or acquiring information from them.

30. ☑ **B.** A USB data blocker is a physical device that sits between a USB charging source and the device that needs to be charged, enabling device charging but not data exchange.
☒ **A, C,** and **D** are incorrect. Air gapping isolates a sensitive network through a lack of connectivity to other networks. Degaussing uses a powerful magnet to erase data from magnetic storage media such as conventional spinning hard disks. Faraday cages enclose electronic equipment to prevent data emanation and to protect components from external static charges.

31. ☑ **C.** In a data center, cold aisles optimize cold airflow to equipment intake fans. Cool air is often fed under raised floors with perforated vents to feed equipment.
☒ **A, B,** and **D** are incorrect. Hot aisles optimize hot air equipment exhaust flow by directing it away from equipment to the outside. Air gapping isolates a sensitive network through a lack of connectivity to other networks. Degaussing uses a powerful magnet to erase data from magnetic storage media such as conventional spinning hard disks.

32. ☑ **C.** Degaussing is a secure disposal mechanism that applies to hard disks. It involves using a powerful magnet to erase data from magnetic storage media such as conventional spinning hard disks.
☒ **A, B,** and **C** are incorrect. Degaussing is designed to erase magnetically stored data, not electrical shielding devices (Faraday cages), paper documents, or solid state drives, which do not store data magnetically.

Chapter 15

Application Attacks and Security

QUESTIONS

Applications, including web sites, must be created with security in mind at all phases of development. App usage must be monitored to identify performance and security problems.

Secure coding is a programming concept that emphasizes security at all times when creating or modifying code. This helps mitigate common attacks such as cross-site scripting, injection attacks, and more. The Open Web Application Security Project (OWASP) provides guidance in securing web applications.

Application code testing can be automated to expedite the continuous delivery of updated secure software solutions. Code testing also ensures that secure coding guidelines have been adhered to.

1. An exploit connects to a specific TCP port and presents the attacker with an administrative command prompt. What type of attack is this?
   A. Botnet
   B. Trojan
   C. Privilege escalation
   D. Logic bomb

2. Which of the following best describes a buffer overflow attack?
   A. Injecting database code via a web page
   B. Using a dictionary file to crack passwords
   C. Sending too much data to an application that allows an attacker to run arbitrary code
   D. Altering the source address of a packet

3. You are analyzing web traffic in transit to your web server, and you notice someone logging on with a username of Bob with a password of "pass' or 1=1--". Which of the following describes what is happening?
   A. XML injection
   B. SQL injection
   C. LDAP injection
   D. Denial of service

4. Which of the following is the most likely to mitigate against buffer overflow attacks?

   A. Static ARP entries

   B. Antivirus software

   C. Firewall ACLs

   D. Patching

5. What type of attack involves the attacker inserting a client-side script into the web page?

   A. XSS

   B. Watering hole

   C. ARP poisoning

   D. SQL injection

6. Your manager has read about SQL injection attacks and is wondering what can be done to best protect against them for applications that were developed in-house. What would you recommend?

   A. Patching

   B. Antivirus

   C. Input validation

   D. Firewall

7. What type of file on your hard drive stores web app preferences and session data?

   A. Cookie

   B. Hosts

   C. LMHOSTS

   D. /etc/shadow

8. Which type of vulnerability results from writing data beyond expected memory boundaries?

   A. Pointer dereference

   B. Integer overflow

   C. Buffer overflow

   D. Memory leak

9. Which application-testing technique is the most likely to uncover improper input handling?

   A. Fuzzing

   B. Overloading

   C. Penetration testing

   D. Vulnerability scanning

10. Which programming problem stems from multiple threads not executing in a predictable, sequential pattern?

   A. Fuzzing

   B. Blue screen of death

   C. Multi-core CPU throttling

   D. Race condition

11. A piece of malware replaces a library of code used as needed by a controlling program. What name describes this type of security issue?

   A. DLL injection

   B. Pointer dereference

   C. Integer overflow

   D. Buffer overflow

12. Which term describes applications that are allowed to run on company computers?

   A. Application approved list

   B. Application block list

   C. Fuzzing

   D. Obfuscation

13. Jane is the lead security officer for your company and is analyzing web server logs. Jane notices suspicious activity related to navigating the file system on a web server. What type of attack was most likely performed?

   A. Integer overflow

   B. Directory traversal/command injection

   C. Malicious add-on

   D. Header manipulation

14. A malicious user deploys a rogue wireless access point that users unknowingly connect to. User traffic is captured, modified, and sent back out on the network in an attempt to send fraudulent user session data. Which type of attack it this?

   A. Replay

   B. Shimming

   C. Refactoring

   D. Pass the hash

15. An attacker tricks a user into clicking a malicious link that causes an unwanted action on a web site the user is currently authenticated to. What type of exploit is this?

   A. Cross-site request forgery

   B. Cross-site scripting

   C. Replay

   D. Pass the hash

16. After testing revealed security flaws, for quality assurance reasons, a software developer would like to harden a custom database API that accepts user parameters. Which hardening techniques should be used? (Choose two.)
    A. Input validation
    B. HTTPS API access
    C. Elasticity
    D. Autoscaling

17. Which type of Public Key Infrastructure (PKI) certificate should software developers use to establish a chain of trust?
    A. Client-side
    B. Subject alternative name
    C. Wildcard
    D. Code-signing

18. Software developers in your company use a centralized code version-control system to track programming code creation, modification, testing, and deployment. You have created automation scripts that are used by this tool to trigger code tests when new code is checked in. Upon successful testing, the code is then packaged and a push notification of the update is sent to mobile app users. Which term best describes this environment?
    A. CI/CD
    B. Input validation
    C. Elasticity
    D. Autoscaling

19. Which non-profit organization focuses solely on securing web applications?
    A. OWASP
    B. NIST
    C. ISO
    D. PCI DSS

20. Which type of attack is depicted in Figure 15-1?
    A. Staging
    B. Normalization
    C. Shimming
    D. SSL stripping

FIGURE 15-1

Web application
attack diagram

21. Which benefits are derived from the use of database stored procedures? (Choose two.)
    A. Code reuse
    B. Shimming
    C. CI/CD
    D. Database object permissions assignment

22. Your team has been tasked with reviewing the source code for a custom application component to identify and mitigate source code vulnerabilities. Which term best describes the procedure?
    A. Dynamic code analysis
    B. Shimming
    C. Static code analysis
    D. CI/CD

23. Which type of software programming vulnerability could allow data to be overwritten in memory, thus affecting the stability of the program?
    A. Buffer overflow
    B. XSS
    C. Cross-site request forgery
    D. Race condition

24. Which action simulates attacks against a web application?
    A. Normalization
    B. Penetration testing
    C. Obfuscation
    D. Configuring deny lists

25. You have configured the **expires** HTTP header on your web server with a value of **-1**. What does this mean?
    A. Cache this HTTP response for 1 hour.
    B. Cache this HTTP response for 1 day.
    C. Do not accept this HTTP response.
    D. Data must be requested before being displayed again.

26. Which HTTP response header is used to require HTTP connections?
   A. X-Frame-Options
   B. Allow
   C. Expires
   D. HSTS

27. Which HTTP response header flags can mitigate XSS attacks and ensure confidentiality over the network? (Choose two.)
   A. X-Frame-Options
   B. HttpOnly
   C. Secure
   D. Expires

28. Which activity can be used to identity and remove dead code?
   A. Dynamic code analysis
   B. Static code analysis
   C. Fuzzing
   D. Shimming

29. Which activity is considered to be a form of penetration testing?
   A. Dynamic code analysis
   B. Static code analysis
   C. Fuzzing
   D. Shimming

30. Your developers must digitally sign scripts before they will be trusted to run on corporate computers. What must be in place before a code-signing certificate can be issued?
   A. PKI
   B. CI/CD
   C. OWASP
   D. Shimming

31. Which of the following security terms is the most closely related to memory management?
   A. Race condition
   B. Cross-site request forgery
   C. Cross-site scripting
   D. Buffer overflow

32. What can be done to mitigate XSS attacks?
   A. Install a device PKI certificate.
   B. Enable the use of stored procedures.
   C. Enable application fuzzing.
   D. Block the use of web browser client-side scripting languages.

A QUICK ANSWER KEY

1.	C	**12.**	A	**23.**	A
2.	C	**13.**	B	**24.**	B
3.	B	**14.**	A	**25.**	D
4.	D	**15.**	A	**26.**	D
5.	A	**16.**	A, B	**27.**	B, C
6.	C	**17.**	D	**28.**	B
7.	A	**18.**	A	**29.**	C
8.	C	**19.**	A	**30.**	A
9.	A	**20.**	D	**31.**	D
10.	D	**21.**	A, D	**32.**	D
11.	A	**22.**	C		

IN-DEPTH ANSWERS

1. ☑ **C.** Privilege escalation occurs when a user gains higher access rights than he or she should have, either because they were given too many rights or because of a security flaw.
    ☒ **A, B**, and **D** are incorrect. A botnet refers to a group of computers under the control of a malicious individual. A Trojan is malware that appears to be benign, commonly by performing a legitimate function in the foreground, while also performing something malicious in the background, without the user's knowledge. Logic bombs are malware triggered by specific conditions or dates.

2. ☑ **C.** A buffer overflow attack occurs when an attacker sends more data to an application or service than it is expecting. The extra data that is sent flows out of the area of memory (the buffer) assigned to the application, which can result in areas of code being overwritten and may cause the application to crash or allow arbitrary execution of commands on the target.
    ☒ **A, B,** and **D** are incorrect. Injecting database code via a web page is an example of an SQL injection attack. Using a dictionary file to crack passwords is known as a dictionary attack—a form of password attack. Altering the source address of a packet is known as spoofing.

3. ☑ **B.** A SQL injection attack occurs when the attacker inserts database (SQL) statements into a backend database, via a web site, that manipulates the way the database stores data. In this example, the attacker is trying to bypass the logon by using "pass' or 1–1--" as a password, thus attempting to display all the database records.
    ☒ **A, C,** and **D** are incorrect. XML injection occurs when the attacker manipulates the logic of the application by inserting XML statements in application messages. An LDAP injection occurs when the attacker inserts an LDAP query into an application to perform search, addition, or modification operations. Denial of service occurs when the attacker tries to overload a target system so that it cannot service valid requests from legitimate clients.

4. ☑ **D.** Buffer overflow attacks can often be mitigated by ensuring that you keep up-to-date with system and application patches. As the vendor finds the vulnerabilities, that vendor will fix the issues through a patch. Input validation is also a common mitigation for buffer overflow attacks.
    ☒ **A, B,** and **C** are incorrect. Static ARP entries will help protect against ARP poisoning. Antivirus software will protect against viruses and other malicious software as long as you keep the virus definitions up to date. Firewall ACL rules can allow/deny specific types of network traffic, but this will not be the most effective way to mitigate buffer overflow attacks.

5. ☑ **A.** Cross-site scripting (XSS) is an attack that involves the attacker inserting script code into a web page so that it is then processed and executed by a client system when a user browses that web page.

   ☒ **B, C,** and **D** are incorrect. A watering hole attack involves an attacker planting malicious code on a web site you trust so that when you navigate to the site, the code results in your system being attacked. ARP poisoning occurs when the attacker inserts incorrect MAC addresses into the target system's ARP cache, thus leading to traffic being forwarded to the attacker's system. In SQL injection, SQL code is inserted into a backend database via a web application in order to manipulate the underlying database or system.

6. ☑ **C.** A SQL injection attack involves the attacker inserting database code via a web application, where it is not expected. The best countermeasure to this is to have your programmers validate any information (check its accuracy) passed into an application.

   ☒ **A, B,** and **D** are incorrect. Although patching a system solves a lot of problems, it will not solve a SQL injection attack for applications that you build. Antivirus software is not going to help you in this instance either, because this is not a virus problem—it is a problem based on your own coding processes and standards. Firewalls are not going to help you, because you need to allow people access to the application, and the problem is not about the type of traffic reaching the system—the problem is about the data that is being inserted into the backend database via a web application.

7. ☑ **A.** A cookie is a text file used by a web browser to store web app preferences and session information. A secure cookie prevents attackers from using the cookie to impersonate a user through XSS attacks by scripting languages such as JavaScript (cookie **HTTPOnly** flag) and allows cookie transmission only over HTTPS (cookie **Secure** flag).

   ☒ **B, C,** and **D** are incorrect. The hosts file stores the FQDNs and matching IP addresses. The LMHOSTS file in Windows stores the computer names and matching IP addresses. The Linux /etc/shadow file stores user account information, including user password hashes.

8. ☑ **C.** Buffer overflows result from writing data beyond expected memory boundaries, which can crash a program or allow arbitrary code execution.

   ☒ **A, B,** and **D** are incorrect. Dereferencing pointers can be used by attackers to trigger program conditions not anticipated by the developer, such as presenting error conditions that could crash a program. Ineffective programming can also lead to memory pointers that can point to null values being manipulated to reference data in memory that should otherwise be inaccessible. Integer numeric values have a specific range of acceptable values—for example, in the Java language, a static **int** variable can have a maximum value of $2^{31}-1$. Improper integer value checking can result in unpredictable application behavior. Memory leaks result from applications not fully deallocating all memory allocated upon program startup.

9. ☑ **A.** Fuzzing provides a large amount of input data, even invalid data, to an application in order to observe its behavior; the idea is to ensure that the application is stable and secure with its input and error handling.

   ☒ **B, C,** and **D** are incorrect. Overloading is not the industry term used to describe the testing of application input handling; fuzzing is. Penetration tests actively seek to exploit vulnerabilities; although this answer is somewhat correct, fuzzing is more specific to input handling. Vulnerability scans passively attempt to identify weaknesses without actively attempting to exploit them. Although they may have an ability to identify basic input handling errors, they're not as comprehensive as fuzzing, which can uncover many more input handling–related vulnerabilities.

10.   ☑ **D.** In a race condition, when code is executed by multiple threads, the timing of dependent events is not predictable, and as a result, a different thread can function in an unintended manner. For example, a piece of code may check the value of a variable and take action later, while that variable's value can change in the interim.

   ☒ **A, B,** and **C** are incorrect. Fuzzing is an application-testing technique to feed large amounts of unexpected data to an application to test its security and stability. A blue screen of death describes a Windows stop error, often attributed to a problem with hardware or hardware drivers. CPU throttling is used to slow down processing, which in turn reduces power consumption and heat; it is not related to the stated problem.

11.   ☑ **A.** Dynamic-link library (DLL) injections insert code into a DLL, which is called by a program at runtime as needed.

   ☒ **B, C,** and **D** are incorrect. Dereferencing pointers can be used by attackers to trigger program conditions not anticipated by the developer, such as throwing error conditions that could crash a program. Integer numeric values have a specific range of acceptable values—for example, in the Java language, a static **int** can have a maximum value of $2^{31}-1$. Improper integer value checking can result in unpredictable application behavior. Buffer overflows result from writing data beyond specific memory boundaries and can be the result of improper input validation.

12.   ☑ **A.** Allowed applications are applications that can run on the company's computer systems. These apps are listed within a policy that applies to computers to control software execution to prevent potentially malicious software from running.

   ☒ **B, C,** and **D** are incorrect. Blocked apps are specifically listed as not being allowed to execute on company computers. Fuzzing provides a large amount of input data, even invalid data, to an application in order to observe its behavior; the idea is to ensure that the application is stable and secure with its input and error handling. Obfuscation is used to make it more difficult to read or understand something such as programming code or sensitive data.

13.   ☑ **B.** Directory traversal, also known as command injection, occurs when the attacker accesses web server directories, which are restricted in order to execute commands found in the operating system of the web server.

   ☒ **A, C,** and **D** are incorrect. Integer overflow is a form of attack that presents security risks because of the unexpected response of a program when a mathematical function is performed, and the result is larger than the space in memory allocated by the programmer. In a malicious add-on, your system downloads a piece of software used by the browser that slows down the system or exploits a vulnerability in the system. Header manipulation occurs when an attacker modifies the header data in the packet in order to manipulate how the application processes the information.

14.   ☑   **A.** Replay attacks involve an attacker first capturing packets of interest, possibly manipulating something in the packet, and then sending it back out on the network. This type of attack can be used to gain access to sensitive resources as a valid user by resending authorized access traffic.
   ☒   **B, C,** and **D** are incorrect. Shimming, in terms of driver manipulation, is an attack in which a piece of software acts as a driver and intercepts and changes commands coming to and from the hardware. A refactoring attack involves changing the internal code of the driver while maintaining the external behavior so it appears to be behaving normally. A pass-the-hash attack involves intercepting a password hash from a legitimate user and using it to authenticate as that user to other resources.

15.   ☑   **A.** Cross-site request forgeries occur when an attacker tricks a user into executing unwanted actions on a web site she is currently authenticated to.
   ☒   **B, C,** and **D** are incorrect. Cross-site scripting occurs when an attacker inserts client-side scripts into a web page that other users will browse to. A replay attack occurs when legitimate network traffic is repeated maliciously. A pass-the-hash attack involves intercepting a hash from a legitimate user and using it to authenticate as that user to other resources.

16.   ☑   **A** and **B.** Software developers must use input validation as a secure coding method to ensure that user-supplied data is expected and valid. Input validation should occur server-side so that validation code is not exposed or potentially modified client-side. To mitigate API attacks, HTTPS can be used to authenticate and encrypt connections to an API.
   ☒   **C** and **D** are incorrect. Elasticity is a computing characteristic that enables the rapid provisioning and deprovisioning of computing resources, often using a self-service web portal. Autoscaling is common in cloud computing to enable an application to provision more underlying virtual machines when application demand increases (scaling out) and remove virtual machines when application demand decreases (scaling in).

17.   ☑   **D.** Code-signing certificates are used by script writers and software developers to digitally sign scripts or software files. Devices that trust the certificate issuer will trust files signed by issued code-signing certificates. Software developers must harden their systems to ensure that their software compilers and certificates are not compromised. Compilers are used to convert programming language code to binary machine-readable language.
   ☒   **A, B,** and **C** are incorrect. Client-side PKI certificates can be used to authenticate a client device, such as a smartphone, to a secure environment such as a VPN. A single Subject Alternative Name (SAN) certificate could be used for multiple DNS domains such as www.acme.uk and www.acme.ca. A wildcard certificate (*.acme.com) could be acquired instead of separate certificates for multiple domains and does not require domain names to be hard-coded into the certificate (as SAN certificates do).

18.   ☑   **A.** Continuous integration and continuous deployment (CI/CD) uses automation to speed up the overall development and delivery of software to interested parties. This can include the monitoring of code check-ins and validating the integrity of code changes through automated testing scripts.

☒ **B, C,** and **D** are incorrect. Software developers must use input validation as a secure coding method to ensure that user-supplied data is expected and valid. Elasticity is a computing characteristic that enables the rapid provisioning and deprovisioning of computing resources, often using a self-service web portal. Autoscaling is common in cloud computing to enable an application to provision more underlying virtual machines when application demand increases (scaling out) and remove virtual machines when application demand decreases (scaling in).

19. ☑ **A.** The Open Web Application Security Project (OWASP) is a vendor-neutral non-profit organization whose focus is to provide guidance and free tools that can be used to secure web applications. Tools include web vulnerability scanners and fuzzers, as well as secure programming libraries supporting security features such as input validation through the OWASP Enterprise Security API (ESAPI).

☒ **B, C,** and **D** are incorrect. While the National Institute of Standards and Technology (NIST), International Standard Organization (ISO), and Payment Card Industry Data Security Standard (PCI DSS) organization do provide guidance related to IT security (PCI DSS focuses on credit card payment system security), they are not focused solely on web application security.

20. ☑ **D.** A Secure Sockets Layer (SSL) stripping attack involves an attacker inserting his system between a client and HTTPS server. Client connections over HTTP are unknowingly sent to the attacker's system (not protected by HTTPS) and the attacker's system then makes an HTTPS connection to the web server. SSL is deprecated and should not be used; instead use Transport Layer Security (TLS).

☒ **A, B,** and **C** are incorrect. Staging is used in software development testing to provide a testing, or staging, area to host and test the application without affecting the production version of the app. Normalization is a data organization process whereby data is organized to reduce the occurrence or repeating data such as customer mailing addresses, e-mail addresses, phone numbers, and so on. Storing customer data once in a customer's table and writing only a unique customer code into a linked transactions table is an example of normalization. Shimming, in terms of driver manipulation, is an attack in which a piece of software acts as a driver and intercepts and changes commands coming to and from the hardware.

21. ☑ **A and D.** Stored procedures are similar to a function or script that can be executed over and over in a database environment. Stored procedures can be assigned permissions to access specific database objects such as tables, and users or database roles are granted the permission to execute stored procedures.

☒ **B and C** are incorrect. Shimming, in terms of driver manipulation, is an attack by which a piece of software acts as a driver and intercepts and changes commands coming to and from the hardware. Shimming is not directly related to database stored procedures. CI/CD uses automation to speed up the overall development and delivery of software to interested parties.

22. ☑ **C.** Static code analysis involves reviewing software source code to identity problems such as security vulnerabilities.

    ☒ **A, B,** and **D** are incorrect. Dynamic code analysis is used to increase code reliability and security. It involves executing and observing the behavior of code, such as with application fuzzing, providing random unanticipated data to a web application. Shimming, in terms of driver manipulation, is an attack in which a piece of software acts as a driver and intercepts and changes commands coming to and from the hardware. CI/CD uses automation to speed up the overall development and delivery of software to interested parties.

23. ☑ **A.** A buffer overflow attack occurs when an attacker sends more data to an application or service than it is expecting. The extra data that is sent flows out of the area of memory (the buffer) assigned to the application, which can result in areas of code being overwritten, and may cause the application to crash or allow arbitrary execution of commands on the target.

    ☒ **B, C,** and **D** are incorrect. XSS is an attack that involves the attacker inserting script code into a web page so that it is then processed and executed by a client system when a user accesses that web page. Cross-site request forgeries occur when an attacker tricks a user into executing unwanted actions on a web site to which she is currently authenticated. In a race condition, when code is executed by multiple threads, the timing of dependent events is not predictable, and as a result a different thread can function in an unintended manner. For example, a piece of code may check the value of a variable and take action later, while that variable's value can change in the interim.

24. ☑ **B.** Simulating attacks against an IT environment, including web applications, is called penetration testing, or pen testing. This type of testing is used to identify security flaws that can be actively exploited. Pen tests can render a web app unusable and must be executed with the direct permission of the system owner.

    ☒ **A, C,** and **D** are incorrect. The listed items are not used for attack simulations. Normalization is a data organization process whereby data is organized to reduce the occurrence or repeating data. Obfuscation is used to make it more difficult to read or understand something such as programming code or sensitive data. Blocked apps are specifically listed as not being allowed to execute on company computers.

25. ☑ **D.** The **-1** value for an **expires** HTTP header means expiration is immediate, and caching for this response does not occur; thus, upon reuse, the data will have to be requested from the server. Caching be sometimes be useful to decrease the amount of time it takes to load web page content and reduce the amount of network traffic sent to a web server. On the server side, caching reduces the number of HTTP requests that must be processed by the web server.

    ☒ **A, B,** and **C** are incorrect. The listed items do not define the purpose of setting **-1** value for the **expires** HTTP header.

26. ☑ **D.** The HTTP Strict Transport Security (HSTS) response header requires HTTPS secured web server connections; it prevents downgrade attacks that may attempt to use HTTP.

☒ **A, B,** and **C** are incorrect. The X-Frames-Options header helps mitigate clickjacking attacks, as it defines whether or not a web browser is able to render a page in a frame. Clickjacking attack involves tricking the user into clicking an object, such as a fake ad on a web page, that does not do what the user expects it to do. The **allow** header lists permitted HTTP actions such as **GET** and **POST**. The **expires** header determines when an HTTP response expires and whether or not responses are cached.

27. ☑ **B** and **C.** The **HTTPOnly** flag prevents client-side script access to a sensitive cookie; it is accessible only by the server. The **secure** flag requires transmission using HTTPS as opposed to the less secure HTTP.

☒ **A** and **D** are incorrect. The X-Frames-Options header helps mitigate clickjacking attacks. The -**1** value for an **expires** HTTP header means expiration is immediate and caching for this response does not occur

28. ☑ **B.** Static code analysis involves reviewing software source code to identity problems such as security vulnerabilities and existing dead code fragments.

☒ **A, C,** and **D** are incorrect. Dynamic code analysis is used to increase code reliability and security. It involves executing and observing the behavior of code, such as with application fuzzing, providing random unanticipated data to a web application. Fuzzing provides a large amount of input data, even invalid data, to an application in order to observe its behavior; the idea is to ensure that the application is stable and secure with its input and error handling. Shimming, in terms of driver manipulation, is an attack in which a piece of software acts as a driver and intercepts and changes commands coming to and from the hardware.

29. ☑ **C.** Fuzzing provides a large amount of input data, even invalid data, to an application in order to observe its behavior; the idea is to ensure that the application is stable and secure with its input and error handling. It's commonly used as a black-box software testing technique.

☒ **A, B,** and **D** are incorrect. Dynamic code analysis is used to increase code reliability and security. It involves executing and observing the behavior of code, such as with application fuzzing, providing random unanticipated data to a web application. Static code analysis involves reviewing software source code to identity problems such as security vulnerabilities. Shimming, in terms of driver manipulation, is an attack in which a piece of software acts as a driver and intercepts and changes commands coming to and from the hardware.

30. ☑ **A.** A PKI is a hierarchy of security certificates used to secure computing environments such as through disk encryption and network authentication and encryption. Developers can use it to sign their source code to ensure that anyone that downloads it is able to confirm the validity of the code.

☒ **B, C,** and **D** are incorrect. CI/CD uses automation to speed up the overall development and delivery of software to interested parties. The OWASP is a vendor-neutral non-profit organization whose focus is to provide guidance and free tools that can be used to secure web applications. Tools include web vulnerability scanners and fuzzers, as well as secure programming libraries supporting security features such as input validation through the OWASP Enterprise Security API (ESAPI). Shimming, in terms of driver manipulation, is an attack in which a piece of software acts as a driver and intercepts and changes commands coming to and from the hardware.

31. ☑ **D.** A buffer overflow attack occurs when an attacker sends more data to an application or service than it is expecting. The extra data that is sent flows out of the area of memory (the buffer) assigned to the application, which can result in areas of code being overwritten, and may cause the application to crash or allow arbitrary execution of commands on the target.

☒ **A, B,** and **C** are incorrect. In a race condition, when code is executed by multiple threads, the timing of dependent events is not predictable, and as a result a different thread can function in an unintended manner. For example, a piece of code may check the value of a variable and take action later, while that variable's value can change in the interim. Cross-site request forgeries occur when an attacker tricks a user into executing unwanted actions on a web site she is currently authenticated to. A cross-site scripting (XSS) attack involves the attacker inserting script code into a web page so that it is then processed and executed by a client system as the user access the web site.

32. ☑ **D.** A XSS attack involves the attacker inserting script code into a web page so that it is then processed and executed by the client web browser, once the user accesses the web page. If the target client web browser blocks languages such as JavaScript from executing in the web browser, the attack is mitigated because the code does not execute.

☒ **A, B,** and **C** are incorrect. The listed options do not mitigate XSS attacks. Device PKI certificates can be used to authenticate to a secured end-point such as an HTTPS web server or a VPN. Stored procedures are similar to a function or script that can be executed over and over in a database environment. Stored procedures can be assigned permissions to access specific database objects such as tables, and users or database roles are granted the permission to execute stored procedures. Fuzzing provides a large amount of input data, even invalid data, to an application in order to observe its behavior; the idea is to ensure that the application is stable and secure with its input and error handling.

Chapter 16

Virtualization and Cloud Security

QUESTIONS

Virtualization is required by cloud computing. Cloud computing enables organizations to provision and deprovision IT services quickly as business needs dictate. Operating system virtualization provides the advantage of maximizing computing hardware resource usage among multiple guest virtual machines. Application containers keep app files and settings confined within a logical boundary called a container. Applications can consist of one or more containers that can be easily moved between hosts and can be started up quickly because they use the underlying host operating system, which is already running.

Organizations must plan for the use and management of cloud services to maximize efficiency, availability, and security while minimizing costs. Options that help achieve this include using templates, replicating data between geographical regions, and preventing the running of unneeded cloud resources.

1. You are a server virtualization consultant. During a planning meeting with a client, the issue of virtual machine point-in-time snapshots comes up. You recommend careful use of snapshots because of the security ramifications. Which security problem is the most likely to occur when using snapshots?
   A. Snapshots can consume a large amount of disk space.
   B. Snapshots could expose sensitive data.
   C. Invoked snapshots will mean that the virtual machine is temporarily unavailable.
   D. Invoked snapshots will have fewer patch updates than the currently running virtual machine.

2. A private medical practice hires you to determine the feasibility of cloud computing, whereby storage of e-mail and medical applications, as well as patient information, would be hosted by a public cloud provider. You are asked to identify potential problems related to sensitive data regulatory compliance. (Choose two.)
   A. Data is stored on the cloud provider's infrastructure, which is shared by other cloud tenants.
   B. HTTPS will be used to access remote services.
   C. Should the provider be served a subpoena, the possibility of full data disclosure exists.
   D. Data will be encrypted in transit as well as when stored.

3. Which of the following are true regarding virtualization? (Choose two.)
   A. Each virtual machine has one or more unique MAC addresses.
   B. Virtual machine operating systems do not need to be patched.

   C. Virtual machines running on the same physical host can belong to different VLANs.

   D. A security compromise of one virtual machine means all virtual machines on the physical host are compromised.

4. Cloud computing offers which benefits? (Choose two.)

   A. Scalability

   B. Fewer hardware purchases

   C. Better encryption

   D. Local data storage

   F. No requirement for on-premises antivirus software

5. You are responsible for three IaaS payroll servers that store data in the cloud. The chief financial officer (CFO) requests observation of access to a group of budget files by a particular user. What should you do?

   A. Create file hashes for each budget file.

   B. Encrypt the budget files.

   C. Configure a HIDS to monitor the budget files.

   D. Configure file system auditing for cloud storage.

6. As the database administrator for your company, you are evaluating various public cloud offerings to test customer database app code changes. Which category of cloud service should you research?

   A. Software as a Service

   B. Platform as a Service

   C. Infrastructure as a Service

   D. Anything as a Service

7. Your company hosts an on-premises Microsoft Active Directory server to authenticate network users. Mailboxes and productivity applications for users are hosted in a public cloud. You have configured identity federation to enable locally authenticated users to connect to their mailboxes and productivity applications seamlessly. What type of cloud deployment model is in use?

   A. Public

   B. Private

   C. Hybrid

   D. Community

8. What type of hypervisor would be required if you wanted to use an existing server with an existing operating system?

   A. Type 1

   B. Type 2

   C. Type 3

   D. Type 4

9. Your manager wants to run every application securely in its own virtualized environment while minimizing application startup time. What should be used for each application?

   A. Virtual machine

   B. Cloud access security broker

   C. VM escape protection

   D. Application container

10. Which cloud computing characteristic relates to how a service can grow in response to workloads?

    A. Scalability

    B. Pulverizing

    C. Templates

    D. Metered usage

11. You have replicated on-premises application servers and data to the cloud in the event of an on-premises network disruption. The servers are kept in sync through replication. Which term best describes the role of the cloud in this configuration?

    A. Warm site

    B. Hot site

    C. Cold site

    D. Glacier site

12. You have configured a cloud-based VDI solution in which client devices run a cloud-based Windows desktop. Which term best describes the connecting user device that may be generally used?

    A. Thick client

    B. Smartphone

    C. Thin client

    D. Tablet

13. You are configuring cloud-based virtual networks without having to connect directly to the cloud provider hardware routers to configure VLANs. What enables this capability?

    A. Software-defined networking

    B. Transit gateway

    C. Software-defined visibility

    D. Serverless architecture

14. Private cloud technicians have configured policies that will shut down and remove virtual machines with no activity for 30 days or more. What are technicians attempting to prevent?

    A. VM escaping

    B. VM resource policy exploitation

C. VM sprawl

D. VM services integration

15. You must ensure that cloud storage is available in the event of a regional disruption. What should you configure?

   A. Cloud storage encryption

   B. Cloud storage permissions

   C. Cloud storage replication within a data center

   D. Cloud storage replication across zones

16. You must control network traffic flow to specific Amazon Web Services (AWS) virtual machines. What should you configure?

   A. Network ACL

   B. Amazon machine image

   C. Elastic IP address

   D. Security group

17. You have deployed a database in an AWS virtual private cloud. You need to limit database access to other AWS resources while ensuring that network traffic does not leave the Amazon network. What should you configure?

   A. VPC endpoint

   B. Transit gateway

   C. Elastic IP address

   D. Security group

18. Which type of provider specializes in providing IT security service offerings?

   A. Microservice API

   B. CASB

   C. MSP

   D. MSSP

19. A cloud firewall solution examines packet headers to allow or deny traffic based on IP addresses and port numbers. To which layer of the OSI model does the type of firewall apply?

   A. 2

   B. 3

   C. 4

   D. 7

20. You have configured a content-filtering firewall for traffic leaving a cloud virtual network. To which layer of the OSI model does this type of firewall apply?

　A.　2

　B.　3

　C.　4

　D.　7

21. Which strategy involves using network edge devices to process and move data into and out of the cloud?

　A.　Quantum computing

　B.　Fog computing

　C.　Hybrid cloud

　D.　Private cloud

22. Which strategy increases the security of cloud-based containerized applications?

　A.　Use a private cloud to host containerized applications.

　B.　Run the containers only on physical servers.

　C.　Create containers only from anonymous public repositories.

　D.　Create containers only from private repositories.

23. Your software developers use security keys to access cloud services. What should you do to harden the use of security keys?

　A.　Rotate cloud keys.

　B.　Use symmetric instead of asymmetric keys.

　C.　Reduce the key length.

　D.　Send copies of keys to all developers via SMTP.

24. You need to deploy virtual machines in the cloud to support big data processing. The virtual machines must not be reachable from the Internet. Data processing summaries will be uploaded from the virtual machines to an on-premises database server. The on-premises network is already configured to allow incoming connections from the Internet. What should you do to allow the required functionality while maximizing security?

　A.　Deploy a public subnet in the cloud with firewall rules.

　B.　Deploy a private subnet in the cloud with an on-premises Internet gateway.

　C.　Deploy a private subnet in the cloud with an Internet gateway.

　D.　Deploy a client-to-site VPN.

25. Over time, you have noticed unauthorized configuration changes made to virtual machine cloud settings. You need a way to track who made these changes and when. What should you do?

 A. Enable virtual machine API integration.

 B. Rotate the cloud access keys.

 C. Deploy an OSI layer 7 firewall.

 D. Enable cloud resource activity auditing.

26. Which capabilities are offered by Next-generation Secure Web Gateways? (Choose two.)

 A. Content filtering

 B. Proxy server

 C. Infrastructure as code

 D. CI/CD

27. Which type of cloud service model is depicted in Figure 16-1?

 A. PaaS

 B. XaaS

 C. SaaS

 D. IaaS

FIGURE 16-1 Amazon Web Services EC2 Instances

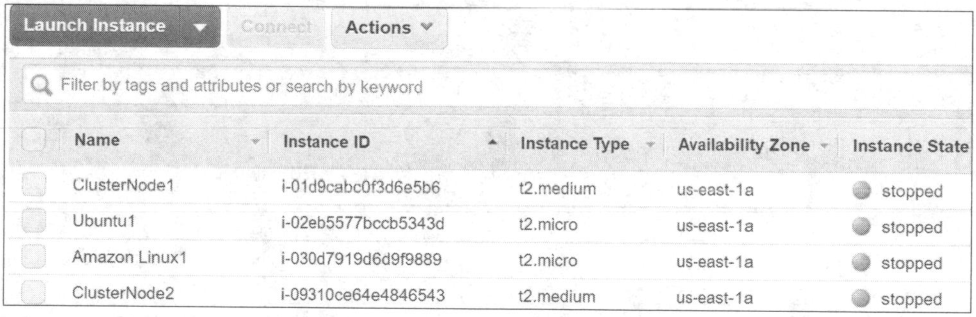

Name	Instance ID	Instance Type	Availability Zone	Instance State
ClusterNode1	i-01d9cabc0f3d6e5b6	t2.medium	us-east-1a	stopped
Ubuntu1	i-02eb5577bccb5343d	t2.micro	us-east-1a	stopped
Amazon Linux1	i-030d7919d6d9f9889	t2.micro	us-east-1a	stopped
ClusterNode2	i-09310ce64e4846543	t2.medium	us-east-1a	stopped

Launch Instance ▼ | Connect | Actions ✓

Filter by tags and attributes or search by keyword

28. Which type of cloud service model is depicted in Figure 16-2?

    A.   PaaS

    B.   XaaS

    C.   SaaS

    D.   IaaS

FIGURE 16-2   Amazon Web Services database creation options

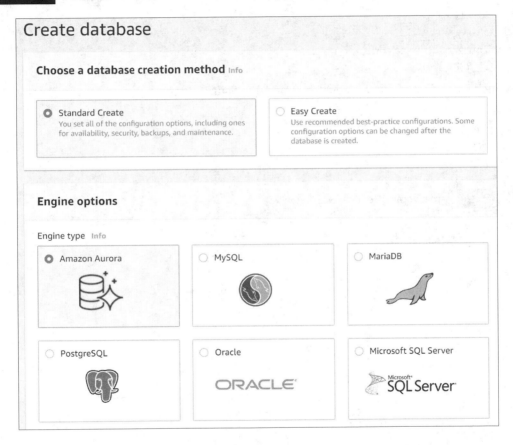

29. You have linked your on-premises and public cloud networks together with a site-to-site VPN. Which type cloud deployment model does this apply to?

    A.   Private

    B.   Community

    C.   Hybrid

    D.   Public

30. Which term best describes Figure 16-3?

    A. Software-defined networking

    B. SaaS

    C. Infrastructure as code

    D. Fog computing

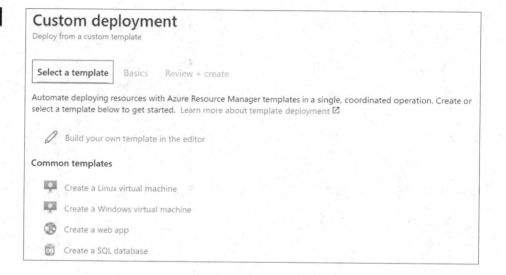

FIGURE 16-3

Microsoft
Azure template
deployment

31. Which type of replication does not wait for data to be committed to the primary replica before synchronizing additional replicas?

    A. Asynchronous

    B. Synchronous

    C. Symmetric

    D. Asymmetric

32. Which term describes breaking out of a virtual machine and attacking the hypervisor?

    A. VM sprawl

    B. VM escape

    C. CASB

    D. OSI layer 7 firewall

QUICK ANSWER KEY

1.	D	**12.**	C	**23.**	A
2.	A, C	**13.**	A	**24.**	C
3.	A, C	**14.**	C	**25.**	D
4.	A, B	**15.**	D	**26.**	A, B
5.	D	**16.**	D	**27.**	D
6.	B	**17.**	A	**28.**	A
7.	C	**18.**	D	**29.**	C
8.	B	**19.**	C	**30.**	C
9.	D	**20.**	D	**31.**	B
10.	A	**21.**	B	**32.**	B
11.	B	**22.**	D		

IN-DEPTH ANSWERS

1. ☑ **D.** Reverting a running virtual machine to an older snapshot could mean going back to a point in time before critical patches or virus scanning updates were applied, thus rendering your virtual machine vulnerable.

   ☒ **A, B,** and **C** are incorrect. Snapshot disk space usage is not directly related to security. Snapshots will not expose sensitive data any more than the current file system on a virtual machine will. Reverting to a snapshot could make a virtual machine temporarily unavailable, but this is not the most prominent potential security issue.

2. ☑ **A** and **C.** Sharing the same cloud computing services with other customers could be forbidden by sensitive data regulations, although cloud tenant data is not accessible by other cloud tenants. Depending on the provider's geographic location, different laws may apply to whether data hosted by the provider can legally be disclosed. However, that's not a risk many organizations are willing to take.

   ☒ **B** and **D** are incorrect. Hypertext Transfer Protocol Secure (HTTPS) is considered a secure transmission protocol for data in transit (while HTTP is not), so this is an advantage not an issue. Data encryption does not cause security concerns; it addresses them.

3. ☑ **A** and **C.** Each virtual machine does have one or more unique MAC addresses that are configurable by the virtual machine administrator. Virtual machines running on the same host can connect to different VLANs (physical or internal); this is a virtual network configuration setting.

   ☒ **B** and **D** are incorrect. Virtualized operating systems must be patched to address stability and security issues that may exist without patching. A single compromised virtual machine does not imply a compromise of all other virtual machines on the same hypervisor; an operating system exploit could provide an attacker with full access to the operating system but not with the ability to "break out" of the virtual machine into the hosting hypervisor operating system.

4. ☑ **A** and **B.** Scalability with cloud computing is possible because a third party (the cloud provider) pools and provides hardware, software, software licensing, and so on. Provisioning additional resources such as more storage on-demand is a characteristic of cloud computing. Because a third party is hosting some (or all) of your IT services, you will require fewer hardware resources on-premises.

   ☒ **C, D,** and **E** are incorrect. Cloud computing does not require that encryption be used and does not necessarily offer better encryption options than may be available on-premises. With cloud computing, data storage is normally hosted by the provider, not locally, unless on-premises data is backed up to the cloud. Even for firms relying exclusively on cloud computing, employees will still use a computing device to connect to cloud services and therefore will need antivirus software.

5.   ☑   **D.** You should configure file system auditing for budget file access by the employee in question. This enables you to track who accessed budget files at any given time.
☒   **A, B,** and **C** are incorrect. File hashing is useful only in determining whether a file has changed, not whether anybody in particular accessed the file. Encryption is used for data confidentiality. A host-based intrusion detection system (HIDS) looks for and reports on abnormal host activity; users who access files with appropriate permissions are generally not considered abnormal.

6.   ☑   **B.** Platform as a Service (PaaS) is primarily of interest to software developers and provides IT services over a network such as databases and programming APIs.
☒   **A, C,** and **D** are incorrect. Software as a Service (SaaS) enables end-user productivity software to be rapidly provisioned over a network. Infrastructure as a Service (IaaS) refers to compute, network, and storage services offered in the cloud. Anything as a service (XaaS) is a general term used to describe IT services delivered over a network.

7.   ☑   **C.** Hybrid cloud solutions combine on-premises IT services with IT services hosted in the cloud.
☒   **A, B,** and **D** are incorrect. Public cloud services are hosted solely on computing resources owned and managed by the public cloud provider. Private cloud services are hosted on computing resources completely owned and managed by a single organization. Community clouds pool computing resources to offer IT services to organizations with similar needs, such as government agencies.

8.   ☑   **B.** Type 2 hypervisors run on top of an existing operating system.
☒   **A, C,** and **D** are incorrect. A Type 1 hypervisor runs directly on the hardware; it is the operating system. Type 3 and Type 4 hypervisors do not exist.

9.   ☑   **D.** Application containers enable the deployment of each app in its own virtualized environment while minimizing app startup time, because the container uses the underlying host operating system that is already running.
☒   **A, B,** and **C** are incorrect. Running apps within virtual machines will work but will not minimize app startup time, since the virtual machine operating system must also be started. Cloud access security brokers are enforcement points that enable enterprise security policies to be applied while accessing cloud resources. VM escape protection is a technique that prevents applications running inside of a virtual machine from accessing the hosting hypervisor.

10.   ☑   **A.** Scalability is a cloud computing characteristic that enables resources to respond to workload changes, such as adding virtual machines (scaling out) when an application becomes busier. Scaling in (removing virtual machines) is also an option when demand declines, and it reduces cloud computing costs.
☒   **B, C,** and **D** are incorrect. Pulverizing is a data destruction technique. Templates are blueprints from which future changes or new item creation can be based. In the cloud, templates are referred to as "infrastructure as code" and serve as a method of automating cloud resource deployment. With cloud computing, metered usage refers to being charged based on cloud resource usage, such as for the amount of time a cloud-based virtual machine is running.

11. ☑ **B.** With disaster recovery, hot alternative sites are mirrored with copies of IT systems and data from a primary site. Configurations and data are kept in sync via replication. Hot sites can be alternate facilities many miles away from the primary site. Public clouds are now commonly used as hot sites, which removes the cost of maintaining a separate facility.

☒ **A, C,** and **D** are incorrect. Warm sites contain equipment and can also contain running IT systems, but they do not have up-to-date data. Cold sites are represented by a physical location to be used in the event that the primary site is unavailable, but they do not contain equipment or data. Glacier site is not a valid disaster recovery term.

12. ☑ **C.** A thin client is an end-user device with limited processing power and storage that connects to a powerful remote server to run operating systems and apps over a network.

☒ **A, B,** and **D** are incorrect. Thick clients are end-user devices with ample processing power and storage. While smartphones and tablets are often used as thin clients, thin client is the best answer because it captures any type of end-user device, while tablets and smartphones capture specific types of devices.

13. ☑ **A.** Software-defined networking (SDN) adds a configuration layer above network infrastructure hardware that enables a simplified and consistent management experience such as through a web GUI or command-line tools. SDN removes the need of cloud customers having detailed technical knowledge related to the configuration of underlying network hardware.

☒ **B, C,** and **D** are incorrect. In the cloud, transit gateways enable cloud virtual network and on-premises network interconnectivity through network linking mechanisms such as VPNs. Virtual networks connected to a centralized transit gateway network would not each need a VPN link to communicate with other networks; instead, they connect through the transit gateway. Software-defined visibility (SDV) provides a holistic approach to managing and monitoring networks with the additional ability to detect and react to real-time security alerts. A serverless architecture still uses an underlying server, but deploying virtual machines and installing code hosting or database software is handled by the cloud service provider (CSP); the cloud tenant configures only higher level services such as creating custom software functions or database objects.

14. ☑ **C.** Because of the ease and speed in which virtual machines can be deployed in the cloud, over time VM sprawl may occur. In VM sprawl, you may not be aware of the existence of numerous virtual machines that are not used or that have been forgotten, yet they still exist and could remain running, thus incurring cloud computing charges.

☒ **A, B,** and **D** are incorrect. VM escape occurs when malicious code running inside of a virtual machine attempts to access the hosting hypervisor operating system. Policies, in some environments such as Amazon Web Services (AWS), are collections of related permissions that can be granted to users or groups to allow resource management or access. Removing unused VMs is not related to VM resource policies or the integration of software services within a VM.

15. ☑ **D.** Replication of cloud-stored data to alternative physical locations, or geographical zones, provides data redundancy in the event of a disruption in one region.

☒ **A, B,** and **C** are incorrect. The listed items do not address the inability to access cloud data during a regional disruption; only replication across zones will do this. Encryption provides confidentiality for data at rest. Setting cloud storage permissions controls data access, and replicating within a single data center is not helpful during a regional outage.

16. ☑ **D.** An AWS security group contains a list of rules that allow traffic into or out of specific virtual machines (called EC2 instances in AWS).

 ☒ **A, B,** and **C** are incorrect. A network access control list (ACL) is used in AWS to allow or deny traffic into and out of cloud subnets, not individual virtual machines. An Amazon machine image (AMI) is a virtual machine template that is selected when deploying a new EC2 instance. An elastic IP address (EIP) is a static unchanging public IP address resource in AWS that can be moved between different virtual machines as needed.

17. ☑ **A.** A virtual private cloud (VPC) is a virtual network defined in the cloud, such as AWS, Google Cloud, or IBM Cloud. A VPC endpoint enables a private connection to resources in a VPC using only internal private IP addresses.

 ☒ **B, C,** and **D** are incorrect. In the cloud, transit gateways enable cloud virtual network and on-premises network interconnectivity through network-linking mechanisms such as VPNs. Virtual networks connected to a centralized transit gateway network would not each need a VPN link to communicate with other networks; instead, they connect through the transit gateway. An elastic IP address (EIP) is a static, unchanging public IP address resource in AWS that can move between different virtual machines as needed. An AWS security group contains a list of rules that allow traffic into or out of specific virtual machines (called EC2 instances in AWS).

18. ☑ **D.** A managed security service provider (MSSP) offers IT security services, such as network DDoS attack mitigation, over a network. MSSP services can be cloud native or offered through third-party providers.

 ☒ **A, B,** and **C** are incorrect. The listed items are not as specific to security service offerings as an MSSP is. A microservice is a mini program that focuses on performing a specific task and can be exposed to other developers as an application programming interface (API). Most modern apps consist of modular independent microservices. Cloud access security brokers (CASBs) are enforcement points that enable enterprise security policies to be applied when accessing cloud resources. A managed service provider (MSP) offers IT services over a network but is not limited to security services as an MSSP is.

19. ☑ **C.** Layer 4, the transport layer of the seven-layer conceptual OSI model, focuses on transporting data either reliably (TCP) or unreliably but more quickly (UDP). Network service port numbers are also called layer 4 addresses; IP addresses are layer 3 (the network layer) addresses. A packet-filtering firewall can examine packet headers containing addressing information, but not the packet payload containing the data being transmitted.

 ☒ **A, B,** and **D** are incorrect. Layer 2 is the OSI data link layer, which is concerned with how transmissions are placed on the network medium. Layer 3 focuses on IP addressing and routing. Layer 7 (the application layer) relates to high-level protocols such as DNS and HTTP, some of which involve user interaction.

20. ☑ **D.** Layer 7 (the application layer) of the OSI model relates to high-level protocols, meaning all packet headers and packet payloads can be examined, as opposed to a layer 4 packet filtering firewall, which can base decisions only on the fields present in packet headers. As a result, layer 7 firewall solutions tend to be more expensive than layer 4 firewall solutions.

☒ **A, B,** and **C** are incorrect. Layer 2 is the OSI data link layer, which is concerned with how transmissions are placed on the network medium. Layer 3 focuses on IP addressing and routing, and layer 4 is responsible for packet transport and delivery.

21. ☑ **B.** Fog computing, also referred to as edge computing, places data processing capabilities on network edge devices between data sources and a public cloud environment, such as a corporate on-premises network. The benefit is that decentralizing processing and placing it nearest where it is needed can speed up data transfers and thus reduce overall processing time.

☒ **A, C,** and **D** are incorrect. Quantum computing is based on the premise of manipulating quantum bits (qbits), which can exhibit multiple states simultaneously, as opposed to current-day computing, which uses bits (0's and 1's) to represent the state of data (only two possibilities). Quantum computing results in the ability to perform multiple calculations quickly, thus increasing compute power. Hybrid clouds combine cloud models such as private and public clouds or combine public clouds with on-premises IT environments such as through VPN connectivity. Private clouds meet all cloud computing characteristics, but a single organization owns and uses the cloud infrastructure.

22. ☑ **D.** A containerized application decouples an application or application component (microservice) from other components or operating system dependencies. A container is a runtime version of a container image and consists of application files and configuration settings but not the OS; the underlying host OS that is already running is used instead. Hosting images in a private repository provides the ability to control which images are used to launch containers, thus enhancing security.

☒ **A, B,** and **C** are incorrect. None of the listed solutions *increases* container security. A private cloud does not offer more security than is available in a public cloud. Whether containers are hosted on physical or virtual machines does not affect the security of the containerized application. An infected or unstable image is more likely to be sourced from an anonymous public repository than a private repository.

23. ☑ **A.** Rotating keys is a standard security practice. Past compromised keys will no longer provide resource access. Software developers must be provided with newly rotated keys for continued cloud resource access.

☒ **B, C,** and **D** are incorrect. Symmetric cryptography uses the same key for encryption and decryption, where asymmetric cryptography uses public and private key pairs to provide security; using symmetric keys does not increase security. Reducing key length does not harden security keys; generally speaking, more bits in a key increase the number of possible key combinations, thus making it more difficult to crack. Sending keys via SMTP is not considered a key-hardening best practice, since SMTP does not encrypt messages; S/MIME would be acceptable, however, since messages are encrypted, but this is not included in the answers.

24. ☑ **C.** A private cloud subnet does not allow incoming connections from the Internet and does not normally allow outgoing connectivity to the Internet. Configuring an Internet gateway will allow cloud virtual machines with only private IP addresses to communicate outside of the private subnet, such as to on-premises resources. Cloud resources are often isolated on segmented networks for security reasons.
     ☒ **A, B,** and **D** are incorrect. Public subnets allow incoming Internet connections, which violates a stated requirement. Because the private network exists in the cloud, so too must the Internet gateway to allow outbound Internet traffic. Client-to-site VPNs allow individual client stations to access a remote network securely; they do not allow cloud resources in a private network to communicate as per the stated requirement.

25. ☑ **D.** Auditing cloud resource activity will provide a log of actions, such as technicians who make configuration changes to cloud-based virtual machines. Most auditing systems have configurable audit data retention periods and filtering options.
     ☒ **A, B,** and **C** are incorrect. The listed items will not track virtual machine configuration changes. API integration allows the interaction of resources such as custom code running within a cloud-based virtual machine that makes API calls to a database running on-premises or in the cloud. Rotating keys is a standard security practice. Past compromised keys will no longer provide resource access, but this does not address the listed tracking requirement. Layer 7 (the application layer) of the OSI model relates to high-level protocols, meaning that layer 7 firewalls can examine all packet headers and packet payloads.

26. ☑ **A** and **B.** A Next-generation Secure Web Gateway (SWG) is an on-premises or cloud-based unified IT security solution that provides services such a malware detection and prevention, network threat detection, forward and reverse proxying, content filtering, data loss protection, and threat reporting.
     ☒ **C** and **D** are incorrect. In the cloud, templates are referred to as "infrastructure as code" and serve as a method of automating cloud resource deployment. Continuous integration and continuous deployment (CI/CD) uses automation to speed up the overall development and delivery of software to interested parties.

27. ☑ **D.** Virtual machine instances are shown in Figure 16-1. The manual deployment and management of virtual machines in the cloud is referred to infrastructure as a Service (IaaS). Infrastructure as a Service (IaaS) refers to compute, network, and storage services offered in the cloud.
     ☒ **A, B,** and **C** are incorrect. The listed cloud service models are not reflected in Figure 16-1. Platform as a Service (PaaS) is primarily of interest to software developers and provides IT services over a network such as databases and programming APIs. Anything as a service (XaaS) is a term used to describe general IT services delivered over a network. Software as a Service (SaaS) enables end-user productivity software to be rapidly provisioned over a network.

28. ☑ **A.** Figure 16-2 shows database creation options in the cloud. Databases apply to Platform as a Service (PaaS), which is primarily of interest to software developers and provides IT services over a network such as databases and programming APIs.

☒ **B, C,** and **D** are incorrect. The listed cloud service models are not reflected in Figure 16-2. XaaS is a term used to describe general IT services delivered over a network. Software as a Service (SaaS) enables end-user productivity software to be rapidly provisioned over a network. Infrastructure as a Service (IaaS) refers to compute, network, and storage services offered in the cloud.

29. ☑ **C.** Hybrid cloud solutions combine cloud deployment models, such as linking a private cloud to a public cloud or linking conventional on-premises IT services with IT services hosted in the public cloud.

☒ **A, B,** and **D** are incorrect. The listed cloud deployment models do not apply to this scenario. Private cloud services are hosted on computing resources owned and managed by a single organization. Community clouds pool computing resources to offer IT services to organizations with similar needs, such as government agencies. Public cloud services are hosted on computing resources owned and managed by the public cloud provider.

30. ☑ **C.** Figure 16-3 shows template deployment options to create cloud resources such as virtual machines, web apps, or databases. Templates can be used to automate the repeated deployment of cloud resources and are text files with instructions related to accomplishing this, and as a result this is referred to as "infrastructure as code."

☒ **A, B,** and **D** are incorrect. The listed terms do not describe what is happening in Figure 16-3. Software-defined networking (SDN) adds a configuration layer above network infrastructure hardware that enables a simplified and consistent management experience such as through a web GUI or command-line tools. SDN removes the need of cloud customers having detailed technical knowledge related to the configuration of underlying network hardware. Software as a Service (SaaS) enables end-user productivity software to be rapidly provisioned over a network. Fog computing, also referred to as edge computing, places data processing capabilities on network edge devices between data sources and a public cloud environment, such as a corporate on-premises network. The benefit is that decentralizing processing and placing it nearest where it is needed can speed up data transfers and thus reduce overall processing time.

31. ☑ **B.** Synchronous replication writes to the primary and replica copies concurrently. This is often used for mission-critical applications and requires sufficient network speeds for replicas spread across great distances.

☒ **A, C,** and **D** are incorrect. Asynchronous replication writes data to the primary replica before synchronizing the committed changes to additional replicas. The terms symmetric and asymmetric are not used in the context of replication.

32. ☑ **B.** VM escape occurs when malicious code running inside of a virtual machine attempts to access the hosting hypervisor operating system. Mitigations against this threat include patching hypervisor and guest operating systems as well as limiting tools that share resources between the hypervisor and guests, such as file sharing.

☒ **A, C,** and **D** are incorrect. VM sprawl refers to being aware of the existence of numerous virtual machines that are not used or have been forgotten about, yet they still exist and could even remain running, thus incurring cloud computing charges. Cloud access security brokers (CASBs) are enforcement points that enable enterprise security policies to be applied when accessing cloud resources. Layer 7 (the application layer) of the OSI model relates to high-level protocols, meaning all packet headers and packet payloads can be examined, as opposed to a layer 4 packet filtering firewall, which can base decisions only on the fields present in packet headers. As a result, layer 7 firewall solutions are more expensive than layer 4 firewall solutions.

Chapter 17

Risk Analysis

CERTIFICATION OBJECTIVES

QUESTIONS

Risk analysis determines the possible threats a business could face and how to minimize their impact effectively. Quantitative risk analysis results in a list of risks prioritized by dollar amount, whereas qualitative risk analysis uses a relative prioritizing system to compare risks to one another and rate them.

Risks to the organization should be centrally listed and ranked by severity in a risk register. The risk register also serves as a centralized list of risk mitigation security controls.

Failure to perform a risk analysis properly could result in violation of laws, loss of customer trust, or even major financial loss in the event of threat occurrence.

1. You are responsible for ensuring that all company IT-related equipment and data are inventoried and given a value. Which term best describes this activity?
   A. Asset identification
   B. Risk assessment
   C. Risk mitigation
   D. Risk register

2. You are identifying security threats to determine the likelihood of virus infection. Identify potential sources of infection. (Choose two.)
   A. USB flash drives
   B. USB keyboard
   C. Smartcard
   D. Downloaded documentation from a business partner web site

3. During a risk analysis meeting, you are asked to specify internal threats being considered. Which item is *not* considered an internal threat?
   A. Embezzlement
   B. Attackers breaking in through the firewall
   C. Employees using corporate assets for personal gain
   D. Users plugging in personal USB flash drives

4. You are an IT security consultant. A client conveys her concern to you regarding malicious Internet users gaining access to corporate resources. What type of assessment would you perform to determine this likelihood?
   A. Threat assessment
   B. Risk analysis

    C.   Asset identification

    D.   Total cost of ownership

5. You are an IT consultant performing a risk analysis for a seafood company. The client is concerned with specific cooking and packaging techniques the company uses being disclosed to competitors. What type of security concern is this?

    A.   Integrity

    B.   Confidentiality

    C.   Availability

    D.   Authorization

6. After identifying internal and external threats, you must determine how these potential risks will affect business operations. Which of the following terms best describes this?

    A.   Risk analysis

    B.   Fault tolerance

    C.   Availability

    D.   Impact analysis

7. When determining how best to mitigate risk, which items should you consider? (Choose two.)

    A.   Insurance coverage

    B.   Number of server hard disks

    C.   How fast CPUs in new computers will be

    D.   Network bandwidth

8. You are listing preventative measures for potential risks. Which of the following would you document? (Choose three.)

    A.   Larger flat-screen monitors

    B.   Data backup

    C.   Employee training

    D.   Comparing reliability of network load balancing appliances

9. An insurance company charges an additional $200 monthly premium for natural disaster coverage for your business site. What figure must you compare this against to determine whether to accept this additional coverage?

    A.   ALE

    B.   ROI

    C.   Total cost of ownership

    D.   Total monthly insurance premium

10. Which of the following is true regarding qualitative risk analysis?

    A.   Only numerical data is considered.

    B.   ALE must be calculated.

    C.   Threats must be identified.

    D.   ROI must be calculated.

11. Which values must be calculated to derive annual loss expectancy? (Choose two.)
    A. Single loss expectancy
    B. Annual rate of occurrence
    C. Monthly loss expectancy
    D. Quarterly loss expectancy

12. You are the server expert for a cloud computing firm. Management would like to set aside funds to respond to server downtime risks. Using historical data, you determine that the probability of server downtime is 17 percent. Past data suggests the server would be down for an average of one hour and that $3000 of revenue can be earned in one hour. You must calculate the ALE. Choose the correct ALE.
    A. $300
    B. $510
    C. $3000
    D. $36,000

13. Your boss asks you to calculate how much money the company loses when critical servers required by employees are down for one hour. You have determined that the probability of this happening is 70 percent. The company has 25 employees, each earning $18.50 per hour. Choose the correct value.
    A. $12.95
    B. $18.50
    C. $323.75
    D. $3885

14. Which term best describes monies spent to minimize the impact that threats and unfavorable conditions have on a business?
    A. Risk management
    B. Security audit
    C. Budgetary constraints
    D. Impact analysis

15. Which risk analysis approach makes use of ALE?
    A. Best possible outcome
    B. Quantitative
    C. ROI
    D. Qualitative

16. You are presenting data at a risk analysis meeting. During your presentation you display a list of ALE values ranked by dollar amount. Bob, a meeting participant, wants to know how reliable the numeracy used to calculate the ALE is. What can you tell Bob?

    A.   The numbers are 100 percent reliable.

    B.   The numbers are 50 percent reliable.

    C.   ALEs are calculated using probability values that vary.

    D.   ALEs are calculated using percentages and are accurate.

17. Which of the following should be performed when conducting a qualitative risk assessment? (Choose two.)

    A.   Asset valuation

    B.   ARO

    C.   SLE

    D.   Ranking of potential threats

18. You are the IT security analyst for a gourmet food company that plans to open a plant in Oranjestad, Aruba, next year. You are meeting with a planning committee in the next week and must come up with questions to ask the committee about the new location so you can prepare a risk analysis report. Which of the following would be the most relevant questions to ask? (Choose two.)

    A.   How hot does it get in the summer?

    B.   How reliable is the local power?

    C.   What kind of physical premise security is in place?

    D.   How close is the nearest highway?

19. Your corporate web site is being hosted by a cloud service provider. How does this apply to the concept of risk?

    A.   Risk avoidance

    B.   Risk transfer

    C.   Risk analysis

    D.   Increase in ALE

20. Which of the following regarding risk management is true?

    A.   Funds invested in risk management could have earned much more profit if spent elsewhere.

    B.   ALEs are only estimates and are subject to being inaccurate.

    C.   IT security risks are all handled by the corporate firewall.

    D.   Qualitative risk analysis results are expressed in dollar amounts.

21. Your competitors are offering a new product that is predicted to sell well. After much careful study, your company has decided against launching a competing product because of the uncertainty of the market and the enormous investment required. Which term best describes your company's decision?

    A. Risk analysis
    B. Risk transfer
    C. Risk avoidance
    D. Product avoidance

22. How can management determine which risks should be given the most attention?

    A. Threat vector
    B. Rank risks by likelihood
    C. Rank risks by probable date of occurrence
    D. Rank risks by SLE

23. Recently your data center was housed in Albuquerque, New Mexico. Because of corporate downsizing, the data center equipment was moved to an existing office in Santa Fe. The server room in Santa Fe was not designed to accommodate all the new servers arriving from Albuquerque, and the server room temperature is very warm. Because this is a temporary solution until a new data center facility is built, management has decided not to pay for an updated air conditioning system. Which term best describes this scenario?

    A. Risk transfer
    B. Risk avoidance
    C. Risk acceptance
    D. Risk reduction

24. You are a member of an IT project team. The team is performing an IT risk analysis and has identified assets and their values as well as threats and threat mitigation solutions. What must be done next?

    A. Perform a cost–benefit analysis of proposed risk solutions.
    B. Calculate the ALE values.
    C. Decide which vulnerabilities exist.
    D. There is nothing more to do.

25. To reduce the likelihood of internal fraud, an organization implements policies to ensure that more than one person is responsible for a financial transaction from beginning to end. Which of the following best describes this scenario?

    A. Probability
    B. Mitigation solution
    C. Impact analysis
    D. Threat analysis

26. What is the difference between risk assessment and risk management?

    A. They are the same thing.

    B. Risk assessment identifies and prioritizes risks; risk management is the governing of risks to minimize their impact.

    C. Risk management identifies and prioritizes risks; risk assessment is the governing of risks to minimize their impact.

    D. Risk assessment identifies threats; risk management controls those threats.

27. Identify the two drawbacks to quantitative risk analysis compared to qualitative risk analysis. (Choose two.)

    A. Quantitative risk analysis entails complex calculations.

    B. Risks are not prioritized by monetary value.

    C. Quantitative analysis is more time-consuming than qualitative analysis.

    D. It is difficult to determine how much money to allocate to reduce a risk.

28. Using Figure 17-1, match the terms on the left to the correct scenario on the right.

FIGURE 17-1

Risk mitigation strategies

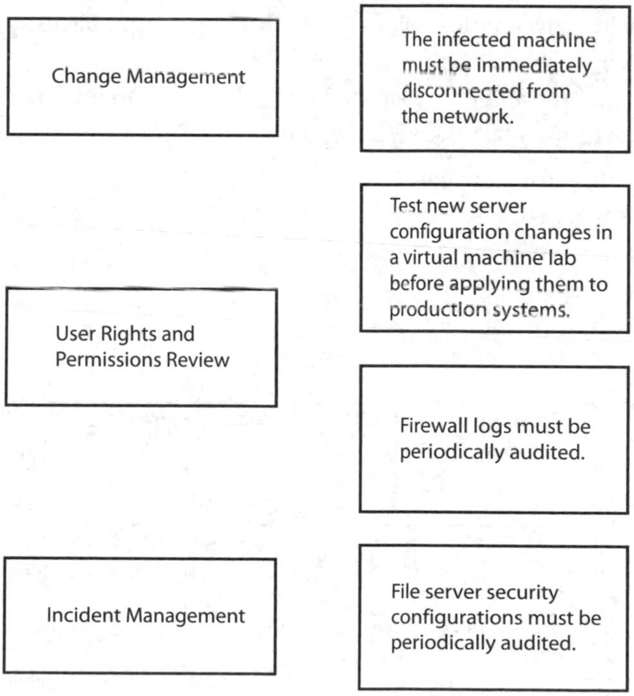

| Change Management | The infected machine must be immediately disconnected from the network. |

| | Test new server configuration changes in a virtual machine lab before applying them to production systems. |

| User Rights and Permissions Review | Firewall logs must be periodically audited. |

| Incident Management | File server security configurations must be periodically audited. |

29. While performing a software licensing compliance scan you discover internal legacy network hosts as well as IoT pump and valve sensor devices running on the network. The hosts run mission-critical software that receives data from the IoT devices. The hosts will be updated with new hardware and software. The IoT devices will not be replaced but will continue to be used. What should you do to best secure this environment? (Choose two.)
   A. Change IoT device default settings.
   B. Deploy a proxy server between users and the legacy hosts.
   C. Place IoT devices on a restricted network.
   D. Change the default port numbers.

30. In preparation for the next IT security meeting for your company, you would like to provide a visual representation of various risks and their likelihood. What should you prepare?
   A. Risk register
   B. Risk heat map
   C. Risk assessment
   D. Risk matrix

31. Which activity is the most closely related to organizational risk transfer?
   A. Requiring new employees to sign an Internet acceptable use policy
   B. Acquiring cybersecurity insurance
   C. Placing a firewall between a screened subnet and an internal network
   D. Configuring a site-to-site VPN tunnel

32. What is being shown in Figure 17-2?
   A. Threat register
   B. Threat heat map
   C. Risk register
   D. Risk heat map

FIGURE 17-2	Description	Likelihood	Impact	Severity	Mitigating Controls
Threats and likelihoods	Ransomwate	Medium	High	9	Employee training E-mail filtering Offline data backups
	Disruption of cloud connectivity	Low	High	8	Dual Internet connections to the cloud using different ISPs
	Public web site going down	Low	High	6	Multiple load balancers in different regions Multiple backend servers hosting web site

QUICK ANSWER KEY

1.	A	**12.**	B	**23.**	C
2.	A, D	**13.**	C	**24.**	B
3.	B	**14.**	A	**25.**	B
4.	A	**15.**	B	**26.**	B
5.	B	**16.**	C	**27.**	A, C
6.	D	**17.**	A, D	**28.**	See "In-Depth Answers."
7.	A, B	**18.**	B, C		
8.	B, C, D	**19.**	B	**29.**	A. C
9.	A	**20.**	B	**30.**	B
10.	C	**21.**	C	**31.**	B
11.	A, B	**22.**	B	**32.**	C

IN-DEPTH ANSWERS

1. ☑ **A.** Asset identification is required before identifying where threats exist. Proper risk management involves identifying assets (including data) and associating a value to them. This information can then be used to justify expenditures to protect these assets.

   ☒ **B, C,** and **D** are incorrect. Risk assessment is the identification of threats. Risk mitigation minimizes the impact of perceived risks; these activities should not be performed until assets within the organization requiring protection are first identified. A risk register is a central list of risks along with their likelihood, impact, severity ratings, and risk control details.

2. ☑ **A and D.** USB flash drives could have files downloaded from the Internet or copied from less secure machines that could infect your network. Business partner documentation downloaded from the Internet could potentially be infected. With proper management approval, conducting a thorough vulnerability assessment of the existing network and its devices, or a more aggressive penetration test, can reveal these potential security holes.

   ☒ **B and C** are incorrect. USB keyboards and smartcards are not likely sources of malware and do not need to be blocked.

3. ☑ **B.** Attackers breaking through a firewall would be considered an external threat.

   ☒ **A, C,** and **D** are incorrect. Anything involving employees and security would be considered a potential internal threat, such users plugging in an infected USB drive, which could then infect one or more devices on the internal network.

4. ☑ **A.** Determining how an entity may gain access to corporate resources would require a threat assessment. Environmental threat assessments consider natural factors such as floods and earthquakes as well as facility environmental factors such as HVAC and physical security. Threat assessment must also consider personmade threats such as war or terrorism. For a completely objective view of threats, assessment should be conducted by an external entity.

   ☒ **B, C,** and **D** are incorrect. Risk analysis is a general term that includes conducting a threat assessment, but threat assessment is a more specific and applicable answer. Asset identification involves determining what items (tangible and nontangible) are of value and associating a value with those items. Cost of ownership enables consumers to determine the true cost of a product or service.

5. ☑ **B.** Confidentiality means keeping data hidden from those who should not see it, such as competitors.
    ☒ **A, C,** and **D** are incorrect. Integrity verifies the authenticity of data; it does not conceal it. Availability ensures that a resource is available as often as possible—for example, clustering a database server. Authorization grants access to a resource once the identity of an entity has been verified through authentication.

6. ☑ **D.** Determining the effect that materialized risks have on the operation of a business is called impact analysis. It is often used to determine whether expenditures against these risks are justified.
    ☒ **A, B,** and **C** are incorrect. Risk analysis is too general a term in this case; impact analysis is a more specific answer. Fault tolerance can reduce the impact if a disk fails, but it is very specific; the question refers to more than a single risk. Availability ensures that resources are available as often as possible to minimize risks, but it does not determine how risks affect a business.

7. ☑ **A** and **B.** Assessing risk includes determining what is and is not covered by various types of insurance coverage and whether the cost of those insurance premiums is justified, such as cybersecurity insurance related to malicious network attacks or intellectual property data theft. The number of server hard disks is definitely risk related. The likelihood of hard disk data loss is minimized when multiple hard disks are configured properly, such as RAID 1 (disk mirroring).
    ☒ **C** and **D** are incorrect. CPU speed and network bandwidth are not directly related to risk assessment; they are related to performance.

8. ☑ **B, C,** and **D.** Backing up data minimizes the risk of data loss. Employee training reduces the likelihood of errors or disclosure of confidential information. Choosing the most reliable network load balancing appliance can reduce the risk of network traffic congestion.
    ☒ **A** is incorrect. Larger flat-screen monitors are not related to risk prevention.

9. ☑ **A.** The annual loss expectancy (ALE) value is used with quantitative risk analysis approaches to prioritize and justify expenditures that help protect against potential risks. For example, an ALE value of $1000 may justify a $200 annual expense to protect against that risk.
    ☒ **B, C,** and **D** are incorrect. The return on investment (ROI) calculates how efficient an investment is. (Does the benefit of a product or service outweigh the cost?) The total cost of ownership exposes all direct and indirect costs associated with a product or service. Using the total monthly premium value to determine whether to accept the additional insurance coverage would be meaningless; it must be compared against the probability of natural disasters in your area.

10. ☑ **C.** Qualitative risk analysis categorizes risks (threats) with general (not hard numerical) terms and numerical ranges—for example, analyzing risks using ratings between 1 (low risk) to 10 (high risk). For this to happen, threats must first be identified.
    ☒ **A, B,** and **D** are incorrect. Although numerical data is important in both quantitative and qualitative risk assessments, qualitative analysis doesn't focus on numerical data. ALE is a cost figure used in quantitative analysis; it uses a relative measurement scale to rank risks. ROI cannot be determined until a risk analysis has been done.

11.   ☑   **A and B.** Annual loss expectancy (ALE) is derived by multiplying the annual rate of occurrence (ARO) by the single loss expectancy (SLE).
      ☒   **C and D** are incorrect. Monthly and quarterly loss expectancies are not used to calculate ALE.

12.   ☑   **B.** Annual loss expectancy is calculated by multiplying the annual rate of occurrence (ARO = 0.17) by the single loss expectancy (SLE = 3000). So, ALE = ARO × SLE, and 0.17 × $3000 = $510.
      ☒   **A, C, and D** are incorrect. None of these numbers expresses the correct ALE figure, which is derived by ALE = ARO × SLE.

13.   ☑   **C.** This question is asking you to calculate the ALE. Multiply the probability (ARO) by the cost associated with a single failure (SLE). ALE = ARO × SLE, and 0.7 × (25 × $18.5) = $323.75.
      ☒   **A, B, and D** are incorrect. None of these numbers expresses the correct ALE figure, which is derived by ALE = ARO × SLE.

14.   ☑   **A.** Risk assessment means determining the impact that threats and less than optimal conditions can have on a business or agency. Risk management involves setting aside the funds to account for these eventualities. Determining the amount of money to set aside may involve many detailed calculations.
      ☒   **B, C, and D** are incorrect. A security audit may be one factor influencing how monies are to be spent to protect a business, but risk management involves actually setting aside the funds. Budgetary constraints do not describe the definition presented in the question. An impact analysis specifically determines the effect threats and unfavorable circumstances have on the operation of a business, but, like a security audit, it would be one of many factors influencing the appropriate number of dollars required to mitigate these issues.

15.   ☑   **B.** The ALE is a specific figure derived from the probability of a loss and the cost of one occurrence of this loss. Because specific dollar values (quantities) are used to prioritize risks, this falls into the category of quantitative risk analysis.
      ☒   **A, C, and D** are incorrect. Best possible outcome is not a risk analysis approach. Return on investment cannot be calculated prior to a risk analysis being completed. The qualitative risk analysis approach uses a relative ranking scale to rate risks instead of using specific figures.

16.   ☑   **C.** ALE values use the probability of a loss in conjunction with the cost of a single incident. Probability values are rarely accurate, but because the future cannot be accurately predicted, they are acceptable. Probability values can be arrived at by referring to past historical data.
      ☒   **A, B, and D** are incorrect. When dealing with probabilities, you cannot state a definite percentage of accuracy. Although the ALE is calculated using a percentage (probability of annual rate of occurrence), you cannot tell Bob that the ALE is accurate.

17.   ☑   **A and D.** Qualitative risk analysis assesses the likelihood of risks that will impede normal business operations and prioritizes; it ranks them relative to one another. Assets that must be protected from identified risks must have an assigned value to determine whether the cost of risk mitigation is justified. This is often done in a risk register.

☒ **B** and **C** are incorrect. Annual rate of occurrence (ARO) and single loss expectancy (SLE) use specific dollar figures (quantitative) to calculate the ALE. Annual loss expectancy (ALE) = annual rate of occurrence (ARO) multiplied by single loss expectancy (SLE).

18. ☑ **B** and **C.** A reliable power source is critical for IT systems. Unreliable power would mean a different plant location or the use of an uninterruptible power supply (UPS) and power generators. Physical security should always be considered during risk analysis
    ☒ **A** and **D** are incorrect. Summer temperatures may be relevant, but power reliability will deal with this since reliable power means reliable heating, ventilation, and air conditioning (HVAC). Unless toxic waste or something similar is being transported on the nearest highway, this is not relevant.

19. ☑ **B.** Risk transfer shifts some or all of the burden of risk to a third party such as the cloud service provider, which in this case is responsible for the underlying infrastructure to support the web site. The cloud customer is responsible for the web site content. The risk transfer combination of cybersecurity insurance when using cloud computing is called multiparty risk.
    ☒ **A, C,** and **D** are incorrect. Risk avoidance is not applicable in this case; risk avoidance mitigates threats by not allowing a party to undertake an action that poses a risk. Risk analysis is the practice of identifying and ranking threats jeopardizing business goals in order to allocate funds to mitigate these threats. ALE is a dollar value associated with the probability of a failure.

20. ☑ **B.** ALE figures are considered inaccurate because part of their calculation is based on probabilities.
    ☒ **A, C,** and **D** are incorrect. Assuming risk analysis was conducted properly, the allocated funds to minimize the impact of risk are probably better invested where they are than in other endeavors. Firewalls do not handle all IT security risks. Qualitative risk analysis reports do not express results in dollar values; instead, risks are weighed against each other and ranked.

21. ☑ **C.** Deciding to invest heavily in a new product for an uncertain market is a gamble. Deciding against it would be classified as risk avoidance.
    ☒ **A, B,** and **D** are incorrect. Risk analysis would aim to provide information to the business so an educated decision is made. Avoiding launching a product may be a decision taken after that risk analysis has been made. Risk transfer would imply some or all risk is assumed by another party. Product avoidance is a fictitious risk management term.

22. ☑ **B.** Whether qualitative or quantitative risk analysis is done, once data has been properly considered, risks should be ranked by likelihood.
    ☒ **A, C,** and **D** are incorrect. A threat vector is a tool or mechanism used by an attacker to exploit a system. In some cases, ranking threats by date can be beneficial, but this is usually factored in when ranking by priority. The single loss expectancy (SLE) is a dollar value associated with a single failure. The annual loss expectancy (ALE) uses the SLE as well as a probability of the incident occurring, resulting in a dollar figure. ALE figures can be sorted by dollar value to determine which threats should be given the most attention, but the SLE by itself is not enough.

23.   ☑   **C.** Accepting the potential consequences of a threat is referred to as risk acceptance and is determined by the organization's appetite for risk. The amount of money to minimize the risk is not warranted, as was the case of a temporary data center in Santa Fe.

   ☒ **A, B,** and **D** are incorrect. Risk transfer shifts risk consequence responsibility to another party. Risk avoidance refers to the disregard of an opportunity because of the risk involved. Risk reduction is the application of mitigation techniques to minimize the occurrence of threats.

24.   ☑   **B.** ALE values must be calculated now that threats have been identified and assets have been valued.

   ☒ **A, C,** and **D** are incorrect. A cost–benefit analysis can be done only after ALE values have been calculated. ALE values give you something to compare threat mitigation costs against to determine whether expenditures are warranted. Deciding which vulnerabilities exist has most probably already been done at this stage. There is much more to be done (such as ALE, cost–benefit analysis, and so on).

25.   ☑   **B.** The implementation of policies for the internal control of transactions encompasses mitigation solutions. The threat is identified, and a solution is put into place.

   ☒ **A, C,** and **D** are incorrect. Probability is a factor used to calculate the ALE. An impact analysis determines the effect various threats can have on business operations. A threat analysis defines threats and possible solutions.

26.   ☑   **B.** Risk assessment requires identification and prioritization of risks using either a relative ranking scale or objective numeric data. Managing those risks involves minimizing their impact on the business.

   ☒ **A, C,** and **D** are incorrect. Risk assessment and management are not the same. Risk assessment identifies and prioritizes risks, while risk management governs risks to minimize their impact. Threat analysis identifies threats, not risk assessment or risk management.

27.   ☑   **A and C.** Quantitative risk analysis involves complex, time-consuming calculations. Results are expressed in specific percentages or monetary values, despite the fact that probability figures are used to arrive at these results.

   ☒ **B and D** are incorrect. Prioritizing risks applies to qualitative risk analysis, where risks are ranked relative to each other but not necessarily by dollar value. Quantitative risk analysis strives to provide a specific dollar amount to facilitate fund allocation.

28.   ☑   Figure 17-3 shows the correct matching of terms and scenarios. Testing new server configurations before applying those changes to production systems falls under change management. Auditing file servers relates to user rights and permission reviews. Removing infected machines from the network is related to incident management.

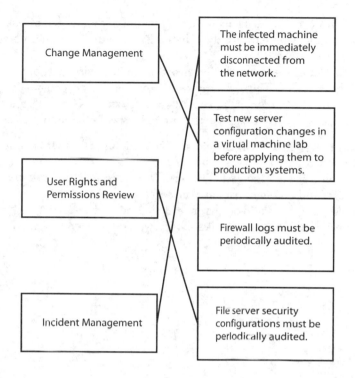

FIGURE 17-3

Risk mitigation strategies—the answer

Change Management

User Rights and Permissions Review

Incident Management

The infected machine must be immediately disconnected from the network.

Test new server configuration changes in a virtual machine lab before applying them to production systems.

Firewall logs must be periodically audited.

File server security configurations must be periodically audited.

29. ☑ **A** and **C**. Hardening Internet of things (IoT) devices is achieved by applying updates, changing default settings, and placing the devices on a restricted network so that a compromised IoT devices will not be on the same network as other assets.
    ☒ **B** and **D** are incorrect. Placing a proxy server between users and internal legacy systems and changing default port numbers can enhance security but are not as prevalent for security hardening in this scenario as changing default settings and network segmentation for IoT devices.

30. ☑ **B**. A risk heat map facilitates with visually communicating risks and occurrence likelihoods, where a high-risk probability of occurrence would be colored red, remote likelihoods would be green, and medium-level risk possibilities would be yellow or orange.
    ☒ **A, C,** and **D** are incorrect. The listed items do not visually represent inherent risks and the likelihood of their occurrence. A risk register (risk matrix) centrally lists and organizes risks by priority and lists risk mitigation controls. Risk assessment is the identification of threats against assets and can also include the recurring assessment of the efficacy of existing risk controls; even the best risk mitigation controls normally result in some degree or residual risk. Unless otherwise stated because of legal, regulatory, or security standards requirements, risk control assessments can be conducted by third parties or by the organization itself.

31. ☑ **B.** With cybersecurity insurance, a portion of the burden of risk related to the occurrence of malicious attacks or sensitive data theft falls upon the insurance company; this is a prime example of risk transfer.

☒ **A, C,** and **D** are incorrect. Because the employee is a part of the organization and a third party is not assuming a risk of any kind, users signing acceptable use policies do not constitute risk transfer. The placement of security devices such as firewalls and configuring VPNs are not considered risk transfer because the risk of realized related threats still falls to the organization.

32. ☑ **C.** A risk register is a central list of risks along with their likelihood, impact, severity ratings, and risk control details.

☒ **A, B,** and **D** are incorrect. The terms *threat register* and *threat heat map* are incorrect; *risk register* and *risk heat map* are the correct terms. A risk heat map facilitates with visually communicating risks and occurrence likelihoods, where a high-risk probability of occurrence would be colored red, remote likelihoods would be green, and medium-level risk possibilities would be yellow or orange.

Chapter 18

Disaster Recovery and Business Continuity

QUESTIONS

Unfavorable circumstances can temporarily or permanently cripple a business both financially and through reputational damage. A disaster recovery plan attempts to minimize the impact that these circumstances, whether caused by nature or by humans, have on a business. The plan should include incident assessment, and it should specify who performs which tasks under specific circumstances.

1. In the event of a server hard disk failure, you have been asked to configure server hard disks as depicted in Figure 18-1. What type of disk configuration is this?

   A. RAID 0
   B. RAID 1
   C. RAID 5
   D. RAID 5+1

FIGURE 18-1

Hard disk configuration

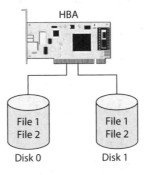

2. A team leader assigns a server administrator the task of determining the business and financial effects that a failed e-mail server would have if it was down for two hours. What type of analysis must the server administrator perform?

   A. Critical systems and components identification
   B. Business impact analysis
   C. Security audit
   D. Risk assessment

3. An airline company has hired you to ensure that its customer reservation system is always online. The software runs and stores data locally on the Linux operating system. What should you do?

   A. Install two Linux servers in a cluster. Cluster the airline software, with its data being written to shared storage.

   B. Install a new Linux server. Ensure that the airline software runs from the first server. Schedule airline data to replicate to the new Linux server nightly.

   C. Configure the Linux server with RAID 5.

   D. Configure the Linux server with RAID 1.

4. A busy clustered web site regularly experiences congested network traffic. You must improve the web site response time. What should you implement?

   A. Ethernet switch

   B. Network load balancing

   C. Fibre Channel switch

   D. Proxy server

5. Your primary e-mail server uses three hot-swappable hard disks in a RAID 5 configuration. When one disk fails, other disks are readily available in the server room, which you can simply plug in while the server is still running. Which term best describes this scenario?

   A. Disk clustering

   B. Hardware fault tolerance

   C. Disk striping

   D. Disk mirroring

6. Your server tape backup routine consists of a full backup each Friday night and a nightly backup of all data changed since Friday's backup. What type of backup schedule is this?

   A. Full

   B. Full and incremental

   C. Full and differential

   D. Disk snapshot

7. You are a network engineer for a San Francisco law firm. After the 1989 earthquake, an emphasis on continued business operation after future earthquakes dominated in the San Francisco business community. What type of plan focuses on ensuring that personnel, customers, and IT systems are minimally affected after a disaster?

   A. Risk management

   B. Fault tolerant

   C. Disaster recovery

   D. Business continuity

8. A server is configured with three hard disks as shown in Figure 18-2. What type of configuration is this?

    A. RAID 0

    B. RAID 1

    C. RAID 5

    D. RAID 5+1

FIGURE 18-2

Hard disk
configuration

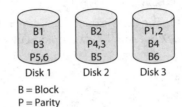

Disk 1 Disk 2 Disk 3

B = Block
P = Parity

9. Windows Server backups are scheduled as follows: full backups on Saturdays at 3 A.M. and incremental backups weeknights at 9 P.M. Write verification has been enabled. Backup tapes are stored off site at a third-party backup vendor location. What should be done to ensure the integrity and confidentially of the backups? (Choose two.)

    A. Have a different person than the backup operator analyze each day's backup logs.

    B. Ensure the user performing the backup is a member of the Administrators group.

    C. Encrypt the backup media.

    D. Use SSL to encrypt the backup media.

10. You are an IT network architect. Your firm has been hired to perform a network security audit for a shipping company. One of the company's warehouses has a server room containing one Windows server and two Linux servers. After interviewing the server administrators, you learn they have no idea what to do if the Linux servers cease to function. What is needed here?

    A. Disaster recovery plan

    B. Risk analysis

    C. Windows servers

    D. Server clustering

11. Which items should be considered when ensuring high availability for an e-commerce web site? (Choose two.)

    A. Use TPM to encrypt server hard disks.

    B. Use redundant Internet links.

    C. Use network load balancing.

    D. Upgrade the server CMOS to the latest version.

12. Which of the following are the most closely related to creating a disaster recovery plan? (Choose three.)

    A. Determining which class of IP addresses are in use

    B. Ranking risks

    C. Disabling unused switch ports

    D. Assigning recovery tasks to personnel

    E. Establishing an alternate location to continue business operations

13. What should be used to make informed decisions regarding your specific disaster recovery plan?

    A. DRP template freely downloaded from a web site

    B. ROI analysis

    C. TCO analysis

    D. Business impact analysis

14. Identify the disaster recovery plan errors. (Choose two.)

    A. Perform a business impact analysis first.

    B. Base your DRP on an unchanged downloaded template.

    C. Data backups are never tested; it costs the company too much money.

    D. Keep existing backup solutions in place even though the software is two versions out of date.

15. You are creating a DRP for a small, independent car dealership. There are four employees who each use a desktop computer; there are no servers. All company data is stored on the four computers. A single high-speed DSL link is shared by all users. What are the best DRP solutions? (Choose two.)

    A. Store data in the cloud instead of locally.

    B. Ensure that employees know exactly what to do in the event of a disaster.

    C. Purchase faster desktops.

    D. Purchase a file server.

16. Your senior network administrator has decided that the five physical servers at your location will be virtualized and run on a single physical host. The five virtual guests are mission-critical and will use the physical hard disks in the physical host. The physical host has the hard disks configured with RAID 1. Identify the flaw in this plan.

    A. The physical server should be using RAID 5.

    B. The physical hard disks must not reside in the physical host.

    C. You cannot run five virtual machines on a physical host simultaneously.

    D. The physical host is a single point of failure.

17. Your company is virtualizing DNS, DHCP, web, and e-mail servers at your location. Each of the four virtual machines will be spread out across two physical hosts. Virtual machines are using virtual hard disks, and these files exist on a SAN. Choose the best virtual machine backup strategy that will enable the quickest granular restore.

    A. Back up the virtual machine hard disks at the SAN level.
    B. Install a backup agent in each virtual machine and perform backups normally.
    C. Duplicate your SAN disk array so that backups are not necessary.
    D. Run all four virtual machines on the same physical host to be backed up.

18. To ensure confidentiality, what should you do when storing server backup disks off site?

    A. Encrypt backed up data.
    B. Generate file hashes for each backed up file.
    C. Place backup tapes in static shielding bags.
    D. Never store backup disks off site.

19. You are the administrator for a recently patched virtual Windows Server running Active Directory Domain Services (AD DS). Recently the server has been randomly rebooting and now cannot boot at all. What should you do?

    A. Run Windows update.
    B. Format the hard disk, reinstall the server, and restore from tape.
    C. Refer to your DRP.
    D. Refer to your BCP.

20. You are the network administrator for a small IT consulting firm. All servers are located at the single site. Employees use a web browser to access their e-mail accounts. After testing the DRP and receiving management approval, you e-mail a copy to all employees for their reference in the event of a disaster. Identify the problem.

    A. The e-mail should have been encrypted.
    B. The e-mail should have been digitally signed.
    C. Only executives should have received the message.
    D. The mail server may not be available in the event of a disaster.

21. You are the network administrator for a small IT consulting firm. All servers are hosted externally in the public cloud. After analyzing threats, creating a DRP, and receiving management approval, you e-mail a copy to all employees for their reference in the event of a disaster. Identify the most serious problem.

    A. The e-mail should have been encrypted.
    B. The DRP was not tested.
    C. The e-mail should have been digitally signed.
    D. Only executives should have received the message.

22. Which of the following regarding disaster recovery are true? (Choose two.)

    A. Once the plan is complete, to save time it need never be revisited.

    B. Once the plan is complete, it must have management approval.

    C. The plan must evolve with the business.

    D. The plan should include only IT systems.

23. Using Figure 18-3, match the descriptions on the left to the corresponding terms on the right.

FIGURE 18-3

Disaster recovery and business continuity terminology

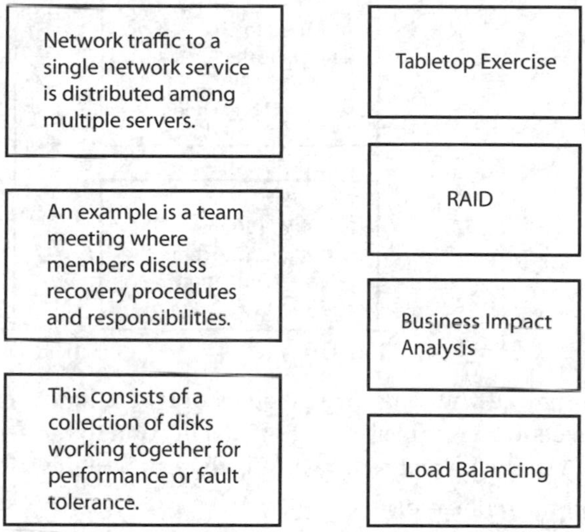

Network traffic to a single network service is distributed among multiple servers.		Tabletop Exercise
An example is a team meeting where members discuss recovery procedures and responsibilities.		RAID
		Business Impact Analysis
This consists of a collection of disks working together for performance or fault tolerance.		Load Balancing

24. You are a web site administrator. You need to minimize web site downtime in the event of a disaster or security compromise. Which of the following terms best describes the reliability of hard disks?

    A. MTBF

    B. MTTF

    C. MTTR

    D. RPO

25. As the IT director, you are comparing public cloud providers. Your company will no longer house on-premises mail or application servers. Which factors under your control must you consider to ensure that e-mail and applications are always available to users?

    A. Updates applied to cloud provider hypervisors

    B. Redundant network links

    C. RAID level used on cloud provider servers

    D. MTTF for cloud provider server hard disks

26. Using Figure 18-4, match the definitions on the left with the correct terms on the right.

FIGURE 18-4

Business impact
terminology

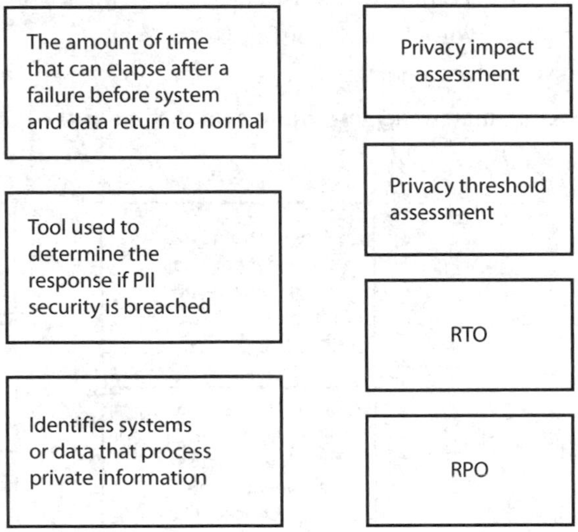

The amount of time
that can elapse after a
failure before system
and data return to normal

Privacy impact
assessment

Tool used to
determine the
response if PII
security is breached

Privacy threshold
assessment

RTO

Identifies systems
or data that process
private information

RPO

27. You have configured your enterprise cloud storage so that it continuously replicates to a cloud
provider data center in a different region. Replication to the secondary region occurs only after
data is written to the primary storage. Which term best describes this resilience configuration?

   A. Synchronous replication

   B. Geographic service dispersal

   C. Dedicated circuit

   D. Load balancing

28. Which storage area network term describes a host using more than one physical path to gain
access to shared network storage?

   A. Multipathing

   B. App load balancing

   C. RAID 0

   D. RAID 1

29. Which configuration provides network traffic load balancing?

   A. Multipath

   B. UPS

   C. NIC teaming

   D. PDU

30. Your Windows server will no longer boot the operating system. No recent updates or configuration changes have been applied. What should you do first to attempt to resolve the problem?

    A. Revert to the last known good configuration.

    B. Reinstall the operating system.

    C. Boot from a Windows Server live media disk and attempt to repair the installation.

    D. Apply a corporate operating system image.

31. Your IT security team has worked with executive management to determine that a company e-commerce web site must never remain down for more than two hours. To which disaster recovery term does this apply?

    A. RPO

    B. RTO

    C. MTTR

    D. MTBF

32. You company backs up on-premises data using a tape backup system that also replicates backup data to the cloud. You need to back data up daily while minimizing backup storage capacity on local backup tapes. What should you do?

    A. Configure daily full backups.

    B. Configure weekly full backups with daily differential backups.

    C. Configure weekly incremental backups.

    D. Configure daily incremental backups.

QUICK ANSWER KEY

1.	B	**10.**	A	**19.**	C	**27.**	B
2.	B	**11.**	B, C	**20.**	D	**28.**	A
3.	A	**12.**	B, D, E	**21.**	B	**29.**	C
4.	B	**13.**	D	**22.**	B, C	**30.**	C
5.	B	**14.**	B, C	**23.**	See "In-Depth Answers."	**31.**	B
6.	C	**15.**	A, B			**32.**	D
7.	D	**16.**	D	**24.**	C		
8.	C	**17.**	B	**25.**	B		
9.	A, C	**18.**	A	**26.**	See "In-Depth Answers."		

IN-DEPTH ANSWERS

1. ☑ **B.** Redundant array of independent disks (RAID) level 1 refers to disk mirroring. Data is written to one disk and duplicated on the second disk. In the event of a single disk failure, the other disk can take over.

   ☒ **A, C,** and **D** are incorrect. RAID 0 involves striping data across multiple disks to increase performance, but there is no fault tolerance since a single disk failure would result in the loss of all data. RAID 5 stripes data across disks (minimum of three disks) but distributes parity (recovery) data on disks so that a single disk failure means data can still be reconstructed. RAID 5+1 is a mirrored RAID 5 array.

2. ☑ **B.** A business impact analysis (BIA), also referred to as a business impact assessment, identifies the effect unwanted events have on the operation of a business.

   ☒ **A, C,** and **D** are incorrect. Identifying mission-critical systems and components (also referred to as mission-essential) is part of determining assets and their worth when performing a risk analysis. A security audit tests how effective security policy implementation is for safeguarding corporate assets. Risk assessments identify assets and their related threats and potential losses; these can be used to create security policies and are an integral part of the overall BIA.

3. ☑ **A.** Clustering software between two servers will enable the customer reservation system to function even if one server fails, because the data is not stored within a single server; it exists on shared storage that both cluster nodes can access. When a cluster node (server) fails, the application fails over to a running cluster node (server).

   ☒ **B, C,** and **D** are incorrect. Scheduling nightly data replication does not ensure that the airline software is always online. Most cloud providers allow cloud-stored data to be replicated between locations separated by long distances. This prevents data loss or downtime resulting from a regional disaster. RAID 1 (mirroring) and RAID 5 (striping with distributed parity) are useless if the server fails.

4. ☑ **B.** Network load balancing (NLB) can distribute network traffic to multiple servers hosting the same content to improve performance. In the cloud, load balancers can use autoscaling to add or remove virtual machines in response to application demand.

   ☒ **A, C,** and **D** are incorrect. Most networks already use Ethernet switches, but that has no effect on web site response time. Fibre Channel switches are used in a storage area network (SAN) environment, not local area networks (LANs) or wide area networks (WANs). A proxy server retrieves Internet content for clients and then optionally caches it for later requests; it would not improve performance here.

5. ☑ **B.** With hardware fault tolerance, a hardware component can fail without completely impeding data access. A single disk failure in a RAID 5 configuration means the failed disk can be hot-swapped with a functional disk. Because RAID 5 stripes data across disks in the array and parity is distributed across disks, user requests for data can be reconstructed dynamically in RAM until the data is reconstructed on the replaced disk.
   ☒ **A, C,** and **D** are incorrect. Disk clustering is a generic term that does not describe the scenario in detail. Disk striping (RAID 0) offers no fault tolerance, only performance increases by writing data segments across a group of disks. Disk mirroring (RAID 1) is not applicable since the question states RAID 5 is in use.

6. ☑ **C.** Differential backups will archive data that has changed since the last full backup. Restoring data means first restoring the full backup and then the latest differential. A full backup, when not used with differential backups, is also called a *copy* backup.
   ☒ **A, B,** and **D** are incorrect. Incremental backups archive data changed since the last incremental backup. Disk snapshots are point-in-time copies of the contents of a disk that enable the restoration of either the entire disk or specific files or folders. Some disk snapshot solutions store pointers of unchanged data to parent snapshots while changed data is stored in its entirety within the new snapshot. Storing an entire disk's state at a point in time is achieved by creating a disk image.

7. ☑ **D.** Business continuity is considered the key goal to which disaster recovery plays a part. Disaster recovery (DR) normally involves implementing steps to get the business operational. Business continuity ensures business operation after the successful implementation of the DRP. Keeping the organization functional sometimes requires the use of an alternate site if the primary site fails, or the use of a recruitment agency (against normal business practices) to employ workers if there is a worker shortage.
   ☒ **A, B,** and **C** are incorrect. Risk management refers to minimizing the impact potential risks could have on business process continuity, business assets, and the safety and lives of personnel. Fault tolerance is not a type of plan; fault tolerance falls under the umbrella of risk management. Disaster recovery involves methodically returning the business to normal operation and is a component of a business continuity plan.

8. ☑ **C.** Distributing data and parity information across disks is referred to as RAID level 5.
   ☒ **A, B,** and **D** are incorrect. RAID 0 (striping) writes data segments across disks without parity, so there is a performance benefit but no fault tolerance. RAID 1 (mirroring) duplicates data written on the first disk to the second disk in case one disk fails. RAID 5+1 mirrors a RAID 5 configuration for additional fault tolerance.

9. ☑ **A** and **C.** To reduce the likelihood of tampering, a different person should review backup logs. For confidentiality, backup tapes stored off site should be encrypted.
   ☒ **B** and **D** are incorrect. There is no need to be a member of the Administrators group, but there is a need to be in the Backup Operators group. SSL encrypts network traffic, not stored data.

10. ☑ **A.** Disaster recovery plans outline exactly who must do what in case unfavorable events occur.
☒ **B, C,** and **D** are incorrect. A risk analysis identifies threats to assets and prioritizes those threats, but actions taken in a disaster are included in a disaster recovery plan (DRP). Windows servers are not needed here; a disaster recovery plan is. Clustering the Linux servers would only make matters worse if they ceased functioning, because clustering introduces more complexity. The administrators should get Linux training, and a DRP addressing the Linux servers should be crafted.

11. ☑ **B** and **C.** High availability makes a resource available as often as is possible. Redundant Internet links allow access to the web site even if one Internet link fails. Network load balancing (which could use the redundant Internet links) distributes traffic evenly either to server cluster nodes or through redundant network links.
☒ **A** and **D** are incorrect. Trusted Platform Module (TPM) is firmware designed to validate machine boot-up integrity and to store cryptographic keys used to encrypt hard disks. Although this addresses integrity confidentiality, it does not address high availability. CMOS upgrades may improve or give new hardware capabilities to the web server, but this does not directly address high availability. If the CMOS update corrects a problem with RAID configurations, then it would address high availability, but the possible answers do not list this.

12. ☑ **B, D,** and **E.** Risks should be ranked to determine which are the most probable. The most attention should be given to the most likely threats. Personnel must be assigned tasks according to the disaster recovery plan (DRP) to minimize confusion and downtime. DRPs also provide details about the order of restoration, such as the order in which software components must be placed back into operation. An alternate site (cold, warm, or hot) should at least be considered. Larger businesses or agencies may be able to justify the cost of maintaining an alternate site.
☒ **A** and **C** are incorrect. IP address classes are more related to network planning than to a DRP. Although unused switch ports should always be disabled, this would not be considered when crafting a DRP.

13. ☑ **D.** A business impact analysis identifies which risks will affect business operations more than others. This is valuable in determining how to recover from a disaster.
☒ **A, B,** and **C** are incorrect. Freely downloadable DRP templates are generic and will not address your specific business or IT configuration. Return on investment (ROI) determines the efficiency of an investment (is the cost justified?). Total cost of ownership (TCO) identifies the true cost of a product or service. Neither ROI nor TCO is tied directly to your DRP like a business impact analysis is.

14. ☑ **B** and **C.** Your DRP should be much more specific than what a downloaded template can provide. DRPs must be tested initially and periodically to ensure their efficiency and efficacy.
☒ **A** and **D** are incorrect. A DRP takes the business impact analysis into account. Backed-up software that is two versions out of date may still function correctly; often there are risks involved with immediately using the newest software.

15. ☑ **A** and **B.** Online data storage in the cloud is an affordable solution to safeguard business data, but the amount of time required to restore from the cloud must be considered; it is affected by factors such as distance to the nearest cloud provider data center and available network bandwidth. Users must know what to do in the event of a catastrophe to ensure the timely resumption of business.

☒ **C** and **D** are incorrect. Faster computers will not have an impact on a DRP for a small business. Purchasing a file server is not justified given the small number of employees and a single site.

16. ☑ **D.** If the single physical host experiences a failure, all five virtual machines will be unavailable. A second server should be clustered with the first, and virtual guests should use shared disk storage versus local disk storage.

☒ **A, B,** and **C** are incorrect. RAID 5 would not solve the problem of the disks being in a single server. Even if shared storage were used, the physical server would still be a single point of failure. Given enough hardware resources, many more than five virtual guests can run simultaneously on a virtualization server.

17. ☑ **B.** If granular restores are required, backing up each virtual machine using a backup agent installed in each VM is the best choice.

☒ **A, C,** and **D** are incorrect. Backing up the SAN means backing up virtual hard disks used by the virtual machines. This presents some difficulty if you must restore specific (granular) files. Backups are always necessary no matter what. If virtual hard disks are on a SAN, all four virtual machines do not have to be running on the same physical host.

18. ☑ **A.** Backup disks stored off site should be encrypted to ensure data confidentiality. Without the correct decryption key, disk contents are inaccessible.

☒ **B, C,** and **D** are incorrect. Generating file hashes for every backed up file is used to detect file changes (integrity); this does not provide data confidentiality. Static shielding bags protect electrical components from electrostatic discharge; they do nothing to protect data stored on backup disks. Off-site backup disk storage is a critical component in a disaster recovery plan but doesn't relate to data confidentiality.

19. ☑ **C.** A disaster recovery plan (DRP) specifies who should do what in case of a disaster, such as in the case of server that will not boot.

☒ **A, B,** and **D** are incorrect. Running Windows update will not likely solve the problem since the virtual machine is already up-to-date. Formatting, reinstalling, and tape restore may need to be done, but the best answer is to refer to your DRP. A business continuity plan (BCP) strives to minimize the business impact of realized threats. The BCP is not as granular as the DRP. The DRP is specific to recovering a specific system.

20. ☑ **D.** The only copy of the disaster recovery plan exists on a mail server that users may not have access to when they need it most. Alternate storage locations and physical copies must be considered.

☒ **A, B,** and **C** are incorrect. Although encrypted and digitally signed e-mail is good practice, these answers are not problems in this scenario. A comprehensive DRP must be made available to applicable employees.

21. ☑ **B.** A DRP changes with the business and must be tested to ensure its success, which is something that doesn't seem to have been done here.

    ☒ **A, C,** and **D** are incorrect. Although encrypted and digitally signed e-mail is good practice, these answers are not problems in this scenario. An IT DRP must be known by all employees.

22. ☑ **B** and **C.** Without management support and approval, a disaster recovery plan will not succeed. The plan must be revisited periodically to ensure that it is in step with changes in the business.

    ☒ **A** and **D** are incorrect. Disaster recovery plans must be periodically revisited. In addition to IT systems, disaster recovery can also include facility restoration and employee relocation systems.

23. ☑ Figure 18-5 shows the correct matching of terms and descriptions. To improve performance, load balancing distributes network traffic to a farm, or collection, of servers offering the same network service. The server that is the least busy and up and running is normally the server that would handle a current request. Tabletop exercises help DR committees ensure that the business continuity plan (BCP) meets the organizational DR goals, including determining the responsibilities of all involved parties. RAID groups physical disks together as logical disks seen by the operating system. This is done to improve disk performance and/or provide redundancy in case of disk failure.

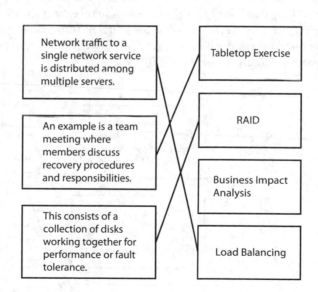

FIGURE 18-5

Disaster recovery and business continuity terminology— the answer

24. ☑ **C.** Mean time to recovery (MTTR) (also sometimes known as mean time to restore) measures the amount of time it takes to return a device, system, or network to normal functionality.

☒ **A, B,** and **D** are incorrect. Mean time between failures (MTBF) is the measure of time between each subsequent failure of a repairable device. Mean time to failure (MTTF) is a statistical measurement applied to non-repairable items such as hard disks. It denotes the average useful life of a device, given that a specific number of those devices are in use. The recovery point objective (RPO) is the amount of time that can elapse after a failure before system and data resume normal operation; for example, a six-hour RPO means data backups can never be more than six hours old. The recovery time objective (RTO) differs in that it denotes the amount of time it will take after an unexpected failure for systems to resume normal operation. Unlike RPO, it does not specify how old the data can be.

25. ☑ **B.** Redundant network links to the Internet will ensure that if one Internet connection fails, the other can be used to access e-mail and application services in the cloud.

☒ **A, C,** and **D** are incorrect. Updating hypervisor servers, RAID disk configuration, and MTTF are not in your control; they are the responsibility of the cloud provider.

26. ☑ Figure 18-6 shows the correct matching of terms and definitions. The recovery point objective (RPO) is a measurement of time between a failure and the resumption of normal business operations. Privacy impact assessments, often required for compliance with privacy regulations, determine which safeguards mitigate threats against sensitive data such as personally identifiable information (PII), and what the incident response will be if this data is compromised. Privacy threshold assessments often precede a privacy impact assessment, because systems that process sensitive data must first be identified.

FIGURE 18-6

Business impact terminology— the answer

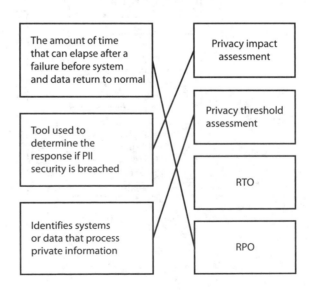

27. ☑ **B.** Geographic dispersal refers to the spreading out of IT services such as cloud storage or virtual machines by replicating across geographical regions to increase resiliency against a regional outage, disaster, or some other kind of disruption. The same configuration can be used for local redundancy within a data center through techniques such as SAN replication.

☒ **A, C,** and **D** are incorrect. Synchronous replication does not wait for data to be written to the primary storage location before replicating to secondary locations, but asynchronous replication does. A dedicated circuit is a private network link that does not traverse the Internet and can be used between a cloud customer on-premises network and the pubic cloud. To improve application performance and increase resiliency related to failed app servers, load balancers accept client app requests and route those requests to a pool of backend servers running the app.

28. ☑ **A.** To improve resiliency against failures, storage area network (SAN) administrators can enable multipathing, which provides hosts with more than one physical path to the shared SAN storage.

☒ **B, C,** and **D** are incorrect. The listed items are not specific to redundant network storage paths. To improve application performance and increase resiliency related to failed app servers, load balancers accept client app requests and route those requests to a pool of backend servers running the app. RAID 0 (striping) writes data segments across disks without parity, so there is a performance benefit but no fault tolerance. RAID 1 (mirroring) duplicates data written on the first disk to the second disk in case one disk fails

29. ☑ **C.** NIC teaming groups multiple server network interface cards (NICs) together to combine network bandwidth, increase resilience against a failed NIC, and to load balance network traffic among the teamed NICs.

☒ **A, B,** and **D** are incorrect. The listed items do not provide network traffic load balancing. To improve resilience against failures, storage area network (SAN) administrators can enable multipathing, which provides hosts with more than one physical path to the shared SAN storage. An uninterruptable power supply (UPS) provides temporary battery power for computing equipment that is plugged into the UPS; this allows for the graceful shutdown of equipment. For longer term power needs during a power outage, a generator should be used. A power distribution unit (PDU) is a power strip with multiple plug-ins for equipment in a data center rack. Some equipment uses dual power supplies for resilience against power supply failure; both power supplies should always be plugged in.

30. ☑ **C.** Booting from a live media CD, DVD, or USB operating system media disk will provide options for repairing the Windows installation. Because this could solve the problem quickly, it should be tried first.

☒ **A, B,** and **D** are incorrect. The Windows last known good configuration option is accessible by pressing F8 only if the machine begins to boot into the Windows operating system. Reinstallation or applying a company OS image may be required, but this option should not be tried first.

31. ☑ **B.** The recovery time objective (RTO) specifies the amount of time it will take after an unexpected failure for systems to resume normal operation. In other words, it denotes the amount of time an application can be non-operational without causing irreparable damage to the business.
☒ **A, C,** and **D** are incorrect. The recovery point objective (RPO) is the amount of time that can elapse after a failure before system and data resume normal operation; for example, a six-hour RPO means data backups can never be more than six hours old. Mean time to recovery (MTTR) measures the amount of time it takes to return a device, system, or network to normal functionality. Mean time between failures (MTBF) is the measure of time between each subsequent failure of a repairable device.

32. ☑ **D.** Daily incremental backups include only those items changed since the previous night's incremental backup and thus results in the least amount of daily backup data.
☒ **A, B,** and **C** are incorrect. Full backups each day will consume more storage space than daily incrementals. Differential backups include new and modified items since the last full backup and therefore take more storage space than daily incrementals. Weekly incrementals do not address the stated daily backup requirement.

Chapter 19

Understanding Monitoring and Auditing

CERTIFICATION OBJECTIVES

QUESTIONS

Monitoring networks and host computers proactively can detect attacks or even prevent their success. Network-based intrusion detection systems (IDSs) detect and report suspicious network activity. Host-based intrusion detection systems (HIDSs) detect and report suspicious host-based activity. Intrusion prevention systems (IPSs) can stop attacks once they have begun.

Log files present a method of tracing activity that has already occurred. Today's networks include logs in many places; you must know which log to consult under specific circumstances. Luckily, centrally monitoring and responding to security incidents is facilitated using security information and event management (SIEM) tools.

1. Which of the following can stop in-progress attacks on your network?
   A. Network IDS
   B. Network IPS
   C. Proxy server
   D. Packet-filtering firewall

2. Which of the following would an administrator most likely use to determine whether there has been unauthorized use of a wireless LAN?
   A. Protocol analyzer
   B. Proxy server
   C. Performance Monitor
   D. Wireless access point logs

3. You are responsible for managing an internal FTP server. A user reports that files available on the server yesterday are no longer available. Where can you look to determine what happened to the missing files?
   A. Firewall log
   B. FTP access log
   C. FTP download log
   D. FTP upload log

4. As a Windows server administrator for server ALPHA, you configure auditing so that you can track who deletes files on the file share SALES. Where will you view the audit results?
   A. Security log
   B. Audit log

C. Application log

D. Deletion log

5. Your manager asks you to configure a honeypot to track malicious user activity. You install the host in the screened subnet without any patches and configure a web site and an SMTP server on it. You have configured nothing else on the host. Identify a problem with this configuration.

A. The honeypot needs to be patched.

B. Honeypots should not run a web site.

C. Honeypot logs are not being forwarded to another secured host.

D. Honeypots should not run SMTP services.

6. Which of the following are true regarding behavior-based network monitoring? (Choose two.)

A. A baseline of normal behavior must be established.

B. Deviations from acceptable activity cannot be monitored.

C. New threats can be blocked.

D. A database of known attack patterns is consulted.

7. You have configured a network-based IPS appliance to prevent web server directory traversal attacks. What type of configuration is this?

A. Behavior-based

B. Signature-based

C. Anomaly-based

D. Web-based

8. An administrator reports that a Windows file server is performing much slower than it normally does. The server is fully patched and has an up-to-date virus scanner. You open an RDP connection to the server to investigate the problem. Which of the following should you first use?

A. Virus scanner

B. Port scanner

C. System restore point

D. Performance Monitor

9. You have inherited the responsibility of managing an office network for which there is no documentation. As you perform desktop support duties over time, by viewing network and host configuration reports you notice many users seem to have more privileges on the network than they need. What should you do?

A. Delete and re-create all user accounts.

B. Conduct a user access and rights review.

C. Check server audit logs.

D. Enforce stronger user passwords.

10. To adhere to new corporate security guidelines, your branch offices must track details regarding web sites visited by employees. What should you install to track this activity?

A. VPN

B. Proxy server

C. Packet-filtering firewall

D. NAT gateway

11. Which of the following are true regarding a network-based IDS? (Choose two.)

A. Network traffic is analyzed for malicious packets.

B. Alerts and notifications can be configured.

C. Malicious packets are dropped.

D. Laptops are protected when disconnected from the LAN.

12. Which of the following is true regarding a HIDS?

A. Suspicious traffic entering the network can be blocked.

B. Encrypted transmissions cannot be monitored.

C. It must be installed on each system where needed.

D. Log files are not analyzed.

13. You are asked to analyze events in a firewall log that occurred six months ago. When you analyze the log file, you notice events go back only two months. What is most likely the problem?

A. You must have administrative access to the logs.

B. The log file size is too small.

C. Firewalls cannot keep logs for more than two months.

D. The firewall is not patched.

14. A Windows administrator must track key performance metrics for a group of seven Windows servers. What should she do?

A. Run Performance Monitor on each host.

B. Use RDP to log into each host and run Performance Monitor.

C. Use RDP to log into each host and check Event Viewer logs.

D. Run Performance Monitor on her machine and add counters from the other seven servers.

15. You are a firewall appliance administrator for your company. Previously restricted outbound RDP packets are now successfully reaching external hosts, and you did not configure this firewall rule. Where should you look to see who made the firewall change and when?

A. Security log

B. Firewall log

C. Audit log

D. Event Viewer log

16. In reviewing your firewall log, you notice a large number of your stations connecting to the web site www.freetripsforyou.com and downloading an EXE file, sometimes in the middle of the night. Your users state they did not visit the web site. Your firewall does not allow any inbound packets initiated from the Internet. What does this most likely indicate?

    A. User stations are connecting to Windows Update to apply patches.

    B. User stations have been hijacked and are downloading malware.

    C. User stations are infected with a password-cracking program.

    D. User stations are being controlled from the Internet through RDP.

17. A corporate network baseline has been established over the course of two weeks. Using this baseline data, you configure your IPSs to notify you of abnormal network activity. A new sales initiative requires sales employees to run high-bandwidth applications across the Internet. As a result, you begin receiving security alerts regarding abnormal network activity. Which of the following types of alerts do you receive?

    A. False positives

    B. False negatives

    C. True positives

    D. True negatives

18. What can be done to prevent malicious users from tampering with and modifying log file entries? (Choose three.)

    A. Store log files on a secured centralized logging host.

    B. Encrypt archived log files.

    C. Run Windows Update.

    D. Generate file hashes for log files.

19. You have been asked to identify any irregularities from the following web server log excerpt:

    ```
    199.0.14.202, -, 03/15/09, 8:33:12, W3SVC2, SERVER, 192.168.1.1, 4502
    12.168.12.79, -, 03/15/09, 8:34:09, W3SVC2, SERVER, 192.168.1.1, 3455
    12.168.12.79, -, 03/15/09, 17:02:26, W3SVC2, SERVER, 192.168.1.1, 4302
    192.16.255.202, -, 03/15/09, 17:03:11, W3SVC2, SERVER, 192.168.1.1, 4111
    ```

    A. 199.0.14.202 is not a valid IP address.

    B. 192.16.255.202 is not a valid IP address.

    C. Web servers cannot use 192.168.1.1.

    D. The log is missing entries for a long period of time.

20. You are the Windows server administrator for a clothing outlet in New York City. Six Windows Server Active Directory computers are used regularly. Files are being modified on servers during nonbusiness hours. You want to audit the system to determine who made the changes and when. What is the quickest method of deploying your audit settings?

    A. Configure audit settings using Group Policy.

    B. Configure each server with the appropriate audit settings.

    C. Configure one server appropriately, export the settings, and import them to the other five.

    D. Delegate the audit configuration task to six other administrators.

21. What is the difference between a packet sniffer and a network-based IDS?

    A. There is no difference.

    B. Packet sniffers put the network card in promiscuous mode.

    C. A NIDS puts the network card in promiscuous mode.

    D. Packet sniffers do not process captured traffic.

22. Your manager has asked you to identify which internal client computers have been controlled using RDP from the Internet. What would be the quickest and most efficient way to accomplish this?

    A. Check the logs on each computer.

    B. Check the logs on your RDP servers.

    C. Check your firewall log.

    D. Contact your ISP and have them check their logs.

23. What is a potential problem with enabling detailed verbose logging on hosts for long periods of time?

    A. There is no problem.

    B. It causes performance degradation.

    C. Network bandwidth is consumed.

    D. Verbose logging consumes a user license.

24. A user reports that his client Windows client station has been slow and unstable since last Tuesday. What should you first do?

    A. Use System Restore to revert the computer state to last Monday.

    B. Check log entries for Monday and Tuesday on the computer.

    C. Run Windows Update.

    D. Reimage the computer.

25. User workstations on your network connect through NAT to a screened subnet, where your Internet perimeter firewall exists. On Friday night, a user connects to an inappropriate web site. You happened to have been capturing all network traffic on the screened subnet at the time. What would be the easiest and fastest way to track which user workstation visited the web site? (Choose two.)

    A. View logs on the NAT router.

    B. View logs on the perimeter firewall.

   C.   View your packet capture.

   D.   View all workstation web browser histories.

26. Using Figure 19-1, match the requirements listed on the left with the solutions listed on the right.

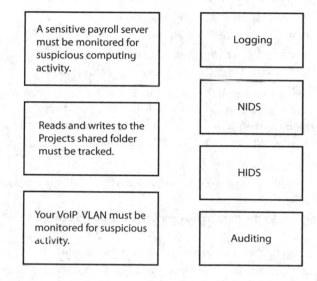

FIGURE 19-1

Security requirements and solutions

27. You are monitoring the performance on a Unix server called ALPHA. ALPHA is used to host concurrent remote sessions for users. You notice that long periods of intense server disk activity on ALPHA coincide with remote users working with large documents stored on a separate Unix server called BRAVO. What might be causing the degraded performance on Alpha?

   A.   There is too much network traffic.

   B.   The CPU is too slow.

   C.   The disks are too slow.

   D.   There is not enough RAM.

28. A server named CHARLIE runs a mission-critical database application. The application encrypts all data from connected client workstations. You would like to monitor CHARLIE for suspicious activity and prevent any potential attacks. What should you deploy?

   A.   Honeypot

   B.   Host-based IPS

   C.   Network-based IDS

   D.   PKI

29. You are reviewing forwarded log entries for your Internet-facing firewall appliance. Last year, your company did some IP restructuring and began using the 172.16.0.0/16 address space internally. You notice abnormally large amounts of traffic within a short time frame coming from the firewall appliance's public interface, 172.16.29.97, destined for UDP port 53. Which of the following might you conclude from this information, assuming default ports are in use?

   A. 172.16.29.97 is an invalid IP address.

   B. 172.16.29.97 is a spoofed IP address.

   C. The logs on the firewall appliance have been tampered with.

   D. An HTTP denial-of-service attack was in progress.

30. A user complains that his machine performance has degraded ever since he downloaded a free file recovery utility. You would like to rule out the possibility of any malicious network services running in the background by viewing all active port numbers and connections on the machine. Which Windows command should you use to do this? _____

31. How do logging and auditing differ?

   A. Logging tracks more than just security events; auditing tracks specifically configured security events.

   B. Auditing tracks more than just security events; logging tracks specifically configured security events.

   C. Logging can track hardware events; auditing cannot.

   D. Auditing can track hardware events; logging cannot.

32. Your network consists of programmable logic controllers (PLCs) that control robotic machinery as well as Linux servers and Windows desktops. Network administrators complain that there are too many similar log events in reports and notifications via e-mail. A solution that can aggregate similar events is needed. What should you suggest?

   A. PowerShell

   B. SIEM

   C. SCCM

   D. Group Policy

33. You have established a baseline of employee login activity on the VPN. You are configuring notifications of abnormal login events to a security orchestration, automation, and response (SOAR) dashboard to reduce security incident response time. Which term is the most closely related to this scenario?

   A. Network IPS

   B. SIEM

   C. User behavior analysis

   D. Sentiment analysis

A

QUICK ANSWER KEY

1.	B	**10.**	B	**19.**	D	**27.**	D
2.	D	**11.**	A, B	**20.**	A	**28.**	B
3.	B	**12.**	C	**21.**	D	**29.**	B
4.	A	**13.**	B	**22.**	C	**30.**	**netstat -a**
5.	C	**14.**	D	**23.**	B	**31.**	A
6.	A, C	**15.**	C	**24.**	B	**32.**	B
7.	B	**16.**	B	**25.**	A, C	**33.**	C
8.	D	**17.**	A	**26.**	See "In-Depth Answers."		
9.	B	**18.**	A, B, D				

IN-DEPTH ANSWERS

1. ☑ **B.** A network-based intrusion prevention system (NIPS) analyzes network traffic patterns, generates event logs and alerts system administrators to events, and sometimes stops potential intrusions. Some implementations have a database of known attack patterns, while others can take notice of abnormal traffic for a specific network. The administrator can then take measures to stop the attack, such as dropping offending packets. IPS and other device logs and alerts can be centrally collected, aggregated, correlated, and reported on by a SIEM system.
    ☒ **A, C,** and **D** are incorrect. A network-based intrusion detection system (NIDS) can detect network anomalies, but it doesn't stop them; instead, it simply triggers an alert or notifies an administrator of the issue. Proxy servers retrieve Internet content on behalf of users; they do not analyze network traffic at all. Packet-filtering firewalls analyze packet headers only to determine whether traffic should be allowed or denied; they are not designed to stop in-progress network attacks, like a NIPS is.

2. ☑ **D.** Wireless access points as well as wireless router logs can reveal all wireless LAN activity. Some access points may require you to enable logging. In an enterprise, log events should be forwarded to a central logging host to facilitate the detection of suspicious activity.
    ☒ **A, B,** and **C** are incorrect. Protocol analyzers capture network traffic; the question asks whether unauthorized WLAN usage in the past can be determined. Proxy servers don't directly relate to WLAN unauthorized access. Performance monitoring measures various performance metrics of a computer system and has nothing to do with traffic analysis.

3. ☑ **B.** File Transfer Protocol (FTP) access logs list file activity on FTP servers, including file deletions or renames.
    ☒ **A, C,** and **D** are incorrect. Firewall logs can list traffic to or from an FTP site, but unless the firewall logs all packet payloads (which is rare, because of performance and space reasons), it cannot reveal who deleted or renamed files on the FTP site. FTP download and upload logs are just that: records of who downloaded files from the FTP server and who uploaded files to the FTP server, respectively.

4. ☑ **A.** Windows machines write audit data to the Event Viewer security log. A centralized SIEM system can store audit log data from many devices in a single repository where the data is written once but can be read many times—write once read many (WORM). WORM functionality is sometimes required for regulatory compliance. An additional benefit is deduplication of similar events, which results in less storage space consumed and quicker searching.

☒ **B, C,** and **D** are incorrect. Windows machines do not have an audit or deletion log. The application log lists events related to specific applications, not audit data.

5. ☑ **C.** The honeypot host is unpatched and is therefore vulnerable, so storing the only copy of log files (a default setting) on a honeypot means attackers could delete the contents of logs to remove all traces of their malicious activity.

☒ **A, B,** and **D** are incorrect. The honeypot does not necessarily need to be patched; a lack of applied patches can be useful so that the honeypot is an easy target for malicious users and malicious code. Honeypots can run web or SMTP mail services if you want to track related malicious activity.

6. ☑ **A and C.** Behavior-based monitoring detects activity that deviates from the norm. A baseline is required to establish what normal is. Because of this, new attacks could potentially be stopped if they do not conform to normal network usage patterns.

☒ **B and D** are incorrect. With behavior-based monitoring, deviations from normal, acceptable activity are detected. Signature-based monitoring uses a database of known attack patterns to compare against current network activity; behavior-based monitoring does not do this.

7. ☑ **B.** Comparing known attacks against current activity is called *signature-based detection*.

☒ **A, C,** and **D** are incorrect. With behavior-based monitoring, deviations from normal, acceptable activity are detected. A deviation from normal behavior is referred to as an *anomaly*; there is no such thing as an anomaly-based configuration, however. Web-based is a fictitious detection method in this context.

8. ☑ **D.** Windows machines include Performance Monitor to measure which aspect of the software or hardware is not performing as well as it should.

☒ **A, B,** and **C** are incorrect. The question states that the virus scanner is up to date, so running a virus scan wouldn't be the most optimal option, since modern virus scanners watch all activity in real-time. Port scanners show only open ports; they cannot identify why a system is slowing down. System restore points can sometimes revert the computer to a previous (and faster) state to solve these types of problems, but Windows servers do not support system restore points. And even if they did, that wouldn't be the first thing you'd do because it's rather invasive in nature.

9. ☑ **B.** A user access and rights review identifies the rights and permissions users must have compared to what they have been given. In this case, the review would reveal what needs to be changed so users have only the rights needed to do their jobs.

☒ **A, C,** and **D** are incorrect. There is no reason to delete and re-create user accounts; existing account permissions and rights could be configured properly instead. Server audit logs could reveal how and when users got so many rights, but this will not help you solve the problem; neither will stronger user passwords, because passwords don't relate to user privileges.

10. ☑ **B.** Proxy servers can track detailed web-surfing activity including site visited, time of day, user account name, and so on. The reliability of this data relies heavily upon time synchronization of all network devices.

    ☒ **A, C,** and **D** are incorrect. Virtual private networks (VPNs) enable secure connections to a private LAN across an untrusted network, but they do not track web-surfing activity. Packet-filtering firewalls cannot track details, although they can log general network traffic allowed to pass through the firewall. Network address translation (NAT) gateways allow hosts with only private IP addresses to access Internet resources through the NAT gateway public IP address; this removes the need for all hosts to have public IP addresses.

11. ☑ **A and B.** A NIDS monitors and analyzes network traffic for malicious packets; if it finds any, it then triggers an alert or notification.

    ☒ **C and D** are incorrect. A NIPS has the ability to drop malicious packets; a NIDS does not. A NIDS does absolutely nothing to protect laptops disconnected from the LAN; a HIDS, however, can detect potential attacks on laptops while they're outside protected networks.

12. ☑ **C.** A HIDS is a host-based solution and thus must be installed on individual hosts. A HIDS has the benefits of being very application specific and being able to monitor each host at all times.

    ☒ **A, B,** and **D** are incorrect. A HIDS cannot block suspicious traffic from entering the network; this is the job of a HIPS. Because a HIDS resides on a host, encrypted network traffic is no longer encrypted by the time a HIDS analyzes it (if it does at all). A HIDS will normally analyze various host log files.

13. ☑ **B.** The firewall is probably configured to overwrite the oldest log entries after the maximum log file size has been reached. Even in this case, however, there are normally log archival options available for configuration.

    ☒ **A, C,** and **D** are incorrect. Administrative rights are definitely required to access firewall logs, but you wouldn't be able to see any entries if you did not have this privilege. Most firewalls can keep logs as long as you configure them to (log archiving). Failure to patch a firewall (software or firmware) would not cause an inability to access archived logs.

14. ☑ **D.** Like many Microsoft administrative tools, Performance Monitor can run locally but can display data (performance counters) added from remote hosts.

    ☒ **A, B,** and **C** are incorrect. Running Performance Monitor on or using Remote Desktop Protocol to log into each host is not an efficient solution, since monitoring can be performed from a single network host. You cannot monitor system performance metrics, at least not easily, with Event Viewer log data.

15. ☑ **C.** Audit logs differ from regular activity logs because they record administrative configuration activities, such as modifying firewall rules.

    ☒ **A, B,** and **D** are incorrect. On Windows machines, the security log shows security events, including Windows auditing events. Firewall logs display normal firewall usage activity, not administrative configuration activity. Windows Event Viewer logs would not display anything related to firewall appliance configurations.

16. ☑ **B.** If a computer is visiting a web site and downloading an EXE file without the user's knowledge, the machine may most likely be under an attacker's control. This activity could commonly result from malware trying to download additional malicious code.

    ☒ **A, C,** and **D** are incorrect. Windows Update does not use the listed URL. Password-cracking programs try to guess passwords; they do not download EXE files without user consent. Because the firewall commonly blocks connections initiated from the Internet, being controlled via RDP is unlikely.

17. ☑ **A.** False positives report there is a problem when in fact there is none, such as in this case, where sales employees are performing legitimate activities. The alert should still be checked to ensure that an attack is not coinciding with this new network activity.

    ☒ **B, C,** and **D** are incorrect. Not reporting a problem when there is one is referred to as a false negative. A true positive depicts a situation in which malicious activity correctly triggers an alert, while a true negative depicts a scenario in which an alert wasn't raised because there was no malicious activity.

18. ☑ **A, B,** and **D.** Log files should be encrypted and stored on secured centralized hosts, so if a machine is compromised, there is still a copy of the log. File hashes ensure that files have not been tampered with in any way; a modified file generates a different hash.

    ☒ **C** is incorrect. Windows Update would not prevent log file tampering.

19. ☑ **D.** There is a large time gap between the second and third lines. Almost nine hours of log activity are unaccounted for. This could indicate that somebody cleared incriminating log entries.

    ☒ **A, B,** and **C** are incorrect. The IP addresses listed are valid. Web servers can commonly use an IP address of 192.168.1.1 (private IP address) if they're internally facing or present on a local machine for testing.

20. ☑ **A.** In an Active Directory environment, Group Policy can be used to deliver settings to domain computers, such as audit settings for servers.

    ☒ **B, C,** and **D** are incorrect. Each listed solution would work, but they take much more time to implement than using Group Policy would.

21. ☑ **D.** Packet sniffers (protocol analyzers) capture network traffic, but they do not process the traffic resulting in a decision to allow, deny, or report on the activity; a NIDS does these things.

    ☒ **A, B,** and **C** are incorrect. There is a difference between a packet sniffer and a NIDS. Packet sniffers capture network traffic passively but do not take action to allow or block or to report the activity. A NIDS analyzes traffic looking for suspicious activity. Promiscuous mode enables a host's NIC to capture and analyze all traffic it intercepts.

22. ☑ **C.** Since RDP connections from the Internet would go through the firewall, it would be quickest and easiest to consult your firewall log.

    ☒ **A, B,** and **D** are incorrect. Checking logs on each computer is too time consuming. Your RDP servers would not be involved with somebody from the Internet RDPing to one of your internal clients. There is no need to contact your ISP; your own firewall should have this information.

23. ☑ **B.** Detailed verbose logging presents much more log data than normal logging; therefore, performance is affected. What is being logged and how much activity is occurring will determine how much performance degradation will occur.

☒ **A, C,** and **D** are incorrect. Verbose logging is useful for troubleshooting, but not for long periods of time, because performance is degraded. Network bandwidth is not affected by verbose logging (unless forwarding log data to a central logging host). Changing logging levels does not consume a user license.

24. ☑ **B.** Before jumping the gun and reimaging or applying a restore point, first check the log files for any indication of changes before the machine became slow and unstable.

☒ **A, C,** and **D** are incorrect. System Restore and reimaging should normally not be performed immediately (unless your corporate policy states to do so); check the logs first. Running Windows Update would most likely not make a difference on the computer.

25. ☑ **A** and **C.** NAT router logs will list which internal addresses were translated and at what time. This could be used in correlation with captured packet time stamps to establish who visited the web site.

☒ **B** and **D** are incorrect. The perimeter firewall most likely will list only the IP address of the NAT router's public interface; all outbound packets assume this IP address. Viewing all client browsing histories would take longer than viewing the NAT log or your packet capture.

26. ☑ Figure 19-2 shows the correct matching of requirements and solutions. HIDS software could be installed on the payroll server to detect suspicious activity and alert security analysts. Tracking any read and write activities to a folder is accomplished with auditing. NIDS monitor networks for suspicious activity.

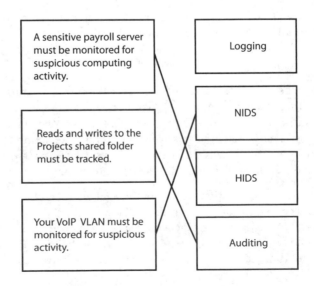

FIGURE 19-2

Security requirements and solutions— the answer

A sensitive payroll server must be monitored for suspicious computing activity.	Logging
Reads and writes to the Projects shared folder must be tracked.	NIDS
Your VoIP VLAN must be monitored for suspicious activity.	HIDS
	Auditing

27. ☑ **D.** Lack of RAM causes the oldest used data in RAM to be swapped to disk to make room for what must now be placed in RAM (many large documents). This sometimes makes it appear as if the disk is the problem.

☒ **A, B,** and **C** are incorrect. The server network connection, CPU, and disks seem fine other than when remote users work with large documents.

28. ☑ **B.** To monitor specific apps running on host computers and prevent potential attacks, you should deploy a HIPS.

☒ **A, C,** and **D** are incorrect. Honeypots are hosts left intentionally vulnerable for the purpose of collecting data regarding attacker patterns and TTPs (tactics, techniques, and procedures). A NIDS analyzes network packets looking for suspicious traffic. Public Key Infrastructure (PKI) is a hierarchy of digital security certificates.

29. ☑ **B.** From the list of choices, the most likely answer is that 172.16.29.97 is a spoofed IP address. IP addresses used on the internal network should not be coming into the network from the outside.

☒ **A, C,** and **D** are incorrect. 172.16.29.97 is a valid IP address. The question states you are reviewing forwarded log entries, not entries on the firewall appliance itself, so log file tampering would not affect you in this case. HTTP normally uses TCP port 80; the question states UDP port 53 (DNS).

30. ☑ The **netstat -a command is a** built-in Windows command that displays local listening ports that can accept connections, as well as which network services (and ports) you are connected to.

31. ☑ **A.** Logging tracks many different types of events related to hardware and software, but auditing specifically tracks security-related events.

☒ **B, C,** and **D** are incorrect. Auditing focuses on tracking access to a specific resource for security purposes. Both logging and auditing could track hardware-related events. For example, logging can track the activity related to a printer, whereas auditing could track smartcard authentication.

32. ☑ **B.** SIEM tools provide a centralized way to monitor and manage security incidents. SIEM solutions also combine, or aggregate, like events to reduce duplicate event notifications and provide reports that correlate data.

☒ **A, C,** and **D** are incorrect. PowerShell provides Windows administrators with a command-line solution that supports scripting to automate repetitive administrative tasks. System Center Configuration Manager is a centralized configuration and change management tool from Microsoft. Group Policy user and computer settings number in the thousands and can be configured locally on a single host or centrally using Active Directory.

33. ☑ **C.** Establishing a baseline of normal user login activity facilitates configuring notifications for login anomalies and sending them to a SOAR dashboard.

☒ **A, B,** and **D** are incorrect. A NIPS analyzes network traffic patterns, generates event logs, and alerts system administrators to events; it also stops potential intrusions. SIEM tools provide a centralized way to monitor and manage security incidents. SIEM solutions also aggregate and deduplicate events and provide reports that correlate data. A sentiment analysis involves analyzing text data to provide context and the emotional origins of messages; it is often used to measure customer satisfaction (or dissatisfaction) with products or services in addition to social media monitoring.

Chapter 20

Security Assessments and Audits

QUESTIONS

Periodic testing of computer systems and networks over time identifies security weaknesses. Security assessments are best conducted by a third party and may be required by government regulation or to acquire business contracts. As a Security+ professional, you must know when to use the various security assessment tools and how to interpret their results.

1. As part of your security audit, you would like to see what type of network traffic is being transmitted on the network. Which type of tool should you use?

    A. Protocol analyzer

    B. Port scanner

    C. Vulnerability scanner

    D. Password cracker

2. Your network consists of 250 computers. You must determine which machines are secure and which are not. Which type of tool should you use?

    A. Protocol analyzer

    B. Port scanner

    C. Vulnerability scanner

    D. Password cracker

3. You would like to focus on and track potential future malicious activity for a particular host in your screened subnet. What should you configure?

    A. Honeynet

    B. Honeypot

    C. DMZ tracker

    D. Web server

4. Which of the following would you employ to determine which ports are open on a host?

    A. Vulnerability scanner

    B. Packet sniffer

    C. Performance Monitor

    D. Port scanner

5. A technician must identify deviations from normal network activity. Which task must she first perform?

   A. Trend analysis

   B. Baseline analysis

   C. Performance monitoring

   D. Risk analysis

6. A Windows computer has not been patched and unnecessary services have not been disabled. Which of the following statements is true regarding security?

   A. The computer will perform faster.

   B. The computer has a large attack surface.

   C. The computer has a small attack surface.

   D. The computer will perform slower.

7. A network security auditor simulates various network attacks against a corporate network. Which term best defines this procedure?

   A. Vulnerability analysis

   B. Network mapping

   C. Penetration testing

   D. Risk assessment

8. Your manager asks you to configure a collection of purposely vulnerable hosts in a DMZ for the purpose of tracking malicious attacker attempts. What term best describes what you are configuring?

   A. Honeynet

   B. Honeypot

   C. Firewall

   D. Proxy server

9. You run a vulnerability scan on subnet 192.168.1.0/24. The results state that TCP ports 135 through 139 are open on most hosts. What does this refer to, assuming default ports are being used?

   A. File and Print Sharing

   B. Web server

   C. Mail server

   D. Remote Desktop Protocol

10. After careful log examination, you realize that somebody has hacked into your WEP-secured home wireless network. What can you do to improve the security of wireless traffic?

   A. Use WPA2 Enterprise.

   B. Use WPA2 PSK.

   C. Disable SSID broadcasting.

   D. Change the ESSID.

11. What should be done to ensure that your network security is effective?

    A. Patch all operating systems.

    B. Update the BIOS on all systems.

    C. Periodically test network security controls.

    D. Upgrade to the latest version of Microsoft Office.

12. Which of the following are considered passive security testing? (Choose two.)

    A. Capturing network traffic

    B. Brute-force password attack

    C. Dictionary-based disk decryption

    D. OS fingerprinting

13. From the following list, identify the security misconfiguration:

    A. A domain administrative account is used as a service account.

    B. An Active Directory account is used as a service account.

    C. Windows stations receive updates from a WSUS server instead of the Internet.

    D. The Windows Guest account is disabled.

14. A security-auditing team has been hired to conduct network penetration tests against a network. The team has not been given any data related to the network or its layout. What type of testing will the team perform?

    A. Unknown environment

    B. Known environment

    C. Partially known environment

    D. Blue box

15. Refer to Figure 20-1. Which of the following statements are true, knowing default ports are in use? (Choose two.)

    A. The web server IP address is 66.220.151.75.

    B. The web server IP address is 192.168.2.12.

    C. The web site is not using SSL.

    D. Packet 24 is going to the web site.

FIGURE 20-1	Wireshark packet capture

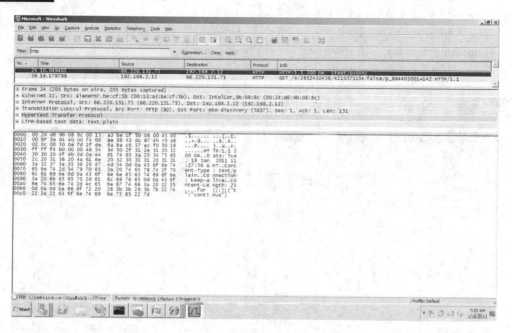

16. You are having trouble pinging host 192.168.17.45; there are no replies. One of your users must use the Remote Desktop Protocol (RDP) against the host to run an application. You cannot test RDP for the user, because you are currently logged on locally to a Linux server with only a command line. What can you use to determine quickly whether RDP is running on 192.168.17.45?

    A. Packet sniffer

    B. Virus scanner

    C. Wireless scanner

    D. Port scanner

17. After conducting a security audit, you inform the network owner that you discovered two unencrypted wireless networks. Your client asks how best to secure wireless traffic. Which of the following is the most secure form of wireless network encryption?

    A. WEP

    B. WPA

    C. WPA2

    D. WPA4

18. Refer to Figure 20-2. Which configuration errors would a security audit find? (Choose two.)

    A. The Administrator account should be deleted.

    B. The Administrator account is enabled and has not been renamed.

    C. The Guest account is enabled and has not been renamed or disabled.

    D. The Guest account should be deleted.

FIGURE 20-2   Local user accounts on a Windows server

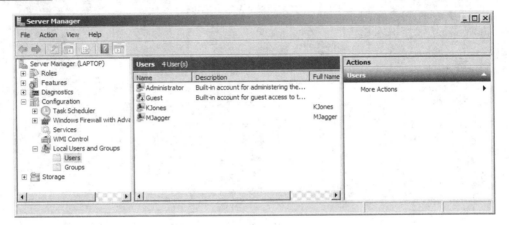

19. A security auditor must determine which types of servers are running on a network. Which type of tool should be used?

    A. Network mapper

    B. Protocol analyzer

    C. Port scanner

    D. Virus scanner

20. A security auditor discovers open wireless networks. She must recommend a secure solution. Which of the following is the most secure wireless solution?

    A. 802.1x

    B. WEP

    C. WPA PSK

    D. Disabling SSID broadcast

21. While auditing a Windows Active Directory environment, you discover that administrative accounts do not have configured account lockout policies. Which of the following are security concerns? (Choose two.)

    A. If account lockout is enabled, administrative accounts could be locked out as a result of repeated password attempts.

    B. If account lockout is not enabled, administrative accounts could be subject to password attacks.

   C. If account lockout is enabled, administrative accounts could be subject to password attacks.

   D. If account lockout is not enabled, administrative accounts could be locked out as a result of repeated password attempts.

22. Which type of security testing provides network configuration information to testers?

   A. Known environment

   B. Unknown environment

   C. Partially known environment

   D. Blue box

23. You are reviewing password policies during a security audit. Refer to Figure 20-3 and identify two security problems. (Choose two.)

   A. The minimum password age is 0 days.

   B. The password history is set to only 5.

   C. The Store Passwords Using Reversible Encryption option is disabled.

   D. Passwords do not meet complexity requirements.

FIGURE 20-3   Local security policy password settings on a Windows computer

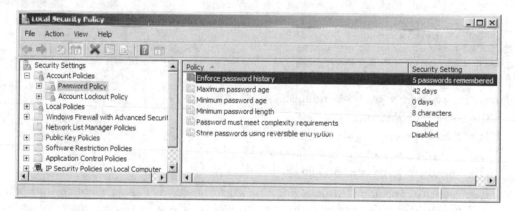

24. Which type of tool scans for known security threats on a group of computers?

   A. Packet sniffer

   B. Vulnerability scanner

   C. Risk scanner

   D. Port scanner

25. You would like an unused host to log zero-day exploit activity. What should you configure?

   A. Patch server

   B. Honeynet

   C. Honeypot

   D. Virus scanner

26. A large wireless network currently uses WPA PSK. As part of your network audit findings, you recommend a centralized wireless authentication option. What should you recommend?

    A.   RADIUS
    B.   WEP
    C.   WPA2 PSK
    D.   TKIP

27. You are performing a network penetration test for a client. From a command prompt, you issue the command **telnet smtp1.acme.com 25** to see what information is returned. Which term refers to what you have done?

    A.   Denial of service
    B.   Port scan
    C.   Banner grab
    D.   Mail grab

28. FakeCorp Inc. recently hired a security consulting firm to perform a security audit of its network at its Vulcan, Alberta, location. An excerpt of the audit findings is listed here:

```
Date: March 6, 2020 4:53am EST
Task performed: Network vulnerability scan
Performed by: Lennard Kneemoy
IP Subnet: 14.65.0.0 / 16
Credential used: FakeCorp\Administrator
Results: We were able to connect to most hosts without specifying a password.
Recommendation: Harden network hosts.
```

    Identify the problem with these findings.

    A.   The subnet mask is incorrect.
    B.   The IP address range is incorrect.
    C.   The consultant ran a noncredentialed scan.
    D.   The consultant ran a credentialed scan.

29. You are a security consultant. After performing a threat assessment on a client network, you recommend actions that should be taken. In Figure 20-4, draw a line linking the requirements on the left to the correct solutions on the right.

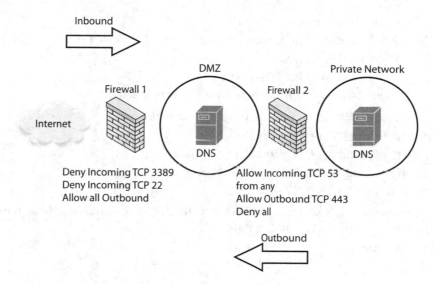

FIGURE 20-4

Security requirements and solutions

30. You are a newly hired IT security officer. An existing network diagram for the Halifax location has been provided, as shown in Figure 20-5. Which recommendations should you make to secure the network infrastructure? (Choose two.)

A. Do not allow all outbound traffic through the firewalls.

B. Allow DNS replication traffic only between specific DNS hosts.

C. Do not place DNS servers in a DMZ (screened subnet).

D. Do not allow outbound TCP 443 traffic.

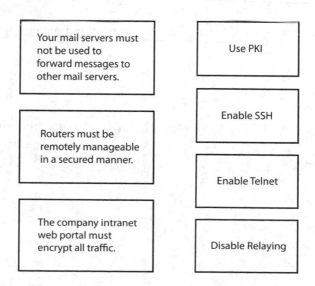

FIGURE 20-5

Halifax network diagram

31. When is baseline reporting useful?
    A. When conducting a penetration test
    B. When hardening DNS servers
    C. When hardening HTTPS servers
    D. When comparing normal activity with current activity

32. Why are penetration tests sometimes not recommended?
    A. They can identify security threats.
    B. They could degrade network performance.
    C. They could generate too much logging data.
    D. They are expensive.

33. You need to verify whether DNS servers allow DNS zone transfers to all hosts. Which built-in Windows command should you use?
    A. **netstat**
    B. **arp**
    C. **ping**
    D. **nslookup**
    E. **tracert**

34. You are creating an IT threat assessment for your organization. You are using tools that gather IT security threat details from multiple sources. Which term best describes this scenario?
    A. Threat feeds
    B. Intelligence fusion
    C. Threat advisories
    D. Threat bulletins

35. Which type of vulnerability scan tests the security and stability of a web application?
    A. Penetration test
    B. Debugging
    C. Port scan
    D. Fuzzing

36. Which IT industry standard uses a scoring system to determine the severity of specific threats?
    A. CVE
    B. Metasploit
    C. CVSS
    D. Bug bounty

37. You have been hired as a member of an IT security red team that will exploit discovered vulnerabilities. Which type of activities will you perform?

A. War driving

B. War flying

C. Data sanitizing

D. Penetration testing

38. Which Linux command was used to create the result in the output shown in Figure 20-6?

A. **route**

B. **curl**

C. **dnsenum**

D. **scanless**

FIGURE 20-6							
	% Total	% Received	Average Speed Dload	Upload	Time Total	Time Spent	Time Left	Current Speed
Linux command output	100 4811k	100 4811k	27.8M	0 --:--:--	--:--:--	--:--:--	27.9M

39. Which Linux command is used to display the entire contents of a text file?

A. **cat**

B. **head**

C. **tail**

D. **grep**

40. You are creating a Linux shell script that will SSH into a target system, change file system permissions, capture network traffic, and then write a custom log entry. Which Linux commands will be used in the script?

A. **chmod, tcpdump, ssh**

B. **chmod, openssl, logger**

C. **chmod, tcpreplay, logger**

D. **chmod, tcpdump, logger**

41. What type of script is the most likely to contain the following command?

```
Get-Service | Where{$_.status -eq "Running"}
```

A. Linux shell script

B. Python script

C. Batch file

D. PowerShell script

QUICK ANSWER KEY

1. A	**12.** A, D	**23.** A, D	**33.** D
2. C	**13.** A	**24.** B	**34.** B
3. B	**14.** A	**25.** C	**35.** D
4. D	**15.** A, C	**26.** A	**36.** C
5. B	**16.** D	**27.** C	**37.** D
6. B	**17.** C	**28.** D	**38.** B
7. C	**18.** B, C	**29.** See "In-Depth	**39.** A
8. A	**19.** A	Answers."	**40.** D
9. A	**20.** A	**30.** A, B	**41.** D
10. B	**21.** A, B	**31.** D	
11. C	**22.** A	**32.** B	

IN-DEPTH ANSWERS

1. ☑ **A.** Protocol analyzers use a promiscuous mode network card driver that enables the capture of all network traffic. Each switch port is a collision domain that prevents capturing unicast traffic related to other hosts; however, some switches enable mirroring of all switch traffic to a specific port. Be aware that packet forgery is easy with freely available tools such as hping.
☒ **B, C,** and **D** are incorrect. Port scanners identify running services on a host. For example, a running web server may show TCP port 80 as being open if default ports are being used. Vulnerability scanners test network devices and hosts for weaknesses and will often generate reports, and they should be used only after proper authorization has been granted. Password crackers use repeated attempts to guess a password and are often automated.

2. ☑ **C.** Vulnerability scanners scan computers for known security vulnerabilities.
☒ **A, B,** and **D** are incorrect. Protocol analyzers capture network traffic. Port scanners list some or all open ports on one or more hosts. Password crackers repeatedly attempt to determine a password. Although port scanners and password crackers could be used to test system security, a vulnerability scanner provides a much more in-depth check, often including identification of open ports and vulnerable password settings.

3. ☑ **B.** A honeypot is an intentionally vulnerable host used to attract and track malicious activity.
☒ **A, C,** and **D** are incorrect. The question stated activity tracking on a single host, not a network of hosts (which would point to a honeypot). There is no such thing as a DMZ or screened subnet tracker. Web servers are not tools to track malicious activity; web servers deliver content to web browsers.

4. ☑ **D.** Port scanners identify open ports on hosts similar to operating system commands such as **netstat**. Personal firewall software may impede the success of port scanners. Note that port scanning can be detected fairly easily by most modern network-based intrusion protection and detection tools.
☒ **A, B,** and **C** are incorrect. Vulnerability scanners can detect open ports as well as many more items; if all that is required is a list of open TCP and UDP ports, a port scanner is a better (and faster) choice. The question doesn't indicate that only TCP and UDP ports should be listed. Packet sniffers capture network traffic, and from that captured traffic you can see port numbers in the TCP and UDP packet headers; you cannot identify exactly which ports are open on a host, just what's included in the packet capture. Performance Monitor is a Windows tool used to measure and monitor performance metrics of a Windows computer; it does not scan for open ports.

5. ☑ **B.** A baseline analysis establishes what is normal on a given network. Without this data, it is difficult to determine deviations from the norm.

 ☒ **A, C,** and **D** are incorrect. Trend analysis refers to the collection of data in hopes of identifying a pattern. Performance Monitor is a tool for Windows computers that measures performance metrics such as CPU and memory utilization. Risk analysis identifies assets and related risks along with methods to minimize business disruption.

6. ☑ **B.** Computers with many potential vulnerabilities (software, physical) are said to have a larger attack surface than patched machines that run only software that is required. A larger attack surface means a higher degree of possibility of a machine becoming compromised.

 ☒ **A, C,** and **D** are incorrect. The question asks about security, not faster performance. Computers generally run faster with patches applied and fewer services running. Because unnecessary services have not been disabled, the machine has a larger, not a smaller, attack surface than it otherwise should. In addition, the computer may be performing slower because extra unnecessary services may be running.

7. ☑ **C.** Penetration testing (pen testing) is an active, or intrusive, type of test that involves simulating malicious activity against hosts or entire networks to assess how secure they are and to identify threats. Proper written consent outlining the rules of engagement must be obtained prior to performing this type of testing, since testing could disrupt hosts and networks.

 ☒ **A, B,** and **D** are incorrect. Vulnerability analysis identifies and classifies potential threats and is considered passive, or non-intrusive, since it does not attempt to exploit weaknesses. Network mapping plots the network layout using a discovery tool such as nmap. Risk assessment does not simulate network attacks; it is used to identify business threats and how to mitigate them.

8. ☑ **A.** A honeynet is composed of two or more honeypots. These are intentionally vulnerable hosts used to track malicious activity.

 ☒ **B, C,** and **D** are incorrect. The question stated a collection of hosts, not a single (honeypot) host. Firewalls and proxy servers should never be left intentionally vulnerable.

9. ☑ **A.** Windows File and Print Sharing generally uses TCP ports 135 to 139 to enable resources to be discoverable on a local network.

 ☒ **B, C,** and **D** are incorrect. Web servers typically use TCP port 80 (clear text) or 443 (SSL/TLS). Mail servers use a variety of ports depending on their type and role. For example, Simple Mail Transfer Protocol (SMTP) servers listen on TCP port 25. Remote Desktop Protocol (RDP) uses TCP port 3389.

10. ☑ **B.** Wi-Fi Protected Access (WPA2) pre-shared key (PSK) is considered more secure than Wired Equivalent Privacy (WEP) and would be the most suitable solution for a home router.

 ☒ **A, C,** and **D** are incorrect. WPA2 Enterprise requires a central authentication server; the average user will not have one at home. This is mostly encountered in medium- to large-scale enterprises. Disabling the Extended Service Set Identifier (ESSID) suppresses the WLAN name from appearing in Wi-Fi beacon packets, but this is easily circumvented with freely available tools. Changing the ESSID name may make it difficult for a hacker to identify what he is breaking into, but WPA2 PSK is a much more secure solution. Changing the name will only help in adding confusion about the target network's functionality; it won't make the network more secure.

11. ☑ **C.** Periodic network testing, perhaps even penetration testing, is valuable to ensure that your network security controls remain valid over time and that previously uncompromised hosts have not been compromised and used for persistent attacker connectivity. Compromised hosts or network devices could allow attackers to use one vulnerable device to gain access, and from there scan for and exploit other vulnerable devices on the network (pivoting) through lateral movement.

☒ **A, B,** and **D** are incorrect. Patching an operating system, updating the BIOS, and upgrading Microsoft Office are all important for host security, but the question asks about network security; therefore, option C is the best answer.

12. ☑ **A and D.** The passive testing of security controls does not interfere with the normal operation of a computer system or network. Capturing network traffic simply takes a copy of network packets already being transmitted, and OS fingerprinting attempts to determine the OS used by a device by analyzing network traffic responses from a host.

☒ **B and C** are incorrect. Brute-force password attacks and disk decryption must interact directly with a computer system and may affect the performance or normal operation of that host.

13. ☑ **A.** A Windows service (and UNIX/Linux daemons) must run under the context of a standard user account. Assigning a powerful domain administrative account presents a major threat if the service is compromised; the hacker would then have escalated domain administrative privileges. Service accounts should have only the rights and permissions required to function—nothing more. Many administrators do not force periodic password changes for service accounts, which presents yet another security risk.

☒ **B, C,** and **D** are incorrect. Some services run on Windows domain controller computers and must use an Active Directory account. Using Windows Server Update Services (WSUS) to update client workstations is considered a best practice; this is not a security misconfiguration. The Windows Guest account is disabled by default in newer Windows versions. It should not be enabled in the interest of security and user auditing.

14. ☑ **A.** Unknown environment testing refers to the process by which computer software or networks are tested and the testers have no information about how the software or networks are designed.

☒ **B, C,** and **D** are incorrect. Known environment testing means the testers have been given full details regarding the item they are testing, such as software source code or network diagrams. Testers have a minimal knowledge of the internals of software or network configuration when conducting partially known environment testing. This enables testers to make better informed testing decisions. Blue-box testing does not exist; in the past, a blue box was a device used to make free long-distance telephone calls.

15. ☑ **A** and **C.** Packet 24 shows the packet coming from 66.220.151.75 with a source port of 80 (look at the middle of the figure at the Transmission Control Protocol, Src Port area). Because web servers use port 80, we now know the IP address of the web server. Because the packet payload (bottom-right panel) contains readable text, we know the packet is not encrypted with Secure Sockets Layer (SSL). We could determine this another way as well; SSL web servers normally use TCP port 443, not 80.

☒ **B** and **D** are incorrect. The client station IP address is 192.168.2.12 (look at the Transmission Control Protocol destination port of 3837 in packet 24). If this were the web server, traffic would be going either to port 80 or 443. Web browsing clients are assigned a dynamic port value above 1024 (such as 3837) that is used when receiving data from the web server. Packet 24 is originating from the web server, not sent to it.

16. ☑ **D.** A port scanner is a quick, simple way to determine which ports are open on a host. Even though ping packets may be blocked, RDP packets may not be. Tools such as Netcat can be used on Linux and Windows to test communication with TCP and UDP ports.

☒ **A, B,** and **C** are incorrect. A packet sniffer captures transmitted network traffic, but it cannot determine whether RDP is available on 192.168.17.45. Virus scanners, including malware analysis tools such as Cuckoo, look for malicious code; they do not test for open ports on remote hosts. Wireless scanners list wireless networks within range; they do not perform port scans.

17. ☑ **C.** WPA2 is the most secure option from the presented list. Unlike WPA, WPA2 must be tested and certified by the Wi-Fi Alliance. WPA2 also uses a stronger encryption implementation in the form of AES, the U.S. government–accepted encryption standard.

☒ **A, B,** and **D** are incorrect. WEP encryption is easily broken, sometimes within seconds with freely available tools, and the same goes for WPA. WPA supersedes WEP, but WPA2 is superior to WPA. WPA4 does not exist commercially (yet).

18. ☑ **B** and **C.** Default administrative accounts must be renamed or disabled because malicious users will try default admin accounts before moving on. Consider renaming the default admin account and creating (as a regular user) a new account named "Administrator" with no rights or permissions. You should always have more than one inconspicuous administrative account.

☒ **A** and **D** are incorrect. The Windows Administrator and Guest accounts cannot be deleted because they are built-in accounts, but they can, and should, be renamed or disabled.

19. ☑ **A.** Network mapping utilities such as the open source Cheops-ng tool can map out a network's layout and identify operating systems running on hosts.

☒ **B, C,** and **D** are incorrect. Protocol analyzers capture only transmitted network traffic; they do not scan for network hosts or network configuration. Port scanners identify listening ports. Virus scanners protect against malicious software on a host; they do not scan entire networks.

20. ☑ **A.** 802.1x requires that connecting hosts or users first authenticate with a central authentication server before even gaining access to the network. This is considered the most secure of the listed choices, since WEP and WPA PSK do not require authentication to get on the network; only a passphrase is required. Neither WEP nor WPA PSK uses a centralized authentication server.

☒ **B, C,** and **D** are incorrect. WEP encryption is easily defeated with freely available tools, so it is not a secure choice. WPA PSK is more secure than WEP, but as mentioned, both have the limitation of requiring only a passphrase, which an attacker can identify and use to connect to the network. Disabling the SSID broadcast will stop only very inexperienced attackers.

21. ☑ **A** and **B.** These answers present a catch-22 scenario. The best solution to prevent this problem is to authenticate admin accounts with a smartcard. This would eliminate remote attacks on admin accounts because of the requirement of possessing a physical smartcard.
☒ **C** and **D** are incorrect. Account lockout impedes the success of password attacks by locking the account for a time after a small number of successive incorrect passwords. Not configuring account lockout means some password-cracking tools such as Hydra could run against admin accounts incessantly; through persistence, attackers would most likely crack account passwords.

22. ☑ **A.** A known environment test provides testers with detailed configuration information regarding the software or network they are testing.
☒ **B, C,** and **D** are incorrect. Unknown environment testing provides no information at all to system testers. Partially known environment testing provides some, but not detailed, information to testers, which enables a more informed testing environment. Blue-box testing does not exist in this context.

23. ☑ **A** and **D.** The minimum password age prevents users from immediately changing their password a number of times (password history) to return to one they have already used that is easy to remember. Complexity requirements on Windows systems means the password cannot contain any variation of the username, it must be at least six characters long, and it must contain characters from three of the four categories: uppercase character, lowercase character, number, and non-alphabetic character (for example, !, $, #, %).
☒ **B** and **C** are incorrect. Compared to answers A and D, a password history of 5 is not a security issue. Storing passwords using reversible encryption is meant to be used by specific software needing the user password. Enabling this option does not store the passwords in a secure manner.

24. ☑ **B.** Vulnerability scanners such as Nessus normally use an updated database of known security vulnerabilities and misconfigurations for various operating systems and network devices. This database is compared against a single host or a network scan to determine whether any hosts or devices are vulnerable. Reports can then be generated from the scan. Network scans can also reveal the presence of rogue systems, including rogue DHCP servers that dole out incorrect IP configurations to disrupt network communications or to re-route traffic through attacker systems for unauthorized detailed traffic examination.
☒ **A, C,** and **D** are incorrect. Packet sniffers such as the UNIX-based tcpdump or the Windows- and Linux-based Wireshark are not designed to look for vulnerabilities; they simply capture transmitted network packets. There is no such thing as a risk scanner. Port scanners do not identify security threats; they list open TCP and UDP ports.

25. ☑ **C.** Honeypots are intentionally exposed systems used to attract the attention of attackers to study attackers' methods and extract operational tactics and procedures.

☒ **A, B,** and **D** are incorrect. Patch servers ensure that software on network hosts is kept up to date. Honeynets are a collection of two or more honeypots; the question specifically states a single host. Virus scanners would not detect zero-day exploits. A zero-day exploit is a vulnerability that has not yet been made known to the software author or virus scanner.

26. ☑ **A.** Remote Authentication Dial-In User Service (RADIUS) is a central server that authenticates users connecting to a network. Failure to authenticate to the RADIUS server means access to the network is denied.

☒ **B, C,** and **D** are incorrect. WEP is not a centralized authentication mechanism; it must be configured on each access point and client station. WPA2 PSK must also be configured on each access point and client. Temporal Key Integrity Protocol (TKIP) uses key mixing and packet sequence counters to enhance security. TKIP is used with WPA to address the lack of security offered by WEP.

27. ☑ **C.** A banner grab is used to probe the listening port of a network service with the intent of learning more, such as what version of software is running.

☒ **A, B,** and **D** are incorrect. Denial-of-service attacks render a network service unavailable for legitimate use; in this case, we have nothing more than information gathering. Port scanning returns ports in use on a host; in this example, we already know that port 25 is in a listening state. Mail grab is not a legitimate term.

28. ☑ **D.** The consultant ran the vulnerability scan with administrative credentials. Although this is fine, a noncredentialed scan should have also been run.

☒ **A, B,** and **C** are incorrect. The subnet mask and IP address are correct and can be verified on a Windows host using **ipconfig** and on a Linux host using **ifconfig** or **ip addr show**. The consultant did not run a noncredentialed scan; he ran a credentialed scan.

29. ☑ Figure 20-7 shows the correct matching of requirements and solutions. Relaying is often used by attackers to send spam messages. SSH encrypts connections when remotely administering routers. PKI uses certificates to secure network transmissions including the encryption of intranet web portal traffic.

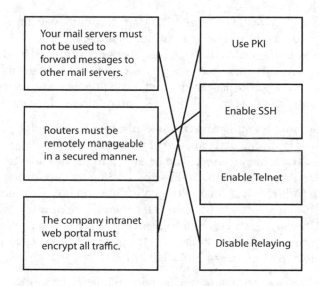

FIGURE 20-7

Security requirements and solutions— the answer

Your mail servers must not be used to forward messages to other mail servers.	Use PKI
Routers must be remotely manageable in a secured manner.	Enable SSH
	Enable Telnet
The company intranet web portal must encrypt all traffic.	Disable Relaying

30. ☑ **A** and **B.** Firewalls should scrutinize not only incoming network traffic but also traffic leaving a network. This can prevent SMTP relaying, spam, DDoS attacks, and many more attacks initiated from your network to a victim host or network. Attackers use tools such as theHarvester to scour the Internet looking for valid e-mail addresses that can be spammed or sent phishing messages. DNS servers must replicate only with other known DNS servers to prevent replicating DNS records to rogue DNS hosts.

☒ **C** and **D** are incorrect. DNS servers can be placed in a DMZ as long as the appropriate firewall rules are in place and as long as private network DNS records are not replicated to the DMZ DNS host. HTTPS uses TCP 443, and in most cases this type of traffic should be allowed to leave a private network so users can connect to secured web sites.

31. ☑ **D.** A baseline establishes what system performance looks like under normal conditions. This can be compared to current conditions to determine whether anything is out of the norm.

☒ **A, B,** and **C** are incorrect. Penetration testing involves security technicians first gathering information through reconnaissance techniques and then issuing common attacks against networks and hosts to identify threats. Pen test rules of engagement often require system cleanup after attacking hosts, which could involve reconfiguring or reimaging devices or hosts. To mimic malicious user techniques, security consultants will often use exploitation framework tools such as The Browser Exploitation Framework to test system security. After taking advantage of initial weaknesses such as gaining network access, technicians can further exploit additional vulnerabilities such as hosts unprotected by firewalls. This technique is called *pivoting*. Hardening hosts is unrelated to baseline reporting.

32. ☑ **B.** Penetration testing can be risky. Many techniques are involved, but degrading network performance or crashing hosts is a distinct possibility.

☒ **A, C,** and **D** are incorrect. Penetration tests are supposed to identify security threats; this is a good thing. Generating excessive logging and pen test costs are not the best reasons listed to skip a penetration test, as the danger involved is too important to ignore. In addition, logging can be appropriately configured and the test cost can be assessed to determine the best option.

33. ☑ **D.** The name server lookup (**nslookup**) command is built into Windows, whereas the **dig** command is specific to Linux and offers similar capabilities.

☒ **A, B, C,** and **E** are incorrect. The **netstat** command is used to display TCP, UDP, IP, and ICMP protocol statistics for both IPv4 and IPv6 on modern operating systems such as Windows 10. The **arp** (Address Resolution Protocol) command is used to view and manage configurations related to IP address–to–MAC address mappings. The **ping** and **tracert** commands use ICMP to test whether or not a network host responds to ping echo requests. The Windows **pathping** command combines the functionality of the **ping** and **tracert** commands in a single utility. Take note that most modern firewalls block ICMP traffic automatically.

34. ☑ **B.** Intelligence fusion brings together multiple threat sources such as threat feeds, advisories, bulletins, and open source intelligence (OSINT) resources to be used for a comprehensive threat assessment.

☒ **A, C,** and **D** are incorrect. Threat feeds, advisories, and bulletins serve as sources for intelligence fusion, which gathers threats from multiple sources and brings them together.

35. ☑ **D.** Fuzzing is a technique used to test the stability and security of an application. Fuzzing feeds random or unexpected data to the app. The app's behavior is observed during fuzzing to bring to light any security or stability problems through the fuzz testing.

☒ **A, B,** and **C** are incorrect. A penetration test is not a type of vulnerability scan; vulnerability scanning tools such as sn1per identify but do not necessarily actively exploit discovered flaws as penetration tests do. The sn1per tool can also be used to execute pen tests. Debugging is not specifically considered an app vulnerability scanning testing technique, although debugging helps software developers identify and solve programming problems. Port scans can be executed using tools such as nmap or are used to identify which TCP and UDP network service ports are open on a device.

36. ☑ **C.** The Common Vulnerability Scoring System (CVSS) is used to evaluate the severity of IT threats and is used by many vulnerability scanning tools such as Nessus.

☒ **A, B,** and **D** are incorrect. Common vulnerabilities and exposures (CVEs) are a centralized public listing of common IT threats, each consisting of a unique number and descriptive detail. Metasploit is an open source exploitation framework consisting of numerous tools such as password crackers and footprinting utilities that can be used during penetration testing to discover (footprinting) and actively exploit (password cracking) IT-related vulnerabilities. Bug bounties are payments offered by companies when third-party IT security specialists discover previously unknown problems or vulnerabilities in their hardware and software products.

37. ☑ **D.** Red teams conduct penetration tests. The company's IT security staff is collectively referred to as the blue team, and the team's job is to put security controls in place in alignment with organizational security policies to protect digital assets against exploits. White teams set the rules of engagement for penetration testing and analysis security testing results. Purple teaming combines attack results (red team) with security defense techniques (blue team) to enhance the organization's security posture.

☒ **A, B,** and **C** are incorrect. The listed actions do not actively exploit discovered vulnerabilities as pen testing does. The act of driving around scanning for wireless networks is called war driving. War flying uses unmanned aerial vehicles (UAVs), or drones, to scan for wireless networks from the air instead of from the ground. Data sanitizing is a technique that destroys data on a storage device to prevent its partial or complete retrieval.

38. ☑ **B.** The Linux client URL (**curl**) command is a data transfer tool that supports many protocols such as FTP, HTTP, and HTTPS.

☒ **A, C,** and **D** are incorrect. The listed commands would not result in the shown output. The Linux **route** command is used to view or manage IP routes to control TCP/IP network traffic flow. The **dnsenum** tool enumerates DNS servers to details such as hostnames and IP addresses; this is considered to be a network reconnaissance tool. Scanless is a Python-based tool that uses online web-based port scanners to conduct a port scan on your behalf.

39. ☑ **A.** The Linux **cat** command, such as **cat /etc/hosts**, shows the entire contents of a text file.

☒ **B, C,** and **D** are incorrect. The **head** command shows the specified first number of lines from a text file (normally 10 by default): **head -n 5 /etc/hosts**. The **tail** command shows the specified last number of lines from a text file (normally 10 by default): **tail /etc/hosts**. The **grep** command is a line-filtering command: **cat /etc/hosts | grep server1**.

40. ☑ **D.** The Linux **chmod** command is used to set file system permissions, such as granting read and write permissions to the owning user of a file with the command **chmod u +rw file1.txt**. The **tcpdump** command is used to capture network traffic on a specific or all network interfaces: **tcpdump -i any**. The **logger** command writes a custom log entry such as with **logger "This is a sample log entry"**.

☒ **A, B,** and **C** are incorrect. The **ssh** command is used to open a remote SSH session with a target host: **ssh user1@server1**. The **openssl** command is used to perform PKI cryptographic operations such as generating public and private key pairs and certificate signing requests. The **tcpreplay** command can be installed on Windows and Linux hosts; it has many command-line options and enables captured network traffic to be modified and replayed on the network.

41. ☑ **D.** PowerShell uses a noun–verb style syntax. The listed example will display only running services on the host where the command is executed.

☒ **A, B,** and **C** are incorrect. **Get-Service** is a PowerShell command, not a standard Linux shell script, Python script, or Windows batch file command.

Chapter 21

Incident Response and Computer Forensics

CERTIFICATION OBJECTIVES

QUESTIONS

All electronic devices we use daily, from our cars and cell phones, to laptops and personal computers, leave digital footprints. *Computer forensics* refers to the documentation, acquisition, and preservation of this digital data for use as evidence. It's vitally important that you ensure that the proper steps are taken to respond to security incidents and to perform data acquisition legally.

Incident preparation activities such as periodic drills, incident simulations and walkthroughs, and tabletop exercises ensure that team members are familiar with their roles and the appropriate response actions that must be taken.

1. What must be determined by the first responder to an incident?
   A. The severity of the event
   B. Which other personnel must be called in
   C. The dollar amount associated with the incident
   D. Who is at fault

2. After seizing computer equipment alleged to have been involved in a crime, it is placed in a corridor unattended for ten minutes while officers subdue a violent suspect. The seized equipment is no longer admissible as evidence because of what violation?
   A. Order of volatility
   B. Damage control
   C. Chain of custody
   D. Time offset

3. A warrant has been issued to investigate a server believed to be used by organized crime to swap credit card information. Following the order of volatility, which data should you collect first?
   A. Electronic memory (RAM)
   B. Hard disk
   C. USB flash drive
   D. CMOS

4. While capturing network traffic, you notice an abnormally excessive number of outbound SMTP packets. To determine whether this is an incident that requires escalation or reporting, what else should you consult?

A. The contents of your inbox
B. The mail server log
C. The mail server documentation
D. The web server log

5. You decide to work late on a Saturday night to replace wiring in your server room. Upon arriving, you realize that a break-in has occurred and server backup tapes appear to be missing. What should you do as law enforcement officials arrive?

A. Clean up the server room.
B. Sketch a picture of the area that was illegally entered on a notepad.
C. Alert officials that the surveillance video is on the premises.
D. Check the surrounding area for the perpetrator.

6. Which of the following best visually illustrates the state of a running computer at the time it was seized by law enforcement?

A. Digital photograph of the motherboard
B. Digital photograph of the screen
C. Visio network diagram
D. Steganography

7. Choose the correct order of volatility when collecting digital evidence:

A. Hard disk, DVD-R, RAM, swap file
B. Swap file, RAM, DVD-R, hard disk
C. RAM, DVD-R, swap file, hard disk
D. RAM, swap file, hard disk, DVD-R

8. What can a forensic analyst do to reduce the number of files that must be analyzed on a seized disk?

A. Write a Visual Basic script that deletes files older than 30 days.
B. Delete files thought to be operating system files.
C. Ensure that the original disk is pristine and use a hash table on a copy of the files.
D. Modify file metadata on the original disk to label files.

9. A professional who is present at the time of evidence gathering can be summoned to appear in court or to prepare a report on her findings for use in court. This person referred to as what?

A. Plaintiff
B. Defendant
C. Auditor
D. Forensic expert witness

10. Which of the following best describes chain of custody?

    A. Delegating evidence collection to your superior

    B. Preserving, protecting, and documenting evidence

    C. Capturing a system image to another disk

    D. Capturing memory contents before hard disk contents

11. While working on an insider trading case, you are asked to prove that an e-mail message is authentic and was sent to another employee. Which of the following should you consider? (Choose two.)

    A. Was the message encrypted?

    B. Was the message digitally signed?

    C. Are user public keys properly protected?

    D. Are user private keys properly protected?

12. What type of evidence would be the most difficult for a perpetrator to forge?

    A. IP address

    B. MAC address

    C. Cell phone SIM card

    D. Documents on a USB flash drive

13. What is the purpose of disk forensic software? (Choose two.)

    A. Using file encryption to ensure copied data mirrors original data

    B. Using file hashes to ensure copied data mirrors original data

    C. Protecting data on the original disks

    D. Creating file hashes on the original disks

14. You are preparing to gather evidence from a cell phone. Which of the following is false?

    A. CDMA mobile devices do not use SIM cards.

    B. CDMA phones store user data directly on the mobile device.

    C. GSM mobile devices do not use SIM cards.

    D. GSM mobile devices use SIM cards.

15. You must analyze data on a digital camera's internal memory. You plan to connect your forensic computer to the camera using a USB cable. What should you do to ensure that you do not modify data on the camera?

    A. Ensure that the camera is turned off.

    B. Flag all files on the camera as read-only.

    C. Log in with a non-administrative account on the forensic computer.

    D. Use a USB write-blocking device.

16. What can be used to ensure that seized mobile wireless devices do not communicate with other devices?

    A. SIM card
    B. Faraday bag
    C. Antistatic bag
    D. GPS jammer

17. Robin works as a network technician at a stock brokerage firm. To test network forensic capturing software, she plugs her laptop into an Ethernet switch and begins capturing network traffic. During later analysis, she notices some broadcast and multicast packets as well as her own computer's network traffic. Why was she unable to capture all network traffic on the switch?

    A. She must enable promiscuous mode on her NIC.
    B. She must disable promiscuous mode on her NIC.
    C. Each switch port is an isolated collision domain.
    D. Each switch port is an isolated broadcast domain.

18. A network intrusion detection device captures network traffic during the commission of a crime on a network. You notice NTP and TCP packets from all network hosts in the capture. You must find a way to correlate captured packets to a date and time to ensure the packet captures will be considered admissible as evidence. What should you do? (Choose two.)

    A. Nothing. NTP keeps time in sync on a network.
    B. Nothing. Packet captures are time stamped.
    C. Without digital signatures, date and time cannot be authenticated.
    D. Without encryption, date and time cannot be authenticated.

19. You arrive at a scene where a computer must be seized as evidence. The computer is powered off and has an external USB hard drive plugged in. What should you do first?

    A. Turn on the computer.
    B. Unplug the external USB hard drive.
    C. Thoroughly document the state of the equipment.
    D. Place the computer in a Faraday bag.

20. You are asked to examine a hard disk for fragments of instant messaging conversations as well as deleted files. How should you do this?

    A. Use bitstream copying tools.
    B. Log in to the computer and copy the original hard drive contents to an external USB hard drive.
    C. Map a drive across the network to the original hard drive and copy the contents to an external USB hard drive.
    D. View log files.

21. How can a forensic analyst benefit from analyzing metadata? (Choose three.)
    A. JPEG metadata can reveal specific camera settings.
    B. Microsoft Word metadata can reveal the author name.
    C. Microsoft Excel metadata can reveal your MAC address.
    D. PDF metadata can reveal the registered company name.

22. Which of the following rules must be followed when performing forensic analysis? (Choose two.)
    A. Work only with the original, authentic data.
    B. Work only with a copy of data.
    C. Seek legal permission to conduct an analysis.
    D. Seek your manager's permission to conduct an analysis.

23. The IT director is creating the following year's budget. You are asked to submit forensics dollar figures for your Cloud Security Incident Response Team (CSIRT). Which item should you *not* submit?
    A. Travel expenses
    B. Man-hour expenses
    C. Training expenses
    D. ALE amounts

24. At 9:30 A.M., users report that network performance has been severely degraded since the workday began at 8 A.M. After network analysis and a quick discussion with your IT security team, you conclude that a worm virus has infected your network. What should you do to contain the damage? (Choose two.)
    A. Determine the severity of the security breach.
    B. Unplug SAN devices.
    C. Shut down all servers.
    D. Shut down Ethernet switches.

25. A suspect deletes incriminating files and empties the Windows recycle bin. Which of the following statements are true regarding the deletion? (Choose two.)
    A. The files cannot be recovered.
    B. The files can be recovered.
    C. Deleted files contain all of their original data until the hard disk is filled with other data.
    D. Deleted files contain all of their original data until the hard disk is defragmented.

26. Using Figure 21-1, match the incident response definitions on the left to the terms on the right.

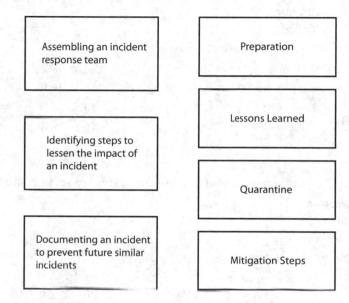

FIGURE 21-1

Incident response definitions and terms

Assembling an incident response team

Identifying steps to lessen the impact of an incident

Documenting an incident to prevent future similar incidents

Preparation

Lessons Learned

Quarantine

Mitigation Steps

27. Which built-in Linux operating system tool can be used to create an exact copy of a disk volume for forensic analysis?
  A. memdump
  B. dd
  C. WinHex
  D. Autopsy

28. You are reviewing existing network security controls and need to get up to speed on current lateral movement attacks commonly used by malicious users. What should you consult?
  A. Diamond model
  B. Cyber kill chain
  C. Mitre Att&ck
  D. COOP

29. Which of the following items can enforce the RTO for a failed server?
  A. Disaster recovery plan
  B. Communication plan
  C. Stakeholder management
  D. COOP

30. You need to review log files to determine whether network reconnaissance to learn of hostnames and IP addresses has occurred. Where will you most likely find this information?

    A. rsyslog configuration

    B. VoIP traffic log

    C. Directory server authentication log

    D. DNS server log

31. Which Linux command is specifically designed to view systemd logs?

    A. **NXLog**

    B. **IPFIX**

    C. **journalctl**

    D. **echo**

32. Which SOAR component is used to automate IT-related security incident response?

    A. Playbook

    B. Legal hold

    C. E-discovery

    D. Runbook

A

QUICK ANSWER KEY

1.	A	**12.**	C	**23.**	D
2.	C	**13.**	B, C	**24.**	A, D
3.	A	**14.**	C	**25.**	B, C
4.	B	**15.**	D	**26.**	See "In-Depth Answers."
5.	C	**16.**	B		
6.	B	**17.**	C	**27.**	B
7.	D	**18.**	A, B	**28.**	C
8.	C	**19.**	C	**29.**	A
9.	D	**20.**	A	**30.**	D
10.	B	**21.**	A, B, D	**31.**	C
11.	B, D	**22.**	B, C	**32.**	D

IN-DEPTH ANSWERS

1. ☑ **A.** A quick assessment of the situation severity by the first responder will determine who needs to be called or what should be done next, based on the incident response policy.
   ☒ **B, C,** and **D** are incorrect. Until the severity has been determined, the first responder will not know who to call. Calculating financial loss is not the first thing that should be done; it can be done once the situation is under control. Pointing fingers also isn't a first response, and it won't help the incident investigation.

2. ☑ **C.** Chain of custody has been violated. Chain of custody involves documenting evidence being collected thoroughly and legally while ensuring that the evidence cannot be tampered with. If the chain of custody has not been maintained because the equipment was unattended, it could result in evidence being deemed inadmissible by a court of law.
   ☒ **A, B,** and **D** are incorrect. Order of volatility determines what type of data is most easily lost—for example, data in electronic memory (RAM) versus data stored on a DVD or a disk volume snapshot used for backup purposes. Damage control involves minimizing further damage in the case of an unfavorable event. Time offset is used to validate the date and time stamps of digital forensic evidence.

3. ☑ **A.** The order of volatility determines which data is most at risk of loss. Electronic memory (RAM) data is lost when a device is powered off, as are the contents of the CPU cache; therefore, data must be properly collected before the other listed items.
   ☒ **B, C,** and **D** are incorrect. Hard disks and stored data, such as temporary swap or page files, USB, and CMOS data, exist even without power, although operating system settings can be set to clear temporary swap files upon reboot. CMOS chips on the motherboard require a small battery to retain their configurations (boot sequence, date/time, and so on) and can provide power for up to an average of five years.

4. ☑ **B.** The mail server log will reveal SMTP activity such as excessive outbound SMTP traffic. Real-time active monitoring of logs and long-term trend analysis can alert administrators immediately; this is the function of a security sensor such as an intrusion detection system (IDS), which can forward security alerts to a centralized security information and event management (SIEM) dashboard. SIEM dashboards can be secured so that sensitive alerts are available only to the appropriate security personnel. Documentation from previous similar incidents contains lessons learned that can aid in quick remediation.

☒ **A, C,** and **D** are incorrect. Your inbox is not related to general outbound SMTP traffic unless you have configured your mail server to notify you. Mail server documentation will detail what you must do to ensure that the server functions properly, but it will not specifically address this issue. The web server log will not contain SMTP outbound traffic details.

5. ☑ **C.** Video surveillance provides important evidence that could be used to solve this crime. For the organization, analyzing data retention policies for backups should be consulted to determine which data was compromised.

 ☒ **A, B,** and **D** are incorrect. You must not disturb the crime scene. Because there is surveillance video, there is no need for a sketch. Never seek out those who have committed a crime; leave that to law enforcement.

6. ☑ **B.** A digital photograph of a screen can prove relevant to the particular crime because it may reveal what was happening on the system at the time it was seized.

 ☒ **A, C,** and **D** are incorrect. A picture of the motherboard would generally be useless; user data is not exposed when viewing a motherboard. A Visio network diagram, while useful as network documentation, is not as valuable as a screenshot when seizing equipment. Steganography is the art of concealing data within other data (for example, messages hidden within pictures); this does not apply in this case.

7. ☑ **D.** Digital forensic evidence must first be collected from the most fragile (power-dependent) locations such as RAM and the swap file. Swap files contain data from physical RAM that were paged to disk to make room for something else in physical RAM. Hard disks are the next most vulnerable, because hard disk data can simply be deleted and the disk can be filled with useless data to make data recovery difficult. A DVD-R is less susceptible to data loss than hard disks since it is read-only.

 ☒ **A, B,** and **C** are incorrect. RAM is much more volatile (power-dependent) than swap files and hard disks. Swap files are more volatile than DVD-Rs.

8. ☑ **C.** A hash table calculates file hashes for each file. Known standard operating system file hashes can be compared to your file hashes to quickly exclude known authentic operating system files that have not been modified.

 ☒ **A, B,** and **D** are incorrect. Writing a Visual Basic script to delete files is not recommended; all data must be retained. Deleting files that are thought to belong to the operating system is not a thorough method of reducing files that must be analyzed. The original data evidence must never be modified, so adding file metadata to the original disk should not be done.

9. ☑ **D.** A forensic expert witness has specialized knowledge and experience in a field beyond that of the average person, and thus her testimony is deemed authentic.

 ☒ **A, B,** and **C** are incorrect. The plaintiff is the party who initiates a lawsuit, and the defendant is the party against which charges are alleged. An auditor examines records of some type to ensure their thoroughness and authenticity.

10. ☑   **B.** Preserving, protecting, and documenting evidence is referred to as chain of custody. The legally required implementation of evidence preservation is referred to as "legal hold."

☒   **A, C,** and **D** are incorrect. Delegation, disk imaging, and capturing memory contents are all tasks that could be performed when gathering forensic evidence, but they do not describe the entire chain of custody, which includes keeping a paper trail that shows the seizure, custody, control, transfer, analysis, and disposal of physical or electronic evidence.

11. ☑   **B and D.** Digitally signing an e-mail message requires a user's unique private key to which only he has access, which means he had to have sent the message and cannot dispute this fact (nonrepudiation). One factor used to arrive at this conclusion is how well protected user private keys are. If user private keys are simply stored on a hard disk without a password, anybody could have digitally signed the message, in which case user interviews and video surveillance may be used to place a user at a device where he may have access to a private key.

☒   **A and C** are incorrect. Encryption is separate from verifying message sender authenticity; it scrambles data to ensure confidentiality. Public keys need not be protected; that is why they are called public keys. Their mathematically related counterpart (private keys) must be safeguarded, however.

12. ☑   **C.** Cell phone subscriber identification module (SIM) cards contain unique data such as a serial number, the user's contacts, text messages, and other relevant mobile subscriber data. This is used in Global System for Mobility (GSM) communication mobile devices and enables the user to use any GSM mobile device as long as a SIM card is inserted.

☒   **A, B,** and **D** are incorrect. IP and MAC addresses, as well as documents on a USB drive, could all be easily forged (spoofed) with freely available tools.

13. ☑   **B and C.** A generated file hash, also called a checksum, is unique to the file on which it was based. Any change to the file invalidates the file hash. This is a method to digitally ensure that the correct version of a file is being analyzed and is part of document provenance, which strives to verify data origin and how it was processed and stored. Data on a seized hard disk must remain intact. Forensic disk software runs on a separate device or boots using its own operating system and uses bitstream copying to copy entire hard disk contents. File hashes should never be generated on the source hard disk; it is imperative that it remain undisturbed.

☒   **A and D** are incorrect. File encryption does not ensure that copied data is the same as the source; instead, it scrambles the data so only authorized persons with the correct decryption key can view it. You should never create file hashes on the original disk; its state at the time of seizure must be preserved.

14. ☑   **C.** Global System for Mobile (GSM) communication devices use SIM cards. This means you could purchase a new GSM mobile device and simply insert your SIM card without having to contact your mobile wireless service provider.

☒   **A, B,** and **D** are incorrect. Code-division multiple access (CDMA) and GSM devices use SIM cards and can store user data on the mobile device.

15. ☑ **D.** USB write-blocking devices ensure that data can travel in only one direction when collecting digital evidence from storage media, such as a digital camera's internal memory. If this tool is used, this fact must be documented to adhere to chain-of-custody procedures.
☒ **A, B,** and **C** are incorrect. The camera should remain in its seizure state, so you should not power it off if it is powered on. You should not flag anything on the camera as read-only; you must not disturb the state of the camera. Simply logging on to a forensic computer using an administrative or non-administrative account has nothing to do with not modifying data on the camera.

16. ☑ **B.** A Faraday bag is a mobile device shield that prevents wireless signals to or from the mobile device. This must be used immediately upon seizure of a wireless mobile device to ensure that data stored on it is not modified through wireless remote communications.
☒ **A, C,** and **D** are incorrect. SIM cards contain user mobile data, but in the question you do not know whether we are inserting or removing the SIM card. Antistatic bags shield sensitive electronic components from electrostatic discharge (ESD) but do nothing to prevent wireless signals. Global Positioning System (GPS) jammers prevent unwanted GPS tracking but do not prevent normal wireless communication.

17. ☑ **C.** Ethernet switches isolate each port into its own collision domain. When capturing network traffic, this means you will not see traffic to or from other computers plugged into other switch ports, other than broadcast and multicast packets. Some switches allow you to copy all switch traffic to a monitoring port, but the scenario did not mention this.
☒ **A, B,** and **D** are incorrect. Promiscuous mode is required to capture network traffic, but it is not the problem in this case. Each switch port is a collision domain, but all switch ports can be grouped into virtual local area networks (VLANs); each VLAN is a broadcast domain, similar to each router port.

18. ☑ **A** and **B.** Network Time Protocol (NTP) keeps computers synchronized to a reliable time source. Captured network traffic is time stamped and includes offset time stamps from when the capture was started.
☒ **C** and **D** are incorrect. Digital signatures ensure the authenticity of the message as well as the sender, but their time stamps are not guaranteed. Encryption secures data but has nothing to do with ensuring that date and time stamps are authentic.

19. ☑ **C.** Thoroughly documenting the state of equipment before it is seized is critical to adhere to chain-of-custody procedures. Failure to do so will render collected evidence inadmissible.
☒ **A, B,** and **D** are incorrect. Never turn on a computer that was turned off. Turning it on could destroy valuable data. Do not unplug the USB hard drive. You must not disturb the state of the equipment until it has been documented. Placing the computer in a Faraday bag may be appropriate if it has a wireless interface, but the scene must be documented first.

20. ☑ **A.** Bitstream forensic copying tools copy hard disk data at the bit level, not at the file level. When a file is deleted, it may disappear from the file system, but the file data in its entirety is intact on the hard disk until the hard disk is filled with new data. Deleted files are not copied with file-level copying, but they are with bitstream copying.

☒ **B, C,** and **D** are incorrect. Never log in to a seized computer to copy disk contents. Use an external forensic tool instead. Do not copy data from a seized computer across the network; this will affect log entries on the target computer and will disturb the original state of the data. Viewing log files could reveal data regarding e-mail and instant messaging, but it will not reveal deleted data. Log analysis covering a range of hosts and networks can provide a wealth of strategic intelligence data used to make informed IT security decisions.

21. ☑ **A, B,** and **D.** Metadata, also called tags, is information that describes data. For example, a JPEG picture stored on a web server taken with a digital camera could contain hidden data including camera settings as well as date and time stamps. Metadata also applied to e-mail message transmission path details and mobile device details such as operating system version. Microsoft Word and Portable Document Format (PDF) documents contain metadata such as the document author name, registered company name, and so on.

☒ **C** is incorrect. Excel documents do not record your computer's network card hardware address (MAC address).

22. ☑ **B** and **C.** You must obtain proper legal permission to seize and analyze data. Perform analysis on a forensic copy of data; never work on the original data, because this will render evidence inadmissible.

☒ **A** and **D** are incorrect. You should never work with the original digital data. This disturbs the data's original state; work only on a forensic copy of the data. Your manager may not have the authority to grant permission for you to examine data; ensure that proper legal permission is obtained before commencing an investigation.

23. ☑ **D.** Annual loss expectancy (ALE) is used to calculate the probability of asset failure over a year. It is used when performing a risk assessment and doesn't relate to a forensics budget.

☒ **A, B,** and **C** are incorrect. Travel, man hours, and training expenses are valid IT forensics budget items.

24. ☑ **A** and **D.** Once the severity of the issue has been determined, the quickest way to control the spread of a worm virus is to eliminate network connectivity.

☒ **B** and **C** are incorrect. Unplugging storage area network (SAN) devices may protect data on SAN disks from infected servers, but the worm could still spread to other devices. To eradicate a malware outbreak properly, it may be necessary to unplug a wired device from a network switch to contain or isolate the malware. Containment, including quarantining infected devices, eradication, and system recovery tasks, should be executed by incident response team members in accordance with an incident response plan (IRP). Shutting down all servers takes longer than simply powering down network switches.

25. ☑ **B** and **C**. Emptying the Windows recycle bin makes deleted files inaccessible to Windows users; however, the entire file contents are still on the disk until the disk is filled with other data. A third-party tool must be used to recover the deleted items in this case.

    ☒ **A** and **D** are incorrect. The files can be recovered using freely available tools, even if the recycle bin is emptied. Hard disk defragmentation doesn't relate to file recovery.

26. ☑ Figure 21-2 shows the correct matching of terms and definitions. Preparing an incident response team before problems occur means problems can be dealt with in an efficient manner because team members are aware of their roles and responsibilities. Mitigation steps lessen the impact of problematic incidents. Documenting incident types, categories, and their solutions can help when similar future events occur.

FIGURE 21-2

Incident response definitions and terms—the answer

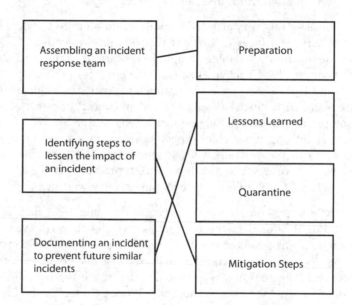

27. ☑ **B**. The built-in Linux **dd** command can be used to copy a disk volume to an image file for future analysis while leaving the original file system intact. A commercial tool equivalent is FTK Imager.

    ☒ **A, C,** and **D** are incorrect. The **memdump** command is available in some Linux distributions such as Ubuntu Linux and is used to copy (dump) the contents of electronic memory to a file for further analysis. Activity related to dump files can be logged to ensure dump file integrity. The commercial WinHex hexadecimal editing tool can be used to recover deleted or damaged data from disk, and Autopsy is a commercial forensic tool that can be used to perform a forensic analysis on many different types of storage media and mobile devices, but these tools are not built into Linux.

28. ☑ **C.** The Mitre Att&ck knowledge base will provide details regarding current malicious user techniques used for lateral movement from a compromised host.

☒ **A, B,** and **D** are incorrect. The listed items are not sources of up-to-date attacker techniques. The Diamond model is an intrusion analysis framework in which each malicious event, or diamond, is used to map out malicious activity; each diamond has a relationship defined with infrastructure components, the adversary executing the malicious activity and their capabilities, and an intended target or goal. The cyber kill chain is a framework used to trace malicious activity from the initial reconnaissance all the way through to the intended system compromise or malware infection and actions on objectives. Continuity of operation planning (COOP), similar to a business continuity plan (BCP), is the preparation for dealing with disruptions to a process, specifically a business process with the BCP, to minimize the impact of that disruption. COOP focuses more on public and government agency preparedness.

29. ☑ **A.** A disaster recovery plan (DRP) outlines the steps to be taken to recover from a disruptive incident. A server DRP can enforce the recovery time objective (RTO) for a given server, which specifies the maximum tolerable amount of downtime. Period DRP drills should be conducted as a proof of concept (PoC) activity to ensure the efficacy of the DRP.

☒ **B, C,** and **D** are incorrect. A communication plan can be included as part of an incident response plan (IRP), which can specify incident contact information such as that for managers, escalation to other parties, legal, public relations, and so on. With IT security and business continuity, managing stakeholder expectations can influence where the focus of time and resources for cybersecurity lies. COOP, similar to a BCP, is the preparation for dealing with disruptions to a process, specifically a business process with the BCP, to minimize the impact of that disruption. COOP focuses more on public and government agency preparedness.

30. ☑ **D.** DNS servers contain resource records detailing items such as host names and corresponding IP addresses; these records are consulted to resolve friendly names to IP addresses. As a result, reconnaissance scans that attempt to enumerate DNS servers will be shown in DNS server logs. As a measure of counterintelligence against attackers, a fake honeypot DNS server with incorrect information may be installed to throw off attackers.

☒ **A, B,** and **C** are incorrect. Some newer versions of UNIX and Linux systems use either the rsyslog or syslog-ng daemon to control logging on the local host as well as the forwarding of log messages to other network hosts. These logging options supersede the older UNIX and Linux syslog daemon and include additional capabilities such as the ability to filter log items based not only on metadata but actual log message contents. Voice over IP (VoIP) devices and related routers will log voice traffic activity and Session Initiation Protocol (SIP) traffic used by many VoIP implementations. Directory server authentication logs capture user, software, and device authentication traffic respectively. None of these logs types captures hostname and IP address scans, but DNS server logs do.

31. ☑ **C.** The Linux **journalctl** command is used to view systemd logs and includes filtering capabilities, such as **journalctl –b** to view only those log entries related to the most recent system boot (as this will show you journal entries that have been collected since the most recent reboot).

☒ **A, B,** and **D** are incorrect. NXLog is a logging utility that supports log forwarding for centralized logging. NXLog works on UNIX, Linux, and Windows hosts. IP flow information export (IPFIX) is a multi-platform solution designed to collect network traffic information for bandwidth monitoring and is commonly used to identify network performance problems, which could indicate malicious activity. Cisco's proprietary IPFIX equivalent protocol, NetFlow, works on devices such as routers and switches to collect network traffic. Another protocol, sFlow, is used to sample network traffic and works on many different types of vendor equipment and hosts.

32. ☑ **D.** Security orchestration, automation, and response (SOAR) is a software solution designed to make incident response more efficient by reducing response time through automation. Runbooks contains series of actions to be executed based on conditions—such as a DDoS attack occurring against the company network.

☒ **A, B,** and **C** are incorrect. SOAR playbooks are sequential incident response steps to be taken and are often influenced by regulations. Playbooks normally involve human intervention more than runbooks do. As part of the electronic data discovery phase (e-discovery) of an investigation, legal hold can be put in place, such as with data stored in the cloud, to ensure that existing data cannot be modified for the purposes of evidence admissibility in a court of law.

Appendix A

Pre-assessment Exam

QUESTIONS

This pre-assessment exam will gauge your knowledge of security-related concepts that you are expected to understand to pass exam SY0-601. This pre-assessment includes 40 questions, so you should allow yourself a maximum of 40 minutes to complete all 40 questions. To mimic the real exam environment, make sure you are in quiet place where you will not be interrupted. Afterward, refer to the self-grading section that appears after the answer section to determine your best course of action to ensure your success in passing exam SY0-601.

1. Which prevention and mitigation measures best protect against the impact of a ransomware attack? (Choose two.)
    A. ICMP blocking rules
    B. Alert e-mail notifications
    C. System imaging
    D. Data backups

2. A company executive complains that her online banking credentials no longer work. After further investigation, you determine that the user clicked a link in a fraudulent e-mail meant to deceive bank customers. Which type of attack occurred?
    A. Impersonation
    B. Tailgating
    C. Hoax
    D. Phishing

3. Which type of attack involves an attacker injecting malicious executable code into a web site page that will be viewed by others?
    A. Buffer overflow
    B. Cross-site request forgery
    C. Cross-site scripting
    D. DoS

4. A malicious user enters a coffee shop and configures a Wi-Fi hotspot that uses the same name used by the legitimate public Wi-Fi available in the coffee shop. What has the malicious user configured?

A. MAC spoofing
B. IP spoofing
C. Evil twin
D. Screened subnet

5. What will detect network or host intrusions and take actions to prevent an intrusion from continuing?
    A. IPS
    B. IDS
    C. IPSec
    D. Screened subnet

6. A router must be configured to allow traffic from certain hosts only. How can this be accomplished?
    A. ACL
    B. Subnet
    C. Proxy server
    D. NAT

7. Your company issues smart phones to employees for business use. Corporate policy dictates that all data stored on smart phones must be encrypted. To which fundamental security concept does this apply?
    A. Confidentiality
    B. Integrity
    C. Availability
    D. Accountability

8. To give a contractor network access quickly, a network administrator adds the contractor account to the Windows Administrators group. Which security principle does this violate?
    A. Separation of duties
    B. Least privilege
    C. Job rotation
    D. Account lockout

9. Complex passwords are considered which type of security control?
    A. Management
    B. Technical
    C. Physical
    D. Operational

10. An insurance company charges an additional $200 monthly premium for natural disaster coverage for your business site. What figure must you compare this against to determine whether to accept this additional coverage?
    A. ALE
    B. ROI
    C. Total cost of ownership
    D. Total monthly insurance premium

11. Which of the following physical access control methods do not normally identify who has entered a secure area? (Choose two.)
    A. Access control vestibule
    B. Hardware locks
    C. Fingerprint scan
    D. Smartcard

12. Juanita uses the Firefox web browser on her Linux workstation. She reports that her browser home page keeps changing to web sites offering savings on consumer electronic products. Her virus scanner is running and is up-to-date. What is the most likely cause of the problem?
    A. Firefox on Linux automatically changes the home page every two days.
    B. Juanita is experiencing a denial-of-service attack.
    C. Juanita's user account has been compromised.
    D. Juanita's browser configuration is being changed by adware.

13. Which of the following refers to unauthorized data access of a Bluetooth device over a Bluetooth wireless network?
    A. Bluejacking
    B. Bluesnarfing
    C. Packet sniffing
    D. Port scanning

14. The process of disabling unneeded network services on a computer is referred to as what?
    A. Patching
    B. Fuzzing
    C. Hardening
    D. Debugging

15. How can you best prevent rogue machines from connecting to your network?
    A. Deploy an IEEE 802.1x configuration.
    B. Use strong passwords for user accounts.
    C. Use IPv6.
    D. Deploy an IEEE 802.11 configuration.

16. You want to focus and track malicious activity to a particular host in your screened subnet. What should you configure?

    A. Honeynet

    B. Honeypot

    C. Screened subnet tracker

    D. Web server

17. A security auditor must determine which types of servers are running on a network. Which tool or technique is best suited for this task?

    A. OS fingerprinting

    B. Protocol analyzer

    C. Port scanner

    D. Virus scanner

18. Which type of security testing provides network configuration information to testers?

    A. Known environment

    B. Unknown environment

    C. Partially known environment

    D. Blue box

19. The web developers at your company are testing their latest web site code before going live to ensure that it is robust and secure. During their testing, they provide malformed URLs with additional abnormal parameters as well as an abundance of random data. Which term describes their actions?

    A. Cross-site scripting

    B. Fuzzing

    C. Patching

    D. Debugging

20. Which solution can centrally authenticate users between different organizations?

    A. RADIUS

    B. RADIUS federation

    C. EAP-FAST

    D. EAP-TTLS

21. What can be done to protect data after a handheld device is lost or stolen?

    A. Enable encryption.

    B. Execute a remote wipe.

    C. Enable screen lock.

    D. Disable Bluetooth discovery.

22. Which firmware solution can store keys used for storage media encryption?
    A. TPM
    B. DLP
    C. EFS
    D. NTFS

23. Your company has issued Android-based smart phones to select employees. Your manager asks you to harden the phones and ensure that data confidentiality is achieved. How should you address your manager's concerns while minimizing administrative effort?
    A. Implement SCADA, screen locking, device encryption, and antimalware, and disable unnecessary software on the phones.
    B. Implement PKI VPN authentication certificates, screen locking, and antimalware, and disable unnecessary software on the phones.
    C. Implement screen locking, device encryption, patching, and antimalware, and disable unnecessary software on the phones.
    D. Implement HTTPS and screen locking, enable antimalware scanning, and disable unnecessary software on the phones.

24. Stored data is referred to as:
    A. Data-in-process
    B. Data-in-transit
    C. Data-at-rest
    D. Data-at-security

25. Which term best describes sensitive medical information?
    A. PHI
    B. TLS
    C. PII
    D. AES

26. Which of the following is considered multifactor authentication?
    A. Username/password
    B. Fingerprint scan/retinal scan
    C. Username/security questions
    D. Smartcard/PIN

27. You are evaluating public cloud storage solutions. Users will be authenticated to a local server on your network that will allow them access to cloud storage. Which identity federation standard could be configured to achieve this?
    A. LDAP
    B. SSL
    C. PKI
    D. SAML

28. Which data forensic term encompasses documenting all aspects of evidence to ensure its integrity?
- A. Legal hold
- B. Volatility
- C. Encryption
- D. Chain of custody

29. The Human Resources department in your company has a policy for conducting thorough background checks before hiring new employees. What type of control is this?
- A. Administrative
- B. Least privilege
- C. Technical
- D. Physical

30. Which type of card can be used to access computer systems as well as buildings? (Choose the best answer.)
- A. Smartcard
- B. CAC
- C. Proximity card
- D. Hardware token

31. Which cryptographic approach uses points on a curve to define public and private key pairs?
- A. RSA
- B. DES
- C. ECC
- D. PKI

32. Your colleagues report that there is a short time frame in which a revoked certificate can still be used. Why is this?
- A. The CRL is published periodically.
- B. The CRL is published immediately but must replicate to all hosts.
- C. The CRL lists only revoked certificate serial numbers; it is not checked to prevent usage of revoked certificates.
- D. The CRL is dependent on network bandwidth.

33. Which term best reflects what is happening in Figure A-1?
- A. TLS
- B. DNS
- C. AES
- D. IPSec

FIGURE A-1

Windows
nslookup
command output

```
C:\Users\>nslookup
Default Server:  cns01.eastlink.ca
Address:  24.222.0.94

> www.mheducation.com
Server:  cns01.eastlink.ca
Address:  24.222.0.94

Non-authoritative answer:
Name:     ecom-prod-alb-ext-501715900.us-east-1.elb.amazonaws.com
Addresses:  54.144.200.169
            3.231.87.241
            54.172.126.195
            52.5.102.115
            107.20.63.228
            52.202.68.133
Aliases:  www.mheducation.com
```

34. Which type of VPN configuration can use the Internet connection of a VPN client device to access Internet resources as opposed to the VPN-connected network's Internet connection?
    A. Split tunnel
    B. Full tunnel
    C. IPSec
    D. HTTPS

35. You are enjoying a cup of coffee at a local coffee shop. When you attempt to use your smart phone to connect to the coffee shop Wi-Fi, you are presented with the web page shown in Figure A-2. What has been configured to require web page authentication prior to your gaining Internet access?
    A. IPSec
    B. HTTPS
    C. Identity federation
    D. Captive portal

FIGURE A-2

Internet access
confirmation
page

Free WiFi

From our friends at Google

Accept & Connect

36. Which standard specifies the syntax used to represent cybersecurity information?
   A. TAXII
   B. XML
   C. STIX
   D. JSON

37. Which tool enables web page viewing on the dark web?
   A. Tor web browser
   B. VPN client
   C. Google Chrome web browser
   D. Botnet

38. Which type of security tool can reduce incident response time by automating security incident response tasks?
   A. Botnet
   B. IPS
   C. SOAR
   D. IDS

39. You are deploying cloud storage for your organization through a public cloud provider. Which type of cloud service model does this apply to?
   A. IaaS
   B. PaaS
   C. XaaS
   D. SaaS

40. Which Linux command is used to view log data captured by the systemd daemon?
   A. **dd**
   B. **chmod**
   C. **tcpdump**
   D. **journalctl**

QUICK ANSWER KEY

1.	C, D	**11.**	A, B	**21.**	B	**31.**	C
2.	D	**12.**	D	**22.**	A	**32.**	A
3.	C	**13.**	B	**23.**	C	**33.**	B
4.	C	**14.**	C	**24.**	C	**34.**	A
5.	A	**15.**	A	**25.**	A	**35.**	D
6.	A	**16.**	B	**26.**	D	**36.**	C
7.	A	**17.**	A	**27.**	D	**37.**	A
8.	B	**18.**	A	**28.**	D	**38.**	C
9.	B	**19.**	B	**29.**	A	**39.**	A
10.	A	**20.**	B	**30.**	B	**40.**	D

IN-DEPTH ANSWERS

1. ☑ **C** and **D.** In the event of a ransomware infection, systems can be quickly returned to an operational state by applying a system image. Frequent data backups enable the restoration of data prior to the ransomware outbreak.

   ☒ **A** and **B** are incorrect. Neither is a ransomware prevention technique. Internet control message protocol (ICMP) blocking rules stop traffic generated by tools such as ping and tracert. E-mail notifications help technicians respond to incidents quickly.

2. ☑ **D.** Phishing scams attempt to convince victims to divulge sensitive information such as online banking credentials.

   ☒ **A, B,** and **C** are incorrect. Impersonation occurs when an attacker pretends to be somebody else on the phone or through communication software in an attempt to gain access to a system. Tailgating is the act of following somebody closely as they unlock doors to sneak in behind them. Hoaxes are fictional scenarios that are designed to trick people into believing they are true.

3. ☑ **C.** Cross-site scripting attacks result from victims using a web site that a malicious user has injected with malicious code. The victim's web browser then executes that code. This can result from ineffective web form field input validation.

   ☒ **A, B,** and **D** are incorrect. Buffer overflows result from data being written beyond a preset memory boundary, which can result in crashing a system or an attacker gaining elevated privileges. A cross-site request forgery results from an attacker compromising a user system so that the attacker is authenticated to a web application and using that web app authentication without the actual user's consent. The attacker then uses those session credentials to execute malicious activities. Denial of service (DoS) attacks render an IT system unusable for legitimate purposes. A DoS attack could, for example, intentionally crash a server.

4. ☑ **C.** An evil twin is an additional Wi-Fi network configured by an attacker to appear as an existing legitimate Wi-Fi network, in hopes that unsuspecting users will connect to it.

   ☒ **A, B,** and **D** are incorrect. None of these is directly related to Wi-Fi hotspots. MAC spoofing forges the 48-bit hardware addresses in a packet, IP spoofing forges the IP addresses in the IP header, and a demilitarized zone (SCREENED SUBNET) is used for placing services that should be directly reachable from the Internet.

5. ☑ **A.** An intrusion prevention system (IPS) actively monitors network or system activity for abnormal activity and can be configured to take steps to stop or contain it. Abnormal activity can be detected by checking for known attack patterns (signature-based) or variations beyond normal activity (anomaly-based).

   ☒ **B, C,** and **D** are incorrect. Like an IPS, an intrusion detection system (IDS) monitors network or system activity for irregular activity, but an IDS does not attempt to stop this activity. IP Security (IPSec) provides data confidentially and integrity to network transmissions and does not detect or prevent intrusions. A screened subnet does not detect or prevent attacks; it is a network segment that hosts services (and ideally an IPS) that are accessible by an untrusted network.

6. ☑ **A.** Access control lists (ACLs) are router settings that allow or deny various types of network traffic from or to specific hosts.

   ☒ **B, C,** and **D** are incorrect. A subnet cannot restrict network traffic; it is a network segment in which IT services and network devices can be located. Routers and layer 3 switches can be used to divide larger networks into smaller subnets, but a subnet is not related to router configuration. The question specifically states that you are configuring a router, and proxy hosts should have routing disabled, although proxy servers do have the ability to limit network access from certain hosts. NAT does not restrict network traffic from certain hosts; instead, it uses a single external IP address to allow many internal computers access to an external network.

7. ☑ **A.** Confidentiality ensures that data is accessible only to those parties who should be authorized to access the data. Encrypting data stored on smart phones protects that data if the phone is lost or stolen.

   ☒ **B, C,** and **D** are incorrect. Integrity ensures that data comes from the user or device it appears to have come from and that the data has not been altered. Availability involves ensuring that data is available when needed. Accountability ensures that people are held responsible for their actions, such as modifying a file. This is accomplished most often through auditing.

8. ☑ **B.** The least privilege principle states that users should be given only the rights needed to perform their duties and nothing more. Adding a contractor to the Administrators group violates this principle by granting the contractor too much privilege.

   ☒ **A, C,** and **D** are incorrect. With separation of duties, each person in a working group is required to perform a specific job. Job rotation is a strategy that exposes employees to various facets of a business and has nothing to do with security. Account lockout relates to security but is not violated by giving a user too many permissions.

9. ☑ **B.** Technical security controls such as complex passwords are used to protect computing resources such as files, web sites, databases, and so on. Complex passwords can help prevent malicious access to IT systems and data.

   ☒ **A, C,** and **D** are incorrect. Management controls are written policies that determine acceptable activities and how they should be conducted. Physical controls such as door locks and fences protect organizational assets from threats. Operational controls such as data backups ensure business continuity.

10.   ☑   **A.** The annual loss expectancy (ALE) value refers to the yearly cost related to the loss of the use of a service or business process. ALE is used with quantitative risk analysis approaches to prioritize and justify expenditures that protect from potential risks. For example, an ALE value of $1000 might justify a $200 annual expense to protect against that risk.

  ☒   **B, C,** and **D** are incorrect. The return on investment (ROI) calculates how efficient an investment is over time (does the benefit of a product or service outweigh the cost?). Total cost of ownership exposes all direct and indirect dollar figures associated with a product or service. Using the total monthly premium value to determine whether to accept the additional insurance coverage would be meaningless; it must be compared against the probability of natural disasters in your area.

11.   ☑   **A** and **B.** Access control vestibules are designed to trap trespassers in a restricted area. Some access control vestibule variations use two sets of doors, one of which must close before the second one opens. Traditional access control vestibules do not require access cards. Hardware locks simply require possession of a key. Neither verifies the person's identity.

  ☒   **C** and **D** are incorrect. Fingerprints identify the user via biometric authentication. Smartcard authentication identifies the user through a unique PIN or PKI certificate in a smartcard.

12.   ☑   **D.** Adware attempts to expose users to advertisements in various ways, including through pop-ups or changing the web browser home page. Spyware often analyzes user habits so that adware displays relevant advertisements. Some antivirus software also scans for spyware, but not in this case.

  ☒   **A, B,** and **C** are incorrect. Firefox on Linux does not change the home page every two days. Denial-of-service attacks prevent legitimate access to a network resource; Juanita is not being denied access. The presence of spyware or adware does not imply the user account has been compromised. Often these types of malware are silently installed when a user visits web sites or installs freeware.

13.   ☑   **B.** Bluesnarfing is the act of connecting to and accessing data from a device over a Bluetooth wireless connection. It is considered much more invasive than packet sniffing or port scanning.

  ☒   **A, C,** and **D** are incorrect. Bluejacking does not access data from a Bluetooth device; instead, it sends an unsolicited message to another Bluetooth device. The question specifies accessing data. Packet sniffing captures network traffic; it does not access data from a wireless device. Port scanning enumerates running services on a host, but it does not access data stored on the host.

14.   ☑   **C.** Hardening includes actions such as disabling unneeded services to make a system more secure.

  ☒   **A, B,** and **D** are incorrect. Patches fix problems with software. Fuzzing refers to testing software for vulnerabilities. Debugging is the methodical testing of software to identify the cause of a flaw.

15. ☑ **A.** The IEEE 802.1x standard requires that devices be authenticated before being given network access. For example, it might be configured for VPN appliances, network switches, and wireless access points that adhere to the standard.
☒ **B, C,** and **D** are incorrect. Strong passwords may prevent a compromise of user accounts, but it will not prevent rogue machines from connecting to the network. IPv6 does not prevent rogue machine network connections. IEEE 802.11 defines the Wi-Fi standard; this does not prevent rogue machine network connections.

16. ☑ **B.** A honeypot is an intentionally vulnerable host used to attract and track malicious activity.
☒ **A, C,** and **D** are incorrect. A honeynet attracts malicious activity to a network of hosts, but the question stated activity tracking on a single host. There is no such thing as a screened subnet tracker. Web servers are not a tool to track malicious activity; web servers deliver content to web browsers.

17. ☑ **A.** Network mapping and vulnerability scanning utilities can map a network's layout and identify operating systems running on hosts using OS fingerprinting. This technique analyzes network packets to and from the host to identify the operating system in use.
☒ **B, C,** and **D** are incorrect. Protocol analyzers capture only transmitted network traffic; they are not specifically designed to scan for network hosts or network configuration. Port scanners identify listening ports. Virus scanners protect against malicious software on a host; they do not scan entire networks.

18. ☑ **A.** A known environment test provides testers with detailed configuration information regarding the software or network they are testing.
☒ **B, C,** and **D** are incorrect. Unknown environment testing provides no information at all to system testers. Partially known testing provides some, but not detailed, information to testers, which allows for a more informed testing environment. Blue-box testing does not exist in this context.

19. ☑ **B.** Fuzzing is a means of injecting data into an application that it does not expect to ensure that no weaknesses are present in the application.
☒ **A, C,** and **D** are incorrect. Cross-site scripts do not ensure that applications are secure; they are a type of attack. Patching would occur after flaws were discovered. Debugging implies that software flaws are already known.

20. ☑ **B.** RADIUS federation required a trusted identify provider in one organization. Edge devices forward authentication requests only to a RADIUS server located on a protected network.
☒ **A, C,** and **D** are incorrect. RADIUS itself does not involve multiple organizations using federated identities. Extensible Authentication Protocol – Flexible Authentication via Secure Tunneling (EAP-FAST) is a Cisco protocol that can use certificates for authentication. Extensible Authentication Protocol – Tunneled Transport Layer Security (EAP-TTLS) doesn't require the client to be authenticated with a signed PKI certificate. EAP-FAST and EAP-TTLS do not make up a central authentication solution between organizations.

21. ☑ **B.** Mobile device administrators can configure devices such that sensitive apps and data can be removed remotely, or wiped, if the device is lost or stolen.
☒ **A, C,** and **D** are incorrect. Encryption is not normally enabled after a device is lost or stolen; it's done beforehand. Screen locking and disabling options such as Bluetooth are common mobile device hardening techniques used before mobile devices are lost or stolen. By far, the most common method of data protection for this scenario involves remotely wiping the device.

22. ☑ **A.** Trusted Platform Module (TPM) chips can store cryptographic keys or certificates used to encrypt and decrypt drive contents. If the drive were moved to another computer (even one with TPM), the drive would remain encrypted and inaccessible.
☒ **B, C,** and **D** are incorrect. Data loss prevention (DLP) refers to fault tolerance and related mechanisms for ensuring that data is safe, such as preventing sensitive data from being copied while it is being viewed (data in use). Encrypting File System (EFS) is purely software, not a firmware chip. The NT File System (NTFS) uses access control lists (ACLs) to control access to data, but the data is not encrypted.

23. ☑ **C.** Hardening a smart phone includes configuring automatic screen locking, encrypting data on the device, patching the OS and required apps, installing and updating antimalware, and disabling unnecessary features and software.
☒ **A, B,** and **D** are incorrect. Supervisory Control and Data Acquisition (SCADA) is a special system used in industrial environments to monitor operations and to provide alarms if any system is tampered with. The question asks about securing data on the phone, not through the network with a VPN. HTTPS will not protect data on the phone, only data in transit between the web browser and a secured web site.

24. ☑ **C.** Data-at-rest is data stored on media.
☒ **A, B,** and **D** are incorrect. Data-in-process refers to data currently in use. Data-in-transit refers to network transmitted data, and data-at-security is an invalid term.

25. ☑ **A.** Protected health information (PHI) refers to sensitive medical information stored and accessed in a secured manner.
☒ **B, C,** and **D** are incorrect. Transport layer security (TLS) is a method of securing network traffic. Personally identifiable information (PII) is more general than PHI and does not focus on medical information. Advanced Encryption Standard (AES) is a symmetric encryption algorithm.

26. ☑ **D.** A smartcard constitutes "something you have," while knowledge of the smartcard PIN constitutes "something you know." When used together, they are considered multifactor authentication.
☒ **A, B,** and **C** are incorrect. A username, a password, and security questions are all considered "something you know." Fingerprint and retinal scans are considered "something you are." None of these combinations are considered multifactor authentication; they are single factor authentication.

27. ☑ **D.** Security Assertion Markup Language (SAML) is an XML standard that defines how authentication and authorization data can be transmitted in a federated identity environment.
☒ **A, B,** and **C** are incorrect. Lightweight Directory Access Protocol (LDAP) is a protocol defining how to access a replicated network database. Secure Sockets Layer (SSL) provides a method to secure application-specific network transmissions. A Public Key Infrastructure (PKI) is a hierarchy of digital security certificates that can be used with computing devices to provide data confidentiality, authentication, and integrity services.

28. ☑ **D.** The chain of custody ensures that the whereabouts of evidence can be accounted for at all times, along with who accessed the evidence.
☒ **A, B,** and **C** are incorrect. Legal hold is a formal requirement to keep potential evidence available without manipulating it. Volatility refers to electronic systems that rely on power such as memory contents as opposed to disk storage. Encryption itself is not directly related to forensic data acquisition.

29. ☑ **A.** Hiring practices are administrative controls.
☒ **B, C,** and **D** are incorrect. None of these are related to hiring practices. The concept of least privilege grants a user only those permissions required to complete a task. Technical controls include safeguards such as firewall rulesets. Physical controls include safeguards such as locked doors and perimeter fencing.

30. ☑ **B.** Common access cards (CAC) grant access to multiple items such as computers and buildings.
☒ **A, C,** and **D** are incorrect. Although the listed items are used to enable access to resources, a common access card is the best answer. Smartcards can be used for system authentication including for buildings. Proximity cards store less information than smartcards and are commonly used to gain access to a room or floor of a building using only the card's ID number, as opposed to user-specific items such as PKI certificates that may be embedded into a smartcard. Hardware tokens display a periodically changing PIN that users enter to gain access to a system, often a VPN.

31. ☑ **C.** Elliptic Curve Cryptography (ECC) is public key cryptography based on points on an elliptic curve.
☒ **A, B,** and **D** are incorrect. RSA is an asymmetric cryptographic standard. DES is a symmetric standard. PKI does involve public and private key pairs but has nothing specifically to do with elliptic curve points.

32. ☑ **A.** The certificate revocation list (CRL) is not published immediately; it is published either manually or on a schedule, so there may be a small time frame in which revoked certificates can still be used.
☒ **B, C,** and **D** are incorrect. The CRL is not published immediately when a certificate is revoked; it is published on a periodic interval. Once the CRL is published, it is referenced by clients. Network bandwidth does not affect when the CRL is published.

33. ☑ **B.** The name server lookup (**nslookup**) command is used to test DNS, as shown in Figure A-1. The web site www.mheducation.com is being queried against the DNS server at 24.222.0.94, which results in the listed of IP addresses shown under "Non-authoritative answer."
     ☒ **A, C,** and **D** are incorrect. Transport Layer Security (TLS) is a method of securing network traffic. Advanced Encryption Standard (AES) is a symmetric encryption algorithm. IP Security (IPSec) provides data confidentially and integrity to network transmissions.

34. ☑ **A.** VPNs with a split tunnel configuration direct traffic for resources available on the other side of the VPN through the VPN tunnel. VPN clients accessing Internet resources will use the VPN client's Internet connection, hence split tunnel.
     ☒ **B, C,** and **D** are incorrect. With full-tunnel VPN connections, all network traffic goes through the VPN tunnel, even VPN client Internet resource traffic. IP Security (IPSec) provides data confidentially and integrity to network transmissions. HTTPS secures network traffic in transit between HTTP clients such as web browsers and secured web sites using a PKI certificate.

35. ☑ **D.** Figure A-2 shows a web page captive portal, which requires user confirmation, and sometimes sign-in and payment, before Internet access is allowed.
     ☒ **A, B,** and **C** are incorrect. IPSec provides data confidentially and integrity to network transmissions. HTTPS secures network traffic in transit between HTTP clients such as web browsers and secured web sites using a PKI certificate. Identity federation uses a single centralized identity provider to authenticate users and devices, after which access to resources such as file servers or web sites is allowed, based on assigned permissions. One benefit of identity federation is that each resource does not need its own authentication mechanism.

36. ☑ **C.** The Structured Threat Information eXpression (STIX) standard defines the syntax used to represent cybersecurity information.
     ☒ **A, B,** and **D** are incorrect. The Trusted Automated Exchange of Indicator Information (TAXII) standard defines how cybersecurity intelligence information is shared among entities. Extensible Markup Language (XML) is a data descriptor language, as is JavaScript Object Notation (JSON). JSON uses key-value pairs. Neither XML nor JSON are specific to sharing cybersecurity information.

37. ☑ **A.** The Tor web browser is designed to provide anonymous access to the Internet and the dark web.
     ☒ **B, C,** and **D** are incorrect. VPN clients make secured connections to VPN endpoints over an untrusted network. Google Chrome is a standard web browser, and botnets are collections of infected computers under a single malicious user's control; none of these is designed to view web pages on the dark web.

38. ☑ **C.** Security Orchestration, Automation, and Response (SOAR) is a software solution designed to make incident response more efficient by reducing response time through automation.
☒ **A, B,** and **D** are incorrect. A botnet is a collection of infected computers under a single malicious user's control. An intrusion prevention system (IPS) actively monitors the network or system for abnormal activity and can be configured to take steps to stop or contain it. Like an IPS, an intrusion detection system (IDS) monitors a network or system for irregular activity, but it does not attempt to stop this activity.

39. ☑ **A.** Infrastructure as a Service (IaaS) refers to compute, network, and storage services offered in the cloud.
☒ **B, C,** and **D** are incorrect. Platform as a Service (PaaS) is primarily of interest to software developers and provides IT services over a network such as databases and programming APIs. Anything as a service (XaaS) is a general term used to describe IT services delivered over a network. Software as a Service (SaaS) enables end-user productivity software to be rapidly provisioned over a network.

40. ☑ **D.** The Linux **journalctl** command is used to view systemd logs and includes filtering capabilities such as **journalctl –b** to view only those log entries related to the most recent system boot (this will show you journal entries that have been collected since the most recent reboot).
☒ **A, B,** and **C** are incorrect. The built-in Linux **dd** command can be used to copy a disk volume to an image file for future analysis while leaving the original file system intact. The Linux **chmod** command is used to set file system permissions, such as granting read and write permissions to the owning user of a file with the command **chmod u +rw file1.txt**. The **tcpdump** command is used to capture network traffic on a specific or all network interfaces, for example, **tcpdump -i any**.

Create Your Study Plan

Congratulations on completing the Security+ pre-assessment! You should now take the time to analyze your results with two objectives in mind.

1. Identify the resources you should use to prepare for the Security+ exam.
2. Identify the specific topics you should focus on in your preparation.

Review Your Score

Use the following table to help you gauge your overall readiness for the Security+ exam. Total your score from the pre-assessment questions for an overall score out of 40.

Number of Answers Correct	Recommended Course of Study
1–25	We recommend you spend a significant amount of time reviewing the material in the *CompTIA Security+ Certification Study Guide, Fourth Edition (Exam SY0-601)* before using this book.
26–30	We recommend you review your scores to identify the particular areas that require your focused attention and use the *CompTIA Security+ Certification Study Guide, Fourth Edition (Exam SY0-601)* to review that material. Once you have done so, you should proceed to work through the questions in this book.
31–40	We recommend you use this book to refresh your knowledge and prepare yourself mentally for the actual exam.

Appendix B

About the Online Content

This book comes complete with TotalTester Online customizable practice exam software with more than 300 practice exam questions, a pre-assessment exam with 40 questions, and other book resources including simulated performance-based questions.

System Requirements

The current and previous major versions of the following desktop browsers are recommended and supported: Chrome, Microsoft Edge, Firefox, and Safari. These browsers update frequently, and sometimes an update may cause compatibility issues with the TotalTester Online or other content hosted on the Training Hub. If you run into a problem using one of these browsers, please try using another until the problem is resolved.

Your Total Seminars Training Hub Account

To get access to the online content, you will need to create an account on the Total Seminars Training Hub. Registration is free, and you will be able to track all your online content using your account. You may also opt in if you wish to receive marketing information from McGraw Hill or Total Seminars, but this is not required for you to gain access to the online content.

Privacy Notice

McGraw Hill values your privacy. Please be sure to read the Privacy Notice available during registration to see how the information you have provided will be used. You may view our Corporate Customer Privacy Policy by visiting the McGraw Hill Privacy Center. Visit the **mheducation.com** site and click **Privacy** at the bottom of the page.

Single User License Terms and Conditions

Online access to the digital content included with this book is governed by the McGraw Hill License Agreement outlined next. By using this digital content you agree to the terms of that license.

Access   To register and activate your Total Seminars Training Hub account, simply follow these easy steps.

1. Go to this URL: **hub.totalsem.com/mheclaim**
2. To register and create a new Training Hub account, enter your e-mail address, name, and password on the **Register** tab. No further personal information (such as credit card number) is required to create an account.

   If you already have a Total Seminars Training Hub account, enter your e-mail address and password on the **Log in** tab.
3. Enter your Product Key: **j69b-tp5d-wrpv**
4. Click to accept the user license terms.
5. For new users, click the **Register and Claim** button to create your account. For existing users, click the **Log in and Claim** button.

You will be taken to the Training Hub and have access to the content for this book.

Duration of License   Access to your online content through the Total Seminars Training Hub will expire one year from the date the publisher declares the book out of print.

Your purchase of this McGraw Hill product, including its access code, through a retail store is subject to the refund policy of that store.

The Content is a copyrighted work of McGraw Hill, and McGraw Hill reserves all rights in and to the Content. The Work is © 2021 by McGraw Hill.

Restrictions on Transfer   The user is receiving only a limited right to use the Content for the user's own internal and personal use, dependent on purchase and continued ownership of this book. The user may not reproduce, forward, modify, create derivative works based upon, transmit, distribute, disseminate, sell, publish, or sublicense the Content or in any way commingle the Content with other third-party content without McGraw Hill's consent.

Limited Warranty   The McGraw Hill Content is provided on an "as is" basis. Neither McGraw Hill nor its licensors make any guarantees or warranties of any kind, either express or implied, including, but not limited to, implied warranties of merchantability or fitness for a particular purpose or use as to any McGraw Hill Content or the information therein or any warranties as to the accuracy, completeness, correctness, or results to be obtained from, accessing or using the McGraw Hill Content, or any material referenced in such

Content or any information entered into licensee's product by users or other persons and/or any material available on or that can be accessed through the licensee's product (including via any hyperlink or otherwise) or as to non-infringement of third-party rights. Any warranties of any kind, whether express or implied, are disclaimed. Any material or data obtained through use of the McGraw Hill Content is at your own discretion and risk and user understands that it will be solely responsible for any resulting damage to its computer system or loss of data.

Neither McGraw Hill nor its licensors shall be liable to any subscriber or to any user or anyone else for any inaccuracy, delay, interruption in service, error or omission, regardless of cause, or for any damage resulting therefrom.

In no event will McGraw Hill or its licensors be liable for any indirect, special or consequential damages, including but not limited to, lost time, lost money, lost profits or good will, whether in contract, tort, strict liability or otherwise, and whether or not such damages are foreseen or unforeseen with respect to any use of the McGraw Hill Content.

TotalTester Online

TotalTester Online provides you with a simulation of the CompTIA Security+ exam. Exams can be taken in Practice Mode or Exam Mode. Practice Mode provides an assistance window with hints, references to the book, explanations of the correct and incorrect answers, and the option to check your answer as you take the test. Exam Mode provides a simulation of the actual exam. The number of questions, the types of questions, and the time allowed are intended to be an accurate representation of the exam environment. The option to customize your quiz allows you to create custom exams from selected domains or chapters, and you can further customize the number of questions and time allowed.

To take a test, follow the instructions provided in the previous section to register and activate your Total Seminars Training Hub account. When you register you will be taken to the Total Seminars Training Hub. From the Training Hub Home page, select **CompTIA Security+ Practice Exams (SY0-601) TotalTester** from the Study drop-down menu at the top of the page, or from the list of Your Topics on the Home page. You can then select the option to customize your quiz and begin testing yourself in Practice Mode or Exam Mode. All exams provide an overall grade and a grade broken down by domain.

Pre-Assessment Test

In addition to the exam questions, the TotalTester also includes a CompTIA Security+ pre-assessment test to help you assess your understanding of the topics before reading the book. To launch the pre-assessment test, click **Security+ Pre-Assessment**. The CompTIA Security+ pre-assessment test has 40 questions. When you complete the test, you can review the questions with answers and detailed explanations on the Detailed Results screen by clicking **I Would Like To Review My Test**. Once you've completed the pre-assessment test, refer to Appendix A, "Pre-Assessment Exam," to get a recommended study plan based on your results. The pre-assessment questions printed in the book are the same questions featured in the online pre-assessment, and you can choose to take your pre-assessment using your book or the Total Tester online.

Other Book Resources

The following sections detail the other resources available with your book. You can access these items by selecting the **Resources** tab, or by selecting **CompTIA Security+ Practice Exams (SY0-601) Resources** from the Study drop-down menu at the top of the page or from the list of Your Topics on the Home page. The menu on the right side of the screen outlines all of the available resources.

Performance-Based Questions

In addition to multiple-choice questions, the CompTIA Security+ exam includes performance-based questions (PBQs), which, according to CompTIA, are designed to test your ability to solve problems in a simulated environment. More information about PBQs is provided on CompTIA's website. You can access the performance-based questions included with this book by navigating to the **Resources** tab and selecting **Performance-Based Questions Quiz**. After you have selected the PBQs, an interactive quiz will launch in your browser.

Technical Support

For questions regarding the TotalTester or operation of the Training Hub, visit **www .totalsem.com** or e-mail **support@totalsem.com**.

For questions regarding book content, visit **www.mheducation.com/customerservice**.